Effective Management of Coding Services

Edited by Lou Ann Schraffenberger, MBA, RHIA, CCS

AHIMA
AMERICAN HEALTH INFORMATION ®
MANAGEMENT ASSOCIATION

ISBN 1-58426-103-X
AHIMA Product Number AC100001
Production Number IPC-1500-102

American Health Information Management Association
233 North Michigan Avenue, Suite 2150
Chicago, Illinois 60601-5800

http://www.ahima.org

Contents

Contributors

About the Editor

Lou Ann Schraffenberger, MBA, RHIA, CCS, CCS-P, is the manager of clinical data in the Clinical Quality Improvement Department of Advocate Health Care in Oak Brook, Illinois. Her position is dedicated to systemwide health information management (HIM) and clinical data projects, clinical coding education, data quality improvement, and coding compliance issues. In 1997, Lou Ann was awarded the first AHIMA Volunteer Award. She has served as chair of the Society for Clinical Coding (2000), and she is a former member of the AHIMA Council on Certification and the Certified Coding Specialist (CCS) Examination Construction Committee. She has also served as author of AHIMA's publication, *Basic ICD-9-CM Coding,* since 1999.

About the Authors

Nadinia A. Davis, MBA, CIA, CPA, RHIA, is an Assistant Professor in the Health Information Management Program at Kean University in Union, New Jersey.

Margaret M. Foley, MBA, RHIA, CCS, is an Assistant Professor at Temple University, Department of Health Information Management, in Philadelphia, Pennsylvania.

Marion K. Gentul, RHIA, CCS, is an independent health information management consultant in Parsippany, New Jersey.

Cheryl L. Hammen, RHIT, is Assistant Vice President of Health Information Management for Community Health Systems, Brentwood, Tennessee.

Desla R. Mancilla, MPA, RHIA, holds the position of Information Protection Officer for the Community Hospital in Munster, Indiana.

Loretta S. Miller, RHIA, CCS-P, serves as Managing Principal at MKM Healthcare Consulting in Akron, Ohio.

Anita Orenstein, RHIT, CCS, CCS-P, is the Health Information Services Compliance Coordinator for Intermountain Health Care in Salt Lake City, Utah.

Ann H. Peden, MBA, RHIA, CCS, is an Associate Professor in Health Information Management at the University of Mississippi Medical Center, Jackson Mississippi.

Vickie L. Rogers, MS, RHIA, is President of VL Rogers & Associates, Powell, Ohio.

Rita A. Scichilone, MHSA, RHIA, CHC, CCS, CCS-P, is Director of Coding Products and Services for AHIMA, Chicago, Illinois.

Lois M. Yoder, RHIT, CCS, is President of the enVision Group, Inc., in Naples, Florida.

Preface

Effective management of coding services has never been more crucial to the stability of healthcare organizations than it is today. These organizations depend on timely and accurate coded data for a variety of reasons. The products of a coding department—ICD-9-CM codes, CPT codes, and abstracted medical information—once produced a clinical database for healthcare statistics and research. Although this clinical database, now often combined with financial information, is still valuable, the products of a coding department now supply the healthcare organization with many more resources for making sound business decisions.

Using Codes for Reimbursement

ICD-9-CM and CPT codes are required on all insurance claims submitted to third-party payers. Government payers, including Medicare and Medicaid, use codes to determine actual reimbursement. Other insurance companies use the coded data to determine medical necessity and the benefits covered for each individual patient. Essentially, the coded data determine if and how much the healthcare organization will be paid for its services.

For years, the focus of attention for most coding services has been the inpatient record. Medicare's diagnosis-related groups (DRGs) demanded complete reporting of a patient's diagnoses and procedures, with special emphasis on the principal diagnosis and procedure, for a hospital to be paid appropriately. Now more than ever, the outpatient record has taken on new meaning. The demands of Medicare's ambulatory payment classification (APC) reimbursement system has illuminated the importance of complete documentation, coding, and billing for hospital outpatients.

Running on a parallel track with the APC system for outpatient reimbursement is Medicare's medical necessity requirements as defined in local medical review policies (LMRPs). Fiscal intermediaries have been producing LMRPs to define Medicare coverage of outpatient services at a feverish rate. The LMRPs include lists of diagnoses that define a medically reasonable and necessary diagnosis for the service. This has required a reexamination of the sparse information contained in many outpatient records so that documentation can be improved. The APC system looks at all the services rendered to an outpatient on a single day on a procedure-by-procedure basis. Thus, hospital coders must look at the documentation with a more critical eye.

Using Codes in the Clinical Database

Coded data produce the foundation for an organization's clinical database. Along with the abstracted information collected for each patient, such as physicians' names, dates of services, number of consultations, and special data collected for different patient types, the coded diagnoses and procedures describe what services were rendered. Various departments in a hospital use this information. For example, quality management departments use this information on a daily basis for clinical studies, process improvement of hospital services, and utilization review of services rendered. Endless questions can be asked about a hospital's patient population and services rendered by querying the clinical database:

- How many patients were admitted with pneumonia?

- How many patients had the principal diagnosis of respiratory failure?

- What was the most common outpatient surgical procedure for patients over age fifty?

- How many patients had a primary cesarean section?

- How many consultations did Doctor Jones have?

- What are the top-ten diagnoses of hospital emergency room visits?

Using Codes for Decision Support

The clinical database becomes a richer information tool when it is combined with the financial information for each patient visit. The merging of clinical and financial data produces a database, commonly referred to as a decision support system, that is used for many business processes. For example, information can be gathered about the cost of hospital services compared to charges and to the actual reimbursement. Financial planners use these data for budgeting and forecasting. Individuals involved with managed care and other insurance contracts can use the clinical and financial information to negotiate payment contracts. The decision support system provides valuable information about the organization's business in both clinical and financial terms.

Management of Coding Services

To support the information needs of an organization, clinical coded data must be timely, accurate, complete, and easily accessible. Accomplishing these goals requires effective management of coding services. This involves a coordinated effort between the coding manager and the medical staff, the financial departments, the registration or admitting departments, the information systems department, and the facility's administration.

The Coding Manager in Various Facilities

In a large facility, a dedicated coding manager may direct a staff of a dozen or more coders and clerical support staff. This manager may not actually do coding but, instead, facilitates communication between departments. The coding manager also provides support within the health information management (HIM) department that enables coders to perform their tasks with the necessary information for accurate coding. In a medium-size facility, the coding manager may be a supervisor who codes part of the day while maintaining the communication link with other departments. In a small facility with only one or two coders, the HIM department manager assumes the role of coding manager. This manager should keep in touch with coding-related issues and interdepartmental relationships.

Skills Required of Coding Managers

Coding managers need a unique balance of technical, communication, and process improvement skills that enable them to manage people, processes, and systems. These skills include the ability to:

- Appreciate the requirements of various coding systems for clear documentation and for adherence to coding guidelines and principles, especially if the manager does not have clinical coding skills

- Support the coding staff with effective recruitment, hiring, mentoring, and counseling skills

- Assume the role of "teacher" to keep the staff members up-to-date on new coding issues and requirements

- Work effectively through strong interpersonal communication skills with people who have an impact on documentation and patient information outside the coding department

- Understand information systems and the transfer of patient care data between software applications by asking:

  —How do ICD-9-CM and CPT codes appear on the insurance claim?

  —What are the system's barriers to data transfer?

- See the "big picture" of healthcare data across the organization by appreciating the clinical needs of the organization as well as the financial or accounting requirements

Not all coding managers possess all these skills. For example, one coding manager may have strong technical coding skills, but little understanding of management skills. Another coding manager may have strong management skills but may not understand the complexities of the coding systems and the documentation needed to support coding. The authors and publisher of *Effective Management of Coding Services* hope that coding managers will use the information and ideas presented here to improve their skill level in all areas necessary to the coding process.

Introducing *Effective Management of Coding Services*

Effective Management of Coding Services provides a resource for coding managers across the continuum of healthcare settings, with a special emphasis on acute care and hospital-based ambulatory settings. Relevant terminology appears in boldface type in the text and is included in the glossary at the end of the book.

Part I: Scope and Organization of Clinical Coding Data

Part I, chapters 1 through 5, addresses the scope and organization of clinical coding data. Chapter 1 provides a general overview of the main coding and reimbursement systems in healthcare today and explains why healthcare organizations should place a great emphasis on coding systems. This chapter introduces the various prospective payment systems (PPSs) and other reimbursement issues tied directly to coding. In addition, chapter 1 discusses standards for healthcare data for future electronic record systems.

Chapter 2 examines the increased use of coded data, shifts in coding procedures, changes in the physical layout of healthcare settings, and the impact of technology and other major changes on the regulatory environment of healthcare. This chapter also addresses the how, when, who, and where of coding practice.

Chapter 3 looks at structuring and organizing the coding function within an organization. Because the primary resource of any coding area is qualified staff, chapter 3 defines the competent coder, the available coding credentials one can earn, and the tools and resources needed to support the coder and the coding function.

Chapter 4 takes a comprehensive look at recruitment, retention, recognition, and reward systems needed to staff a functional coding area. Because healthcare organizations compete for qualified staff, the chapter also examines alternative staffing and work arrangements such as job sharing, telecommuting, and use of external agencies to support the coding function.

Chapter 5 examines the role of the chargemaster in the overall coding process. The implications of the chargemaster, quality data collection, reimbursement, and the organization of outpatient services are explained. In the past, the health information manager and clinical coder have had limited roles in chargemaster development and maintenance. Their roles have changed as new emphasis has been placed on the importance of accurate clinical codes in the chargemaster.

Part II: Monitoring for Excellence of Service Delivery

Part II, chapters 6 through 9, examines strategies and techniques for monitoring the delivery of quality coding services. Chapter 6 considers performance management and process improvement and how to maintain the balance between coding quality and productivity. Coding quality versus quantity productivity is an important issue for the efficiency of the coding staff. The coding manager must take the lead in working with staff members to develop standards that address both quality and productivity.

Chapter 7 examines quality control issues by offering a plan for designing and implementing a data quality improvement program. The importance of auditing and of monitoring the coding of inpatient and outpatient records is reviewed. This chapter also shows how Medicare's Payment Error Prevention Program (PEPP) can contribute to internal quality control procedures. Finally, chapter 7 looks at the use of coding consultants as independent quality review resources. How to make the best use of an external consultant for coding assessment is emphasized.

The important topic of compliance is addressed in chapter 8. The potential conflict between reimbursement optimization and ethical practices in coding is highlighted. AHIMA's standards for ethical coding are presented as part of a compliance program. The opportunity for clinical coders to contribute to an organization's compliance program to prevent healthcare fraud and abuse is another focus of this chapter.

Chapter 9 examines reporting issues. This chapter can be used as a vehicle to define:

- The sources of data as they relate to the coding process

- The type of information necessary for creation of reports based on coded data

- How various users throughout the organization need and use clinical coded data

Part III: Financial Implications

Part III, chapters 10 and 11, considers the financial implications of coded data. Chapter 10 defines the link between coding services and the patient accounting department. It discusses how managing accounts receivable has become a joint effort between the patient accounting manager and the clinical coding manager. This chapter also examines the impact of registration functions and the effective management of coding services on accounts receivable. The timeliness of coding services and its impact on other departments' functions is also emphasized. This chapter also stresses that the coding manager must be familiar with patient accounting functions to contribute to the overall efficiency of the healthcare organization.

Chapter 11 examines the complex subject of case-mix management. Often misunderstood by financial managers, case mix is influenced by coding practices, but not completely driven by coded data. This chapter emphasizes that the coding manager must completely understand how case-mix numbers are determined to appreciate their role in the coding process as well as to defend them when they might be inappropriately "blamed" for a case-mix decline.

Part IV: Future Considerations

Part IV, chapter 12, concludes the book. This final chapter examines the changing landscape of the professional coding community and looks ahead to what the future holds for the clinical coding process.

The goal of this book is to equip coding managers with a unique resource that focuses on the effective management of coding services. Whether they are prospective coding managers, new coding managers, or seasoned veterans—whether they have a professional health information background or have come to coding from another clinical healthcare area—this book provides coding managers with information essential to providing high-quality coding services. By taking advantage of the wealth of information supplied here, health information managers can advance their professional skills and contribute to an important organizational objective—the effective management of coding services.

Acknowledgments

AHIMA is indebted to the following people who served as content reviewers for this book and contributed their interest, enthusiasm, and helpful suggestions to the project:

Claire R. Dixon-Lee, PhD, RHIA, President, MC Strategies, Inc., Atlanta, Georgia

Reesa Gottschalk, MS, RHIA, Health Information Consultant, Glendale, Wisconsin

Launa L. Graham, MPH, RHIA, CCS, Data Quality Manager, Veterans Administration Medical Center, Augusta, Georgia

M. Susan Humm, RHIT, CCS-P, Assistant Professor in HIM Technology, Oakton Community College, Des Plaines, Illinois

Lynn M. Kuehn, MS, RHIA, CCS-P, FAHIMA, Director of Operations, Children's Medical Group, Milwaukee, Wisconsin

Kathleen M. LaTour, MA, RHIA, Chair of the Department of Health Information Management, College of St. Scholastica, Duluth, Minnesota

Elizabeth J. Layman, PhD, RHIA, CCS, FAHIMA, Professor and Chair, East Carolina University, Greenville, North Carolina

Patricia L. Shaw, MEd, RHIA, Assistant Professor, Weber State University, Ogden, Utah

Gail I. Smith, MA, RHIA, CCS-P, Program Chair, Cincinnati State Technical Community College, Cincinnati, Ohio

In addition, we wish to thank AHIMA staff members **Harry B. Rhodes,** RHIA, HIM Professional Practice Manager, and **Rita A. Scichilone,** MHSA, RHIA, CCS, CCS-P, CHC, Director, Coding Products and Services, who served as technical reviewers for this publication.

Part I

Scope and Organization
of Clinical Coding Data

Chapter 1

Scope of Services

Ann H. Peden, MBA, RHIA, CCS

Over the years, coded data have become increasingly important in the delivery and reporting of healthcare services. In the twenty-first century, healthcare practitioners often view coding classification systems either as a method to facilitate the computerization of data or as a mechanism to facilitate reimbursement. Although coding systems can serve both of these functions, healthcare data were maintained in coded form long before the introduction of computers or the inception of current reimbursement methods.

Data classification systems were first used for public health purposes, such as mortality reporting. The *International Classification of Diseases, Ninth Revision, Clinical Modification* (ICD-9-CM) has its roots in the Bertillon Classification, or International List of Causes of Death, that dates back to 1893 (World Health Organization 1992). In the twentieth century, hospitals began using coding systems to index manually diseases and operations for research purposes. For many years, accrediting organizations, such as the Joint Commission on Accreditation of Healthcare Organizations (JCAHO), have promulgated standards requiring coding and indexing of clinical information.

Coding systems are necessary to retrieve data for various purposes in healthcare organizations. Such purposes include provider credentialing, quality improvement, and utilization management. However, today's emphasis is on coding systems as they pertain to reimbursement and to the development of computer-based patient record systems. Numerous coding systems exist, and each system provides different functions. By understanding the wide range of systems available, individuals and organizations can select appropriate coding systems to achieve a variety of purposes.

Standards for Healthcare Data

The increasing emphasis on computer-based patient records (CPRs) and electronic data interchange (EDI) has resulted in a quest for standards to facilitate data manipulation and transfer.

Standard-Setting Organizations

Groups such as the American Society for Testing and Materials (ASTM) and the American National Standards Institute (ANSI) have been conducting voluntary standard setting for issues related to healthcare data for many years. ANSI accredits groups such as Health Level Seven (HL7), one of several ANSI-approved standards-developing organizations focusing on the healthcare industry. The mission of HL7 is to "provide standards for the exchange, management and integration of data that support clinical patient care and the management, delivery and evaluation of healthcare services" (HL7 2001).

Another ANSI-chartered subgroup is the Accredited Standards Committee X12 (ASC X12). This group develops and maintains EDI standards for billing transactions (Brandt 2000).

Standards under the Health Insurance Portability and Accountability Act

Standards that were developed voluntarily are now becoming mandatory as a result of the Health Insurance Portability and Accountability Act of 1996 (HIPAA). Under the Administrative Simplification (AS) provisions of HIPAA, the secretary of health and human services (HHS) promulgates standards through the federal rule-making process. (U.S. Department of Health and Human Services 2001). The U.S. Department of Health and Human Services (DHHS) published the first of several HIPAA-mandated final rules in the *Federal Register* on August 17, 2000. This rule dealt primarily with electronic transactions, including standard code sets (Rode 2001), and also established several designated standards maintenance organizations (DSMOs). The DSMOs are (*Federal Register* 2000a, 50373):

- ASC X12

- Dental Content Committee of the American Dental Association

- HL7

- National Council for Prescription Drug Programs

- National Uniform Billing Committee (NUBC)

- National Uniform Claim Committee (NUCC)

In addition to ASC X12 and HL7, the NUBC and the NUCC are of interest to coding professionals. These two committees are responsible for the processes by which and the forms on which codes are submitted for payment.

The Centers for Medicare and Medicaid Services (CMS)—formerly the Health Care Financing Administration (HCFA)*—adopted billing and claim forms originally developed by the American Hospital Association (AHA) and the American Medical Association (AMA). The NUBC maintains the UB-92, or HCFA-1450, form that is used for hospital billing (NUBC 2001). (See figure 1.1.) The NUCC maintains the HCFA-1500 form used by the noninstitutional healthcare community, including physicians, for filing insurance claims (NUCC 2001). (See figure 1.2.) Both the UB-92 (HCFA-1450) form and the HCFA-1500 form can be used in paper or electronic versions. Copies of these forms and instructions for their use may be obtained from the CMS Web site at <http://www.hcfa.gov> or <http://www.cms.gov>.

HIPAA final rules have established certain standards for EDI, which include the ASC X12 standard. Frequently asked questions (FAQs) about the HIPAA transaction standards may be found at the U.S. Department of Health and Human Services' (DHHS) Web site on administrative simplification, <http://aspe.os.dhhs.gov/admnsimp/faqtx.htm>.

---

*The Health Care Financing Administration became the Centers for Medicare and Medicaid Services on June 14, 2001. This book uses the acronym CMS when referring to this agency.

Figure 1.1. **HCFA-1450 (UB-92) form**

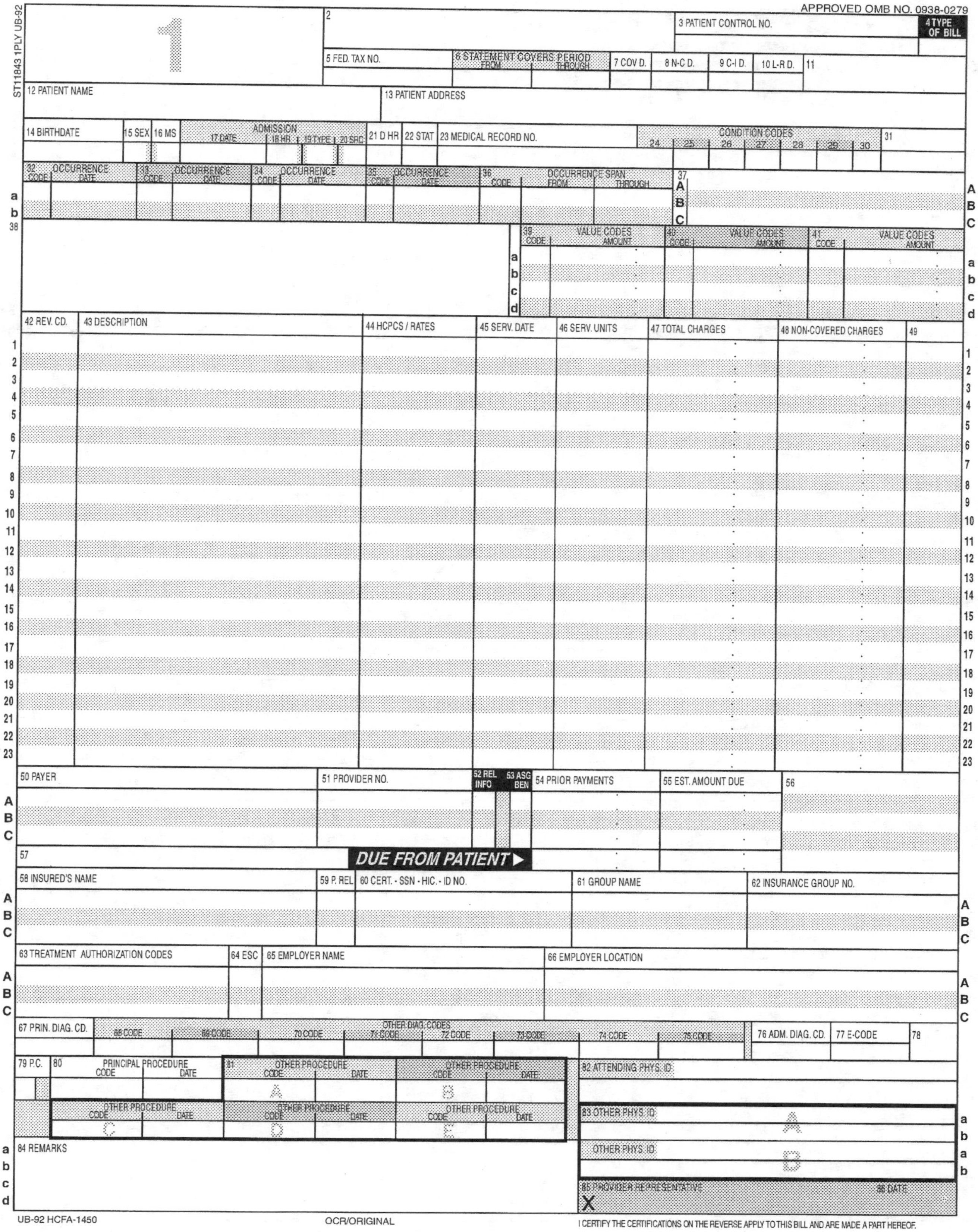

Figure 1.2.   **HCFA-1500 form**

PLEASE
DO NOT
STAPLE
IN THIS
AREA

APPROVED OMB-0938-0008

CARRIER

HEALTH INSURANCE CLAIM FORM

| | | PICA | | | | | | | | | | PICA | | |

| 1. MEDICARE   MEDICAID   CHAMPUS   CHAMPVA   GROUP HEALTH PLAN   FECA BLK LUNG   OTHER | 1a. INSURED'S I.D. NUMBER   (FOR PROGRAM IN ITEM 1) |

(Medicare #)   (Medicaid #)   (Sponsor's SSN)   (VA File #)   (SSN or ID)   (SSN)   (ID)

2. PATIENT'S NAME (Last Name, First Name, Middle Initial)

3. PATIENT'S BIRTH DATE   MM   DD   YY   SEX   M   F

4. INSURED'S NAME (Last Name, First Name, Middle Initial)

5. PATIENT'S ADDRESS (No., Street)

6. PATIENT RELATIONSHIP TO INSURED   Self   Spouse   Child   Other

7. INSURED'S ADDRESS (No., Street)

CITY   STATE

8. PATIENT STATUS   Single   Married   Other

CITY   STATE

ZIP CODE   TELEPHONE (Include Area Code) ( )

Employed   Full-Time Student   Part-Time Student

ZIP CODE   TELEPHONE (INCLUDE AREA CODE) ( )

9. OTHER INSURED'S NAME (Last Name, First Name, Middle Initial)

10. IS PATIENT'S CONDITION RELATED TO:

11. INSURED'S POLICY GROUP OR FECA NUMBER

a. OTHER INSURED'S POLICY OR GROUP NUMBER

a. EMPLOYMENT? (CURRENT OR PREVIOUS)   YES   NO

a. INSURED'S DATE OF BIRTH   MM   DD   YY   SEX   M   F

b. OTHER INSURED'S DATE OF BIRTH   MM   DD   YY   SEX   M   F

b. AUTO ACCIDENT?   PLACE (State)   YES   NO

b. EMPLOYER'S NAME OR SCHOOL NAME

c. EMPLOYER'S NAME OR SCHOOL NAME

c. OTHER ACCIDENT?   YES   NO

c. INSURANCE PLAN NAME OR PROGRAM NAME

d. INSURANCE PLAN NAME OR PROGRAM NAME

10d. RESERVED FOR LOCAL USE

d. IS THERE ANOTHER HEALTH BENEFIT PLAN?   YES   NO   *If yes*, return to and complete item 9 a-d.

READ BACK OF FORM BEFORE COMPLETING & SIGNING THIS FORM.

12. PATIENT'S OR AUTHORIZED PERSON'S SIGNATURE I authorize the release of any medical or other information necessary to process this claim. I also request payment of government benefits either to myself or to the party who accepts assignment below.

SIGNED _____   DATE _____

13. INSURED'S OR AUTHORIZED PERSON'S SIGNATURE I authorize payment of medical benefits to the undersigned physician or supplier for services described below.

SIGNED _____

PATIENT AND INSURED INFORMATION

14. DATE OF CURRENT: ILLNESS (First symptom) OR INJURY (Accident) OR PREGNANCY(LMP)   MM   DD   YY

15. IF PATIENT HAS HAD SAME OR SIMILAR ILLNESS. GIVE FIRST DATE   MM   DD   YY

16. DATES PATIENT UNABLE TO WORK IN CURRENT OCCUPATION   MM   DD   YY   FROM   TO   MM   DD   YY

17. NAME OF REFERRING PHYSICIAN OR OTHER SOURCE

17a. I.D. NUMBER OF REFERRING PHYSICIAN

18. HOSPITALIZATION DATES RELATED TO CURRENT SERVICES   MM   DD   YY   FROM   TO   MM   DD   YY

19. RESERVED FOR LOCAL USE

20. OUTSIDE LAB? $ CHARGES   YES   NO

21. DIAGNOSIS OR NATURE OF ILLNESS OR INJURY. (RELATE ITEMS 1,2,3 OR 4 TO ITEM 24E BY LINE)

1. |___.___   3. |___.___

2. |___.___   4. |___.___

22. MEDICAID RESUBMISSION CODE   ORIGINAL REF. NO.

23. PRIOR AUTHORIZATION NUMBER

24. A DATE(S) OF SERVICE		B Place of Service	C Type of Service	D PROCEDURES, SERVICES, OR SUPPLIES (Explain Unusual Circumstances)		E DIAGNOSIS CODE	F $ CHARGES	G DAYS OR UNITS	H EPSDT Family Plan	I EMG	J COB	K RESERVED FOR LOCAL USE
From MM DD YY	To MM DD YY			CPT/HCPCS	MODIFIER							
1												
2												
3												
4												
5												
6												

PHYSICIAN OR SUPPLIER INFORMATION

25. FEDERAL TAX I.D. NUMBER   SSN EIN

26. PATIENT'S ACCOUNT NO.

27. ACCEPT ASSIGNMENT? (For govt. claims, see back)   YES   NO

28. TOTAL CHARGE $

29. AMOUNT PAID $

30. BALANCE DUE $

31. SIGNATURE OF PHYSICIAN OR SUPPLIER INCLUDING DEGREES OR CREDENTIALS (I certify that the statements on the reverse apply to this bill and are made a part thereof.)

SIGNED _____ DATE _____

32. NAME AND ADDRESS OF FACILITY WHERE SERVICES WERE RENDERED (If other than home or office)

33. PHYSICIAN'S, SUPPLIER'S BILLING NAME, ADDRESS, ZIP CODE & PHONE #

PIN#   GRP#

(APPROVED BY AMA COUNCIL ON MEDICAL SERVICE 8/88)   ***PLEASE PRINT OR TYPE***   FORM HCFA-1500 (12-90), FORM RRB-1500, FORM OWCP-1500

Code Set Standards under HIPPA

Of particular interest to coding professionals are the HIPAA standards for medical data code sets. The code sets are (*Federal Register* 2000, 50370):

- *International Classification of Diseases, Ninth Edition, Clinical Modification* (ICD-9-CM), Volumes 1 and 2

- *International Classification of Diseases, Ninth Edition, Clinical Modification* (ICD-9-CM), Volume 3 Procedures

- *National Drug Codes* (NDC)

- *Code on Dental Procedures and Nomenclature, Second Edition* (CDT-2)

- The combination of *Health Care Common Procedure Coding System* (HCPCS) and *Current Procedural Terminology, Fourth Edition* (CPT)

HIPAA Standards for the Future

In future years, HIPAA could establish changes and additions to these initial code sets. For example, ICD-10-CM and ICD-10-PCS (Procedure Coding System) provide more specificity in coding than does ICD-9-CM. Future HIPAA rules could make these more specific systems the standard instead of ICD-9-CM. Also, because HIPAA includes "tables of terms" and "medical concepts" in its definition of code sets, future implementations of HIPAA could include standards for clinical terminologies (Health Insurance Portability and Accountability Act of 1996 2001).

Classifications, Nomenclatures, and Clinical Terminologies

A **classification** is a system that groups related entities to produce necessary statistical information. ICD-9-CM is an example of a classification system. The term **nomenclature** literally means "name calling." A nomenclature is a system of names used in any science or art. In medicine, a nomenclature presents preferred terminology for naming disease processes. An example of a nomenclature was the classic coding system of the mid-twentieth century, the *Standard Nomenclature of Diseases and Operations*.

The idea of a standardized **clinical terminology** is a newer concept than that of a classification or a nomenclature. The first National Conference on Terminology for Clinical Patient Description defined a clinical terminology as:

Standardized terms and their synonyms which record patient findings, circumstances, events and interventions with sufficient detail to support clinical care, decision support, outcomes research, and quality improvement; and can be efficiently mapped to broader classifications for administrative, regulatory, oversight, and fiscal requirements (Computer-Based Patient Record Institute 1999).

An example of a clinical terminology is *Systematized Nomenclature of Human and Veterinary Medicine International Clinical Terminology* (SNOMED-CT). More information is provided on specific classifications, nomenclatures, and clinical terminologies later in this chapter.

Several structural terms are related to classifications, nomenclatures, and terminologies. For example, a system that is **hierarchical** is structured with broad groupings that can be further subdivided into more narrowly defined groupings or detailed entities. A system that is **multi-axial** can classify an entity in several different ways. For example, a neoplasm can be classified by site, by morphology, and by behavior—three axes. Many systems are both hierarchical and multiaxial. The **granularity** of a system refers to the level of detail the system is able to capture. A highly granular system captures finer details of data than a less granular system.

Overview of Coding Systems

The most commonly used coding systems in the United States are those used for reimbursement. These include the ICD-9-CM, HCPCS, and CPT coding systems.

ICD-9-CM Codes

ICD-9-CM Volumes 1 and 2 provide diagnosis codes for a variety of healthcare providers, including hospitals, home health providers, long-term care facilities, and physicians. ICD-9-CM Volume 3 provides procedure codes for hospital inpatient billing.

HCPCS and CPT Codes

HCPCS and CPT codes are used to bill physicians' procedures and services—both inpatient and outpatient. Hospitals use HCPCS/CPT codes to bill Medicare and other insurers for hospital outpatient procedures. (See table 1.1.) (A few insurers prefer to use ICD-9-CM Volume 3 procedure codes for hospital outpatients, but this will change with implementation of the HIPAA standardized code sets.) Traditionally, there have been three levels of HCPCS codes. (See table 1.2.)

Level I Codes

Level I codes are CPT codes developed by the AMA. CPT codes contain five numeric characters; for example, 00540.

Table 1.1. **Typical reimbursement uses of ICD-9-CM and HCPCS/CPT**

Coding System	Hospital Use	Physician Use
ICD-9-CM Volumes 1 and 2	Diagnoses for inpatients and outpatients	Diagnoses for inpatients and outpatients
ICD-9-CM Volume 3	Procedures for inpatients	None
HCPCS/CPT	Procedures for outpatients	Procedures for inpatients and outpatients

Table 1.2. **Levels of HCPCS**

Level	Name	Origin	Code Structure	Example
I	CPT Codes	AMA	5 numeric characters	00540
II	National Codes	CMS/HCFA	Alphanumeric codes beginning A–V	J0150
III*	Local Codes	Local Carriers	Alphanumeric codes beginning W–Z	W0001

*HIPAA eliminates Level III local codes.

Level II Codes

Level II codes are national codes developed by CMS. They are alphanumeric codes that begin with the letters A–V; for example, J0150. In informal usage, the term "HCPCS codes" often refers to Level II codes.

Level III Codes

Level III codes are local codes developed by local carriers. Local codes are alphanumeric codes that begin with the letters W–Z; for example, W0001.

HIPAA rules have scheduled the elimination of Level III codes. With the final implementation of the HIPAA code sets, users of local codes must apply to either the AMA or CMS to request the new Level I or Level II codes needed to replace Level III codes (U.S. Department of Health and Human Services 2000).

International Classification of Diseases

Volumes 1 and 2 of ICD-9-CM classify diseases and are based on ICD-9, which was developed and is published by the World Health Organization (WHO). Because ICD-9 was designed primarily for mortality classification, it was clinically modified as ICD-9-CM for use in the United States for morbidity reporting as well. The National Center for Health Statistics (NCHS) maintains the disease classification in the United States.

Volume 3 of ICD-9-CM classifies procedures and was created for use in the United States. Therefore, it has no corresponding section in the WHO ICD-9. CMS maintains Volume 3.

Rules and Guidelines for Using ICD-9-CM

The Cooperating Parties develop coding rules and guidelines for correct use of ICD-9-CM. The Cooperating Parties are the American Health Information Management Association (AHIMA), the AHA, CMS, and the NCHS.

Coding Clinic

Coding Clinic is a publication that contains coding advice and decisions made by the Cooperating Parties. It is published quarterly by the AHA's Central Office on ICD-9-CM. Because the Cooperating Parties agree to content and guidelines before publication, information appearing in *Coding Clinic* is considered to be authoritative advice on the correct use of ICD-9-CM.

Other Guidelines

The Cooperating Parties also have approved "Official ICD-9-CM Guidelines for Coding and Reporting." This document contains official coding guidelines and combines selected coding and reporting rules in one source (AHA 2001). It was named in the HIPAA regulations as part of the ICD-9-CM standard code set. The "Official ICD-9-CM Guidelines for Coding and Reporting" is available free of charge online at the Centers for Disease Control and Prevention (CDC) Web site under the NCHS classification of diseases initiative, <http://www.cdc.gov/nchs/data/icdguide.pdf>.

ICD-10

WHO published the *International Statistical Classification of Diseases and Related Health Problems, Tenth Revision* (ICD-10), in 1992. ICD-10 is a more comprehensive and detailed classification than ICD-9. Unlike ICD-9, the main classification of ICD-10 is alphanumeric. Each code in the classification begins with an alphabetic character followed by numerals. For example, B15.9 is the code for "Hepatitis A without hepatic coma" (World Health Organization 1992, 152). This alphanumeric format expanded the number of codes available without lengthening the number of characters in each code.

ICD-10-CM

The United States has developed ICD-10-CM, a clinical modification of ICD-10. Adopting ICD-10-CM would provide an expanded classification with more clinical detail and would facilitate comparison of U.S. data with data from other countries. However, before ICD-10-CM can be implemented in the United States, it would have to be adopted as a HIPAA standard code set. Then there would be a two-year implementation window from the time the final rule appeared in the *Federal Register* until the new standard would take effect (NCHS 2001).

ICD-10-PCS

Realizing that more detail was needed in the procedural classification as well as in the diagnostic classification, the United States developed ICD-10-PCS (Procedure Coding System) to replace Volume 3 of ICD-9-CM. ICD-10-PCS uses a seven-character, alphanumeric code structure. The classification is divided into sixteen sections. The first character in each code is the letter or number designating the appropriate section (medical and surgical, obstetrics, imaging, and so on) within the classification. Within each section, each position in a code captures a specific concept, and each character used in a position has a meaning specific to that position.

For example, "Open reduction internal fixation of left tibia with plate and screws" would be coded 0QQH04Z. The initial "0" in the code indicates the medical and surgical section; "Q," the body system, "lower bones"; "Q," the root operation, "repair"; "H," the body part, "left tibia"; "0," the approach, "open"; "4," the device, an "internal fixation device"; and "Z," there is "no qualifier" (Averill et al. 1998).

Current Procedural Terminology

Current Procedural Terminology (CPT) is copyrighted and maintained by the AMA. From the beginning, CPT was designed as a means of communication between physicians and third-party payers. CPT codes represent procedures and services performed by physicians in clinical practice. CPT comprises six major sections: Evaluation and Management, Anesthesiology, Surgery, Radiology, Pathology and Laboratory, and Medicine (AMA 2000b).

The AMA also publishes *CPT Assistant*. This monthly newsletter provides authoritative guidance on the correct use of CPT. Transmittals and bulletins from CMS, Medicare carriers, and fiscal intermediaries (FIs) are other sources of guidance on the use of CPT.

A fifth edition of CPT, under development by the AMA, expands the purposes of CPT beyond its traditional billing and administrative uses. The new purposes incorporated in the fifth edition include performance measurement and tracking of new procedures.

To accomplish these new purposes, three new categories of codes have been developed:

- Category I will be composed of five-digit codes as found in the fourth edition of CPT.

- Category II, a new set of codes, will be optional tracking codes used in performance measurement. These will be five-character, alphanumeric codes with a letter in the last field; for example, 1234F.

- Category III codes will be used to track new and emerging procedures and services that have clinical efficacy. In the past, such procedures may have been assigned local codes, which will no longer occur under HIPAA. Like Category II codes, Category III codes will be alphanumeric codes containing a letter in the last field; for example, 1234T.

Both Category II and Category III codes will be located in separate sections of CPT-5, following the Medicine section (Beebe 2001). The first Category III codes became available for use in 2001. The AMA published them on its Web site, <http://www.ama-assn.org/cpt>, and in *CPT Assistant* (AMA 2001a, 5–6).

Other Coding and Classification Systems

Numerous other coding and classification systems have significance in various arenas ranging from electronic transmittal of data to clinical research. The systems mentioned in the following paragraphs are not exhaustive. However, they do provide a glimpse of the many facets of classifications, nomenclatures, and clinical terminologies.

The Unified Medical Language System Metathesaurus

The Unified Medical Language System (UMLS ®) *Metathesaurus* is an ongoing project of the National Library of Medicine (NLM). The Metathesaurus electronically links a broad range of clinical terminologies or vocabularies. It integrates those vocabularies by using a concept unique identifier (CUI) that permits the source vocabularies to maintain their own definitions, but links equivalent concepts across vocabularies (Campbell, Oliver, and Shortliffe 1998, 12–13).

The 2001 edition of the UMLS Metathesaurus included about 800,000 concepts and 1.9 million concept names derived from more than 60 different biomedical vocabularies (NLM 2001). The UMLS includes many of the classification and terminology systems mentioned in this chapter.

Diagnostic and Statistical Manual of Mental Disorders

The *Diagnostic and Statistical Manual of Mental Disorders, Fourth Edition* (DSM-IV), published by the American Psychiatric Association (APA), is an example of a specialized coding system for mental health. DSM-IV code numbers correspond to ICD-9-CM; however, its text and terminology are different (APA 2000a). In 2000, DSM-IV was revised as DSM-IV-TR to update the text and any codes that had been updated in ICD-9-CM (APA 2000b).

The Diagnostic and Statistical Manual of Mental Disorders, Fourth Edition, Primary Care Version (DSM-IV-PC) provides a standard approach to diagnosing mental health disorders, with an emphasis on disorders likely to be detected in the primary care setting (AHIMA 1998, 54). DSM-IV-PC was designed to be useful in education, communication, and research. It facilitates collaboration between primary care and mental health specialists (APA 2000c).

Systematized Nomenclature of Human and Veterinary Medicine

The College of American Pathologists publishes *Systematized Nomenclature of Human and Veterinary Medicine* (SNOMED®) *International.* SNOMED is available in multiple languages and has been voluntarily adopted by numerous organizations in more than forty countries. Although once available in book form, the latest version of SNOMED is available only in electronic form and is updated frequently.

ANSI's Healthcare Informatics Standards Board states:

> The structure of *SNOMED® International,* together with its ability to index and retrieve comprehensive patient information, makes this system a strong candidate for the standard vocabulary and data model that is essential for the computer-based patient record (ANSI 2001).

Studies comparing SNOMED with other systems have shown that it more completely captures clinical concepts (Chute et al. 1996, 224). SNOMED has continued to expand and to evolve as a robust clinical terminology for electronic records. A new design, the *Systematized Nomenclature of Medicine Reference Terminology* (SNOMED-RT®), was released in May 2000. SNOMED-RT covers numerous concepts, as indicated by its multiple root hierarchies, listed below (Systematized Nomenclature of Medicine 2001):

- Findings, Conclusions, and/or Assessments
- Procedures
- Body Structures
- Biological Functions
- Living Organisms
- Substances (Chemicals and Drugs)
- Physical Agents, Activities, and/or Forces
- Occupations
- Social Context
- Modifiers/Linkage Terms and/or Qualifiers

SNOMED has continued to expand its breadth of coverage by developing SNOMED *Clinical Terms* (SNOMED CT). This system will combine terminologies from SNOMED with the United Kingdom's (UK) National Health Service's (NHS) *Clinical Terms Version 3.* The merger of these two systems should provide the most comprehensive clinical terminology available because the primary care focus of *Clinical Terms* complements SNOMED's strength in specialty areas.

Clinical Terms has been known more commonly as the "Read Codes" or *Read Thesaurus.* This terminology and coding system was developed in the early 1980s by Dr. James Read in the UK. It is presently maintained by the UK NHS Centre for Coding and Classification (Schulz, Price, and Brown 1997).

Code Sets Used in Preliminary Standards

Logical Observation Identifiers, Names, and Codes (LOINC®) is a terminology and coding system for reporting laboratory results and other observations for the CPR (Prophet 1997). LOINC has been used in preliminary X12 standards, such as standards 277/275, Health Care

Claim Request for Additional Information and Response. Similarly, *Data Elements for Emergency Department Systems* (DEEDS), developed by the National Center for Injury Prevention and Control (NCIPC), is also included as a code set in HL7 messages in preliminary ASC X12N standards for attachments. Those standards are expected to be included in future HIPAA rules (Washington Publishing Company 2001).

International Classification for Primary Care

The *International Classification for Primary Care* (ICPC-2) was developed by the World Organization of Family Doctors (WONCA) International Classification Committee (WICC). (Note: The World Organization of Family Doctors is the currently accepted short name for the World Organization of National Colleges, Academies, and Academic Associations of General Practitioners/Family Physicians [Rabold 1995].)

ICPC-2 is a merger of the following three earlier classifications:

- *Reason for Encounter Classification* (RFEC)

- *International Classification of Process in Primary Care* (IC-Process-PC)

- *International Classification of Health Problems in Primary Care, Second Edition, Defined* (ICHPPC-2-D) (Jamoulle and Humbert 2001)

An electronic version of the ICPC classification, ICPC-2-E, was developed for use with electronic patient records. Both ICPC-2 and ICPC-2-E have been mapped to ICD-10 (Okkes et al. 2000, 101).

ABC Codes

The ABC codes are another interesting classification system. Copyrighted by Alternative Link, Inc., ABC codes describe "what is said, done, ordered, prescribed, or distributed by providers of alternative medicine" (Prophet 1999, 65).

ABC codes were developed for electronic transactions that require a code for complementary and alternative medicine (CAM) services, as well as for services rendered by more conventional healthcare practitioners. ABC codes are available for acupuncture, chiropractic, holistic medicine, homeopathy, massage therapy, midwifery, naturopathy, and osteopathy, as well as for services provided by physician assistants, nurse practitioners, and others. The ABC codes have also been incorporated into the NLM's UMLS Metathesaurus (Alternative Link, Inc. 2001).

Classification Systems for Nursing

Several classification systems for nursing have been developed in North America. The American Nurses Association (ANA) established the Nursing Information and Data Set Evaluation Center (NIDSEC) to develop standards and to evaluate vendor products related to nursing information systems (Henry et al. 1998, 51). As of the year 2000, NIDSEC had recognized the following twelve languages or classification systems that meet ANA standards (ANA 2000):

- North American Nursing Diagnosis Association (NANDA)

- *Nursing Interventions Classifications* (NIC)

- *Nursing Outcomes Classification* (NOC)

- *Omaha System*

- *Home Health Care Classification* (HHCC)

- *Patient Care Data Set* (PCDS)

- *Nursing Management Minimum Data Set* (NMMDS)

- *Perioperative Nursing Dataset*

- SNOMED-RT

- *Nursing Minimum Data Sets* (NMDS)

- *International Classification for Nursing Practice* (ICNP®)

- Alternative Link

Some of these systems have been discussed previously and apply to other areas of healthcare as well as to nursing. Of the systems that deal wholly with nursing, one of the first groups to formally identify and classify nursing diagnoses was NANDA (NANDA 2001), which primarily names and classifies problems that nurses treat. NIC classifies nursing interventions or the treatments that nurses perform. NOC classifies the outcomes of those treatments. Both NIC and NOC are maintained by the University of Iowa's Center for Nursing Classification (University of Iowa College of Nursing 2001).

Other systems, such as the *Omaha System* and the *Home Health Care Classification,* provide ways to classify data in all three areas—diagnoses, interventions, and outcomes (Henry et al. 1998, 50).

The *International Classification for Nursing Practice* (ICNP) can map concepts from one nursing classification system to another. The International Council of Nurses developed this classification system, which was released in Beta version in 1999. ICNP is a terminology that also classifies nursing diagnoses, interventions, and outcomes (International Council of Nurses 2001).

In addition to providing a unifying framework for the various nursing classification systems, ICNP serves as a classification system for use in countries in which no established system exists. ICNP should facilitate the description and comparison of nursing practices across nations (Clark 1998).

Other Special-Purpose Classifications and Terminologies

Also in the international arena are several other special-purpose classifications and terminologies.

Medical Dictionary for Drug Regulatory Affairs

The *Medical Dictionary for Drug Regulatory Affairs* (MedDRA) has been developed for the purpose of pharmaceutical regulation. Pharmaceutical companies use MedDRA internationally to report adverse drug reactions. As a standardized medical terminology, MedDRA includes terms for symptoms, signs, diseases, and the results of investigations rather than the names of drugs. MedDRA is both hierarchical and multiaxial and also incorporates other terminologies that were in use prior to its development (Rulon 2000).

International Classification of Diseases for Oncology

The *International Classification of Diseases for Oncology* (ICD-O) is used throughout the world for data collection and analysis in cancer registries. ICD-O is based on ICD-10 and uses codes for topography, morphology, and behavior of neoplasms (WHO 2001b).

International Classification of Functioning, Disability, and Health

Another international classification system is WHO's *International Classification of Functioning, Disability, and Health* (ICIDH-2). (The 1980 version is known as the *International Classification of Impairments, Disabilities, and Handicaps.*) ICIDH-2 classifies disabilities by body function and structure, by activities and participation, and by environmental factors. It was released in Beta version in 1999 (WHO 2001a).

Arden Syntax for Medical Logic Modules

Arden Syntax for Medical Logic Modules (MLM) is useful in generating clinical alerts and in developing decision support systems (Department of Medical Informatics 2001). Although some writers list MLM as a coding system, it is not a coding system in the sense of a classification, nomenclature, or terminology.

MLM is more accurately termed a "modeling language" (Van der Maas et al. 2001, 146). Instead of providing a set of codes, it provides a standardized method of representing medical knowledge in modules. This allows sharing of expert knowledge between otherwise incompatible systems (Berthelsen 2001). Fittingly, *Arden Syntax for Medical Logic Modules Version 2.0* is now sponsored by HL7 (HL7 2001), an organization whose purpose is to facilitate the exchange of healthcare data.

Historical Coding Systems

Several twentieth-century coding systems have historical importance. Health information managers assisting with research projects may occasionally have to retrieve data from the following older disease or operation indexes:

- The *Standard Nomenclature of Diseases and Operations* (SNDO) was a dual classification that used site and etiology as disease axes and site and procedure as operation axes. For example, the site "aorta" is represented by "461," and the procedure "biopsy" is represented by "16." Therefore, "Biopsy of the aorta" would be coded "461-16" (Cofer 1994, 324). The AMA last published SNDO in the 1960s. A modification of SNDO continued to be used into the 1990s by Shriners Hospitals.

- The AMA also published *Current Medical Information and Terminology* (CMIT), which used nonsemantic identifiers; that is, the characters comprising the codes carried no meaning. In addition to codes, CMIT provided concise information, such as etiology, signs, symptoms, lab findings, and so on, for the diseases it listed.

- The *Standard Nomenclature of Pathology* (SNOP), published by the College of American Pathologists, was the forerunner to SNOMED. SNOP used four axes— topography, morphology, etiology, and function.

- The *International Classification of Diseases, Adapted for Use in the United States, Eighth Edition* (ICDA-8) was the forerunner to ICD-9-CM.

- The *Hospital Adaptation of ICDA* (H-ICDA), a contemporary of ICDA-8, was published by the Commission on Professional and Hospital Activities (Cofer 1994, 335). The Mayo Foundation for Medical Education and Research still uses a modification of H-ICDA in some of its research databases.

Further Uses of Coded Data

Coded healthcare data are used in many ways in the United States, including their use in case-mix, severity-of-illness, and risk-adjustment systems.

Case-Mix Systems

Case-mix systems provide information about the types of patients treated by a facility. Most case-mix systems group cases that are clinically similar and that ordinarily use similar resources. Some case-mix systems have been used directly in reimbursement systems. Other systems are used more for internal data analysis and benchmarking purposes. Various case-mix systems, such as the diagnostic-related group (DRG) system and the ambulatory payment classification (APC) system, have been used to analyze inpatient and outpatient data.

Diagnosis-Related Group System

Since the early 1980s when it was mandated as the prospective payment system (PPS) for Medicare, the diagnosis-related group (DRG) system has been the most widely used inpatient case-mix system. Because DRGs were based on the Medicare population, the first evolutions of this case-mix system were modified for use with other groups. Pediatric-modified DRGs (PM-DRGs) were developed for use in children's hospitals; all-payer DRGs (AP-DRGs) evolved for use with the general population.

Ambulatory Patient Group System

Outpatient case-mix systems began receiving more attention when ambulatory patient groups (APGs) were developed as a possible PPS for hospital-based outpatient services. However, when the hospital outpatient prospective payment system (HOPPS or OPPS) was actually implemented, the system chosen was the ambulatory payment classification (APC) system.

Episodes of Care Systems

Research also has been conducted on case-mix systems that look at episodes of care for both inpatient and outpatient services. One such system is the episode treatment group (ETG). This system facilitates analysis of resource consumption and clinical outcomes for clinically similar episodes of care as identified through inpatient-, outpatient-, and pharmaceutical-claims data (Forthman, Dove, and Wooster 2000, 53).

Severity-of-Illness and Risk-Adjustment Systems

Severity-of-illness and risk-adjustment systems are similar to case-mix systems. The following systems are based on traditional coding systems:

- The all-patient-refined DRG (APR-DRG) is a severity-of-illness system that can be used with all patients, including children. APR-DRGs adjust for severity-of-illness by considering the number of and severity of patient complications, comorbidities, and procedures coded.

- Disease staging is another severity-of-illness/risk-adjustment system that uses administrative data. Stages range from no complications (Stage I) to death (Stage IV).

- Patient management categories (PMCs), a third severity-of-illness system, consider the same types of data as those available from the UB-92. PMCs, however, do not consider sequencing of codes in determining severity (Bowman 1996, 233–34).

Other severity-of-illness systems require more information than is ordinarily needed to assign standard ICD-9-CM codes. The following systems require additional data from the patient record:

- The *Computerized Severity-of-Illness Index* adds a sixth digit to ICD-9-CM codes to establish a severity level.

- The *Atlas System* (formerly the *MedisGroups System*) uses key clinical findings abstracted from the patient record rather than diagnoses to adjust for severity.

- The *Acute Physiology and Chronic Health Evaluation* (APACHE) system uses twelve physiological measures, such as lab values. These measures are then adjusted for other factors to arrive at a severity score for patients in an intensive-care unit (Bowman 1996, 234).

Medicare Risk-Adjustment Proposals

The Medicare program has evaluated several different risk-adjustment proposals for payments to its managed care providers in the Medicare+Choice program. Among the comprehensive proposals that have been considered are ambulatory care groups (ACGs), diagnostic cost groups (DCGs), and hierarchical coexisting conditions (HCCs) (Rulon 1998).

By 2004, CMS plans to implement a system that considers both outpatient and inpatient data when determining risk-adjusted capitation payments to managed care organizations. A DCG/HCC model could meet federal goals of using data from all hospital encounters to adjust payments based on the health risks of the population served (Pope et al. 2000, ES-1).

Principal inpatient diagnostic cost groups (PIP-DCGs), an interim system that considers only inpatient diagnoses, were implemented in the year 2000 (*Federal Register* 2000c, 40306). Because patients who have been hospitalized increase costs for managed care organizations, the PIP-DCG system provides a measure of clinically based risk adjustment. However, the PIP-DCG system is limited in comparison with more comprehensive systems. For example, the risk-adjustment factor for a member who has been hospitalized for a kidney infection might be twice that of an unhospitalized member. Another example would be a member with two hospitalizations, including one for lung cancer. Such a member might have four times the risk-adjustment factor of the "healthy" member. The effect of an increased risk-adjustment factor is to increase the premiums paid to the Medicare+Choice program (Tully and Rulon 2000, 64).

Managed Care Organizations' Use of Coded Data

In addition to risk adjustment, managed care organizations use coded data in other ways. For example, coded data are included among the elements collected in the Health Plan Employer Data and Information Set (HEDIS®). The National Committee for Quality Assurance (NCQA) developed HEDIS, a set of performance measures designed for healthcare purchasers and consumers (HCFA 2000b). To measure quality, HEDIS collects a wide array of data elements, including ICD-9-CM codes, CPT codes, DRGs, and revenue codes, along with other types of data (Willner 1999).

Prospective Payment Systems

Coded data are also used in the variety of prospective payment systems (PPS) initiated by the federal government. Information about these systems can be found in the professional section of the CMS Web site under Medicare Coding and Payment Systems Information for Health Plans and Providers (HCFA 2000d).

PPS regulations for hospitals include the DRG system for hospital inpatients and the APC system for hospital outpatients. PPS regulations also are in place for home health providers and for skilled nursing facilities. Proposed regulations were announced in 2000 for inpatient rehabilitation programs.

Diagnosis-Related Groups

Diagnosis-related groups (DRGs) were originally implemented as a payment mechanism for Medicare inpatients. Today, DRGs are used for many purposes, including the following:

- Reimbursement by other insurers

- Data analysis in negotiating managed care contracts

- Utilization management

There are about 500 DRGs, and each inpatient admission is assigned to only one DRG. Updates to the DRG system are published each year in the *Federal Register.*

Calculating DRGs

A computer program called a grouper calculates DRGs. (See table 1.3 for basic DRG vocabulary.) Decision-tree diagrams depict grouper logic in assigning DRGs. (See figure 1.3 for an example of a decision tree.) The grouper uses coded data—ICD-9-CM codes and other information from the UB-92—to categorize cases into DRGs. Grouper logic ordinarily uses the following pattern or algorithm:

1. In assigning a DRG, the grouper uses the principal diagnosis to place the case in a major diagnostic category (MDC).

2. If the patient had a procedure normally done in an operating room (an OR procedure), the grouper places the case in the surgical partition of the decision tree. If the patient did not undergo an OR procedure, the grouper places the case in the medical partition of the decision tree.

3. Within the surgical partition, the surgical hierarchy determines the next branch of the decision tree taken by the grouper. The surgical hierarchy is an arrangement of surgical procedures in order of resource consumption. If the patient underwent more than one surgical procedure, the procedure highest in the hierarchy would control the choices of DRGs available for that case.

Complications and Comorbidities

Complications and comorbidities (CCs) also play a part in determining the DRG. CCs are additional, or secondary, diagnoses that ordinarily extend the length of stay. A **complication** is a secondary condition that arises during hospitalization, while a **comorbidity** is one that exists at the time of admission. Some DRGs are paired, with one DRG including cases with a CC and the other DRG including the same type of cases, but without a CC. The DRG with the CC is the higher-paying DRG in each pair. Other factors, such as the patient's age and discharge disposition, can also affect DRG assignment.

Relative Weight of DRGs

Each DRG is assigned a relative weight. The **relative weight** is a multiplier that determines reimbursement. For example, a DRG with a relative weight of 2.0000 would pay twice as much

Table 1.3.   Vocabulary related to diagnosis-related groups (DRGs)

Term	Definition
Case-Mix Index (CMI)	The average of the relative weights of all cases treated at a given hospital. The case-mix index can be used to make comparisons between hospitals. The theoretical "average" case-mix index is 1.0000.
CC	A complication or comorbidity
Comorbidity	An additional diagnosis that exists at the time of admission and extends the length of stay in most cases
Complication	An additional diagnosis that arises during hospitalization and extends the length of stay in most cases
Decision Tree	A diagram depicting grouper logic in assigning DRGs
Diagnosis-Related Group (DRG)	A grouping of cases that are similar with respect to diagnoses and treatment
Grouper	A computer program that utilizes coded data to categorize cases into DRGs
Major Diagnostic Category (MDC)	An initial category into which the grouper places the patient based (usually) on the principal diagnosis
Medical Partition	A branch of a decision tree for cases without OR procedures
OR Procedure	A procedure normally done in an operating room
PPS Rate or Blended Rate	A dollar amount that is based on an individual hospital's costs of operating and that is multiplied by the DRG relative weight to calculate that hospital's reimbursement for a given DRG
Principal Diagnosis (PDx)	The condition established after study to be chiefly responsible for occasioning the admission of the patient to the hospital
Relative Weight	A number that is assigned to each DRG and that is used as a multiplier to determine reimbursement
Surgical Hierarchy	An arrangement of surgical procedures in order of resource consumption
Surgical Partition	The branch of a decision tree for cases with OR procedures

as a DRG with a relative weight of 1.0000. The hospital's PPS rate, or blended rate, makes up the other component of the DRG payment calculation. Each hospital's PPS rate is a dollar amount based on that hospital's costs of operating as determined by several blended factors. This blended rate is multiplied by the DRG's relative weight to calculate that hospital's reimbursement for a given DRG. For example, a hospital with a PPS rate of $4,000 would receive $6,000 for a case in a DRG with a relative weight of 1.5000 (1.5000 × $4000 = $6000).

Case-Mix Index and DRG System

A hospital can monitor its performance under the DRG system by monitoring its **case-mix index (CMI).** The CMI is the average of the relative weights of all cases treated at a given hospital. The Medicare CMI for every participating hospital is published annually in the *Federal Register.* The CMI can be used to make comparisons between hospitals and to assess the quality of documentation and coding at a particular hospital. The theoretical "average" case-mix index is 1.0000. Thus, a hospital with a CMI of 1.5000 theoretically has a more severely ill patient population than the average hospital. On the other hand, a hospital with a CMI of 0.9500 theoretically has a less severely ill patient population than the average hospital. If a hospital's case-mix index seems to be low compared with the perceived severity of the patient population, coding staff may be failing to document and code all relevant diagnoses and procedures. (See chapter 11, Case-Mix Management.)

Figure 1.3.   Example of a DRG decision tree

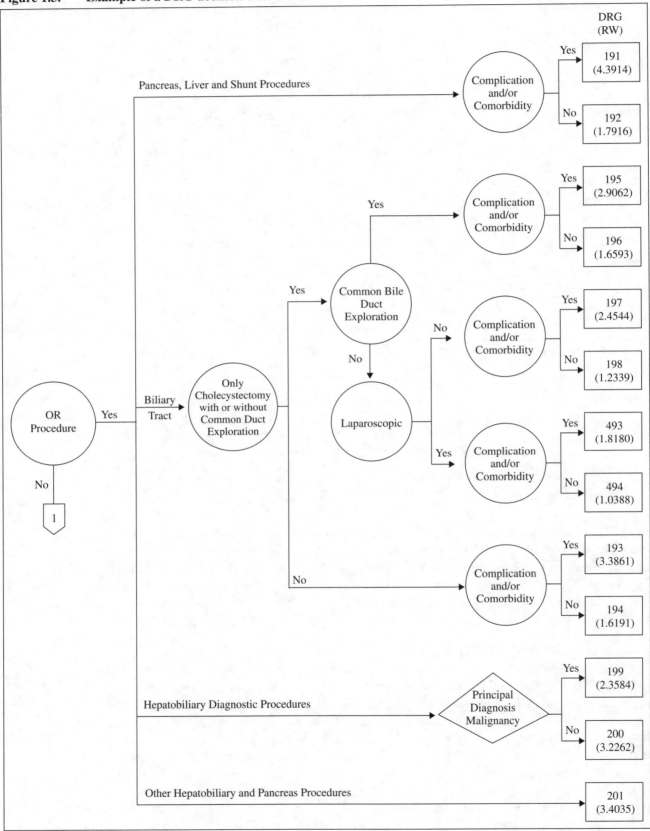

DRG Creep

As hospitals have striven to improve their case-mix indexes year after year, the phenomenon of **DRG creep** has appeared. DRG creep is the rise in the CMI through the coding of higher-paying principal diagnoses and of more complications and comorbidities, even though the actual severity level of the patient population did not change. Because an improved CMI could be viewed as an indication of fraud or abuse, coders must adhere to established coding guidelines and ethical principles in code assignment. Legitimate improvements in the quality of coding and documentation can lead to a legitimate rise in the case-mix index.

Ambulatory Payment Classifications

The ambulatory payment classification (APC) system was created as a result of provisions in the Balanced Budget Act of 1997. Its purpose was to implement a PPS for hospital outpatient services for Medicare patients. APCs were implemented in August 2000 (HCFA 2000c).

The APC system groups procedures that have similar clinical characteristics with similar costs based on the CPT/HCPCS codes assigned. Diagnosis codes do not affect APC assignment per se. However, diagnostic codes may affect reimbursement by indicating (or failing to indicate) the medical necessity of the services provided. There are about 1,000 APCs, which include the following groupings:

- Significant procedures, therapies, or services

- Medical visits

- Ancillary tests and procedures

- Partial hospitalization

- Drugs and biologicals

- Devices

APCs changed frequently in 2000–2001. The final rule implementing APCs was published in the *Federal Register,* April 7, 2000 (18433–18820). However, numerous updates and corrections to the rule were published during the first year of implementation, either through the *Federal Register* or through CMS program memoranda and transmittals.

APC System versus DRG System

One major difference between the APC and DRG systems is in the assigning of codes. An outpatient may be assigned more than one APC code per hospital encounter, whereas an inpatient is assigned only one DRG code per hospital admission. For example, a patient's emergency department visit includes evaluation and management, X-ray diagnosis of a fractured radius, and treatment of the fracture. This encounter will generate several APCs. The payment to the hospital would include amounts for each APC as indicated in table 1.4.

Table 1.4.   Example of APC reimbursement for an emergency department visit

Code	Procedure	Payment *
APC 0044	Closed treatment fracture/dislocation	$105
APC 0260	Level I plain film except teeth	$40
APC 0611	Mid-level emergency visit	$95
		Total $240

* Dollar amounts are for illustrative purposes only and do not represent actual payments.

Evaluation and Management Codes

Medical visits present several interesting aspects of the APC. For the most part, APCs follow the CPT coding rules as set forth by the AMA. However, for medical visits, hospitals may develop their own criteria for assigning the evaluation and management (E & M) codes that determine the level of the visit. In addition, hospitals do not have to follow the same guidelines that physicians do. The AHA recommends that hospitals develop a system for E & M code assignment that (1) reasonably reflects the medical necessity of services provided and (2) is based on documentation found in the patient record (Holbrook et al. 2001).

In a hospital clinic or emergency department, cases are classified according to one of three levels of service—low level, mid-level, or high level—based on E & M coding. However, the three levels of service used in clinic and emergency department APCs do not apply to the one medical visit APC that is assigned for interdisciplinary team conferences.

Discounted Payment for Multiple Procedures

Although the example in table 1.4 indicates full payment for each APC, there are actually several situations in which the payment could be reduced or discounted. One such situation is when multiple procedures are performed during a single encounter. The APC system recognizes that, when several procedures are performed at the same time, certain efficiencies occur that reduce costs. For example, only one operating room is used, and the patient is prepared only once.

Use of APC Status Indicators in Discounted Payments

The APC status indicator of the given service determines whether the service will be discounted in such a situation. If the status indicator is "T," multiple-procedure reductions apply. For example, the surgery or procedure with the highest APC rate may be paid at 100 percent, but any other surgical procedures performed may be paid at 50 percent. However, if the status indicator is "S," each procedure is paid at full APC value. In addition to "T" and "S" status indicators, several other status indicators provide information about each APC. (See table 1.5.)

Table 1.5.   APC status indicators

Status Indicator	Explanation
A	Services paid under a fee schedule (if payable)
C	Inpatient services; must admit patient and bill as inpatient; no payment under OPPS
E	Noncovered items or services
F	Acquisition of corneal tissue; paid at reasonable cost
G	Current drug/biological pass-through; additional payment
H	Device pass-through; additional payment
J	New drug/biological pass-through; additional payment
K	Non-pass-through drug/biological; paid under OPPS
N	Incidental services, packaged into APC rate (no separate payment is made for these procedures)
P	Partial hospitalization APC; paid per diem
S	Significant procedure, not discounted when multiple procedure (100% paid); paid under OPPS
T	Significant procedure, multiple-procedure reduction applies; paid under OPPS
V	Visit to clinic or emergency department; paid under OPPS
X	Ancillary service; paid under OPPS

Use of Modifiers in Discounted Payment for Terminated Procedures

Another type of discounting may occur when procedures are terminated or discontinued. A CPT modifier indicates that a procedure was terminated or discontinued. For example, modifier -74 indicates that surgery was terminated after induction of anesthesia had started. Hospital costs are essentially the same when a procedure is discontinued after induction of anesthesia as when the procedure is completed. Therefore, a procedure discontinued after induction of anesthesia is paid at 100 percent of the APC rate. However, if the procedure is terminated after the patient is prepared, but before anesthesia is started, modifier -73 is used and 50 percent of the APC rate is paid.

OPPS and APC Payments

The OPPS provides transitional pass-through payments. The purpose of these payments is to cover additional costs of innovative medical devices, drugs, and biologicals. Transitional pass-through payments provide separate payments in addition to APC payments. Payments for a given drug, device, or biological can be made on a pass-through basis for at least two, but not more than three, years. CMS's Web site explains the process for submitting a new item for consideration for pass-through payments (*Federal Register* 2000b, 18438).

OPPS and Provider-Based Clinics

Another issue in the OPPS is that of provider-based hospital clinics. When a Medicare patient is seen in a provider-based hospital clinic, the clinic receives an APC payment and the physician receives a reduced payment for services. The rationale for the reduction in the payment to the physician is that his or her practice expense has been shifted to the hospital. However, the total of the two payments in this situation is greater than the full-fee schedule payment that a physician in a freestanding clinic would receive. Therefore, CMS is very cautious about awarding provider-based status to a clinic that has not previously held that status.

APC Coding Edits

The outpatient code editor (OCE) operates in the systems of fiscal intermediary (FI) contractors. The OCE provides a series of flags that can affect APC payments because it identifies coding errors in claims. National Correct Coding Initiative (NCCI or CCI) edits also apply to the APC system. The main purpose of CCI edits is to prohibit unbundling of procedures. CCI edits are updated quarterly.

Resource-Based Relative Value Scale System

Medicare reimburses physician outpatient services on a different basis from that of hospital outpatient services. As previously explained, hospitals receive APC payments from Medicare for their outpatient services. Physicians, on the other hand, receive resource-based relative value scale (RBRVS) payments for their services. Both systems are based on CPT/HCPCS codes.

The RBRVS system has been in effect for physicians since 1992. This system is used by Medicare to develop fee schedules for Part B payments to physicians. Although RBRVS is the name commonly used for this system, CMS regulations refer to this system in terms of relative value units (RVUs). RVUs function in a manner similar to relative weights in the DRG system, with an RVU of 2.00 paying twice as much as an RVU of 1.00.

The components that make up the total RVU for a given procedure are physician work, practice expense, and malpractice expense. The RVUs for each of these three components and the total for each CPT/HCPCS procedure code are listed annually in the *Federal Register.* An oversimplified example of RVUs is provided in table 1.6. (For a complete table, see the annual

Medicare physician fee schedule in the *Federal Register*.) To arrive at a fee schedule amount for each procedure, the RVUs are multiplied by a national conversion factor and adjusted by a geographic practice-cost index (GPCI).

Skilled Nursing Facility Prospective Payment System

Federal data collection in skilled nursing facilities (SNFs) is based on the resident assessment instrument (RAI) process. A key component of this process is the periodic completion of a comprehensive resident assessment. This assessment is included as part of the minimum data set (MDS) form.

Although the PPS for SNFs was implemented July 1, 1998, the RAI/MDS process has been in effect for all nursing home residents since 1991. If the data abstracted on the MDS indicate that the resident is affected by any one of eighteen conditions that correlate to the functional well-being of the patient, a resident assessment protocol (RAP) is generated or "triggered." Examples of conditions that will trigger a RAP include the following:

- Cognitive impairment

- Pressure ulcers

- Delirium

- Feeding tubes

- Falls

- Urinary incontinence

- Use of physical restraints

The RAP summary provides guidelines for further assessment of the patient. RAP concepts are incorporated into the resident's care plan (Hawes et al. 1995).

Identification of diagnoses and ICD-9-CM coding is a part of the MDS process. One section of the MDS form captures diagnoses of diseases relating to the resident's activities-of-daily-living (ADL) status. (See Section I in figure 1.4.) Although some diagnoses can be reported using the check boxes in parts one and two of Section I, the third part of this section provides space for reporting more detailed diagnoses with ICD-9-CM codes (HCFA 2000f).

The SNF PPS system uses a case-mix adjustment based on the MDS. For each resident, the SNF receives per diem payments that are case-mix adjusted using the resident classification system, or resource utilization group version III (RUG-III). RUGs are based on data from resident assessments (MDS 2.0), and relative weights are developed from staff-time data (HCFA 2000a).

Table 1.6.   Examples of relative value units (RVUs)

CPT/ HCPCS Code	Description	Physician Work RVUs	Practice Expense RVUs	Malpractice RVUs	Total RVUs
10040	Acne surgery of skin abscess	1.18	1.58	0.05	2.81
10060	Drainage of skin abscess	1.17	1.29	0.08	2.54

*CPT five-digit codes and/or nomenclature are copyrighted by the American Medical Association.

Figure 1.4. **Portion of MDS 2.0 form**

Resident _____ Numeric Identifier _____

2.	BATHING	How resident takes full-body bath/shower, sponge bath, and transfers in/out of tub/shower (EXCLUDE washing of back and hair.) ***Code for most dependent*** in self-performance and support. (A) BATHING SELF-PERFORMANCE codes appear below	(A)	(B)
		0. Independent—No help provided		
		1. Supervision—Oversight help only		
		2. Physical help limited to transfer only		
		3. Physical help in part of bathing activity		
		4. Total dependence		
		8. Activity itself did not occur during entire 7 days *(Bathing support codes are as defined in Item 1, code B above)*		

3.	TEST FOR BALANCE (see training manual)	(Code for ability during test in the *last 7 days*) 0. Maintained position as required in test 1. Unsteady, but able to rebalance self without physical support 2. Partial physical support during test; or stands (sits) but does not follow directions for test 3. Not able to attempt test without physical help	
		a. Balance while standing	
		b. Balance while sitting—position, trunk control	

4.	FUNCTIONAL LIMITATION IN RANGE OF MOTION (see training manual)	(Code for limitations during *last 7 days* that interfered with daily functions or placed resident at risk of injury) (A) RANGE OF MOTION (B) VOLUNTARY MOVEMENT 0. No limitation 0. No loss 1. Limitation on one side 1. Partial loss 2. Limitation on both sides 2. Full loss	(A)	(B)
		a. Neck		
		b. Arm—Including shoulder or elbow		
		c. Hand—Including wrist or fingers		
		d. Leg—Including hip or knee		
		e. Foot—Including ankle or toes		
		f. Other limitation or loss		

5.	MODES OF LOCOMO-TION	(*Check all that apply* during *last 7 days*)		
		Cane/walker/crutch	a.	
		Wheeled self	b.	
		Other person wheeled	c.	
		Wheelchair primary mode of locomotion	d.	
		NONE OF ABOVE	e.	

6.	MODES OF TRANSFER	(*Check all that apply* during *last 7 days*)		
		Bedfast all or most of time	a.	
		Bed rails used for bed mobility or transfer	b.	
		Lifted manually	c.	
		Lifted mechanically	d.	
		Transfer aid (e.g., slide board, trapeze, cane, walker, brace)	e.	
		NONE OF ABOVE	f.	

7.	TASK SEGMENTA-TION	Some or all of ADL activities were broken into subtasks during *last 7 days* so that resident could perform them 0. No 1. Yes	

8.	ADL FUNCTIONAL REHABILITA-TION POTENTIAL	Resident believes he/she is capable of increased independence in at least some ADLs	a.
		Direct care staff believe resident is capable of increased independence in at least some ADLs	b.
		Resident able to perform tasks/activity but is very slow	c.
		Difference in ADL Self-Performance or ADL Support, comparing mornings to evenings	d.
		NONE OF ABOVE	e.

9.	CHANGE IN ADL FUNCTION	Resident's ADL self-performance status has changed as compared to status of **90 days ago** (or since last assessment if less than 90 days) 0. No change 1. Improved 2. Deteriorated	

SECTION H. CONTINENCE IN LAST 14 DAYS

1.	CONTINENCE SELF-CONTROL CATEGORIES (*Code for resident's PERFORMANCE OVER ALL SHIFTS*)
	0. *CONTINENT*—Complete control [includes use of indwelling urinary catheter or ostomy device that does not leak urine or stool]
	1. *USUALLY CONTINENT*—BLADDER, incontinent episodes once a week or less; BOWEL, less than weekly
	2. *OCCASIONALLY INCONTINENT*—BLADDER, 2 or more times a week but not daily; BOWEL, once a week
	3. *FREQUENTLY INCONTINENT*—BLADDER, tended to be incontinent daily, but some control present (e.g., on day shift); BOWEL, 2-3 times a week
	4. *INCONTINENT*—Had inadequate control BLADDER, multiple daily episodes; BOWEL, all (or almost all) of the time

a.	BOWEL CONTI-NENCE	Control of bowel movement, with appliance or bowel continence programs, if employed	
b.	BLADDER CONTI-NENCE	Control of urinary bladder function (if dribbles, volume insufficient to soak through underpants), with appliances (e.g., foley) or continence programs, if employed	

2.	BOWEL ELIMINATION PATTERN	Bowel elimination pattern regular—at least one movement every three days	a.	Diarrhea	c.
				Fecal impaction	d.
		Constipation	b.	NONE OF ABOVE	e.

3.	APPLIANCES AND PROGRAMS	Any scheduled toileting plan	a.	Did not use toilet room/commode/urinal	f.
		Bladder retraining program	b.	Pads/briefs used	g.
		External (condom) catheter	c.	Enemas/irrigation	h.
		Indwelling catheter	d.	Ostomy present	i.
		Intermittent catheter	e.	NONE OF ABOVE	j.

4.	CHANGE IN URINARY CONTI-NENCE	Resident's urinary continence has changed as compared to status of **90 days ago** (or since last assessment if less than 90 days) 0. No change 1. Improved 2. Deteriorated	

SECTION I. DISEASE DIAGNOSES

Check only those diseases that have a relationship to current ADL status, cognitive status, mood and behavior status, medical treatments, nursing monitoring, or risk of death. (Do not list inactive diagnoses.)

1.	DISEASES	(If none apply, CHECK the NONE OF ABOVE box)				
		ENDOCRINE/METABOLIC/ NUTRITIONAL		Hemiplegia/Hemiparesis	v.	
				Multiple sclerosis	w.	
		Diabetes mellitus	a.	Paraplegia	x.	
		Hyperthyroidism	b.	Parkinson's disease	y.	
		Hypothyroidism	c.	Quadriplegia	z.	
		HEART/CIRCULATION		Seizure disorder	aa.	
		Arteriosclerotic heart disease (ASHD)	d.	Transient ischemic attack (TIA)	bb.	
		Cardiac dysrhythmias	e.	Traumatic brain injury	cc.	
		Congestive heart failure	f.	**PSYCHIATRIC/MOOD**		
		Deep vein thrombosis	g.	Anxiety disorder	dd.	
		Hypertension	h.	Depression	ee.	
		Hypotension	i.	Manic depression (bipolar disease)	ff.	
		Peripheral vascular disease	j.	Schizophrenia	gg.	
		Other cardiovascular disease	k.	**PULMONARY**		
		MUSCULOSKELETAL		Asthma	hh.	
		Arthritis	l.	Emphysema/COPD	ii.	
		Hip fracture	m.	**SENSORY**		
		Missing limb (e.g., amputation)	n.	Cataracts	jj.	
		Osteoporosis	o.	Diabetic retinopathy	kk.	
		Pathological bone fracture	p.	Glaucoma	ll.	
		NEUROLOGICAL		Macular degeneration	mm.	
		Alzheimer's disease	q.	**OTHER**		
		Aphasia	r.	Allergies	nn.	
		Cerebral palsy	s.	Anemia	oo.	
		Cerebrovascular accident (stroke)	t.	Cancer	pp.	
		Dementia other than Alzheimer's disease	u.	Renal failure	qq.	
				NONE OF ABOVE	rr.	

2.	INFECTIONS	(If none apply, CHECK the NONE OF ABOVE box)				
		Antibiotic resistant infection (e.g., Methicillin resistant staph)	a.	Septicemia	g.	
				Sexually transmitted diseases	h.	
		Clostridium difficile (c. diff.)	b.	Tuberculosis	i.	
		Conjunctivitis	c.	Urinary tract infection in **last 30 days**	j.	
		HIV infection	d.	Viral hepatitis	k.	
		Pneumonia	e.	Wound infection	l.	
		Respiratory infection	f.	NONE OF ABOVE	m.	

3.	OTHER CURRENT OR MORE DETAILED DIAGNOSES AND ICD-9 CODES	a.		•	
		b.		•	
		c.		•	
		d.		•	
		e.		•	

SECTION J. HEALTH CONDITIONS

1.	PROBLEM CONDITIONS	(Check all problems present in *last 7 days* unless other time frame is indicated)				
		INDICATORS OF FLUID STATUS		Dizziness/Vertigo	f.	
				Edema	g.	
		Weight gain or loss of 3 or more pounds within a 7 day period	a.	Fever	h.	
				Hallucinations	i.	
				Internal bleeding	j.	
		Inability to lie flat due to shortness of breath	b.	Recurrent lung aspirations in **last 90 days**	k.	
		Dehydrated; output exceeds input	c.	Shortness of breath	l.	
				Syncope (fainting)	m.	
		Insufficient fluid; did **NOT** consume all/almost all liquids provided during **last 3 days**	d.	Unsteady gait	n.	
				Vomiting	o.	
		OTHER		NONE OF ABOVE	p.	
		Delusions	e.			

The Home Health PPS

The home health PPS (HH PPS) became the basis for Medicare payments to home healthcare providers on October 1, 2000. The case-mix system used in home health is called home health resources groups (HHRGs). The unit of payment is a sixty-day episode, paid in two split payments (HCFA 2000d). The amount received by the home healthcare provider is adjusted according to the level of the HHRG for that case.

Data for the HH PPS come from a comprehensive patient assessment in a manner similar to the MDS assessment process for SNF residents. The comprehensive assessment used for home health is the outcomes and assessment information set (OASIS). OASIS data are used to group cases to the appropriate HHRG. On claims, HHRGs are represented by health insurance prospective payment system (HIPPS) codes. HIPPS codes for HH PPS are five-position alphanumeric codes that represent specific patient characteristics from which Medicare payment determinations are made. The second, third, and fourth characters of an HIPPS code are alpha characters that represent the three domains of the HHRG system—clinical, functional, and service. See table 1.7 for examples of HHRGs, their corresponding HIPPS codes, and the three HHRG domains (HCFA 2000e).

Inpatient Rehabilitation Facility PPS

On August 7, 2001, the final rule describing the inpatient rehabilitation facility PPS (IRF PPS) was published in the *Federal Register* (*Federal Register* 2001). The IRF PPS uses a patient assessment instrument to classify patients into case-mix groups (CMGs). Determination of the CMG for a given case depends on rehabilitation impairment codes (RICs), motor admission score, cognitive admission score, age, and medical complications (Campbell and Thomas 2000).

As with previously discussed case-mix systems, one of the items included in the IRF patient assessment instrument is the ICD-9-CM code. Figure 1.5 shows the placement of the ICD-9-CM codes on the assessment form (*Federal Register* 2001).

Summary

The scope of services provided by various coding systems is far greater than the typical consumer of a given coding system may realize. Clinical concepts can be translated into a wide variety of codes. These codes can be used to:

- Manipulate and transmit data in a computerized system

- Map concepts from one coding system to another

- Classify cases into broad groupings

Table 1.7.   Examples of HHRGs with corresponding HIPPS codes and domain levels

HHRG	HIPPS Code	Clinical Domain	Functional Domain	Service Domain
C0F0S0	HAEJ1	Min	Min	Min
C0F0S1	HAEK1	Min	Min	Low
C0F0S2	HAEL1	Min	Min	Mod

Figure 1.5.   Portion of IRF patient assessment instrument

APPENDIX BB Patient_____   Numeric Identifier_____

4.	BOWEL CONTINENCE (Code for last 7-14 days)	0. CONTINENT— Complete control, does not use ostomy device 1. CONTINENT WITH OSTOMY—Complete control with use of an ostomy device that does not leak stool 2. BIWEEKLY INCONTINENCE—Incontinent episodes less than once a week (i.e., once in last 2 weeks) 3. WEEKLY INCONTINENCE—Incontinent episodes once a week 4. OCCASIONALLY INCONTINENT—2-3 times a week 5. FREQUENTLY INCONTINENT—4+ times a week but not all of time 6. INCONTINENT—All of time 8. DID NOT OCCUR— No bowel movement during the entire 14 day assessment period	

5.	BOWEL APPLIANCES (Code for last 3 days)	CODE: 0. No 1. Yes	
		a. Bedpan	c. Medication for control
		b. Enema	d. Ostomy

6.	BOWEL APPLIANCE SUPPORT (Code for last 24 hours)	0. No appliances (in item F5) 1. Use of appliances, did not require help or supervision 2. Use of appliances, required supervision or setup 3. Minimal contact assistance (light touch only) 4. Moderate assistance; patient able to do 50% or more of tasks 5. Maximal assistance; patient able to do 25-49% of all sub-tasks 6. Total dependence	

4.	OTHER CURRENT OR MORE DETAILED DIAGNOSES AND ICD-9-CM CODES (Any new diagnosis at reassessment or discharge is to be recorded here)	A. CODE ICD-9-CM diagnosis code B. CODE: 1. Other primary diagnosis/diagnoses for current stay (not primary impairment) 2. Diagnosis present, receiving active treatment 3. Diagnosis present, monitored but no active treatment

	A ICD-9-CM	B
a. _____	| | | | • | |	
b. _____	| | | | • | |	
c. _____	| | | | • | |	
d. _____	| | | | • | |	
e. _____	| | | | • | |	

5.	COMPLICA-TIONS/ COMOR-BIDITIES	Code the ICD-9-CM diagnostic code. Refer to manual to code comorbidities.

DIAGNOSIS	ICD-9-CM
a. _____	| | | | • | |
b. _____	| | | | • | |
c. _____	| | | | • | |
d. _____	| | | | • | |

SECTION G. DIAGNOSES

1.	IMPAIRMENT GROUP	Refer to manual for coding of impairment group
		| | | • | | |

2.	OTHER DISEASES	CODE: [Blank] Not present 1. Other primary diagnosis/diagnoses for current stay (not primary impairment) 2. Diagnosis present, receiving active treatment 3. Diagnosis present, monitored but no active treatment [If no disease in list, check G2aq None of Above item]

ENDOCRINE
a. Diabetes mellitus (250.00)
b. Hypothyroidism (244.9)
HEART/CIRCULATION
c. Cardiac arrythmias (427.9)
d. Congestive heart failure (428.0)
e. Coronary artery disease (746.85)
f. Deep vein thrombosis (451.1)
g. Hypertension (401.9)
h. Hypotension (458.9)
i. Peripheral vascular disease (arteries) (443.9)
j. Post acute MI (within 30 days) (410.92)
k. Post heart surgery (e.g., valve, CABG) (V45.81)
l. Pulmonary embolism (415.1)
m. Pulmonary failure (518.8)
n. Other cardiovascular disease (429.2)
MUSCULOSKELETAL
o. Fracture - hip (V43.64)
p. Fracture - lower extremity (812.40)
q. Fracture(s) - other (829.0)
r. Osteoarthritis (715.90)
s. Osteoporosis (733.00)
t. Rheumatoid arthritis (714.0)
NEUROLOGICAL
u. Alzheimer's disease (331.0)

v. Aphasia or Apraxia (784.3,784.69)
w. Cerebral palsy (343.9)
x. Dementia other than Alzheimer's disease (290.0)
y. Hemiplegia/hemiparesis — left side (342.90)
z. Hemiplegia/hemiparesis — right side (342.90)
aa. Multiple sclerosis (340)
ab. Parkinson's disease (332.0)
ac. Quadriplegia (344.00 - 344.09)
ad. Seizure disorder (780.39)
ae. Spinal cord dysfunction—non-traumatic (336.9)
af. Spinal cord dysfunction—traumatic (952.9)
ag. Stroke (CVA) (436)
PSYCHIATRIC/MOOD
ah. Anxiety disorder (300.00)
ai. Depression (311)
aj. Other psychiatric disorder (300.9)
PULMONARY
ak. Asthma (493.9)
al. COPD (496)
am. Emphysema (492.8)
OTHER
an. Cancer (199.1)
ao. Post surgery - non-orthopedic, non-cardiac (V50.9)
ap. Renal failure (586)
aq. NONE OF ABOVE

3.	INFECTIONS	CODE: [Blank] Not present 1. Other primary diagnosis/diagnoses for current stay (not primary impairment) 2. Diagnosis present, receiving active treatment 3. Diagnosis present, monitored but no active treatment (If no infections, check NONE OF ABOVE item G3l)

a. Antibiotic resistant infection (e.g., methicillin resistant staph - (041.11), VRE - (041.9))
b. Cellulitis (682.9)
c. Hepatitis (070.9)
d. HIV/AIDS (042)
e. Pneumonia (486)
f. Osteomyelitis (730.2)
g. Septicemia (038.9)

h. Staphylococcus infection (other than item "G3a") (041.10)
i. Tuberculosis (active) (011.90)
j. Urinary tract infection (599.0)
k. Wound infection (958.3, 998.59,136.9)
l. NONE OF ABOVE

SECTION H. MEDICAL COMPLEXITIES

1.	VITAL SIGNS	Vital signs (pulse, BP, respiratory rate, temperature) Score for the most abnormal vital sign 0. All vital signs were normal/standard (i.e., when compared to standard values) 1. Vital signs abnormal, but not on all days during assessment period 2. Vital signs consistently abnormal (on all days)

2.	PROBLEM CONDITIONS (In last 3 days)	(CHECK all problems present in the last 3 days unless otherwise noted)

FALLS/BALANCE
a. Dizziness/vertigo/light-headedness
b. Fell (since admission or last assessment)
c. Fell in 180 days prior to admission
CARDIAC/PULMONARY
d. Advanced cardiac failure (ejection fraction < 25%)
e. Chest pain/pressure on exertion
f. Chest pain/pressure at rest
g. Edema - generalized
h. Edema - localized
i. Edema - pitting

j. Impaired aerobic capacity/endurance (tires easily, poor task endurance)
FLUID STATUS
k. Constipation
l. Dehydrated; output exceeds input; or BUN/Creat ratio > 25
m. Diarrhea
n. Internal bleeding
o. Recurrent nausea/vomiting
p. Refusal/inability to take liquids orally
OTHER
q. Delusions/hallucinations
r. Fever
s. Hemi-neglect (inattention to one side)
t. Cachexia (severe malnutrition)
u. Morbid obesity
v. End-stage disease, life expectancy of 6 or fewer months
w. NONE OF ABOVE

3.	RESPIRATORY CONDITIONS (In last 3 days)	(CHECK all problems present in the last 3 days)

a. Inability to lie flat due to shortness of breath
b. Shortness of breath with exertion (e.g., taking a bath)
c. Shortness of breath at rest
d. Oxygen saturation < 90%

e. Difficulty coughing and clearing airway secretions
f. Recurrent aspiration
g. Recurrent respiratory infection
h. NONE OF ABOVE

4.	PRESSURE ULCERS (Code for last 24 hours)	a. Highest current pressure ulcer stage 0. No pressure ulcer (if no, skip to H5) 1. Any area of persistent skin redness (Stage 1) 2. Partial loss of skin layers (Stage 2) 3. Deep craters in the skin (Stage 3) 4. Breaks in skin exposing muscle or bone (Stage 4) 5. Not stageable (necrotic eschar predominant; no prior staging available)

b. Number of current pressure ulcers

SELECT THE CURRENT LARGEST PRESSURE ULCER TO CODE THE FOLLOWING—calculate three components (c through e) and code total score in f

c. Length multiplied by width (open wound surface area)
0. 0 cm²   4. 1.1–2.0 cm²   8. 8.1–12.0 cm²
1. <0.3 cm²   5. 2.1–3.0 cm²   9.12.1–24.0 cm²
2. 0.3–0.6 cm²   6. 3.1–4.0 cm²   10. > 24 cm²
3. 0.7–1.0 cm²   7. 4.1–8.0 cm²

d. Exudate amount
0. None   1. Light   2. Moderate   3. Heavy

Codes and their groupings can be used for many purposes, including the following:

- Public health surveillance and epidemiology
- Research
- Maintenance of computer-based patient records
- Reimbursement

The knowledgeable coding consumer keeps these many purposes in mind when compiling or using coded data.

References

Alternative Link, Inc. 2001. Coding and systems solutions for CAM and nursing. <http://www.alternativelink.com/> (Accessed May 8, 2001).

American Health Information Management Association. 1998. DSM-IV gets a fresh look. *Journal of the American Health Information Management Association* 69(5): 54.

American Hospital Association Central Office on ICD-9-CM. 2001. *Coding Clinic for ICD-9-CM.* <http://www.icd-9-cm.org/clinic.htm> (Accessed May 9, 2001).

American Medical Association. 2001a. CPT category III temporary codes. *CPT Assistant,* February, 5–6.

_____. 2001b. *Current Procedural Terminology.* Chicago: American Medical Association.

American National Standards Institute. 2001. Supporting standards: Healthcare Informatics Standards Board inventory of health care information standards pertaining to the Health Insurance Portability and Accountability Act (HIPAA) of 1996 (P.L. 104-191). <http://aspe.os.dhhs.gov/datacncl/hisbinv0.htm> (Accessed April 28, 2001).

American Nurses Association. 2000. Nursing Information and Data Set Evaluation Center (NIDSEC). <http://www.ana.org/nidsec/index.htm> (Accessed May 10, 2001).

American Psychiatric Association. 2000a. APA about to publish text revision of DSM-IV. *Psychiatric News.* <http://www.psych.org/pnews/00-05-05/publish.html> (Accessed May 12, 2001).

_____. 2000b. *Diagnostic and Statistical Manual of Mental Disorders,* 4th ed. (DSM-IV), Primary Care Version. <http://www.psych.org/clin_res/dsm_iv_pc.cfm> (Accessed May 12, 2001).

———. 2000c. DSM-IV questions and answers. <http://www.psych.org/clin_res/q_a.cfm> (Accessed May 12, 2001).

Averill, R. F., et al. 1998. Development of the ICD-10 procedure coding system (ICD-10-PCS). *Journal of the American Health Information Management Association* 69(5): 65–72.

Beebe, M. 2001. Coding notes: CPT-5 supports performance measurement, technology. *Journal of the American Health Information Management Association* 72(4).

Berthelsen, C. 2001. Interview. Jackson, Mississippi, May 8.

Bowman, E. D. 1996. Coding and classification systems. In *Health Information: Management of a Strategic Resource,* edited by M. Abdelhak et al. Philadelphia: W. B. Saunders Company.

Brandt, M. D. 2000. Health informatics standards: A user's guide. *Journal of the American Health Information Management Association* 71(4): 39–43.

Campbell, K. E., D. E. Oliver, and E. H. Shortliffe. 1998. The unified medical language system: Toward a collaborative approach for solving terminologic problems. *Journal of the American Medical Informatics Association* 5(1): 12–16.

Campbell, M., and C. Thomas. 2000. Inpatient rehabilitation prospective payment system. Paper presented at Healthcare Financial Management Association (HFMA) Conference, October 30, Tuscon, Arizona.

Centers for Disease Control and Prevention, National Center for Health Statistics. 2001. Official ICD-9-CM guidelines for coding and reporting. <http://www.cdc.gov/nchs/data/icdguide.pdf> (Accessed May 9, 2001).

Chute, C. G., et al. 1996. The content coverage of clinical classifications. *Journal of the American Medical Informatics Association* 3(3): 224–33.

Clark, J. 1998. The international classification for nursing practice project. *Online Journal of Issues in Nursing.* <http://www.nursingworld.org/ojin/tpc7/tpc7_3.htm> (Accessed May 9, 2001).

Cofer, J., ed. 1994. *Health Information Management,* 10th ed. Berwyn, Illinois: Physicians' Record Company.

Computer-Based Patient Record Institute. 1999. National Conference on Terminology for Clinical Patient Description. Terminology II: Establishing the consensus, lessons from experience. April 27–29. Tysons Corner, Virginia. <http://www.amia.org/cpri/terminology2/overview.html> (Accessed October 23, 2001).

Department of Medical Informatics, Columbia University. 2001. Arden Syntax overview. <http://www.cpmc.columbia.edu/arden/> (Accessed April 26, 2001).

Federal Register. 2000a. Health insurance reform: Standards for electronic transactions; announcement of designated standard maintenance organizations; final rule and notice. 65(160): 50312–50373. Or <http://aspe.os.dhhs.gov/admnsimp/final/txfinal.pdf> and <http://aspe.os.dhhs.gov/admnsimp/final/dsmo.htm> (Accessed April 27, 2001).

———. 2000b. Hospital outpatient services: Prospective payment system. 65(68): 18433–18820.

———. 2000c. Medicare+Choice program: Final rule. 65(126): 40169–40332.

———. 2000d. Medicare: Physician fee schedule (2001 CY), payment policies. 65(212): 65375–65603.

———. 2001. Medicare program; prospective payment system for inpatient rehabilitation facilities, final rule. 66(152): 41315–41430.

Forthman, M. T., H. G. Dove, and L. D. Wooster. 2000. Episode treatment groups (ETGs): A patient classification system for measuring outcomes performance by episode of illness. *Topics in Health Information Management* 21(2): 51–61.

Hawes, C., et al. 1995. Reliability estimates for the Minimum Data Set for nursing home resident assessment and care screening (MDS). *The Gerontologist* 35(2): 172–78. Or <http://www.rti.org/publications/RAI_gerontologist.cfm> (Accessed May 12, 2001).

Health Care Financing Administration. 2000a. Case-mix prospective payment for SNFs: Balanced Budget Act of 1997. <http://www.hcfa.gov/medicare/overview.htm> (Accessed May 12, 2001).

———. 2000b. HEDIS ® data release. <http://www.hcfa.gov/stats/hedis.htm> (Accessed May 11, 2001).

———. 2000c. Hospital outpatient prospective payment system. <http://www.hcfa.gov/medicare/hopsmain.htm> (Accessed May 11, 2001).

———. 2000d. Information for health plans and providers. <http://www.hcfa.gov/audience/planprov.htm> (Accessed May 11, 2001).

———. 2000e. Medicare Home Health Agency Manual: Transmittal 296. <http://www.hcfa.gov/pubforms/transmit/R296HHA.pdf> (Accessed: September 25, 2000).

———. 2000f. September update to the MDS form. <http://www.hcfa.gov/medicaid/mds20/mds0900b.pdf> (Accessed May 12, 2001).

Health Insurance Portability and Accountability Act of 1996. Public Law 104–191. <http://aspe.os.dhhs.gov/admnsimp/pl104191.htm> (Accessed April 27, 2001).

Health Level Seven. 2001. About HL7. <http://www.hl7.org/about/> (Accessed April 26, 2001).

Henry, S. B., et.al. 1998. Nursing data, classification systems, and quality indicators: What every HIM professional needs to know. *Journal of the American Health Information Management Association* 69(5): 48–55.

Holbrook, J., et al. 2001. APC coding for facility levels. American Hospital Association outpatient prospective payment system resources. <http://www.aha.org/opps/resources/appcoding700.asp> (Accessed May 11, 2001).

International Council of Nurses. 2001. International Classification for Nursing Practice (ICNP®) information sheet, March. <http://www.icn.ch/icnp.htm> (Accessed May 9, 2001).

Jamoulle, M., and J. Humbert. 2001. ICPC structure. <http://www.ulb.ac.be/esp/wicc/structen.html> (Accessed April 30, 2001).

National Center for Health Statistics. 2001. *International Statistical Classification of Diseases, 10th Revision, Clinical Modification* (ICD-10-CM). <http://www.cdc.gov/nchs/about/otheract/icd9/abticd10.htm> (Accessed April 28, 2001).

National Library of Medicine. 2001. Fact sheet: UMLS metathesaurus. <http://www.nlm.nih.gov/pubs/factsheets/umlsmeta.html> (Accessed July 17, 2001).

National Uniform Billing Committee. 2001. About the NUBC. <http://www.nubc.org/about.html> (Accessed April 27, 2001).

National Uniform Claim Committee. 2001. Standardized data set. <http://www.nucc.org/> (Accessed April 27, 2001).

North American Nursing Diagnosis Association. 2001. <http://www.nanda.org/> (Accessed May 10, 2001).

Okkes, I. M., M. Jamoulle, H. Lamberts, and N. Bentzen. 2000. ICPC-2-E: The electronic version of ICPC-2. Differences from the printed version and the consequences. *Family Practice* 17(2): 101–107.

Pope, G. C., et al. 2000. Diagnostic cost group hierarchical condition category models for Medicare risk adjustment: Final report. December 21. <http://www.cms.gov/ord/dcg.pdf> (Accessed May 11, 2001).

Prophet, S. 1997. Classification systems: Taking a broader look. *Journal of the American Health Information Management Association* 68(5): 46–50.

———. 1999. Alternative medicine: Growing trend for the new millennium, part II. *Journal of the American Health Information Management Association* 70(5): 65–71.

Rabold, J. 1995. World Organization of Family Doctors. Department of Community and Family Medicine, Duke University Medical Center. <http://cfm.mc.duke.edu/chair/wonca/WOFD.htm> (Accessed April 30, 2001).

Rode, D. 2001. Understanding HIPAA transactions and code sets. *Journal of the American Health Information Management Association* 72(1): 26–33.

Rulon, V. 1998. Medicare managed care: Risk adjustment and coding implications. *Journal of the American Health Information Management Association* 69(4): 58–65.

———. 2000. A global language for pharmaceutical regulation. *Journal of the American Health Information Management Association* 71(1).

Schulz, E. B., C. Price, and P. J. B. Brown. 1997. Symbolic anatomic knowledge representation in the Read Codes Version 3: Structure and application. *Journal of the American Medical Informatics Association* 4(1): 38–48.

Systematized Nomenclature of Medicine. 2001. <http://www.snomed.org/> (Accessed April 30, 2001).

Tully, L., and V. Rulon. 2000. Evolution of the uses of ICD-9-CM coding: Medicare risk adjustment methodology for managed care plans. *Topics in Health Information Management* 21(2): 62–67.

U. S. Department of Health and Human Services. 2001. *Administrative Simplification*. <http://aspe.os.dhhs.gov/admnsimp/> (Accessed April 27, 2001).

———. 2000. Frequently asked questions about code set standards adopted under HIPAA. <http://aspe.os.dhhs.gov/admnsimp/faqcode.htm> (Accessed April 27, 2001).

University of Iowa College of Nursing. 2001. Center for Nursing Classification. <http://www.nursing.uiowa.edu/cnc/> (Accessed May 10, 2001).

Van der Maas, A. A. F., A. H. M. ter Hofstede, and A. J. ten Hoopen. 2001. Requirements for medical modeling languages. *Journal of the American Medical Informatics Association* 8(2): 146–62. Or <http://www.jamia.org/cgi/reprint/8/2/146.pdf> (Accessed May 10, 2001).

Washington Publishing Company. 2001. ANSI ASC X12N HIPAA implementation guides. <http://hipaa.wpc-edi. com/HIPAA_40.asp> (Accessed April 30, 2001).

Willner, S. 1999. HEDIS® 2000. Society for Clinical Coding 1999 annual meeting presentation highlights. <http://www.sccoding.org/index.html> (Accessed April 30, 2001).

World Health Organization. 1992. *International Statistical Classification of Diseases and Related Health Problems, 10th revision* (ICD-10). Geneva: World Health Organization.

_____. 2001a. Introduction. *ICIDH-2: International Classification of Functioning, Disability and Health.* <http://www.who.int/icidh/intro.htm> (Accessed May 20, 2001).

_____. 2001b. Publications: Disease classification, nomenclature. <http://www.who.int/dsa/cat98/disease8.htm> (Accessed May 10, 2001).

Chapter 2

The Practice of Coding

Lois M. Yoder, RHIT, CCS

Coding practice is based on the simple concept of transforming descriptions of diseases, injuries, conditions, and procedures from words to alphanumerical designations. The purpose of coding in healthcare settings is to utilize code sets, such as ICD-9-CM, ICD-10, CPT, and HCPCS, or morphology codes, to classify patient encounters or episodes of care for historical and clinical reference. The actual code set used is determined by country, healthcare setting, regulatory agency, or reimbursement system.

Although the concept of coding is straightforward, the practice of coding is expanding and diversifying in many of today's healthcare environments. This expansion can be attributed to the following factors:

- Increased use of coded data

- Shifts in coding procedures

- Changes in the physical layout of healthcare settings

- The impact of technology

- Major changes in the regulatory environment of healthcare

The coding of clinical data has been a responsibility of health information services since medical librarians established the profession in the early 1900s. For many years, coding has enabled healthcare facilities and associated agencies to tabulate, store, and retrieve disease-, injury-, and procedure-related data. However, coding has taken on increased significance with the passage of legislation, as shown in the following time line:

- 1983—Prospective payment for hospital coding was instituted.

- 1991—All Medicare outpatient visits were first required to have some form of code attached to the encounter as a condition for reimbursement.

- 2000—The outpatient prospective payment system (OPPS) was implemented.

Coding under Prospective Payment

The prospective payment system (PPS) marked the beginning of a new era for health information services. Hospitals are now expected to provide the codes on discharged Medicare patients within five days of discharge. Medical staff policies regarding incomplete health records have been strengthened and are being firmly enforced in many hospitals.

With prospective payment for inpatients, coding is directly linked to a hospital's survival. ICD-9-CM codes are a primary element of the diagnosis-related group (DRG) system, an inpatient classification scheme that categorizes patients who share similar clinical and cost characteristics. Medicare inpatient payment rates are based on DRGs. Billing cannot be done until the codes are available.

Implementation of OPPS in August 2000 brought major changes in the reporting and reimbursement processes of hospital-based outpatient health services. OPPS legislation affects payments for the following types of facilities and services:

- Hospital outpatient departments

- Community mental health centers

- Certain services provided by comprehensive outpatient rehabilitation facilities

- Home health agencies

- Hospice services provided to patients for the treatment of nonterminal illness

OPPS uses the ambulatory payment classification (APC) system in which outpatient services that are similar both clinically and in use of resources are assigned to separate groups for payment. To be paid accurately under OPPS, hospitals now must list all HCPCS codes for all outpatient services provided.

The new Medicare reimbursement methodologies, which are based on the DRG and APC systems, require coders to have a thorough knowledge of the ICD-9-CM and CPT/HCPCS coding systems. Coders today must have a sophisticated understanding of both procedural and diagnostic coding, as well as the ability to analyze and interpret patient health data.

An effective health information service is essential to the success of the hospital. A high demand for the expertise of credentialed health information management (HIM) professionals exists in hospitals today because data quality is increasingly emphasized both internally and externally.

The Role of the Coding Professional

Coding professionals are persons who perform the coding function. Coders' abilities or skill sets can be measured in terms of education, experience, aptitude, quality, and productivity.

Beginning Coders

Beginning coders who have just completed their coding course work in a college or technical school program generally test out at a basic level, making them eligible for basic coding jobs. Beginning coders may be assigned limited responsibilities, such as coding only diagnoses in primary care clinics or coding ancillary testing encounters in hospitals or ambulatory care settings. Many healthcare institutions provide critical on-the-job training that molds beginning coders into coding professionals with the fundamental skills, practice, and experiences that are valued by coding teams, departments, and organizations throughout the healthcare industry.

Experienced Coders

Because the variety of settings that require coding expertise is expanding, candidates for a coding position may be required to demonstrate a mastery skill level in several code sets. For example, a freestanding ambulatory care center or hospital outpatient department may require coding expertise in both ICD-9-CM and CPT coding systems. These facilities must use ICD-9-CM codes for diagnoses and CPT codes for procedures to report the services they provide to patients.

Experienced coding professionals sometimes have strong preferences about the types of cases they want to code. Some coders prefer to maintain a high skill level in ICD-9-CM coding and to practice only in acute care hospitals. Although subspecializing may limit their practice options, it allows coders to become true experts in a particular area of coding.

Experienced ICD-9-CM coders with several years of acute care hospital experience and with a demonstrated mastery skill level would probably be assigned the responsibility of coding complex, acute care hospital cases. Such coders might be physically located in a healthcare facility's coding department, or they might work at home if the technology is available to support electronic coding at a remote site. (See the discussion of e-coding later in this chapter.)

Knowledge of the Coding Function

The process of coding may vary among settings; however, the function of assigning codes does not change. Coders take clinical information—diagnostic terms and procedure descriptions—and assign a numeric code to each one according to a set of official guidelines designed to standardize coding. Coders take this clinical information from the physician's or primary caregiver's portion of the health record. The primary caregiver is responsible for providing coders with proper information. Information used to assign codes must be part of an official health record, not part of an unofficial document such as a surgery log or registration list.

Regardless of the healthcare setting, official health records should be used. In rare circumstances, exceptions to this rule may occur. However, an approved policy and procedure for these exceptions should be available to coders.

Coders must be able to assign codes to all codable information. Sometimes, however, the only information available to code consists of signs and symptoms. In such instances, coders must know where to look for pertinent clinical information for coding, as well as how to identify information that is not pertinent. The coding professional does not make assumptions or employ personal preferences for a particular code. Coding guidelines absolutely preclude such practices.

Titles for Coding Professionals

Some of the most common titles for coding professionals are coder, coding specialist, data quality technician, inpatient coder, outpatient coder, service-line coder, and coder/biller. Titles for coding professionals have proliferated in recent years because the nature of the work varies from setting to setting, and the level of a coder's expertise can be better denoted with a specific title. For example, coding specialists are responsible for coding only inpatient or outpatient cases, whereas data quality technicians may be responsible for specific abstracting functions and for handling some parts of internal audits in addition to coding.

Because no official national coding titles exist, a coder's title might simply be the title selected for the coders at a particular facility. No matter what the title, the fundamentals of the job are essentially the same—assigning codes to clinical data or to encounters for the purpose of requesting payment or of recording healthcare activity for studies or archiving.

Coders

The title of **coder** denotes only that the person holding that position is assigned solely to the function of coding. The volume of work is such that a full-time position has been created to support the coding function without extra roles and responsibilities.

Service-Line Coders

Service-line coders are proficient in all coding areas, but they excel in one particular service line, such as oncology or cardiology. They code inpatient and/or outpatient accounts for only one particular service line and, therefore, can maintain a high level of coding accuracy. Service-line coders are also responsible for maintaining a dialogue with the clinical staff on their unit regarding documentation issues and yearly coding and reimbursement changes. Service-line coders routinely ensure that appropriate clinical information is recorded in the health record. They are often considered educators to the degree that they communicate with clinical and finance staff regarding coding, documentation, and compliance matters.

Because service-line coders function in a subspecialty unit, they become part of the care-management team. Coders who subspecialize are responsible for maintaining their level of expertise for both inpatient and outpatient coding guidelines and for all information regarding proper reporting of the unit's business for purposes of payment. They communicate routinely with patient fiscal services personnel, the coding manager or director, and the medical staff. Answering questions for physicians and nurses, who must continually review their documentation practices to ensure proper recording of patient care, is an important part of the service-line coder's job description. However, coding remains the most important function of this job, no matter how the nuances of the position may vary.

Outpatient Coders

Outpatient coders are responsible for assigning ICD-9-CM and CPT codes to ambulatory surgery or emergency department cases each day. The scope of their work remains in one of these settings and does not cross over into inpatient or physician-office settings. In teaching hospitals, an outpatient coder may be responsible for coding clinic cases in which patients who are considered outpatients see physicians in a clinic within a teaching environment. The coding of clinic cases could be considered a subspecialty service line in an office-type setting.

Coders/Billers

Coders/billers work in ambulatory care and physician-office settings. They are generally responsible for processing the **superbill,** or office form, that has been initiated by the physician and that states the diagnoses and other information for each patient encounter. Coders/billers take the information about patient encounters and then process claims, or bills, for the patient's insurance company, or for patients who are self-pay or who choose to submit the claims themselves. Coders/billers may use a computerized software program called an **encoder** to assign codes, or they may have only a computerized listing of codes to reference. (See chapter 3 for a detailed discussion of encoders.)

Physical Setting of the Coding Function

The physical setting in which the coding function actually occurs has changed subtly over the years. Historically, coding has been a hospital-based function housed in the health records department. Now, however, coding is performed in numerous settings—hospitals, ambulatory care centers, clinics, physician's offices, skilled nursing facilities, insurance companies, managed care organizations, workmen's compensation agencies, health statistics agencies, veterinary clinics, prisons, behavioral healthcare settings, pathology and diagnostic centers, research centers, and educational institutions.

Physical Layout of Coding Areas

Over the years, many organizations and agencies have come to understand the need to employ professional coders. The physical layout of the area in which coding is performed, however, remains a frequent concern of those working in the field. Because coders require a certain amount of concentration when reviewing clinical data or health records, the physical layout of the setting in which they work is important.

Some employers and managers who hire coders neither appreciate the importance of the coding function nor understand the basic requirements of the coding professional. As a result, they may limit the physical layout of a coding department or workstation. For example, a coder in a physician's office or ambulatory care center may be given a single desk in a room with other employees who perform other functions, such as registration, billing, or charge-entry tasks.

Coders in other settings, however, may be located in the business office in close proximity to the billers. In these situations, coders and billers may be able to set up effective teams to accomplish their tasks. Hospitals commonly allocate space for a coding team in the HIM department.

Most recently, alternative locations for coders have been expanding. Some coders are now located in surgery suites, in medical units, closer to physician's offices in teaching hospitals, and even at home.

E-Coding

Since the advent of e-coding, some coders have been working from their homes. They code health records over the Internet or via a protected interface with the hospital's mainframe. With physical space at a premium in hospitals and other healthcare settings, the option of having coders work at home is appealing to some healthcare administrators and coding managers.

E-coding provides an alternative for managing an increased number of coders in an HIM department. The concept of placing coders at home to work via computer is similar to the model used by medical transcriptionists. Before a hospital or healthcare provider can use e-coding, it must have an information system capable of routing computerized health records and scanned documents in on-line form to the coder's off-site location. E-coding interface programs allow home-based coders to access patient health data and the encoder concurrently to code each record that is routed to them.

The advantages of e-coding include the following:

- The coder may have more flexible work hours.

- Space in the HIM department is available for other employees.

Some disadvantages of e-coding include the following:

- Transcription models have proven that when employees work from home, they are removed from the daily activities and structure of a work environment.

- Some employees do not work well in a home environment and opt to come back to a more structured setting.

To prevent the negative aspects of e-coding from occurring, some facilities require the coder to work one week per month in the HIM department. In this way, e-coders maintain contact with other coders and with management.

Coding Practice for Various Settings

Coding practice varies from setting to setting based on clinical factors, reimbursement issues, types of services provided, uses of coded information, time factors, staff availability, technology, and coding classification system(s) used.

Coding of Inpatients in the Hospital Setting

Coding of acute care or hospital inpatient accounts is the most standardized model of coding. In this practice model, coders complete the following steps in the coding process:

Step 1.   Receive inpatient health records, in most cases after patients have been discharged to home or other facilities.

Step 2.   Review the health record in a standardized fashion, looking for important clinical information from the physician that will assist them in assigning ICD-9-CM codes for diagnoses and procedures.

Step 3.   Input clinical information into the encoder program and answer several Uniform Hospital Discharge Data Set (UHDDS) questions, such as age, gender, and discharge disposition.

Step 4.   Begin to enter clinical information into the system, prompting the software to a code selection. If coders are not comfortable with the code mapping in the system, they reference code books and follow the manual process of assigning a specific code. They then use both manual and encoder processes to make a final determination.

Step 5.   Complete a clinical abstract and route the coded information to the patient fiscal services department for claims processing.

Step 6.   Sign off on the health record and print a final coding summary that they attach to the health record.

Coders who work in the usual and customary setting of a hospital HIM department, away from the activity and noise of a medical unit or office, commonly find that environment comfortable. Some coders in acute care inpatient settings have little interaction with others in the department and no direct contact with physicians or other healthcare providers. Other coders in hospital settings, however, go directly to medical and surgical units in the hospital to review cases, obtain clinical information for coding, and engage in dialogue with physicians. The practice environment depends to a large extent on whether the hospital follows a retrospective or a concurrent model of coding.

Retrospective Coding

As indicated in step 1 of the coding process, hospital inpatient cases are most frequently coded retrospectively. **Retrospective coding** takes place after the patient has been discharged and the entire health record has been routed to the HIM department. Because the health record is the main source document used in the coding function, it must be complete. Physicians must have dictated all pertinent documents, such as consultations and discharge summaries, and have completed all progress notes. In retrospective coding, coders perform the following tasks:

1. Review the health record, primarily the physician portion, the ancillary studies, and therapeutic modalities of care.

2. Match up the physician's documentation with coding guidelines to establish the principal diagnosis (the reason after study for the encounter) and all other pertinent diagnoses and procedures.

3. Use the encoder to assign ICD-9-CM diagnoses and procedure codes.

4. Finalize the abstract.

Concurrent Coding

In some hospitals, however, inpatient cases are coded concurrently. **Concurrent coding** takes place while the patient is still in the hospital and receiving care. Under the concurrent coding model, coders may be located near the physician's "incomplete" area of the HIM department so they can query physicians during the patient's stay if documentation is vague, unclear, or incomplete. In concurrent coding, coders complete the following tasks:

1. Receive notification when a patient is admitted.

2. Travel to the medical and surgical units to review the case.

3. Begin a problem or diagnosis list from physician documentation.

4. Assign ICD-9-CM codes while the patient is in-house.

5. Review each case on an average of every other day.

After the patient is discharged, health records are still routed to the coding department. However, coders spend much less time reviewing the records because they have already initiated the coding process. At that point, coders complete the encoding process and the abstract. The coding process is thus finalized.

Coding of Outpatients in Ambulatory Care Services

In ambulatory care centers, coders are often located close to actual areas of patient care so they can interact more readily with caregivers. They serve not only as coders, but also as documentation specialists and health record completion "cops." These additional functions seem to merge with coding tasks in smaller settings. Coders in ambulatory care settings are likely to code a higher volume of cases per day because of the limited amount of information they must review in each case. Sometimes ambulatory care coders are also responsible for communicating with insurance companies and with prior-authorization firms that represent the patient's benefits plan.

For ambulatory surgery, emergency department, and other ambulatory care services, coders follow a method of coding practice similar to that used for inpatients in hospitals. They receive copies of health records in their work areas, review each record, and assign both ICD-9-CM diagnosis codes and procedure codes to each account.

When portions of health records are stored on-line, coders may be required to access those portions on a computer screen and incorporate the information into their code assignment process. Coders then print out a final code summary and attach it to the hard-copy health record, thus signing off on the case.

When the entire ambulatory care record is on-line, coders utilize a split-screen program to view the health record on one side of their computer screen and the encoder on the other side. Then, they follow the same basic process of assigning codes and finalizing the account.

Accounts that coders deem incomplete are flagged in the computer system via the abstract or billing screen to be held until a complete health record has been compiled.

Coding in Physician-Office and Clinic Settings

Coders in physician-office and clinic settings commonly are placed in their own area with one or two desks, close to the billing staff. Alternatively, coders in these settings may be placed in the registration and discharge area of the clinic or office because the coding function is tied to the actual process of generating a **demand bill**—one that patients can take with them. In such situations, coders must rely on a computerized program that assigns ICD-9-CM diagnosis codes and CPT procedure codes, as well as "visit" or evaluation and management (E & M) codes.

The coding function takes place at the same time that the claim with assigned charges is being generated. This arrangement may limit a coder's access to the physician's documentation in the health record. The handwritten notes compiled by the physician during the office visit may be incomplete or lack a true description of the entire episode of care. The coder must be able to think quickly and know when to question or to ask for clarification of clinical information used to assign codes.

More commonly, however, the physician checks off information on a superbill or encounter form that lists the many visit/procedure options and diagnoses. The medical visit level and any procedures and diagnoses are then taken from that form and entered into the coding or billing system to finalize the HCFA-1500 claim form. After the patient's claim has been created, the coder/biller's job is essentially complete. The patient's record is returned to storage or is routed back to the clinical staff.

Drawbacks for Coders in Clinic and Physician-Office Settings

One drawback for coders in a clinic or physician-office setting is that coding tools or references are generally more limited than they are in the hospital environment. Code books are frequently used in these settings when encoders are not available. In such circumstances, if the coders/billers are not properly trained in coding, they may tend to use "cheat sheets" to assign codes.

Other drawbacks for coders/billers in clinic and physician-office settings include the following:

- Administrative personnel may have excessively high expectations for coders' productivity.

- Other staff may not have an appreciation of the importance of correct coding.

- Source documents may be limited at the time of coding because physicians have just dictated the office visit notes so they are not yet available to coders.

- Coders often must rely on handwritten notes in the patient record and in the superbill information.

Additional Responsibilities of Coders in Clinics and Physician-Office Settings

In some clinic and physician-office settings, coders/billers have additional responsibilities. If on-line billing software is available to execute the claim on behalf of the patient, the coder/biller initiates the billing process. Payers such as Medicare and Blue Cross often sell or license use of a software program that allows claims to be submitted electronically. The coder/biller can initiate an electronic "send" of the day's activities to a designated payer authorizing an electronic transmission. This ultimately completes the coding process for that day.

If the electronic data interchange (EDI) edits the file and identifies errors in the claims data, such as an incorrect ICD-9-CM code or insurance number, it will return that particular claim to the coder for correction. Often coders/billers are also responsible for monitoring the payments received from insurance companies. Coders/billers then determine if claims were paid in full or if more work is required to receive the expected payments.

Coding in Long-Term Care Facilities

Coders in skilled nursing facilities, rehabilitation centers, home health agencies, and other long-term care facilities practice much as coders in hospitals do. They work from health records to assign ICD-9-CM and/or CPT codes for each patient's encounter, commonly on a monthly basis because most long-term care services are billed every thirty days.

For these services, payers like Medicare or Medicaid are likely to require that codes be submitted in a specific format at the beginning of the encounter, or at the start of the patient's stay. The codes are then reported again each month and on final discharge. The coder follows the payer's instructions about when and how codes are submitted, for example, by electronic format or manual processes. Code books are used to complete the coding function. Encoders and abstracting systems are not necessarily available as work tools except in larger institutions.

Coding guidelines vary for long-term care settings because information about the patient's complete clinical picture, including manifestations of conditions, is needed to support the level of care assigned for each patient. Coding in these settings could be considered a concurrent coding process because the patient is in-house and may be a resident for a long period of time. Diagnoses are not likely to change much over the duration of the stay. However, the coder's ability to identify the onset of new conditions or diseases throughout the stay is important and requires a specific coding skill set. The coder is also responsible for communicating with the nursing and therapy staffs to ensure that they understand the coding process and the necessary documentation required to assign codes.

Coding in Behavioral Healthcare Settings and Prisons

Behavioral healthcare institutions and prisons frequently set up designated work areas for coders similar to those in acute care hospitals. In these settings, coders utilize the health record to assign codes, to follow the reporting process, and possibly to complete a clinical abstract for each patient.

Behavioral Healthcare Settings

Coders in behavioral healthcare settings, both inpatient and outpatient, function much as those in hospitals and ambulatory care centers. They take care of the facility's coding and abstracting needs. Coders in behavioral healthcare settings use DSM-IV codes to classify behavioral healthcare patients. DSM-IV codes are not that different from ICD-9-CM codes. However, distinct variances in the numeric DSM-IV codes create a more specific coding hierarchy with which to report the characteristics of certain behaviors and mental health conditions. The process of coding in behavioral healthcare settings is also similar to that in hospitals.

Prisons

Prison systems have begun to maintain a comprehensive healthcare delivery system. With such a system comes the need for an HIM department that includes coding and recording of all healthcare activity. Most prisons have only an infirmary or ambulatory care setting. Some prisons, however, are expanding healthcare services to meet the needs of the prison population internally, thus reducing the number of transfers to external healthcare providers. Although coders who work in prison settings are generally classified as ambulatory care coders, coding positions in prisons may carry unique titles and responsibilities.

Coding in Veterinary Clinics

Veterinary clinics have found a need for coders in their environment as well. To better classify cases and diseases, code sets are also a valuable method of recording clinical data in animal medicine. Unique code sets have been created to classify disease processes. These code sets are recorded in an abstract designed for veterinary settings. Coders record and code patient assessment information along with diagnoses and procedures documented by the veterinarian. Coders in large veterinary environments may have full-time positions, whereas smaller veterinary clinics only require a part-time coder.

Coding in Insurance Companies and in Other Settings

Insurance companies benefit greatly by hiring skilled coders from clinical or hospital settings. These coders are a valuable asset to insurance companies for several reasons:

- They can interpret and classify clinical-coded data for their nonclinical counterparts.

- They serve as data analysts by reviewing claims information from providers.

- They assist in linking coverage policy with codes.

- They analyze incoming claims data to identify trends for future benefits planning.

Coders who work in insurance companies, managed care organizations, research offices, or statistical agencies generally spend a good portion of their time analyzing and validating data that have already been coded. These coders validate data for the following purposes:

- To prepare data to be entered into a provider file or master database

- To use them to analyze a healthcare delivery system

- To adjudicate payment for services rendered

- To correct or remove coding errors, thus ensuring a clean batch of statistical data

After coders complete their initial tasks, the data are stored in data banks for future analysis of hospitals, physicians, or other providers. Institutions such as insurance companies utilize coded data to make assumptions about terms of coverage, benefits plans, and rate setting; to analyze methods of healthcare delivery; and to project future needs in patient care.

Sometimes coders in insurance companies may re-code data to meet the needs of their internal, standardized set of codes or coding methodology. Coders may also re-code data in research or teaching institutions in which a classification system such as ICD-9-CM may not meet the mark in terms of data collection or specificity of clinical classification. In such instances, coders may be trained to utilize an internal coding system that is unique to the institution in which they work.

Insurance companies, managed care firms, and statistical agencies are beginning to realize the value of coding experts. These organizations now aggressively recruit coding professionals to maintain the continuity of their clinical data.

Source Documents and the Coding Function

Source documents play an important part in the coding function because coders glean important clinical information from them. The following source documents make up the patient's health record:

- Health history and physical examination

- Progress notes

- Consultations

- Operative reports/procedure notes

- Discharge summaries

When physicians record less-than-complete healthcare data because of time constraints or other influences on their daily schedules, the quality of documentation diminishes. To improve documentation, a concurrent documentation program that prompts physicians to be more specific in their documentation may be put into place.

Concurrent documentation programs, similar to concurrent coding, are being implemented in some hospitals. In such programs, care managers and coders are paired up for education and training in the basics of documentation. Coders then train clinical staff about clinical terms and coding terms so that staff members become concurrent resources for physicians in the unit. Only documentation is focused upon at that time. The coding function remains a retrospective process to be completed after the patient has been discharged.

The Abstracting Function

In hospitals, the abstracting function is usually considered part of the coding process. To carry out the abstracting process, coders utilize encoders to assign ICD-9-CM or CPT codes. The encoder automatically incorporates the codes into the clinical abstract for each episode of care and calculates DRG assignments or other payment-driven categories.

The Clinical Abstract

A **clinical abstract** is a computerized file that summarizes the following patient information:

- Demographics

- Reason for admission

- Diagnoses

- Procedures

- Physician information

- Other information deemed pertinent by the facility

Information such as resident information (in a teaching hospital) and blood transfusion data may also be captured in an abstract. The abstract is maintained as a long-term document. Each time a patient presents as an inpatient, or as an ambulatory surgery or emergency department patient, an abstract is triggered by the registration.

Coders and the Abstracting Process

Coders generally complete the abstract during the coding process. They abstract certain data elements in health records for the purpose of recording specific events, providers, or other clinical information that is of interest to the hospital, state agency, research agency, or teaching facility. In large hospitals, the abstracting function may be assigned to dedicated staff.

Abstracting in Ambulatory Care Centers

In small ambulatory care settings, such as teaching clinics or solo-practice physician offices, a clinical abstract is most likely not created in the computer system. A brief, single-page (or single-screen) abstract of the patient's visit may be recorded, including items such as visit date, visit type, and other demographics. Larger clinics or multiphysician practices, on the other hand, do opt for abstracting systems that provide more sophisticated business reports and processing capability of patient data.

Tools Used in the Coding Function

Coders use both manual and software tools to carry out the coding process. Manual tools include the following:

- Current code books

- Official coding guideline publications

- Clinical references such as pharmacy formularies and anatomy plates

- Other clinical or coding references

Many encoder (software) products now include official coding references and anatomic references. These features make it easier for coders to validate code assignments.

Both encoders and code books must be updated several times during the year, most importantly when the annual ICD-9-CM code changes and the CPT/HCPCS updates become available. Other official updates may be released throughout the year if errors or omissions have been published. Coding managers should make all updated information available to coders as soon as possible.

Third-Party Reporting Requirements and Regulations

Third-party reporting requirements and regulations should also be made available to coders. Payers often have specific reporting requirements that have a direct impact on reimbursement. For example, two-digit modifiers are often required with CPT procedure codes on Medicare outpatient claims. To explain certain care scenarios more precisely, such as a bilateral procedure rather than a common unilateral one, coders would use a specific two-digit code attached to the base CPT procedure code, if the code does not already describe a bilateral component. Failure to properly follow such reporting guidelines tends to reduce some payments and prolong others because the edits in the payers' claims edit systems recognize when these reporting guidelines are not followed.

The Charge Description Master or Chargemaster

A common method of coding for outpatient procedures and services comes in the form of the **charge description master (CDM)** or **chargemaster.** The chargemaster is the entire list of eligible charges by department within a hospital. This document is stored in the main computer as a text file. The CDM lists all services that are eligible for reporting on a patient's claim in each department by **charge code**—the key code selected to report a service or item that is attached.

For certain services such as radiology, HCPCS procedure codes are included for each line item, along with the text description of the test, the revenue code (an address code that indicates the type of department reporting the item), and the charge. When a service is rendered, the technician selects the proper charge code with the associated procedure description and code. The technician then enters that information onto a computerized charge screen or onto a hard-copy charge ticket. That information then is routed to the patient's bill for final processing.

Diagnosis codes that are assigned retrospectively by other coders are matched up on the claim with the HCPCS codes generated in the radiology department. Because the HCPCS codes remain in the chargemaster over time, radiology personnel often require assistance from coders in updating codes or in clarifying correct HCPCS code assignments for certain procedures. Coders are becoming recognized as valuable resources for department managers who may require help revising their codes when the official updates are published each January. (See chapter 5 for a detailed discussion of the chargemaster.)

Other Practice Opportunities for Coding Professionals

Coders are in the unique position not only of understanding the clinical data needs of today's healthcare organizations, but also of piloting the technology that is emerging to support those needs. The perspective that coders bring to the healthcare environment is opening up new practice opportunities for them, expanding their leadership roles, and offering them initiatives and incentives for professional growth.

Coders as Chargemaster Coordinators

Coders are sometimes placed in the role of chargemaster coordinator. As such, they are responsible for mentoring other staff and assisting each department with its line item updates each year. They are also responsible for maintaining their own level of expertise in HCPCS coding throughout the year.

Coders responsible for the chargemaster document may be given a title such as chargemaster coordinator so that all staff members know the focus of their position. The chargemaster coordinator meets routinely with departments to discuss issues such as:

- New technology or equipment

- Changes in procedure codes

- Changes in reimbursement methodologies that require a revision of charges or text descriptions associated with the department's business

Chargemaster Coordinators and Local Medical Review Policies

Chargemaster coordinators also pass on information from local medical review policies (LMRPs) published by CMS. LMRPs outline diagnoses considered medically necessary for a certain test or procedure. LMRPs are revised by CMS every few years with regard to coverage policy. Chargemaster coordinators review LMRPs with departments and with registration personnel to ensure proper administration of benefits for Medicare patients. LMRPs generally list CPT/HCPCS and ICD-9-CM diagnosis codes within their memoranda. Chargemaster coordinators share this information with each department affected because revisions to line items in the chargemaster may be necessary.

Other Responsibilities of Chargemaster Coordinators

Chargemaster coordinators may also be responsible for reconciling any billing issues that arise from chargemaster-driven coding. If claims do not pass to a designated payer, the patient fiscal services staff may look to the chargemaster coordinator for assistance in resolving the claim in order to complete the billing process.

Another responsibility of chargemaster coordinators may be conducting random internal audits. These audits occur when procedure codes are generated from the chargemaster to ensure the integrity of data within the healthcare system. Outcomes from this type of auditing merge nicely with internal audits from the HIM coding areas, thus making the coding audit process more comprehensive.

Coders as Patient Screening and Referral Assistants

According to some payer regulations, hospitals and ambulatory care centers must screen referral information from physicians when patients register for some types of ambulatory care. Certain payers require that their beneficiaries be notified in writing prior to receiving a service if that service is not covered by their benefits plan.

For example, a physician orders a CBC serum test for a particular Medicare patient and writes a diagnosis on the referral form along with the test requisition. A registrar or technician at the hospital must review that requisition and compare it against Medicare coverage to determine whether the CBC is considered a covered service with the diagnosis indicated. If the CBC is not considered "covered," the registrar or technician issues a written notice to the patient stating that the clinical indication noted for the test is not covered by Medicare.

Because referral information is of such importance, some hospitals and ambulatory care centers place coders in or near the registration area. Coders then screen referrals before the patient receives the service. This action ensures proper coding of the diagnosis and supports the process of notifying patients of noncoverage. Such screening assistance is a new role for outpatient coders.

Coders and External Audits

In any healthcare setting, coders may be given the responsibility of responding to outside queries or external audits. If external auditors are scheduled to come into the facility to conduct an audit, the coding staff may be required to prepare or verify the health record **pull list**— the list of requested records to be pulled and provided to the auditors. Coders may also meet with the auditors after the audit is complete. For off-site coding audits, mail-in requests for copies of health records may first be routed to coders and then to the release-of-information department for processing.

More recently, state peer review organizations (PROs), particularly those with Medicare contracts, are conducting focused coding and documentation audits at the direction of CMS. As part of those audits, some review organizations are notifying hospitals that they must conduct internal audits and submit the findings to them. Those audits may be routed to coders to initialize the audit process, particularly in rural settings.

Coders in Rural Healthcare Settings

In rural healthcare settings, highly skilled coders are difficult to employ because they may not live close to the rural hospital or the physician's office. If a rural hospital does employ a coder, that person may be required to work in many capacities, including as medical staff secretary. Coders in rural hospitals may also be assigned responsibilities associated with health record processing, abstracting, and managing incomplete health records. Because the average census in a rural hospital may not support a full-time coder, the mix of other duties ensures a full workweek.

In rural hospitals, retrospective coding is most commonly performed because the coder may not have time to go out to the units and review cases. If utilization management (UM) responsibilities, such as reviewing documentation for medical necessity or for appropriate use of health resources, are assigned to the coder, then coding and UM duties can be merged.

Some healthcare providers have developed innovative ways to deal with the shortage of professional coders in rural settings. For instance, a facility might hold health records for coding until a traveling coder comes to the facility and codes all the accounts that are ready for billing. The traveling coder then moves on to the next facility and codes accounts that are waiting there.

Other healthcare facilities in rural settings use express mailing to send copies of health records to off-site coders. These records are coded within twenty-four hours and sent back to the facility. The codes are then entered into the facility's billing system.

Contract Coders

Many providers or facilities now use **contract coders**—coders hired on a temporary basis to work on-site. They either help with coding backlogs or maintain the current coding workload.

The employment of contract coders gives a facility time to recruit new coders to fill open positions. Contract coders utilize the same process to assign codes for each case as coders who are regular employees. It is not uncommon for coders to leave full-time employment and to embark on contract coding careers that may offer them travel to other regions of the country.

Conclusion

The practice of coding varies according to the type of healthcare facility involved and the services the facility offers. Numerous other factors can also have an impact on the practice of coding, including:

- New applications for coded data

- Government reimbursement regulations

- Third-party reporting guidelines

- Official coding guidelines

- Physical layout of the coding department

- Tools and technology

- Content of the health record

- Staffing patterns

- Preferences of coding professionals

Today, the coding function is most often carried out retrospectively—after the patient has received the service or has been discharged from the facility. All clinical information is then available to the coder, and codes can be properly assigned.

In the future, health records will be computerized. At that time, artificial intelligence in the **computerized patient record (CPR)** will support concurrent coding because the provider or clinician will enter data into the system. Coders will then become data quality validators to ensure that codes are assigned correctly.

When this transition occurs, coders will be looking at data both concurrently and retrospectively. For a period of time, coders will map back the codes automatically assigned with the actual documentation dictated into the CPR. Through dictation, voiced terms are translated into text or characters in a CPR. Because voice-recognition systems are still in their infancy, they will require constant validation and review.

As new technology becomes available, the practice of coding will continue to change and expand along with coders' titles, job descriptions, roles, and responsibilities.

References and Bibliography

Abdelhak, M., S. Grostick, M.A. Hanken, and E. Jacobs. 2001. *Health Information: Management of a Strategic Resource.* 2d ed. Philadelphia: W.B. Saunders Company.

Huffman, Edna K. 1994. *Health Information Management.* 10th ed. Berwyn, Ill.: Physicians' Record Company.

Chapter 3

Structure and Organization of the Coding Function

Marion K. Gentul, RHIA, CCS
Nadinia A. Davis, MBA, CIA, CPA, RHIA

Recent changes in healthcare delivery and reimbursement have brought about corresponding changes in the practice of clinical coding. The coding manager brings stability to this changing environment by structuring and organizing the coding function around certain basic resources.

The main resources of a successful HIM department of any size or setting include the following:

- Qualified staff
- Up-to-date tools and adequate information systems
- A well-designed physical environment

In addition, the coding manager is responsible for organizing the coding process so that documentation can be converted into meaningful data that meet the facility's various needs.

Qualified Staff

The primary resource in any coding area is qualified staff. Although credentials are not always part of the job description for a coding position, a credentialed coder is always a most desirable candidate. The person who has earned and who maintains a credential demonstrates measurable coding aptitude and knowledge.

Coding Credentials

The two industry-recognized professional organizations that award coding credentials are the American Health Information Management Association (AHIMA) and the American Academy of Professional Coders (AAPC). Each of these organizations conducts credentialing examinations at various times throughout the year.

AHIMA offers the certified coding specialist (CCS) and the certified coding specialist—physician based (CCS-P) credentials. The CCS exam emphasizes and tests the applicant's knowledge of hospital inpatient coding, specifically, the ICD-9-CM and associated coding rules and guidelines. The CCS-P exam also tests the applicant's knowledge of ICD-9-CM. However, the CCS-P exam emphasizes outpatient, ambulatory care, and physician practice-based coding, and it covers the HCPCS/CPT coding rules and nationally applicable reporting.

AAPC also offers two coding credentials. The certified professional coder (CPC) credential acknowledges competency for physician practice-based coding. The certified professional coder—hospital (CPC-H) credential recognizes competency for hospital-based coding.

Although the credentials that AHIMA and AAPC offer may sound similar, there is a significant difference in the competency levels demonstrated by successful examinees. AHIMA's current credentials are mastery-level credentials with underlying competencies that reflect significant record-analysis training and work experience. A new entry-level coding examination will be offered by AHIMA in late 2002. AAPC credentials are entry-level credentials for which a brief course of study can prepare examinees. Although credentials offer a degree of confidence in the motivation and professional commitment of the individual, they are not the final word on competence. (See chapter 4 for more information about the importance of credentials.)

In general, hospital-based staff whose primary function is to perform inpatient coding should hold the CCS credential. Staff performing outpatient coding in hospital outpatient departments, ambulatory care settings, or physician practices may appropriately have the CCS-P, CPC, or CPC-H credential. Many coders hold coding credentials from both AHIMA and AAPC. Coders also must meet continuing education requirements to retain their credentials.

Some local colleges, trade schools, or Internet sites offer various sorts of "coding credentials" or "coding certificates." On an individual, case-by-case basis, a person possessing such a credential or certificate may meet the requirements for a coding job. However, it cannot be assumed that this person has achieved the same level of coding competence as one holding a credential from AHIMA or AAPC. Coding managers should encourage all staff members to work toward obtaining the credential or credentials most pertinent to their job functions.

In addition to coding credentials, AHIMA offers two HIM credentials: the registered health information administrator (RHIA) and the registered health information technician (RHIT). These credentials demonstrate competence in general HIM practice and are useful in supporting job enhancement and enrichment opportunities for coding staff. See table 3.1 for a summary of coding and HIM credentials.

Table 3.1.   Summary of coding credentials and other HIM credentials

Credential	Title	Granting Organization	Requirements	Continuing Education
CCS	Certified coding specialist	AHIMA	Passing national examination	10 hours per year
CCS-P	Certified coding specialist—physician office based	AHIMA	Passing national examination	10 hours per year
CPC	Certified professional coder	AAPC	Passing national examination, plus experience	18 hours per year
CPC-H	Certified professional coder—hospital	AAPC	Passing national examination, plus experience	18 hours per year (24 if both CPC credentials are held)
RHIT	Registered health information technician	AHIMA	Graduation from an accredited associate degree program, and passing national examination	20 hours biannually
RHIA	Registered health information administrator	AHIMA	Graduation from an approved or accredited degree program, and passing national examination	30 hours biannually

Membership in Professional Organizations

Professional coding organizations support coding initiatives and provide educational programs and services for coders. Without belonging to at least one professional association, coding professionals would find it difficult, if not impossible, to keep abreast of coding changes, reporting rules, and relevant legislation.

AHIMA, the national association of HIM professionals, is a diverse organization. Its members include coding staff personnel, as well as those who oversee coding functions and manage coding staff personnel. AHIMA offers coding resources, training, and continuing education, as well as the Society for Clinical Coding (SCC), a designated Community of Practice within the association. The membership of SCC includes coding professionals who work in settings throughout the healthcare continuum. AHIMA is also a member of the Cooperating Parties, which includes the AHA, CMS, and the National Center for Health Statistics (NCHS). The Cooperating Parties coordinate and maintain the ICD-9-CM coding system.

AAPC is a privately owned, professional coding organization. It offers both national and local continuing education opportunities, an informative bimonthly publication called *The Coding Edge,* and a strong network of local chapters.

Depending on the individual's job function and work setting, a coder might benefit from belonging to both AHIMA and AAPC. On the other hand, staff members within the same healthcare facility who have memberships in different associations may share information with one another. Departments should budget funds for coding staff memberships in professional associations.

Experience

In recent years, the ability of many healthcare organizations to hire new coders has been hampered by industrywide economic pressures to reduce the number of coding positions and to keep salaries low in the face of declining inpatient occupancies. Meanwhile, the need for qualified coders in outpatient and other nonacute care settings has increased because the focus has been on data quality and data integrity, in conjunction with corporate compliance and the electronic patient record. Because training a new coding professional can take a minimum of six months to a year, facilities have tended to drop training programs in favor of recruiting experienced coders.

In general, coders who have the appropriate credentials for their job functions, as well as two years of successful coding experience, are the most desirable candidates for coding positions. Unfortunately, even experienced coders may have difficulty adapting to different facility-specific guidelines and must also be trained and supervised. On the plus side, coders in new settings may provide their facilities with fresh alternatives and improvements to current practices. Coding experience in one setting may not always translate to success in another setting. A common misconception among noncoders is that "all coding is the same," or "a coder is a coder." This is not the case because competency levels and documentation requirements differ from setting to setting.

For example, a coder with many years of experience at a local community hospital may not be proficient initially in a major teaching medical center. Similarly, inpatient coders who are moved to outpatient settings and outpatient coders who are moved to inpatient settings will also need additional training because of differences in coding systems and reimbursement reporting guidelines.

Continuing Education

Ongoing continuing education is vital to ensure accurate coding. Healthcare facilities should have specific policies and a formal process for continuing education for all coding staff positions.

Such action would be in response to current compliance guidelines from the Department of Health and Human Services, Office of the Inspector General (DHHS OIG), that mention the need for keeping coding staff up-to-date with regulatory requirements.

Internal Continuing Education

Much continuing education can be accomplished without sending staff to costly outside seminars or workshops. The coding manager should consider the following suggestions for internal continuing education:

- Ask physicians from the medical staff to present short clinical topics pertinent to the patient population in a particular setting. Allow time for coders to ask questions of physicians within the different medical specialty areas.

- Have coders research pertinent clinical topics and present them to their colleagues. This activity can be done individually or in teams. Allow a specific amount of work time for staff to research the topics in the medical staff library, the local library, or on the Internet. The presentation should provide applicable coding assignments for the topics and include discussion of DRG or APC impact as appropriate.

- In hospital settings, allow coding staff to attend physicians' continuing education programs or "Grand Rounds." Ask the medical staff office for a list of upcoming topics and obtain permission for coding staff members to attend.

- Consider using a "Lunch-and-Learn" format. Provide lunch to participants as a time-saver rather than using regular work hours for this activity. Busy physicians in particular will appreciate this accommodation. If the coding staff is large enough, consider forming coding teams and awarding token prizes, such as free food or movie tickets, for outstanding presentations. When creativity and fun are encouraged, the process can be motivating.

- Keep a log of topics presented by and programs attended by staff. Routine documentation presents a strong case to management and auditors that the HIM department and the facility are committed to data quality and accuracy.

- Ensure that employees attending in-house programs receive a certificate of attendance, or other documentation, that can be used as evidence of continuing education for maintenance of credentials.

External Continuing Education

AHIMA and AAPC offer numerous external continuing education opportunities, often at local sites or by teleconference. Members of these organizations have the option of being automatically informed of upcoming events and topics.

Many highly regarded training companies and consulting firms also offer pertinent education and training. Training companies and individual trainers are often able to customize presentations and materials specifically to meet an organization's needs. Code book vendors or coding outsourcing firms are other sources of continuing education activities. To receive notice of these opportunities, coders should put their names on mailing lists. They should also review notices about continuing education in professional journals.

State hospital associations and the American Hospital Association (AHA) also offer educational opportunities. The AHA periodically offers satellite presentations concerning clinical topics and coding changes.

When coders take part in external continuing education activities, their coding managers should document the continuing education credits awarded and the areas in which they apply. Coders should obtain a certificate of attendance for their personal files. Coding managers also should maintain a record of coders' attendance in the HIM department's file as evidence of coding education.

Tools of the Trade

Coding tools include code books, groupers, encoders and other software applications, official coding guidelines, dictionaries, texts, and other resource materials.

Code Sources

The type of facility in which a coder works dictates the source of the diagnosis and procedure codes that are assigned. It is imperative that only current code sources be used. Regardless of the setting or the coding system utilized, an encounter that takes place in 2001 cannot be coded accurately with a 1997 code book. The following sections contain brief explanations of the current code sources that are available and when they need to be updated. (See table 3.2 for a summary of code sources.)

ICD-9-CM

The *International Classification of Diseases, 9th Edition, Clinical Modification* (ICD-9-CM) is currently used to code diagnoses in most settings, such as acute care, long-term care, rehabilitation, and ambulatory care. Volume III of ICD-9-CM is used for the coding of procedures in acute care and in other inpatient settings. Annual changes in ICD-9-CM codes become effective for discharges after October 1, coinciding with the beginning of the U.S. government's fiscal year.

All coding materials related to ICD-9-CM must be updated annually so that new and revised codes and descriptions can be correctly assigned on a timely basis. Coding materials can be ordered in advance from a chosen vendor or vendors for delivery as soon as they are available.

Table 3.2.   Summary of code sources

Codes	Description	Uses	Updated	Maintained by
ICD-9-CM	3 volumes: Volumes 1 and 2: Diagnosis Tabular and Index Volume 3: Procedures	All diagnosis coding Procedure coding in inpatient settings	Annually Effective for discharges after October 1	Cooperating Parties: CMS NCHS AHA AHIMA
CPT	Procedures and other services performed by or under the direction of physicians	Procedure coding in ambulatory settings; capturing charges in inpatient settings	Annually Effective for encounters after January 1	AMA
HCPCS	Procedures, services, supplies, and durable medical equipment	Procedure coding and capturing charge	Annually	CMS

Printed code books are available in both updateable ring-binder form and in bound versions. Layout, font size, color, and resources in these books vary significantly among vendors and generate definite preferences among individual coders. Unless a significant price difference that materially affects the budget exists between books, coders should be allowed to choose the vendor and format of their choice. Budgets should allow for one book per coder, plus at least one book for general office reference.

Some coders prefer to own and maintain their own coding materials. Coding managers must appropriately supervise this practice to ensure that correct versions are always being used.

HCPCS

The Healthcare Current Procedural Coding System (HCPCS) is a three-tiered system of procedural codes used primarily for ambulatory care and for physician services. HCPCS codes are also frequently attached to inpatient chargemasters for convenience and to facilitate communication between providers and payers about services and supplies included in the CPT or HCPCS Level II or Level III systems. (See chapter 5 for a detailed discussion of the chargemaster.)

Level I: Current Procedural Terminology (CPT), developed and maintained by the American Medical Association (AMA), is the first level of the HCPCS coding system. CPT is a nomenclature designed to standardize communication between physicians and payers. It is used primarily for claims-processing purposes for physician services and for reporting ambulatory care services. The primary focus of CPT is to describe to the payer the physician's care of the patient. When used for facility reporting, CPT reflects facility services rather than the professional services of the physician.

The AMA updates CPT annually, with most codes effective January 1. Although CMS and other payers generally allow a three-month grace period to implement new and revised CPT codes, facilities are nevertheless advised to obtain updated versions of the codes and to orient coding staff to them as soon as possible. Some CPT codes may be released with an effective date other than January 1.

Printed code books for CPT, like those for ICD-9-CM, can vary somewhat in their features and formats. Comments about coder preferences apply here as well. The budget should include a CPT code book for every coder who is responsible for outpatient coding, plus one extra book for general office reference.

Level II: Level II codes are applicable to selected physician and nonphysician services, durable medical goods, drugs, and supplies. These codes, developed and maintained by CMS, are updated as needed—currently, each quarter. The updates become effective when announced. Level II codes are used primarily for reporting purposes in ambulatory care for claims processing. Although many insurance plans recognize HCPCS Level II codes, the possibility exists that selected plans will reject these codes.

Level III: Level III codes apply to certain new procedures, new devices, and services performed by providers not found in Levels I and II. Level III codes are defined by the individual fiscal intermediary (FI) or carrier and, therefore, vary by location or payer. Over time, as they become more widely used, these services are often incorporated into Level II and, if they are physician based, into CPT. This practice can be problematic for billing purposes because the provider may use the new code while the payer still only recognizes the Level III code. For this reason, it is important for provider personnel to have excellent working relationships with payers. With the implementation of the standard transaction code sets required by the Heath Insurance Portability and Accountability Act (HIPAA), the use of Level III HCPCS codes will be phased out.

Groupers

As discussed in chapter 1, two main types of Medicare grouping programs are used: DRGs for inpatient cases and APCs for outpatient cases. **Grouping** refers to a system of assigning patients to a classification scheme (DRG or APC) via a computer software program. Such a program is normally purchased from a vendor by a facility's information systems (IS) department.

In addition to Medicare, selected payers may adopt other grouping programs for non-Medicare inpatients. Other grouping programs may or may not use the same relative weights as the Medicare (CMS) grouper. The use of other grouping programs for non-Medicare patients varies from state to state.

DRGs and APCs: Similarities and Differences

The grouper systems for DRGs and APCs are similar in the following ways:

- Both grouper systems are driven by coded data.

- Patient admissions or encounters are classified using grouping methodologies.

- Payments are weighted in both systems.

The **weight** is the numerical assignment that is part of the formula by which a specific dollar amount, or reimbursement, is calculated for each DRG or each APC.

Significant differences, including the following, also exist between DRGs and APCs:

- Under DRGs, facilities are reimbursed for each admission.

- Under APCs, facilities are reimbursed for each outpatient encounter.

- One DRG is assigned for each inpatient admission.

- One or more APCs may be assigned for each outpatient encounter.

Groupers and Diagnosis-Related Groups

Diagnosis-related groups, or DRGs, are used for hospital inpatient reimbursement. In 1983, Congress amended the Social Security Act to include a national DRG-based hospital prospective payment system (PPS) for all Medicare acute care inpatients. CMS oversees this program. Acute care facilities are reimbursed for inpatient Medicare cases according to the DRG category to which each case is assigned by the CMS grouper.

Under contract with CMS, 3M Health Information Systems has performed all annual updates or revisions to the grouper. Each revision is called a grouper version. The revisions are necessary because annual changes are made in ICD-9-CM, as well as to the grouper itself. Updates are effective at the beginning of the federal fiscal year. For example, version 18.0 was the grouper version effective during the time period from October 1, 2000, to September 30, 2001. Upcoming changes to the DRG grouper are published in the *Federal Register* several months in advance of the effective date.

From a coding management standpoint, inpatient cases of patients discharged on October 1 must be grouped using the new *grouper version*. The HIM department should be in communication with the IS department to verify that the necessary software updates have been made by the time cases are to be entered into the facility's coding/abstracting system. Testing of some cases in which changes have been made may be necessary to verify that the updated software is functioning properly.

Even though grouper versions change yearly, historical data reflect the grouper version assigned at any given time. New DRGs have been added and others have been deleted over time. To ensure that year-to-year DRG comparisons are valid, the Definitions Manual of each grouper version may be utilized. This manual is essentially a printout of all data elements contained within each DRG.

Groupers and Ambulatory Payment Classifications

Ambulatory payment classifications (APCs) are used in the outpatient prospective payment system (OPPS). While facilities are reimbursed for each inpatient admission under DRGs, they are reimbursed for each patient encounter under APCs.

As with DRGs, CMS oversees APCs and OPPS. 3M Health Information Systems, under contract with CMS, provides the APC grouper and updates. The initial final regulations for OPPS and APCs can be found in the *Federal Register* 65, no. 68 (April 7, 2000): 18438–18820, with updates published subsequently. Because APCs are a relatively new regulatory requirement, CMS has devoted a special section of its Web site to OPPS at <www.hcfa.gov/medlearn/refopps.htm>. Coding managers should periodically review this Web site because it includes OPPS updates, corrections, frequently asked questions (FAQs), pricer logic, outpatient code editor (OCE) specifications and revisions, and program memoranda. The Web site also contains the Medicare OPPS Training Manual. Many excellent publications that focus on code selection and the impact of APC implementation on the HIM department are also available from vendors.

Groupers and Other PPSs

The administration of other PPSs and the role of HIM personnel vary widely by type of facility. For example, in long-term care facilities, coded data are not the primary determinant of Medicare reimbursement. However, regardless of the HIM setting or the PPS under which it operates, groupers must be updated and tested by the effective dates. Likewise, personnel must be appropriately informed about any changes in the grouper, as well as the impact those changes may have on coding practices and on reimbursements to the facility.

Computer-Based Coding Sources

Printed coding materials are rapidly being supplemented with, or replaced by, computer-based coding sources. These sources include both simple code look-up software and comprehensive encoders.

Code Look-Up Software

A **code look-up** is merely a computer file with all of the indexes and codes recorded on magnetic disk or CD-ROM. Because the coder still must search the index for the correct code and then verify the code in the tabular section of the system, the code look-up is not an efficient application for routine coding. However, when employed as accessory files to applications in which the code is already known, look-ups can be used to fill in code description text.

Encoder Software

The most effective computer-based application for routine code assignment is the encoder. An encoder is a software program that generates specific codes to accurately portray patient encounters and to comply with all current coding guidelines. With an encoder, the coder uses technology and software assistance to find and assign codes correctly.

Advantages of Using an Encoder

One advantage of using an encoder can be illustrated with the following example:

> A health record indicates that the patient has "arteriovenous (A-V) malformation of the intestines." The coder is not familiar with "A-V malformation." The code book index does not specifically list this term in the alphabetic index. "Malformation" does not have a subterm for either "arterio" or "venous." Even creative searching leads only to congenital codes. Before proceeding to code this diagnosis, the coder obtains a medical dictionary to find out the definition of "A-V malformation." Unsuccessful in this pursuit, the coder turns to *Coding Clinic.* While searching *Coding Clinic,* the coder finds a reference that links A-V malformation to angiodysplasia and gives the correct code. Only then is the coder able to proceed with the code selection. This scenario occurs often enough that productivity can be dramatically affected for a coder encountering this type of problem for the first time.

In the scenario just described, an encoder with built-in resource references would allow the coder to look up the definition within the computer program. In addition, most encoding software contains references that the coder can access with just a keystroke or mouse click. Some references are: *Coding Clinic, CPT Assistant,* a CPT/ICD-9-CM Volume III crosswalk, a medical dictionary, a pharmacology reference, an anatomy and physiology reference, laboratory value resources, National Correct Coding Initiative (NCCI) edits, and reimbursement weights. The ability to access these references seamlessly within the encoding process makes encoding software a valuable tool. Even experienced coders can appreciate the convenience, accuracy, and productivity gains these resources can generate.

In addition to these obvious procedural advantages, encoders also contain validity edits and other edits to help the coder decide whether certain codes are correct or if reporting requirements have been met. For example, an encoder can prevent "childbirth" from accidentally being assigned to a male patient's health record.

Finally, an encoder almost always contains grouper capability. Some encoders may only include the federal (Medicare) grouper. However, in many states encoders may provide multiple groupers that are specific to payer and time period. An encoder with such capability enables coders to compare selected cases between groupers, by year, or by version numbers. Encoders and groupers are also used together to apply existing payer edits to a case and to show the impact on reimbursement prior to claims submission.

Encoder Applications

Encoding software products differ in the way they assist with the coding process. The primary application of encoding software is to assign diagnosis and procedure codes to hospital inpatient and ambulatory surgery records through computerization. Therefore, an encoder will always contain ICD-9-CM codes and should also contain HCPCS/CPT codes required for all types of reporting.

Encoders can be used to look up the appropriate code from a text description. They can also be used to verify a known code. Therefore, searches of the tabular index can usually be conducted by keyword or by code. To facilitate ambulatory surgery procedure coding, a software crosswalk may exist between the chosen ICD-9-CM code and the CPT codes. Because there is not always a one-to-one match between the two code sets, the crosswalk may produce a selection of CPT codes from which the coder must choose.

Some types of encoders operate in the same way that code books do by merely supplanting the Volume 2 and Volume 3 indexes with a computer search and look-up. However, because the ICD-9-CM indexes also have embedded coding conventions and rules, a logic-based encoder may be designed to prompt the coder to answer certain questions before returning a response. For example:

The keyword "hypertension" in the ICD-9-CM code book leads to a table of possible codes, including certain comorbidities and complications. The encoder would return a question such as: "Is the hypertension benign, malignant, or unspecified?" The encoder may stop there and return the appropriate code from category 401. Some encoders may take the search further and ask for certain pertinent conditions, such as heart failure or renal failure, and whether the physician has specified a connection between the hypertension and these conditions. Upon coder input, the encoder would return the appropriate code.

Such encoder–coder interaction employing software assistance leads some managers to believe that inexperienced coders can function at a higher level than would ordinarily be indicated by their training and experience. However, unless the coder has been properly and thoroughly trained in coding guidelines, terminology, disease processes, and coding conventions, errors may occur during the encoder–coder interaction. Inexperienced coders may respond erroneously to encoder prompts. Thus, coders with comprehensive coding education, experience, and analytical skills cannot be replaced by encoders.

Disadvantages of Encoders

As previously mentioned, encoders can facilitate the coding process with computerized searches, interactive queries, validity edits, and linked references. Some experienced coders find that using an encoder is slower than doing manual coding because they rely on their book-based notes and on memory to code quickly.

A significant disadvantage occurs when the encoder does not link to the hospital claims management database. When the encoder is linked to the hospital database, codes can simply be entered, grouped, and examined as usual. Without this capability, the information must be entered twice: first to the encoder and then to the hospital indexing or financial database.

Still another disadvantage of using encoders is the need to update the software system. An encoder must be updated at least quarterly to keep current with *Coding Clinic* and *CPT Assistant,* as well as ICD-9-CM and CPT code updates and grouper updates. The coding of records discharged around scheduled code changes should be carefully monitored to ensure that the appropriate version of codes is being used. Coding managers should make sure that encoder vendors are contractually obligated to provide and install timely updates.

Authoritative Coding References

Official coding guidelines and requirements, code changes, clarifications and interpretations of rules, edits, and other authoritative coding references come from the Cooperating Parties for ICD-9-CM. The Coordination and Maintenance Committee of the Cooperating Parties meets in public forum semi-annually to suggest, discuss, and recommend potential changes to ICD-9-CM codes. ICD-9-CM is maintained and updated annually by the Cooperating Parties.

AHA/Coding Clinic

Coding Clinic is the primary, authoritative reference for official coding guidelines pertaining to ICD-9-CM. It is available by subscription through the AHA by calling 1-800-261-6246. *Coding Clinic* is accessible in print, CD-ROM, and computerized formats. As previously mentioned, some encoders include *Coding Clinic* references with their packages.

The AHA is responsible for issuing official advice via an editorial advisory board, on behalf of the Cooperating Parties. Responses to coding questions posed by practitioners are published quarterly in *Coding Clinic for ICD-9-CM*. Individuals should send each coding question with as much clinical detail as possible. No patient or practitioner identifiers should remain on any of the documents submitted. At this time, questions may be sent to: American Hospital Association, ICD-9-CM Central Office, One N. Franklin, Chicago, IL 60606. It should be noted that a published response to a question requiring consideration by the ICD-9-CM Coordination and Maintenance Committee may not appear in *Coding Clinic* for many months.

CMS/Federal Register

Much of the authority for the universal application in the United States of rules pertaining to the use of the ICD-9-CM coding system comes from the federal government. CMS has adopted the ICD-9-CM codes and these rules as the official method of communicating inpatient diagnostic and procedural data between providers and Medicare/Medicaid agencies. Because CMS is a federal agency, coding changes are published in the *Federal Register* as drafts for public comment in the spring and as final codes in August.

AMA/CPT Assistant

The AMA maintains the CPT nomenclature system and publishes *CPT Assistant,* a monthly publication that communicates CPT guidelines and changes and that addresses CPT coding questions. *CPT Assistant* is available by subscription by calling 1-800-621-8335. A separate subscription service for assistance with coding questions is available by calling 1-800-634-6922. The AMA Web site <http://www.ama-assn.org/catalog> contains a full listing of AMA products and services.

Other CPT Sources

HCPCS coding guidelines or conventions may be payer specific and found in payer manuals; however, the CMS Web site <www.hcfa.gov> or <www.cms.gov> contains useful information concerning HCPCS codes. Most Medicare and Medicaid manuals are available on this Web site for downloading.

The NCCI is a set of edits to be applied to CPT codes for physician services and outpatient hospital claims. These edits were created by CMS in anticipation of the APC system and for use by intermediaries and carriers in Medicare Part B claims processing. *The NCCI Coding Policy Manual for Part B Medicare Carriers* can be purchased through the National Technical Information Service (NTIS) by calling 1-800-363-2068. The NTIS Web site can be accessed at <http://www.ntis.gov>. The NCCI edits for hospital outpatients are included in the outpatient code editor (OCE).

Other "Drivers" of Coding

The official coding and reporting guidelines contain the authoritative coding rules that all coders must follow. However, third-party payers and some states also issue reporting guidelines and data collection requirements. These guidelines and requirements can create conflicts and present challenges for practitioners.

Third-Party Payer Requirements

In theory, third-party payers should conform to official coding guidelines and requirements for ICD-9-CM, as promulgated by the Cooperating Parties, or to the AMA's guidelines for use of

CPT. However, situations sometimes require that a facility or physician assign codes according to a third-party payer's reporting guidelines so that the facility is appropriately reimbursed for services. Occasions arise in which third-party payer guidelines appear to be, or are, in conflict with official coding guidelines.

Third-party payers do not necessarily provide their guidelines in writing. Often the only way a practitioner or coding manager can find out what is required is to review all claims rejections and to contact the third-party payer or insurance plan administrator directly regarding a specific case. When contacting the payer, the coding manager should document the conversation. If there is still disagreement with the payer's guidelines, the coding manager should include a copy of the official coding guideline that supports the facility's position in the document. This document can be placed in the billing folder or in a comment field somewhere in the patient accounts section of the computer system. Before sending a copy of the document and attachments to the payer, the coding manager should discuss the situation with the patient accounts manager, practice manager, or whomever is most appropriate. In that way, the facility's administration is aware of the disagreement and of the reason for any resultant delay in reimbursement.

Essentially, the goals are to code cases properly and still get paid; however, both goals may not always be possible to achieve. The coding manager, in conjunction with the patient accounts manager, should develop a written policy for handling situations in which a payer's coding instructions are in direct conflict with official coding guidelines.

Sometimes a facility determines that the more important goal is to be paid. The coding manager should then keep a record of those cases in which coding may have been compromised and what are believed to be the correct codes. In essence, the coding manager creates a separate database. This database may be necessary to track certain diagnoses or procedures in the future. Such a database may also serve as a reference should the third-party payer ever change its guidelines—the facility might be able to resubmit the cases and possibly recoup payment. Maintaining this separate database also demonstrates an effort by the facility to remain in compliance with official coding guidelines.

State-Specific Requirements

Some states have developed their own data collection requirements in addition to the minimum requirements set forth by CMS. For example, the state of New Jersey requires the collection of "Z codes" to describe the physical location at which a traumatic injury occurred (at home, at work, in a public place, and so forth). Such data collection issues pose challenges to practitioners. They often must be extremely creative in devising an appropriate field in which to capture the data without having to recreate the entire patient database.

When finding "space" for the newly required data, practitioners should not compromise the depth of the diagnosis and procedure data that are being collected. Many systems do not allow the capture of more than the maximum number of codes allowed (currently nine diagnosis and six procedure codes) on the standard Medicare billing form—the UB-92. The insertion of a code other than an appropriate diagnostic or procedure code into one of those fields can have a negative impact on the clinical database. Therefore, the practitioner should make every effort to identify and effectively utilize another area of the database.

Facility-Based Coding Guidelines

The purpose of facility guidelines is to ensure accurate, uniform coding within the facility. Facility guidelines should supplement and support, but never contradict, official guidelines.

Facility guidelines may be organized alphabetically, chronologically, or by topic or clinical service. Regardless of the method of organization, it is imperative that the guidelines begin with an index so that they can be referenced quickly and accurately.

All coding guidelines must be freely accessible to the coding staff and physicians to whom they apply. In situations where coders are not physically located in close proximity to one another, multiple copies of guidelines may be necessary, or on-line copies may be placed on the encoding system or on the facility's intranet. Particular care must be taken to ensure that all copies of coding guidelines are complete and updated on a timely basis. Whenever a guideline is updated, all coders must be informed about the new procedure.

Clinical Guidelines

In addition to official guidelines, coders benefit from guidance provided by physicians at the hospital level. Within the facility, certain practices may be standardized so that coders need not query physicians for certain routine events.

Coders may not define clinical parameters for applying specific codes. Such a practice would lead to inconsistency in coding and lack of comparability of databases, both locally and nationally. *Coding Clinic* clearly states that in the absence of specific physician documentation, the coder must query the physician as to the appropriateness of specific codes. However, because clinical practice for certain routine events does not vary dramatically from physician to physician, clinical services may be called upon to define or establish certain parameters within which coders may make specific, defined assumptions, given a predefined set of clinical findings. Such documentation must be clear, written, and universally applicable.

Within a specific clinical service, defined protocols and care plans codify best practices in that service. For example, an insulin-dependent diabetes mellitus patient may be on a sliding scale insulin regimen to effectively manage blood sugar. The patient's blood sugar may be under control with this prescription. However, if the patient's blood sugar is markedly high, even under this prescription, then the patient's condition may be uncontrolled. A coder cannot unilaterally decide that the patient's condition is uncontrolled and assign that code. However, if the endocrinology department's care plan defines "two sequential blood sugars over 600 mg/dL" as uncontrolled, then the coder may assign the code. This is a fairly common facility guideline.

Other common facility guidelines address postoperative blood loss anemia and hypokalemia. Such guidelines must be applicable to every case and be supported by evidence within the record's documentation. Individual physicians should not be encouraged to express personal guidelines because that might lead to corruption of the documentation and coding process.

Operational Guidelines

In addition to clinical guidelines, certain operational guidelines are essential for uniform coding. For example, operational guidelines may address how and when to code blood transfusions, diagnostic radiology, and other procedures. Most inpatient facilities do not code routine chest X-rays using ICD-9-CM Volume III codes. Some inpatient facilities do not use ICD-9-CM Volume III to code any diagnostic radiology except CT scans and MRIs. Because these procedures rarely affect inpatient reimbursement, they are ignored for coding purposes in favor of invasive procedures. When and how to refer questions to physicians should be defined in a coding compliance document.

Supplementary Materials

A variety of additional materials exist that are helpful to the coding staff. Suggested minimum resources include the following:

- Official coding guidelines: For any resource, the quality of the source should be considered. Wherever possible, the original resource is preferable to a derivative. Official guidelines and related publications must be provided to all coding staff.

- Grouper guides: Although the computer routinely performs grouping, the coding department may find it useful to maintain a copy of the appropriate definitions manuals to resolve audit issues and to educate coders when questions arise as to grouping for a particular case.

- Terminology references: Because no coding source contains every possible variation of every term, a recent edition of a medical dictionary is necessary. A good medical dictionary is also useful when physicians refer to diseases using eponyms, which may not be found in the coding source. Because new terms arise continuously, a medical dictionary should be replaced about every five years.

- Anatomy and physiology references: Although many coding sources now include basic anatomic diagrams, coders may encounter unfamiliar or detailed anatomy terms in health records. Unless the coding source specifically identifies the term, the coder may not be able to identify the correct anatomical site from the health record or the coding source. Therefore, an anatomy and physiology text can be useful. Again, this is not an annual expense. Replacement every five to seven years is probably sufficient.

- Pathology references: Although not specifically a coding reference, a good pathophysiology book, such as the *Merck Manual,* can be helpful to a coder in framing a question to a physician.

- Pharmacology references: Part of the coder's analysis of any health record involves review of the physician's orders to determine what conditions are being treated. Coders quickly become familiar with the hospital's formulary; however, new drugs and generic drug names often make matching the drugs with the patient's conditions difficult for the coder. Therefore, a high-quality pharmacology reference is very useful. This reference book should be replaced at least biannually. Sometimes a facility's medical library orders a new one every year. If so, the library's older reference book may be "recycled" into the HIM department.

- Diagnostic test reference: Another key analysis performed by the coder is the review of diagnostic testing. A reference that explains laboratory, radiology, and other diagnostic procedures can help with this process. A good reference will highlight the implications of results that are not within normal limits.

Computer Access

As may be inferred from the preceding discussion, a computer is one of the key tools that should be on a coder's desk. The computer is not only essential for encoding and grouping, but it can also facilitate coder activity, enrich the coder's job, optimize work flow, and encourage continuing education and research.

Clinical Data

Because more clinical data are captured and stored online, coders can access these data on-line and complete the coding process as soon as the information becomes available. Coders need not wait for paper copies to follow the record.

Patient History

As more data become available online, the coder's understanding of patients' clinical situations will be facilitated. All coding of patient encounters or discharges must be based on the documentation that pertains to particular visits or events. The coder cannot use prior documentation to "fill in the gaps" when current health records are not complete. Nevertheless, access to prior records can help the coder frame a query to a physician or better understand existing documentation.

Administrative Data

Coders are often required to abstract specific data from the patient record in order to update the admission or discharge record on-line. The coder can perform this task most efficiently with a computer. However, less costly data-entry personnel may be able to perform this function more economically.

Internet Access

Internet access is fast becoming a necessary tool for coding professionals because it provides research tools, resources, and the opportunity for continuing education from other sources. If coders do not have access to the Internet within the HIM department, access is often available in the medical staff library or in other hospital locations.

With the implementation of the AHIMA Communities of Practice, coders have the opportunity to reach other coders to discuss coding questions, procedural issues, best practices, coding guidelines, and other topics of interest to coders. In addition, the AHIMA Web site provides Internet links, libraries of documentation, continuing education, and other useful research tools for coders.

The following negative aspects to Internet access have also been identified:

- Unauthorized personal use of Internet access

- Excessive time spent posting unnecessary or non-job–related questions

- Potential inappropriate release of information

- Interruptions in service or system "downtime"

These issues must be addressed before access is provided to coders. Clear policies and procedures (appendix 3.1), effective supervision of personnel, and strong confidentiality statements (appendix 3.2) can limit the negative aspects of Internet access.

Physical Environment

As discussed in chapter 2, the location of the department or division responsible for coding in a facility as well as the location of the coders within the department or division are important considerations in terms of access to information and productivity.

Location of the HIM Department

The location of the HIM department in a facility may not be negotiable. However, the location can have a positive or a negative impact on the coding process because coders must have access to sources of information that are not always available within the department or in the health record. Sources of information include physicians, the Internet, and other departments. The types of information needed from these sources include:

- Clarification of documentation within the health record

- Research material, including disease processes and coding regulations

- Source documents, such as pathology reports, that are not present in the health record at the time of coding but are needed for coding

Contact with Physicians

When the HIM department is in a remote area, physicians may be unable or less inclined to visit the HIM department and respond to coding questions. In such a situation, the coder must meet the physician on the patient unit or in some other, more convenient area.

Although physicians may be contacted by phone to clarify documentation, both documentation and coding are most accurate when physicians review the health records face-to-face with coders. At the time of the review and discussion, the physician should be asked to add or modify documentation in the record.

Contact with Other Departments

Because reports necessary for coding are often not available at the time the health record is being coded, they must be accessed on-line or obtained from the appropriate department. These reports can include pathology reports, laboratory reports, and dictation. Retrieval of the reports can easily be handled by clerical personnel rather than by coders because discussion of the content of the reports is not necessary. Collection procedures for these reports should be evaluated for cost-effectiveness.

Coding Staff Location within the HIM Department

Ideally, coders' work areas should be apart from the rest of the staff and away from high traffic areas. In that way, coders can concentrate with a minimum of noise and distractions. Noise from copy machines, overhead pagers, telephones, moving files, radios, and other staff who must be able to perform their functions while talking can be detrimental to productivity and coding accuracy.

Workstation Considerations

Coding workstations should be ergonomically correct and comply with the standards and requirements of the U.S. Department of Labor, Occupational Safety and Health Administration (OSHA). Additional information can be obtained from the OSHA Web site: <http://www.osha-slc.gov/ergonomics-standard/index.html>.

Lighting Issues

Because the coding activity is based on reading, proper lighting is essential to prevent fatigue and eyestrain. Overhead ceiling lights are often inadequate for reading, so coders should have desk lamps that evenly distribute light in the work area. Bar lighting affixed to the bottom of cubicle shelves is one way to provide even distribution of light in the work area. Use of an inexpensive glare shield in front of the computer screen can minimize glare.

Space and Ergonomic Issues

The work space must be large enough to accommodate computers, books, keyboards, and open health records. Desks manufactured prior to the general use of computers in the workplace will probably be inadequate. Whenever possible, the coding manager should involve the coding staff in the selection process of new workstations. Coders are able to provide input that only the persons who perform the tasks every day can give. The coding manager may avoid costly mistakes by obtaining staff input.

When designing or purchasing new workstations, coding managers should consider the following points with regard to space and ergonomics:

- Desk space is needed for one open health record, a stack of health records, a computer with monitor, and a keyboard. Prior to any purchase, these items should be measured and arranged in the work configuration for each individual.

- If some or all of the coders are not currently using computers, the workstation plan should allow for the use of computers by all coding staff in the near future.

- Chairs are of critical importance for coders, who are required to sit most of the day. Although they are expensive, high-quality chairs with adjustable height, back, and tension configurations are a good investment. Chairs should have wheels and be able to swivel. Chairs with arms are probably unnecessary because arms would be in the way for most coding operations.

- Other considerations that can improve coder productivity and reduce downtime include the following:

    —A left-handed mouse for left-handed coders

    —Special access requirements

    —Products designed to prevent carpal tunnel syndrome

    —Overhead shelving with at least one shelf that can be reached from a sitting position

Shared Workstations

At times, coders share workstations. If possible, each individual should be assigned a drawer and a shelf to ensure the security of personal items and to provide a sense of individual space. In shared areas, coders should limit the number of personal items displayed. Coworkers who share space should leave the work area neat and clean for the next person. This holds true whether the work area is shared between employees, outsource personnel, or reviewers.

Organizing the Work Flow: Job Analysis

Each job in the HIM department should be analyzed to ensure that appropriate personnel are performing the tasks and that the flow of work among individuals is optimized. Clearly, staff members find the shifting of records from one side of the room to another to be time-consuming and enervating. Optimum work flow, therefore, is dependent not only on the efficient sequence of record-processing functions, but also on the physical location in which these functions are performed. Although a general discussion of HIM department work flow is outside the scope of this book, the following discussion includes the steps in the process that have an impact on coders.

Availability of Clinical Data

Complete and accurate coding depends on the availability of clinical data in the health record. Those data provide a full report of the conditions treated and the services rendered to the patient and include the following:

- Physician documentation

- Physician communications, or query forms

- Laboratory data

- Pathology data

- Radiology reports

- Nursing notes

- Social service notes

- Admission or discharge data

Physician Documentation

Because clinical coding represents the diagnostic and procedural impressions and decisions of the physician, the documentation by the physician is critical in the coding process. Coders are expected to read the history and physical report, progress notes, orders, operative notes and reports, and the discharge summary. In addition, they should have available the physician's recording of diagnoses and procedures on the patient's registration record, or face sheet. In reality, the pressure on coders to effect reimbursement pushes many coders to "read between the lines" of the health record, even in the absence of or the illegibility of some of this documentation. Most frequently missing are the face sheet notations and the discharge summary. In the absence of this documentation, any coding should be considered preliminary, whether or not it results in a bill.

Physician Communications, or "Query" Forms

When a coder is unsure of a diagnosis or procedure, or when ancillary documentation points to a condition that is not apparently documented by the physician, the coder should query the physician prior to making a final code assignment. Some facilities require that this query, or communication between the coder and the physician, whether oral or written, be formally documented by means of a query form.

If the query form has identified a documentation deficiency, the physician should go back and include the information in the health record. Late entries or corrections to the existing health record should be noted as such and should include the actual date that the late entry was made.

When query forms are to be used for documentation quality improvement purposes, they may be retained in administrative files, organized by physician or service. Trends may be noted and followed up, with the goal of reducing the use of query forms for questions repeatedly asked.

Appendix 3.3 contains the AHIMA practice brief, Developing a Physician Query Process, which provides a detailed discussion of current accepted standards for this area of HIM practice.

Laboratory Data

Coders need laboratory data to ensure that they have captured the patient's entire clinical experience. For example, the finding of "low hemoglobin" on a laboratory report may prompt the physician to order iron supplements. As a condition treated during the stay, this possible "anemia" is a codable event. However, in the absence of physician documentation or specific facility guidelines, the coder might not consider querying the physician regarding "anemia" as a diagnosis unless the laboratory report were available for review.

Pathology Data

Pathology reports are not always complete or available at the time of patient discharge. When a malignancy is suspected, the health record should never be coded without these data. Pathology specimens or tissue samples related to certain routine conditions such as tonsillectomy, appendectomy, and lipoma of cord secondary to inguinal hernias are often coded before the pathology report is available. However, coders are aware that the difference between an acute condition and a chronic condition is sometimes found only in the pathology report. Therefore, the absence of this documentation may directly lead to incorrect coding. Charts with missing pathology reports cannot always be coded with impunity.

Radiology Reports

Unlike pathology reports, radiology reports are usually available prior to discharge. Although radiology reports convey important information to physicians, they are less useful in alerting coders to potential codable events. However, radiology reports often clarify issues that are documented in the progress notes and help confirm ruled-out diagnoses that may not be clearly stated as such.

Nursing Documentation

Coders may not use nursing documentation such as notes and graphics as the sole support for assigning diagnoses and/or procedures to a health record. However, nursing documentation is often a rich source of information that may assist the coder in querying the physician or in confirming illegible or vague physician documentation. In addition, nursing documentation confirms whether a medication has been administered, providing information that supports the coding decision.

Social Service Notes

Social service notes may provide information concerning patient disposition/discharge status that cannot be found elsewhere in the record. For example, the physician may state "discharge to nursing home." If the coder or data-entry person is abstracting the actual name of the nursing home, the only place to find this information may be in the social service note. Often the patient transfer form is located with this note. Another important detail often found in social service notes is whether the patient will be receiving home care, such as a visiting nurse service. The transfer destination at discharge is extremely important because Medicare inpatient DRG reimbursement may be affected.

Admission/Discharge Data

Coders are often asked to "review" data that have been charted or entered into the hospital computer system by clerical staff or nursing staff at the time of admission and at the time of discharge. These data, which are often demographic data, are reviewed for errors that may affect coding. For example, if a patient's gender has been entered incorrectly, as in the case of a female patient having prostate surgery, the system may not accept the correct gender-specific codes. Birth dates may also affect coding. For example, V30.00 would not be used as the principal diagnosis unless the newborn were born during that admission. If the coder were about to code a newborn record and saw that the admission date and birth date did not match, the coder would then be alerted to review the record to see whether:

- The newborn had been born elsewhere and transferred into the facility.

- An error had been made in the recording of the admission date.

- An error had been made in the recording of the birth date.

Access to Prior Admissions

As discussed previously, the coding of each patient encounter must stand on its own documentation. However, access to documentation and coding of prior admissions may assist coders in identifying issues for a physician query. For example, a physician may document "Cancer of the breast with metastasis." The coder needs to determine whether the patient has had surgery—therefore a "history" of cancer of the breast—and exactly where the cancer has metastasized. If the coder has access to documentation from a prior admission, the health record may contain information that can be presented to the physician and enable the physician to document consistently throughout all admissions. The physician must add the documentation to the record for each encounter or admission in order for the correct codes to be assigned.

Posted Charges

In some instances, the health record does not contain enough information to determine whether:

- A procedure was performed.

- A procedure that should have been reported with a code was missed.

- A procedure was coded but not performed.

For example, when coding the health record of a patient seen in the emergency department for a deep laceration, the coder would review the documentation to determine whether the laceration was sutured. If the chart documentation does not indicate the suture was performed, the coder may be able to see if a suture tray was ordered by reviewing the charges posted for the account. Although the presence of an order and a bill for a suture tray suggests that the procedure was performed, it does not justify coding of the procedure. The physician must still document the procedure to support assignment of the code. It may have been that the suture tray was ordered but that the laceration was not sutured because the patient decided to leave against medical advice. In this case, the charge should be deleted. Coders should refer such cases back to the physician for clarification. For such referral, coders should follow the policy or process coordinated between the coding manager and the patient accounts manager or the practice manager.

Process Flow

The coding process can be broken down into the separate subtasks of data access, data assessment, data analysis, code assignment, and post-assignment processing, as well as auxiliary tasks.

Data Access

Coders must have access to pertinent documentation at the time that the codes are assigned. Data may be in the form of a paper record, an electronic record, or a combination of both. For example, laboratory test data are commonly computerized. Rather than search for or wait for a paper laboratory report to catch up with a paper record, the coder may readily access the information via the facility's computer system. In the event of a transcription backlog, the coder should have permission to play back a dictated report and obtain the required information.

Coders who work off-site—whether they are home-based, telecommuting, or outsourced coders—should have the same access to data as on-site coders. If this access cannot be achieved, then off-site coding will not be successful in terms of accuracy and quality of code assignment.

Policies and procedures should be established to ensure that off-site coders have access to all pertinent documentation. Policies and procedures must also be established to facilitate off-site coders' ability to obtain missing documentation. If, for example, incomplete records are forwarded off-site for coding, the determination should be made whether it is necessary to forward the entire record or only parts of the record. For example, when the record is missing the operative report, the coding manager should consider the following questions:

- Will the record still be forwarded?

- Will the record be held until the report is available?

- Will the operative progress note alone suffice?

In addition, the coding manager should ask the following questions:

- Can a clerical staff person make these determinations on a record-by-record basis?

- Does the staff member need to have a certain degree of coding knowledge to ascertain the "codability" of an incomplete record?

- Who will be held accountable if a record is coded incorrectly because a critical piece of the record was not forwarded?

Data Assessment

Coders must assess the completeness of the available documentation. Health records may be coded concurrently at any time during or after the patient's encounter or admission. (See chapter 2 for a complete discussion of concurrent coding.)

However, coding is most commonly performed postdischarge. Even then, the health record is most often not finalized or complete. From a fiscal and practical perspective, coders cannot wait for every health record to be completely finalized prior to coding. They must consider that most regulatory bodies allow the physician thirty days to complete an inpatient hospital health record. Therefore, coders must possess the knowledge to determine which incomplete records can or cannot be coded. The facility must have policies in place to support coders in such a determination. For instance, coders should know whether it is acceptable or not to code a record that does not yet have a final diagnosis or discharge summary. When records are coded without this information, a method should be established to review the code assignments against the information when it becomes available.

Data Analysis

Coders review documentation to identify "codable" diagnoses and procedures. As previously mentioned, information may be noted in ancillary reports or nursing notes. These sources of data are not a substitute for physician documentation and should not be used for coding on their own.

Physicians may document conditions or diagnoses in the final diagnosis or discharge summary that existed previously ("history of") but are not currently being treated, do not affect the patient's care, or have no impact on the patient's length of stay. Coders must be able to identify and distinguish these conditions or diagnoses because they should not be coded.

Many procedures are performed, but not all are coded. For example, it is unlikely that an ICD-9-CM Volume III procedure code for a chest X-ray would be assigned for an inpatient admission. However, a CPT code assigned by the chargemaster would be used if the X-ray were the reason for an outpatient encounter. The determination of which procedures to code or not to code is often facility or encounter based. For inpatient admissions, all procedures affecting DRG assignment must be coded.

Code Assignment

Coders assign the appropriate codes from the appropriate code set—ICD-9-CM and/or CPT. As discussed previously, these code assignments may be made using the code books, the assistance of an encoder, or a combination of both.

Postassignment Processing

Coders abstract the data, including the diagnoses and procedure codes, and enter them into the computer or record them on the health record, or both. Many facilities have coders handwrite the codes and other abstracted data onto the health record face sheet in addition to entering the data into the computer. At first, this abstraction process may be considered redundant. Coders often need a worksheet, however, and use the face sheet for this purpose. Also, in cases in which a coding error has occurred, the handwritten codes may be compared to the codes entered into the system. In that way, it can be determined if a true coding error was made or if a data entry or system interface error was made.

Some facilities have noncoding personnel enter codes into the computer system. This approach enhances productivity because coders do not have to spend time entering data. A disadvantage to this approach is that coders cannot catch errors, such as transposition of numbers in codes, that noncoders might unwittingly enter. In addition, when coders enter data, they are able to note any edits, make changes if necessary, and confirm that the DRG assignment makes sense for each particular case. If a noncoder is entering the codes, a postentry audit process should be in place to ensure that the data were entered correctly.

Auxiliary Tasks

Coders may be required to perform a variety of tasks in addition to specific coding-related activities. Although task assignment is largely a function of staffing, work flow, and worksite, coders' daily noncoding activities should be limited to functions that enrich their work experience and that utilize their training and abilities to the fullest.

Any task that is not directly related to coding should be evaluated to ensure that it moves the goals and objectives of the coding process forward. If a task is not related to coding, the coding manager should evaluate whether noncoding staff could perform it effectively. Coders should not routinely assemble or analyze health records, answer telephones, or handle general correspondence.

Assembly and Analysis

For the most efficient coding, the health record should be assembled and analyzed prior to coding. Assembly and routine quantitative analysis facilitate the reading of the health record and the coder's understanding of the data. In addition, abstracting of data, such as the identification of consultants and surgeons or of the dates of invasive procedures, helps the coder to follow the events described in the record and to recognize whether critical data are missing.

When a coder receives an unassembled record, the coder might decide to assemble it so that it is easier to read. For small records, such as those for ambulatory surgery, clinic visits, and normal newborns, this action may take seconds. For larger records, the minutes involved in assembly can seriously impair productivity. For appropriate utilization of resources, the coding manager should evaluate whether allowing overtime by other staff in the assembly and analysis area is less expensive than paying coders to assemble and analyze charts.

Reporting

Credentialed individuals such as RHITs and RHIAs have received training in statistical methods and can assist in reporting activities. Although coders understand clinical data, they are not always trained in statistical reporting methods. Depending on the facility's computerized support, coders can be trained to run routine reports and to create ad hoc reports. With some training in computerized spreadsheet programs, coders can also prepare other types of analyses.

Statistical and other types of reporting activities can be job enriching for some coders. Although not all coders will view these activities as such, others will welcome the opportunity to add to their job skills and achieve greater visibility within the facility.

Quality Analysis

As previously mentioned, the prescreening of identified record content can be effectively delegated to coders. Not only can this activity enrich the coder's job, but it can also be an effective use of facility resources. As always, the impact of other responsibilities on coding productivity is a concern. If quality analysis activities lead to outsourcing part of the coding function, the departments requesting these services may need to assist in funding them.

Post-Audit Review

Many facilities require coders to pre-audit records that payers and other auditors have requested for review. This activity is of limited benefit because the pre-audit does not prevent the audit itself. The audit findings will be the same whether or not errors have been detected and corrected prior to the audit.

On the other hand, post-audit review of problems is essential. If a payer audit or other audit results in the identification of possible errors, the records containing these errors should be reviewed. First, if the auditor is in error, the facility should resolve this type of finding immediately. Second, the nature of an actual error must be identified and the reason for the error evaluated. Trends in errors found on audit often demonstrate the need for general or targeted retraining. One of the most common reasons for coding "errors" is missing documentation. The coding manager should carefully evaluate the need to complete a health record versus the need to bill quickly, keeping in mind that errors found on audit can lead to payment reductions or denials.

Self-Auditing

Routine quality control audits should be an integral part of the coding function in any facility. The facility should not rely on payer audits to ensure coding quality or to identify problem areas. When resources are limited, coders can audit themselves. Self-auditing, however, may be the least desirable form of review when motivating factors other than data quality are involved. If this type of auditing is performed, it can be done on a rotating basis, with the "auditor" role passing from one coder to the next on a specific schedule. This method works best when all coders are of equivalent experience.

Self-auditing can also be handled as a routine part of daily activities. Depending on the workload, one hour per day or per week can be devoted to reviewing selected records. Some or all of this audit activity can be handled on an overtime basis if the existing workload is heavy. The cost of overtime can be compared with the cost of hiring external quality auditors and consultants.

Finally, the coding supervisor should perform quality audits on a routine basis for performance evaluation. In some facilities, the coding supervisor's role is limited to audit activity and overload or fill-in coding but does not include routine coding.

Expectations of Other Staff Members

Staff members in many departments of healthcare organizations rely on coded data to complete their work. The expectations of these other departments for timely information must be factored into performance standards for coders.

Turnaround Time

Many facilities measure coding turnaround time by days past discharge. For example, a facility may use a threshold of "discharge plus three days" (three days postdischarge) to describe its expectation of when health records should be coded. However, the currency of the coding is not as important as is its accuracy. Waiting a few extra days to assemble all of the necessary documentation is better than forcing the coding of an inadequately documented health record. As previously mentioned, some documentation is more critical to the coding process than other documentation. Although coding managers would wait for a pathology report before billing a suspected neoplasm, they might not delay billing for a tonsillectomy. However, coding managers should be aware that there is a risk in forcing the coding of an incomplete health record.

Delayed Billing

The HIM department is responsible for coding, which in turn affects billing. Even if the patient's payer is not reimbursing the facility, based on a DRG, the payer still wants the chart to be coded. Failure to code can lead to a failure to bill. For that reason, the HIM department should routinely receive a detailed list of all discharges for which no bill has yet been dropped. This list is often called the **discharged not final billed,** or DNFB, list. Although delays in billing may be due to reasons other than coding, the DNFB list is an important tool in managing the coding process. The coding manager should examine the reasons health records have not been billed. Records that account for large amounts of unbilled dollars should be prioritized for timelier coding. This type of proactive management demonstrates the commitment of the HIM department to facilitywide concerns. (See chapter 10 for a detailed discussion of billing issues.)

Medical Staff Office Support

Medical staff offices may request data pertaining to individual practitioners. Reports containing physician-specific data should not be provided without proper authorization as specified by medical staff rules and regulations. An example of routinely approved, reported data concerns physicians on cycle for reappointment to the staff, or "re-credentialing." Often the purpose of such data is to review the types of cases the physician has had over a specified time period. If the physician has performed a certain number of cases in a particular area, he or she may be "promoted" from one staff level to the next, such as from associate physician to attending physician. Accurate coding is paramount to this process because it is the only method used to capture these kinds of data.

The medical staff office may also request data for a particular physician group or specialty. For example, the chair of a department of urology wants the facility to open an impotence clinic and has asked the medical staff office to assist in some of the aspects of market analysis. Data concerning how many impotent patients were seen over the course of a year would be used as part of a market research and feasibility plan.

Organizing the Coding Staff

The primary component of the coding staff is made up of individuals with coding skills and experience. The number of coders, support staff, and supervisors of a coding area is completely dependent on the workload. Because no universally accepted criteria have been established for coding performance and because coders' responsibilities vary by facility and by setting, no exact formula exists for determining how many coders are necessary. (See chapter 4 and chapter 6 for further discussion on staffing issues.)

Coding Skill Sets and Competencies

AHIMA has developed a specific set of work-based task competencies that credentialed coders should possess at both the hospital and physician-office levels. Those competencies are listed in appendix 3.4 and appendix 3.5. In the absence of AHIMA credentials, employers must decide how coders will evidence competency. Employers may choose to make credentials a condition of employment. Alternatively, the hiring process may include a facility-based exam for all candidates.

Job Descriptions

Job or position descriptions normally vary from one facility or organization to another, depending on the following factors:

- The size of the organization

- The services the facility offers

- The size and responsibilities of the coding staff

- The scope, setting, and oversight of the coding functions performed

Job descriptions should be reviewed annually and during an employee's annual performance review. Job descriptions should be updated whenever there are changes in responsibilities, oversight, or systems. They should also be updated if the organization has undergone a merger, acquisition, or reorganization. Facilities should ensure that job descriptions continuously reflect the most recent Joint Commission on Accreditation of Healthcare Organizations' (JCAHO) requirements for job descriptions.

As discussed in chapter 2, job titles also vary from setting to setting. There is no "official" or preferred job title; however, the image conveyed by the title should be professional in tone.

The format of job descriptions also varies from organization to organization, but in general, the format should include:

- Job or position title.

- Department name: All coders within the organization may not be part of the HIM department even though they may have the same job or position title.

- Job or position title that the described position reports to, as it appears in the department table of organization (TO) or organization chart.

- Position summary: A brief statement or paragraph describing the major functions of the position as performed on a daily basis.

- Duties: A detailed explanation of the job functions that expands on the position summary. Duties should be listed in the order that the functions are performed, with the least-occurring functions listed last. Many organizations include as the last duty, "other duties as assigned." If this phrase is not required by the facility or by a union, it is best omitted. When "other duties" become apparent or are part of the coding function, they should be specified in the list of duties.

- Qualifications or requirements, including physical requirements such as lifting, sitting, reaching, computer skills, and specific knowledge of the organization's system. The requirements should specify whether a basic knowledge of the job is sufficient or if the position requires special expertise in certain areas. For example, a coder must have expertise in coding, but not necessarily an extensive knowledge of the patient accounts function.

- Education, credentials, and experience should depend on the needs of the job as discussed previously in this chapter.

A sample job/position description is shown in appendix 3.6.

Control and Supervision

Each coding position also should be listed in the department's table of organization (TO) or organizational chart. Any time a position is added or deleted, or when the job title has changed, the TO should be updated. The TO shows how each position fits within the department and indicates lines of authority. In addition to the department's TO, the overall organizational TO demonstrates the authority and reporting lines and relationships among departments. Relationship and reporting lines within each department and among departments provide structure to the individual and can be used to foster cooperation within the organization.

Most traditional HIM departments have a director or manager who oversees the functions and duties of that department. If the HIM department has a small staff, the coding staff may report directly to the HIM department manager or director. If the coding staff is large, coders may report to an assistant director, an assistant manager, a coding manager, or a coding supervisor. Regardless of their title or other responsibilities, the person who oversees the coding function should have a strong coding background and the ability to act as a mentor and resource for new coders. He or she does not have to be the best coder in the department or understand every detail of the coding process. However, this person must be able to facilitate the coding process and access all resources, professional and organizational, so that coders can function at maximum potential.

In a large organization or an integrated delivery system, coding positions may be delineated by the scope of services the facility or system provides. Because of organizational complexity and the differences between inpatient and outpatient coding, separate job titles and positions may exist. For example, a coder who works in the long-term care division of an organization may have a different coding job title and job description than an acute care coder who works in the same facility. The difference in job descriptions reflects the variability in the scope of service, the setting, and the separate and distinct knowledge that each coder must have to perform the job.

Competency-Based Assessment

Job descriptions must contain measurable criteria for performance against which coders can be evaluated. Performance criteria include, but are not limited to:

- The number of charts coded

- Accuracy of coding as determined by a predefined audit process

- Maintenance of effective relationships with physicians and facility personnel

Coders should be evaluated at least quarterly, with appropriate training needs identified, facilitated, and reassessed over time. Only through this continuous process of evaluation can data quality and integrity be ensured.

Summary

Coders are a valuable resource to their healthcare facilities. Although the competence of coders is reflected in coding quality, credentials, such as CCS, CCS-P, CPC, and CPC-H, can evidence achievement prior to employment. To effectively perform their function, coders require high-quality continuing professional education. They also require specific tools that should be updated appropriately: code books, reference texts, encoders, and groupers. The facility should support coders with access to official and facility-based coding guidelines, as well as to computers and the Internet. The physical environment affects coder productivity and should be evaluated for ergonomics and efficiency.

Coders require specific data to effectively perform their functions. Physician, laboratory, radiology, and pathology data are particularly important. The function of the coder is to assign accurate codes to the clinical data. To do this effectively, distracting tasks such as answering telephones should not be assigned.

In managing the coding function, turnaround time and billing are important considerations. Coders demonstrate professionalism and commitment by fulfilling customer expectations and responding to organizational requirements.

Coders must meet specific competency levels, as detailed in their job descriptions. Control and supervision of the coding function require appropriate supervisory oversight and continuous assessment.

References and Bibliography

AHIMA. 2001. Practice Brief: Developing a coding compliance policy document. *Journal of the American Health Information Management Association* 72(7): 88A–88C.

Bienborn, J. 1999. Automated coding: The next step? *Journal of the American Health Information Management Association* 70(7): 38–42.

Dunn, R. 2001. Developing facility-specific productivity measures. *Journal of the American Health Information Management Association* 72(4): 73–74.

MacDonald, E. 1999. Better coding through improved documentation: Strategies for the current environment. *Journal of the American Health Information Management Association* 70(1): 32–35.

Scichilone, R. 1999. Three perspectives on coding. *Journal of the American Health Information Management Association* 70(7): 44–46.

Wieland, L. 2000. Filling a critical niche: HIM and the corporate compliance committee. *Journal of the American Health Information Management Association* 71(9): 22.

Appendix 3.1

Sample Procedure for Internet Use

Excerpt from AHIMA Position Statement *Confidential Health Information and the Internet*

Background

Recommendations

Health information applications on the Internet have the potential to bring great benefit to patient care but may also result in significant harm if they are improperly designed, monitored, or used. To protect the confidentiality and integrity of patient health information, the American Health Information Management Association (AHIMA) and the Medical Transcription Industry Alliance (MTIA) make the following recommendations:

- Applications on the Internet that contain patient-identifiable health information must be carefully designed to protect the confidentiality of the information.

- Appropriate security measures and available technologies should be employed to protect confidential health information from unauthorized access or alteration. These measures include encryption, secure transmission protocols, and firewalls.

- Text, voice, image and other patient files transmitted or maintained on the Internet should be encrypted to protect their confidentiality. Whenever possible, patient-identifiable information should exist as a separate file rather than part of the transcribed text document.

- Photographs or other images that may identify a patient should be used in Internet applications only with the express written consent of the patient or his/her legal representative.

- When a transcriptionist completes a document, it should be transmitted back to the transcription service bureau with no files (text, voice, or image) remaining on the hard drive of the transcriptionist's computer. Temporary files containing patient-identifiable information should be deleted as soon as they are no longer needed. Files such as patient admission lists should be deleted automatically or returned to the originator when the transcriptionist logs off at the close of each business day. Any files stored outside the transcription service bureau should have the same level of physical and electronic security as files kept by the service bureau.

- Print functions should be limited. Off-site transcriptionists should not be allowed to print copies of reports.

- Audit trails should record all individuals who access, modify, or delete any report.

- If patients and caregivers will use electronic mail to communicate, such communications should be limited to nonconfidential information. If confidential information will be transmitted via electronic mail, that information should be encrypted to protect its confidentiality.

- If caregivers use electronic mail, bulletin boards, or online discussion groups to discuss a patient's case, no patient-identifiable information should be included. If electronic mail is used to discuss a case, that transmission should be encrypted.

- Client-side file caching by an Internet browser should be disabled. This prevents the localized save of patient data on the client machine.

- Transcription service bureaus should educate their employees and contractors about privacy and confidentiality issues, including use of electronic mail and online discussions ("chat rooms"). Written confidentiality agreements addressing these issues should be signed by each employee or contractor at the time of hire. Written acknowledgement should be signed on an annual basis thereafter to remind individuals of their ongoing responsibility for protecting the confidentiality of health information. Such agreements should be updated periodically to address issues raised by the use of new technologies.

- Organizations should develop, implement, and enforce policies and procedures to protect confidential information in Internet applications.

Appendix 3.2

Sample Confidentiality Statement

Employee/Student/Volunteer Nondisclosure Agreement

[Name of healthcare facility] has a legal and ethical responsibility to safeguard the privacy of all patients and to protect the confidentiality of their health information. In the course of my employment/assignment at *[name of healthcare facility]*, I may come into possession of confidential patient information, even though I may not be directly involved in providing patient services.

I understand that such information must be maintained in the strictest confidence. As a condition of my employment/assignment, I hereby agree that, unless directed by my supervisor, I will not at any time during or after my employment/assignment with *[name of healthcare facility]* disclose any patient information to any person whatsoever or permit any person whatsoever to examine or make copies of any patient reports or other documents prepared by me, coming into my possession, or under my control, or use patient information, other than as necessary in the course of my employment/assignment.

When patient information must be discussed with other healthcare practitioners in the course of my work, I will use discretion to ensure that such conversations cannot be overheard by others who are not involved in the patient's care.

I understand that violation of this agreement may result in corrective action, up to and including discharge.

_____

Signature of Employee/Student/Volunteer

_____

Date

Note: This sample form was developed by the American Health Information Management Association for discussion purposes only. It should not be used without review by your organization's legal counsel to ensure compliance with local and state laws.

Appendix 3.3

Practice Brief: Developing a Physician Query Process

Principles of Medical Record Documentation

Medical record documentation is used for a multitude of purposes, including:

- serving as a means of communication between the physician and the other members of the healthcare team providing care to the patient

- serving as a basis for evaluating the adequacy and appropriateness of patient care

- providing data to support insurance claims

- assisting in protecting the legal interests of patients, healthcare professionals, and healthcare facilities

- providing clinical data for research and education

To support these various uses, it is imperative that medical record documentation be complete, accurate, and timely. Facilities are expected to comply with a number of standards regarding medical record completion and content promulgated by multiple regulatory agencies.

Joint Commission on Accreditation of Healthcare Organizations

The Joint Commission's *2000 Hospital Accreditation Standards* state, "the medical record contains sufficient information to identify the patient, support the diagnosis, justify the treatment, document the course and results, and promote continuity among health care providers" (IM.7.2).[1] The Joint Commission Standards also state, "medical record data and information are managed in a timely manner" (IM.7.6).

Timely entries are essential if a medical record is to be useful in a patient's care. A complete medical record is also important when a patient is discharged, because information in the record may be needed for clinical, legal, or performance improvement purposes. The Joint Commission requires hospitals to have policy and procedures on the timely entry of all significant clinical information into the patient's medical record, and they do not consider a medical record complete until all final diagnoses and complications are recorded without the use of symbols or abbreviations.

Joint Commission standards also require medical records to be reviewed on an ongoing basis for completeness and timeliness of information, and action is taken to improve the quality and timeliness of documentation that affects patient care (IM.7.10). This review must address the presence, timeliness, legibility, and authentication of the final diagnoses and conclusions at termination of hospitalization.

Medicare

The Medicare Conditions of Participation require medical records to be accurately written, promptly completed, properly filed and retained, and accessible.[2] Records must document, as appropriate, complications, hospital-acquired infections, and unfavorable reactions to drugs and anesthesia. The conditions also stipulate that all records must document the final diagnosis with completion of medical records within 30 days following discharge.

Relationship Between Coding and Documentation

Complete and accurate diagnostic and procedural coded data must be available, in a timely manner, in order to:

- improve the quality and effectiveness of patient care

- ensure equitable healthcare reimbursement

- expand the body of medical knowledge

- make appropriate decisions regarding healthcare policies, delivery systems, funding, expansion, and education

- monitor resource utilization

- permit identification and resolution of medical errors

- improve clinical decision making

- facilitate tracking of fraud and abuse

- permit valid clinical research, epidemiological studies, outcomes and statistical analyses, and provider profiling

- provide comparative data to consumers regarding costs and outcomes, average charges, and outcomes by procedure

Physician documentation is the cornerstone of accurate coding. Therefore, assuring the accuracy of coded data is a shared responsibility between coding professionals and physicians. Accurate diagnostic and procedural coded data originate from collaboration between physicians, who have a clinical background, and coding professionals, who have an understanding of classification systems.

Expectations of Physicians

Physicians are expected to provide complete, accurate, timely, and legible documentation of pertinent facts and observations about an individual's health history, including past and present illnesses, tests, treatments, and outcomes. Medical record entries should be documented at the time service is provided. Medical record entries should be authenticated. If subsequent additions to documentation are needed, they should be identified as such and dated. (Often these expectations are included in the medical staff or house staff rules and regulations.) Medical record documentation should:

- address the clinical significance of abnormal test results

- support the intensity of patient evaluation and treatment and describe the thought processes and complexity of decision making

- include all diagnostic and therapeutic procedures, treatments, and tests performed, in addition to their results

- include any changes in the patient's condition, including psychosocial and physical symptoms

- include all conditions that coexist at the time of admission, that subsequently develop, or that affect the treatment received and the length of stay. This encompasses all conditions that affect patient care in terms of requiring clinical evaluation, therapeutic treatment, diagnostic procedures, extended length of hospital stay, or increased nursing care and monitoring[3]

- be updated as necessary to reflect all diagnoses relevant to the care or services provided

- be consistent and discuss and reconcile any discrepancies (this reconciliation should be documented in the medical record)

- be legible and written in ink, typewritten, or electronically signed, stored, and printed.

Expectations of Coding Professionals

The AHIMA Code of Ethics sets forth ethical principles for the HIM profession. HIM professionals are responsible for maintaining and promoting ethical practices. This Code of Ethics states, in part: "Health information management professionals promote high standards for health information management practice, education, and research." Another standard in this code states, "Health information management professionals strive to provide accurate and timely information." Data accuracy and integrity are fundamental values of HIM that are advanced by:

- employing practices that produce complete, accurate, and timely information to meet the health and related needs of individuals

- following the guidelines set forth in the organization's compliance plan for reporting improper preparation, alteration, or suppression of information or data by others

- not participating in any improper preparation, alteration, or suppression of health record information or other organization data

A conscientious goal for coding and maintaining a quality database is accurate clinical and statistical data. AHIMA's Standards of Ethical Coding were developed to guide coding professionals in this process. As stated in the standards, coding professionals are expected to support the importance of accurate, complete, and consistent coding practices for the production of quality healthcare data. These standards also indicate that coding professionals should only assign and report codes that are clearly and consistently supported by physician documentation in the medical record. It is the responsibility of coding professionals to assess physician documentation to assure that it supports the diagnosis and procedure codes reported on claims.

Dialogue between coding professionals and clinicians is encouraged, because it improves coding professionals' clinical knowledge and educates the physicians on documentation practice issues. AHIMA's Standards of Ethical Coding state that coding professionals are expected to consult physicians for clarification and additional documentation prior to code assignment when there is conflicting or ambiguous data in the health record. Coding professionals should also assist and educate physicians by advocating proper documentation practices, further specificity, and resequencing or inclusion of diagnoses or procedures when needed to more accurately reflect the acuity, severity, and the occurrence of events. It is recommended that coding be performed by credentialed HIM professionals.[4]

It is inappropriate for coding professionals to misrepresent the patient's clinical picture through incorrect coding or add diagnoses or procedures unsupported by the documentation to maximize reimbursement or meet insurance policy coverage requirements. Coding professionals should not change codes or the narratives of codes on the billing abstract so that meanings are misrepresented. Diagnoses or procedures should not be inappropriately included or excluded, because payment or insurance policy coverage requirements will be affected. When individual payer policies conflict with official coding rules and guidelines, these policies should be obtained in writing whenever possible. Reasonable efforts should be made to educate the payer on proper coding practices in order to influence a change in the payer's policy.

Proper Use of Physician Queries

The process of querying physicians is an effective and, in today's healthcare environment, necessary mechanism for improving the quality of coding and medical record documentation and capturing complete clinical data. Query forms have become an accepted tool for communicating with physicians on documentation issues influencing proper code assignment. Query forms should be used in a judicious and appropriate manner. They must be used as a communication tool to improve the accuracy of code assignment and the quality of physician documentation, not to inappropriately maximize reimbursement. The query process should be guided by AHIMA's Standards of Ethical Coding and the official coding guidelines. An inappropriate query, such as a form that is poorly constructed or asks leading questions, or overuse of the query process can result in quality-of-care, legal, and ethical concerns.

The Query Process

The goal of the query process should be to improve physician documentation and coding professionals' understanding of the unique clinical situation, not to improve reimbursement. Each facility should establish a policy and procedure for obtaining physician clarification of documentation that affects code assignment. The process of querying physicians must be a patient-specific process, not a general process. Asking "blanket" questions is not appropriate. Policies regarding the circumstances when physicians will be queried should be designed to promote timely, complete, and accurate coding and documentation.

Physicians should not be asked to provide clarification of their medical record documentation without the opportunity to access the patient's medical record. Each facility also needs to determine if physicians will be queried concurrently (during the patient's hospitalization) or after discharge. Both methods are acceptable. Querying physicians concurrently allows the documentation deficiency to be corrected while the patient is still in-house and can positively influence patient care.

The policy and procedure should stipulate who is authorized to contact the physician for clarifications regarding a coding issue. Coding professionals should be allowed to contact physicians directly for clarification, rather than limiting this responsibility to supervisory personnel or a designated individual.

The facility may wish to use a designated physician liaison to resolve conflicts between physicians and coding professionals. The appropriate use of the physician liaison should be described in the facility's policy and procedures.

Query Format

Each facility should develop a standard format for the query form. No "sticky notes" or scratch paper should be allowed. Each facility should develop a standard design and format for physician queries to ensure clear, consistent, appropriate queries.

The query form should:

- be clearly and concisely written

- contain precise language

- present the facts from the medical record and identify why clarification is needed

- present the scenario and state a question that asks the physician to make a clinical interpretation of a given diagnosis or condition based on treatment, evaluation, monitoring, and/or services provided. "Open-ended" questions that allow the physician to document the specific diagnosis are preferable to multiple-choice questions or questions requiring only a "yes" or "no" response. Queries that appear to lead the physician to provide a particular response could lead to allegations of inappropriate upcoding

- be phrased such that the physician is allowed to specify the correct diagnosis. It should not indicate the financial impact of the response to the query. The form should not be designed so that all that is required is a physician signature

- include:

  —patient name

  —admission date

  —medical record number

  —name and contact information (phone number and e-mail address) of the coding professional

  —specific question and rationale (that is, relevant documentation or clinical findings)

  —place for physician to document his or her response

  —place for the physician to sign and date his or her response

The query forms should not:

- "lead" the physician

- sound presumptive, directing, prodding, probing, or as though the physician is being led to make an assumption

- ask questions that can be responded to in a "yes" or "no" fashion

- indicate the financial impact of the response to the query

- be designed so that all that is required is a physician signature

When Is a Query Appropriate?

Physicians should be queried whenever there is conflicting, ambiguous, or incomplete information in the medical record regarding any significant reportable condition or procedure. Querying the physician only when reimbursement is affected will skew national healthcare data and might lead to allegations of upcoding.

Every discrepancy or issue not addressed in the physician documentation should not necessarily result in the physician being queried. Each facility needs to develop policies and procedures regarding the clinical conditions and documentation situations warranting a request for physician clarification. For example, insignificant or irrelevant findings may not warrant querying the physician regarding the assignment of an additional diagnosis code. Also, if the maximum number of codes that can be entered in the hospital information system has already been assigned, the facility may decide that it is not necessary to query the physician regarding an additional code. Facilities need to balance the value of marginal data being collected against the administrative burden of obtaining the additional documentation.

Members of the medical staff in consultation with coding professionals should develop the specific clinical criteria for a valid query. The specific clinical documentation that must be present in the patient's record to generate a query should be described. For example, anemia, septicemia, and respiratory failure are conditions that often require physician clarification. The medical staff can assist the coding staff in determining when it would be appropriate to query a physician regarding the reporting of these conditions by describing the specific clinical indications in the medical record documentation that raise the possibility that the condition in question may be present.

When Is a Query Not Necessary?

Queries are not necessary if a physician involved in the care and treatment of the patient, including consulting physicians, has documented a diagnosis and there is no conflicting documentation from another physician. Medical record documentation from any physician involved in the care and treatment of the patient, including documentation by consulting physicians, is appropriate for the basis of code assignment. If documentation from different physicians conflicts, seek clarification from the attending physician, as he or she is ultimately responsible for the final diagnosis.

Queries are also not necessary when a physician has documented a final diagnosis and clinical indicators, such as test results, do not appear to support this diagnosis. While coding professionals are expected to advocate complete and accurate physician documentation and to collaborate with physicians to realize this goal, they are not expected to challenge the physician's medical judgment in establishing the patient's diagnosis. However, because a discrepancy between clinical findings and a final diagnosis is a clinical issue, a facility may choose to establish a policy that the physician will be queried in these instances.

Documentation of Query Response

The physician's response to the query must be documented in the patient's medical record. Each facility must develop a policy regarding the specific process for incorporating this additional documentation in the medical record. For example, this policy might stipulate that the physician is required to add the additional information to the body of the medical record. As an alternative, a form, such as a medical record "progress note" form, might be attached to the query form and the attachment is then filed in the medical record. However, another alternative is to file the query form itself in the permanent medical record. Any documentation obtained post-discharge must be included in the discharge summary or identified as a late entry or addendum.

Any decision to file this form in the medical record should involve the advice of the facility's corporate compliance officer and legal counsel, due to potential compliance and legal risks related to incorporating the actual query form into the permanent medical record (such as its potential use as evidence of poor documentation in an audit, investigation, or malpractice suit, risks related to naming a nonclinician in the medical record, or quality of care concerns if the physician response on a query form is not clearly supported by the rest of the medical record documentation).

If the query form will serve as the only documentation of the physician's clarification, the use of "open-ended" questions (that require the physician to specifically document the additional information) are preferable to multiple-choice questions or the use of questions requiring only a "yes" or "no" answer. The query form would need to be approved by the medical staff/medical records committee before implementation of a policy allowing this form to be maintained in the medical record. Also keep in mind that the Joint Commission hospital accreditation standards stipulate that only authorized individuals may make entries in medical records (IM.7.1.1). Therefore, the facility needs to consider modifying the medical staff bylaws to specify coding professionals as individuals authorized to make medical record entries prior to allowing query forms to become a permanent part of the medical record.

Auditing, Monitoring, and Corrective Action

Ideally, complete and accurate physician documentation should occur at the time care is rendered. The need for a query form results from incomplete, conflicting, or ambiguous documentation, which is an indication of poor documentation. Therefore, query form usage should be the exception rather than the norm. If physicians are being queried frequently, facility management or an appropriate medical staff committee should investigate the reasons why.

A periodic review of the query practice should include a determination of what percentage of the query forms are eliciting negative and positive responses from the physicians. A high negative response rate may be an indication that the coding staff are not using the query process judiciously and are being overzealous.

A high positive response rate may indicate that there are widespread poor documentation habits that need to be addressed. It may also indicate that the absence of certain reports (for example, discharge summary, operative report) at the time of coding is forcing the coding staff to query the physicians to obtain the information they need for proper coding.

If this is the case, the facility may wish to reconsider its policy regarding the availability of certain reports prior to coding. Waiting for these reports may make more sense in terms of turnaround time and productivity rather than finding it necessary to frequently query the physicians. The question of why final diagnoses are not available at the time of discharge may arise at the time of an audit, review by the peer review organization, or investigation.

The use of query forms should also be monitored for patterns, and any identified patterns should be used to educate physicians on improving their documentation at the point of care. If a pattern is identified, such as a particular physician or diagnosis, appropriate steps should be taken to correct the problem so the necessary documentation is present prior to coding in the future and the need to query this physician, or to query physicians regarding a particular diagnosis, is reduced. Corrective action might include targeted education for one physician or education for the entire medical staff on the proper documentation necessary for accurate code assignment.

Patterns of poor documentation that have not been addressed through education or other corrective action are signs of an ineffective compliance program. The Department of Health and Human Services Office of Inspector General has noted in its Compliance Program Guidance for Hospitals that "accurate coding depends upon the quality of completeness of the physician's documentation" and "active staff physician participation in educational programs focusing on coding and documentation should be emphasized by the hospital."[5]

The format of the queries should also be monitored on a regular basis to ensure that they are not inappropriately leading the physician to provide a particular response. Inappropriately written queries should be used to educate the coding staff on a properly written query. Patterns of inappropriately written queries should be referred to the corporate compliance officer.

Prepared by

Sue Prophet, RHIA, CCS

Acknowledgments

AHIMA Advocacy and Policy Task Force
AHIMA's Coding Practice Team
AHIMA Coding Policy and Strategy Committee
AHIMA Society for Clinical Coding
Dan Rode, MBA, FHFMA

Notes

1. Joint Commission on Accreditation of Healthcare Organizations. *Comprehensive Accreditation Manual for Hospitals: The Official Handbook.* Oakbrook Terrace, IL: Joint Commission, 2000.

2. Health Care Financing Administration, Department of Health and Human Services. "Conditions of Participation for Hospitals." Code of Federal Regulations, 2000. 42 CFR, Chapter IV, Part 482.

3. Official ICD-9-CM Guidelines for Coding and Reporting developed and approved by the American Hospital Association, American Health Information Management Association, Health Care Financing Administration, and the National Center for Health Statistics.

4. AHIMA is the professional organization responsible for issuing several credentials in health information management: Registered Health Information Administrator (RHIA), Registered Health Information Technician (RHIT), Certified Coding Specialist (CCS), and Certified Coding Specialist-Physician-based (CCS-P).

5. Office of Inspector General, Department of Health and Human Services. "Compliance Program Guidance for Hospitals." Washington, DC: Office of Inspector General, 1998.

References

AHIMA Code of Ethics, 1998.

AHIMA Standards of Ethical Coding, 1999.

AHIMA Coding Policy and Strategy Committee. "Practice Brief: Data Quality." *Journal of AHIMA* 67, no. 2 (1996).

Appendix 3.4

Hospital-Based Coding Competencies

CCS/CCS-P Competencies

The Council on Certification routinely undertakes a job analysis study of coding specialists. From this job analysis study, the Council on Certification develops cognitive competencies, which serve as the template for construction of the credentialing examinations.

The following are the competencies identified for the CCS and CCS-P examinations:

I. Hospital-based Competencies (taken from CCS coding competencies)

A. Data Identification

1. Read and interpret health record documentation to identify all diagnoses and procedures that affect the current inpatient stay/outpatient encounter visit
2. Assess the adequacy of health record documentation to ensure that it supports all diagnoses and procedures to which codes are assigned
3. Apply knowledge of anatomy and physiology, clinical disease processes, pharmacology, and diagnostic and procedural terminology to assign accurate codes to diagnoses and procedures
4. Apply knowledge of disease processes and surgical procedures to assign non-indexed medical terms to the appropriate class in the classification/nomenclature system

B. Coding Guidelines

1. Apply knowledge of current approved "ICD-9-CM Coding and Reporting Official Guidelines"* to assign and sequence the correct diagnosis and procedure codes for hospital inpatient services
2. Apply knowledge of current "Diagnostic Coding and Reporting Guidelines for Outpatient Services'"
3. Apply knowledge of CPT format, guidelines, and notes to locate the correct codes for all services and procedures performed during the encounter/visit and sequence them correctly
4. Apply knowledge of procedural terminology to recognize when an unlisted procedure code must be used in CPT

C. Regulatory Guidelines

1. Apply Uniform Hospital Discharge Data Set (UHDDS) definitions to select the principal diagnosis, principal procedure, complications and comorbid conditions, other diagnoses and significant procedures which require coding
2. Select the appropriate principal diagnosis for episodes of care in which determination of principal diagnosis is not clear because the patient has multiple problems
3. Apply knowledge of the Prospective Payment System to confirm DRG assignment which ensures optimal reimbursement
4. Refuse to fraudulently maximize reimbursement by assigning codes that do not conform to approved coding principles/guidelines*
5. Refuse to unfairly maximize reimbursement by unbundling services and codes that do not conform to CPT basic coding principles

6. Apply knowledge of the Ambulatory Surgery Center Payment Groups to confirm ASC assignment which ensures optimal reimbursement
7. Apply policies and procedures on health record documentation, coding, and claims processing and appeal
8. Use the HCFA Common Procedural Coding System (HCPCS) to appropriately assign HCPCS codes for outpatient Medicare reimbursement

D. Coding

1. Exclude from coding diagnoses, conditions, problems and procedures related to an earlier episode of care which have no bearing on the current episode of care
2. Exclude from coding ICD-9-CM nonsurgical, noninvasive procedures which carry no operative or anesthetic risk
3. Exclude from coding information such as symptoms or signs characteristic of the diagnosis, findings from diagnostic studies, or localized conditions, which have no bearing on the current management of the patient
4. Apply knowledge of ICD-9-CM instructional notations and conventions to locate and assign the correct diagnostic and procedural codes and sequence them correctly
5. Facilitate data retrieval by recognizing when more than one code is required to adequately classify a given condition
6. Exclude from coding those procedures which are component parts of an already assigned CPT procedure code

E. Data Quality

1. Clarify conflicting, ambiguous, or nonspecific information appearing in a health record by consulting the appropriate physician
2. Participate in quality assessment to ensure continuous improvement in ICD-9-CM and CPT coding and collection of quality health data
3. Demonstrate ability to recognize potential coding quality issues from an array of data
4. Apply policies and procedures on health record documentation and coding that are consistent with official coding guidelines*
5. Contribute to development of facility-specific coding policies and procedures

---

Source: AHIMA. 2001. *CCS Candidate Handbook.* Chicago: American Health Information Management Association.

Appendix 3.5

Physician-Office-Based Coding Competencies

CCS/CCS-P Competencies

The Council on Certification routinely undertakes a job analysis study of coding specialists. From this job analysis study, the Council on Certification develops cognitive competencies, which serve as the template for construction of the credentialing examinations.

The following are the competencies identified for the CCS and CCS-P examinations:

II. Physician-based Competencies (taken from CCS-P coding competencies)

A. Data Identification

1. Read and interpret visit documentation to identify codeable diagnoses and procedures for data capture and billing
2. Read and interpret medical record documentation to identify all diagnoses, conditions, problems, or other reasons for the outpatient encounter and all services and procedures performed during that visit
3. Assess the adequacy of medical record documentation to ensure that it supports the codes assigned
4. Apply knowledge of disease processes to assign codes to conditions/medical terms not found in the index of the coding book to the appropriate class in the classification system

B. Coding Guidelines

1. Understand the use and function of modifiers in CPT
2. Apply the "ICD-9-CM Coding Guidelines for Outpatient Services"* and knowledge of instructional notations and conventions to select and sequence diagnoses, conditions, problems, or other reasons which require coding
3 Apply knowledge of CPT guidelines, format, and notes to locate and correctly sequence codes for all services and procedures performed during the encounter
4 Confirm Evaluation and Management codes based upon medical record documentation using the E/M guidelines
5. Recognize when an unlisted code must be used
6. Demonstrate ability to recognize potential coding quality issues from an array of data (e.g., explanation of benefits, coding database, etc.)

C. Regulatory Guidelines

1. Apply regulatory agency guidelines (i.e., HCFA) to coding principles so that codes are assigned correctly to each visit
2. Observe guidelines on bundling and unbundling
3. Have knowledge of the global surgical package and its components
4. Have knowledge of various reimbursement methodologies, fee schedule and RBRVS
5. Execute policies and procedures on medical record documentation, coding, claims filing, and claims appeal

D. Coding

1. Exclude from coding, those procedures which are component parts of an already assigned procedure code
2. Assign Level II HCPCS codes correctly for services not found in CPT (e.g., administration of drugs, durable medical equipment)
3. Attach modifiers to procedure or service codes when applicable
4. Appropriately code for the professional vs. technical component when applicable
5. Assign ICD-9-CM code(s) for conditions managed or treated during the encounter
6. Assign CPT code(s) for procedures and/or services rendered during the encounter
7. Evaluate the disease processes as related to various ancillary procedures

E. Data Quality

1. Query physicians when additional information is needed for coding and/or to clarify conflicting or ambiguous information
2. Link ICD-9-CM code(s) to proper CPT code(s) to ensure accurate claims submission
3. Verify that the CPT code(s), ICD-9-CM code(s), and Place of Service code(s) on the HCFA 1500 claim form correctly support the services performed
4. Determine educational needs for physicians and staff on coding, reimbursement, and documentation rules as well as penalties and sanction possibilities (e.g., standardized encounter form/progress notes)

Source: AHIMA. 2001. *CCS Candidate Handbook.* Chicago: American Health Information Management Association.

Appendix 3.6

Sample Job Description

Job Title: Certified coding specialist

Job Description: Reviews patient records and assigns accurate codes for each diagnosis and procedure. Applies knowledge of medical terminology, disease processes, and pharmacology. Demonstrates tested data quality and integrity skills.

Education:

A minimum of a high school degree*, plus successful obtainment and maintenance of the American Health Information Management Association (AHIMA) credential—certified coding specialist (CCS)

Qualifications:

Two years of coding and abstracting experience in ICD-9-CM, DRGs, and CPT including modifiers and APCs

Job Skills:

- Thorough knowledge of the related prospective payment systems (PPSs)

- Broad knowledge of pharmacology indications for drug usage and related adverse reactions

- Knowledge of ancillary testing (laboratory, X-ray, EKG)

- Knowledge of anatomy, physiology, and medical terminology

- Understanding of coding practices and guidelines

- Experience with PC and mainframe applications and with encoding systems

- Auditing skills for coding quality and compliance

- Strong process management skills

---

*Many HIM professionals with advanced degrees have taken the CCS in order to demonstrate coding knowledge.

Chapter 4

Coding Staff Recruitment and Retention Issues

Nadinia A. Davis, MBA, CIA, CPA, RHIA
Marion K. Gentul, RHIA, CCS

The goal of coding staff recruitment is to match the needs of the healthcare organization with the needs of the person performing coding functions. Unfortunately, trends of supply and demand in the personnel industry may pressure some HIM department managers to hire candidates who are not fully qualified or adequately trained. Skilled coders are likely to look for facilities that offer incentive plans or other attractive benefits, such as flexible work hours. Moreover, advanced coders are often lured to jobs in the consulting field, where productivity is likely to be matched by compensation that is higher than it is in the healthcare facilities.

This chapter presents basic guidelines that coding managers can use to assess their facilities' needs when recruiting applicants to fill a vacancy in the HIM department. It also discusses alternatives to filling vacancies with full-time employees.

Performing a Needs Assessment

When a vacancy occurs on the coding staff, the first thing the HIM department manager should do is to perform a **needs assessment.** This involves the following tasks:

- Performing a job analysis

- Assessing staff productivity requirements

- Analyzing the experience level of the coding staff

- Conducting a salary survey

Each of these tasks is a key element in helping the healthcare facility determine what coding positions are reasonable and necessary.

Performing a Job Analysis

The coding manager should not automatically try to fill a vacancy with a new coder who is just like the one who left. For example, filling a position vacated by a coder with six years of experience in the facility with a coder from outside the facility who also has six years of experience is not necessarily the best solution. The coding manager first should review his or her options. Questions to ask include:

- Should a new employee be hired and trained to fill the vacancy?

- Can the additional work be divided among current staff members?

- Can a current staff member be promoted to the position vacated?

- Should the department outsource the work?

During the vacating coder's time of service, the department probably has hired, trained, and educated any number of coders, one of whom could be promoted to fill the open position. Obviously, when a current staff member is promoted to fill an open position, the vacancy simply shifts to another position. However, the position vacated by the promoted staff member may be easier to fill if it requires a lower skill level or less experience. Moreover, promotions within the department can boost staff morale, which is often needed when a staff member resigns.

During the time of a staff shortage, the coding manager should periodically review staff productivity and workload to assess their impact on morale and to avoid the loss of additional staff. Moreover, he or she can incorporate staff input when addressing pertinent issues, deciding whether to promote a staff member, or reorganizing work space and job responsibilities. In cases where current staff have to compensate for a vacancy, the coding manager should consider making whatever adjustments are necessary to balance the workload and to delegate some tasks temporarily to noncoding staff.

Finally, when the coding manager finds it necessary to hire a coder to fill a vacated position, he or she must justify that decision to the facility's administration. Thus, it is advisable to have benchmarking data and survey information completely up to date. In addition, the coding manager must know the costs for overtime or for contract coding if the vacant position is not to be filled promptly. The longer a position is left unfilled, the likelier facility administration or owners are to decide that it is not really needed. Moreover, in times of layoffs, unfilled positions are often eliminated automatically.

Assessing Staff Productivity Requirements

The second part of the coding manager's needs assessment addresses staff productivity requirements. One approach is to review coder productivity (for both full- and part-time personnel) during regular hours and shifts. Such a review helps the coding manager determine whether productivity fluctuates at different times of the workday. For example, productivity is likely to be higher at night when fewer distractions or interruptions are present.

To compensate for productivity lost because of a change in personnel, the coding manager might be able to persuade some staff members to shift hours temporarily, perhaps by offering incentives such as a shift-differential increase in compensation. A shift-differential increase in pay may prove to be more cost-effective than overtime compensation.

Another approach to compensating for lost productivity is to arrange for coding staff to work when the HIM department is normally closed. This option requires notifying other departments and physicians as well as security staff that coders will be working after hours.

Average discharges, productivity standards, and normal work hours all should be factored into the calculation of coding staff needs. Coders do not work every day. Vacations, sick days, holidays, downtime, continuing education, and noncoding responsibilities all must be considered. (See chapter 6, Performance Management and Process Improvement, for a detailed discussion of productivity standards and the coding staff complement.)

In addition to assessing the productivity requirements of the HIM staff at his or her facility, the coding manager may want to conduct **benchmarking surveys** to determine the productivity requirements of local healthcare employers or those with a similar service mix. Some facilities may be willing to share this information directly. Local coding vendors also can be a useful source of information. Information items to be requested include hours worked, additional tasks performed, abstracting requirements, data-entry requirements, and vacation/sick days, in addition to the number of health records coded per time period. (See chapter 6 for a detailed discussion of productivity.)

To have information available when recruitment becomes necessary, the coding manager should conduct benchmarking surveys on a routine basis. Routine benchmarking also helps the coding staff avoid complacency or the excessive assumption of unrelated tasks.

Analyzing the Level of Experience of Current Staff

The staff's level of experience is another critical factor to consider when deciding how to fill a vacancy. When the staff's level of experience is strong, hiring a trainee may be a possibility. However, in the absence of experienced leadership or a staff resource person, a skeleton staff or a staff that is relatively inexperienced may be unable to support the hire of an untrained coder. One way to determine the experience level of the staff complement is to review each individual's current productivity and error rates and then compare them with previous productivity rates.

Conducting a Salary Survey

Understanding the economic marketplace is essential to any needs assessment. AHIMA is a good source of general salary information by region for AHIMA-credentialed coding staff. Local outsourcing coding vendors also are good sources of information, as are local colleges and universities with recent survey data for the region.

State hospital associations are another good source because they conduct salary surveys for all the main job categories generally found in hospitals. Hospital administrators and human resources (HR) departments frequently use this information. However, salaries can vary widely within a state, and compensation is typically higher in metropolitan areas than in rural areas.

Salary surveys should be performed every one to two years. The HR department usually conducts them, but the HIM department may want to do job-specific surveys and then compare the results. One reason for this is that the two departments could have different hiring criteria. For example, the HIM department's main objective in hiring a coder is to find the best-qualified candidate whereas the HR department's main objective may be to lower the compensation level for the position. Indeed, some healthcare facilities offer their HR departments incentives to achieve savings in hiring practices. Thus, the coding manager must work with the HR department to ensure a balance in overall hiring goals and objectives.

Moreover, coding managers could use salary surveys done within their local marketplace to help them adjust compensation or environmental factors to better compete for coding employees. However, facilities competing for the same qualified candidates may not want to share information. When salary survey information is unavailable locally, coding managers will need to seek it from facilities with similar profiles that are located outside the immediate marketplace. In that way, competition for the same candidates is less likely.

Surveyors sometimes can increase their success by offering to share the results with everyone who participated in the survey. However, this usually will work only if the surveyors guarantee the participants' anonymity.

Recruiting and Hiring Coding Staff

When the HIM department makes the decision to fill a vacancy with a full-time staff member, it begins its effort to recruit candidates. This involves advertising the position and a sometimes-lengthy interviewing process.

Choosing the Appropriate Advertising Vehicle

Many organizations limit their employment advertisements to local newspapers. However, to reach the maximum number of candidates, ads also may be placed in appropriate trade papers and magazines and on Web sites.

Determining the Content of the Ad

The HR department is responsible for writing and placing job advertisements. When job descriptions are updated annually, the HR department usually has the correct information on hand. However, sometimes inappropriate or outdated credentials have not been changed. An ad for an accredited record technician (ART), for instance, would reflect poorly on the department and the facility, because this credential is no longer valid. Thus, the coding manager should review ads for accuracy before they are placed.

In addition to checking for errors, the coding manager should read the ad for tone. HR departments use standard wording in recruiting advertisements. The coding manager should ensure that both the facility and the HIM department are described in a manner that makes them attractive to candidates and yet communicates a true picture of the working environment. Standard phrases such as "pleasant working conditions," "opportunity for advancement," and "full support for continuing education" are appropriate only when they are true.

Stating the Minimum Requirements

The ad also must specify the minimum requirements for the position. In itself, "high school education" is not an effective requirement for a coding position. Years of experience, if required, should be specified, in addition to all acceptable credentials. Depending on the duties of the coder, CCS, CCS-P, CPC, and CPC-H are the only credentials that pertain specifically to healthcare coding, although RHIT, RHIA, or "eligible" also are acceptable designations.

The issue of credentials can have an impact on employee morale. The coding manager must determine whether to hire a credentialed coder or one who either is not yet certified or is preparing for certification. A staff composed entirely of credentialed coders may resent the hiring of an uncredentialed coder at a market salary. If obtaining an appropriate credential is a job requirement, the new employee may be hired on probation or paid a lower salary until he or she earns the credential. When a trainee is hired, any time limits imposed on obtaining the credential should be made in writing.

Finally, the ad should not state that the facility is willing to hire a trainee. Such a statement suggests that the position pays a trainee salary, which would discourage experienced coders from applying. On the other hand, if the facility is truly looking for a lower-salaried trainee, that should be specified.

Offering Sign-on Bonuses

Sometimes healthcare organizations offer sign-on bonuses to entice employees away from competing facilities. A **sign-on bonus** is a monetary incentive used by a facility to encourage a candidate to accept employment. Any organization that offers a sign-on bonus, however, should specify its criteria for qualifying for the bonus in a written contract. Having such criteria in writing will discourage coders from "job hopping" from one sign-on bonus to another. Examples of such criteria include:

- The new coder must pass a probationary period.

- He or she must remain at the facility for a defined period of time, for example, one year following the probationary period.

- He or she must meet or exceed productivity standards at the milestone performance review.

Finally, when sign-on bonus criteria are not met, the contract might require the employee to reimburse the facility for the bonus amount.

Selecting and Interviewing Candidates

Selecting and interviewing candidates involves a number of steps. These are explained in the following sections.

Reviewing the Resume

The resume is typically the principal element on which organizations base their decision to interview job applicants. When reviewing resumes submitted for coding positions, the recruiter should look for:

- Level of experience

- Satisfaction of the minimum requirements

- Appropriateness of credentials

- Gaps in employment

- Unrelated employment

- Length of service with previous employers

- Job responsibilities during coding employment that are unrelated to coding

Any questions about the content of the resume should be noted.

In addition to content, the recruiter should assess the resume and its cover letter for neatness, organization, spelling, grammar, and punctuation. The way applicants present themselves for employment is a possible indicator of how they will present themselves on the job. However, for many potentially excellent employees, English is a second, or sometimes a third, language. Thus, it may be difficult to determine whether grammar problems are the result of sloppiness or poor language proficiency. When grammar is the only problem with the documentation, it is always best to err on the side of the applicant.

Sometimes, on paper, an applicant will appear to be overqualified for the position, as in the case of a consultant or a former department director. Such individuals should not be dismissed automatically. They may have personal reasons for seeking a position that is less stressful and/or that requires less overtime. Such applicants often have a good understanding of the "big picture" that would enable them to model motivating behavior to others in the department.

Scheduling the Interview

Applicants who pass the resume review process become candidates for the position. Depending on the facility and the job being offered, the candidate will likely be interviewed by individuals in both the HR and HIM departments. If necessary, the interviews can be conducted over several days. Obviously, candidates who are currently working will be unable to schedule multiple interviews on different days during regular work hours. In such cases, interviews should be arranged to accommodate the candidates' schedules and, if possible, to include more than one interviewer at a time.

Certain general questions should be asked of all candidates. (See table 4.1 for some classic interview questions and explanations of their purposes.) The coding manager should not skip any questions simply because he or she knows the candidate. If this is the case, someone from the HR department could join the interview to ask the questions. This strategy makes explanations easier when the candidate is not the best one for the position.

The interview process should include time for questions and replies, as well as time for taking a coding test, if required. Before meeting with the candidate, the interviewer can expedite the process by rehearsing the questions and determining the time required to take the test. If the test needs to be scheduled at a different time than the interview, the candidate should be so informed in advance.

Analyzing the Interview

Interviewers should allow time after each interview to record their impressions. However, they should be extremely careful about what they write in the margins of the resume and on their question notes. The purpose of a resume review and standard interview experience is to

Table 4.1. Common interview questions and their purposes

Questions	Purposes
Describe your biggest accomplishment.	Can identify whether the individual is goal oriented or a team player. Is the biggest accomplishment being promoted or contributing to a major project?
	Illustrates the scope of the candidate's vision. Is the accomplishment related to a particular day's activities or to an organization-wide project?
	Focus on work- or school-related achievements. If the biggest achievement is personal, redirect the question.
What would you do if you were not a coder?	May lead to a discussion of the candidate's professional goals. Does he or she look for advancement to supervision and management? Is coding a step along the way of his or her chosen profession?
	Why the candidate is not doing this other activity may be important. Self-knowledge of lack of talent, for example, shows that the candidate has a realistic view of his or her skills and abilities.
	Some interviewers like to interpret unusual answers. "Broadway singer" might be interpreted as liking to be the center of attention and "baseball player" as a team player. However, this is dangerous territory and should be avoided.
Describe a problem you had and how you solved it.	Regardless of the origin of the problem, pay attention to how it was solved. Is this how you would want an employee to solve problems in your facility? Does the candidate's strategy fit into your corporate/department culture? If you are unsure, pose a problem that your coders have had and ask how the candidate would handle it.
All questions.	If you gain nothing else from the responses, you will gain an understanding of the degree of the candidate's verbal communication skills. Is he or she well prepared and articulate?

eliminate bias and subjectivity in hiring. Interviewers should not subvert that process by using discriminatory language in their interview notes.

Testing for Coding Skills

The coding test may be standardized, with scenarios to which the coder assigns the appropriate codes. Examples of such tests may be taken from routinely published coding handbooks and texts. A local college or university may be able to assist in this process. The HIM department should review the test annually to ensure that it accurately reflects current codes and coding practices, as well as the actual work to be performed, as required by the Occupational Safety and Health Administration (OSHA 1998).

The test also may require the candidate to code health records. Although coding health records can take more time than a standardized test, it gives the coding manager a better idea of the candidate's level of productivity. If health records are used, they should be photocopied, with patient identities obscured or removed. Health records used for this type of test should reflect common coding issues that arise in the facility. For example, if the facility has an active cardiac catheterization laboratory, such a health record should be included.

The test results should be evaluated for accuracy, level of experience, and speed. However these elements are handled, all candidates must be treated equally in the scoring and analysis of the test.

Evaluating for Accuracy

Accuracy is the most important characteristic of the coder's work. An unfamiliar environment may impair the coding candidate's speed but should not affect his or her accuracy. The person evaluating the test should pay close attention to the types of errors made. These can indicate whether the coder merely needs training in a particular area or whether he or she is sloppy or inattentive to detail. If necessary, a test debriefing that queries the candidate about incorrect responses can be scheduled. When errors cannot be explained, the answer key to the test should be checked.

Evaluating for Level of Experience

Test results also should be evaluated to determine the applicant's stated level of coding experience. For example, a coder who has never seen an A/V fistula procedure for renal dialysis may not code it accurately but should at least be close. A coder with years of experience who states that renal procedures were routine at a previous position should be able to code the procedure correctly, without hesitation.

Evaluating for Speed

The least important factor in the coding test is speed. An experienced coder would certainly be expected to complete the test more quickly than a trainee. However, an unfamiliar format and environment can have a negative effect on productivity.

Making the Offer

Depending on a facility's policy, either the HIM department manager or someone in the HR department makes the actual offer of employment. If the coding manager is so designated, the two departments must resolve a number of specific issues, including:

- How long the offer will be in effect
- What leeway the coding manager will have in negotiating salary

- What specific issues or benefits the HR department will handle

- How to schedule preemployment requirements, such as physical examinations and facility orientations

- What the appropriate start date will be

The offer of employment should always be made in writing. Most currently employed individuals will not resign a position without the guarantee of a written offer. After the prospective employee has accepted the offer, it is appropriate to e-mail or fax confirmation of the acceptance.

After the position has been filled, the courteous and common business practice is to inform the other candidates. This notification also should be done in writing as soon as possible.

Taking the New Employee through the Orientation Process

Many, if not most, healthcare facilities have a regularly scheduled, one- or two-day orientation program for all new employees, regardless of job function. The purpose of the orientation program is to introduce new employees to:

- The organization as a whole

- The department in which he or she will work

- The specific job responsibilities

Orientation to the Organization

Depending on the facility's policy, new employees may be required to attend an orientation to the overall organization before attending the department-specific orientation. Therefore, their start date is not necessarily the date they actually begin to produce work. As a practical matter, coding managers should assume that the new employee's first week is devoted primarily to orientation.

Orientation to the overall organization might include discussion of:

- Requirements of the Joint Commission on Accreditation of Healthcare Organizations (JCAHO)

- Requirements of the Occupational Safety and Health Administration (OSHA)

- State requirements

- Employee benefits

- Expectations of conduct

When possible, orientation topics should be presented in order of importance. For example, the facility's confidentiality policies should be presented before the location of the cafeteria is discussed.

Typically, the HR department conducts the orientation to the organization, with support from other departments. For instance, the coding manager may be asked to present the topic of confidentiality to new employees.

Certainly one purpose of this process is to impart the tone and culture of the organization. However, the orientation also gives new employees the opportunity to ask questions they may have thought of since accepting employment.

Orientation to the Department

The new employee's workstation should be ready upon his or her arrival. Orientation to the department should begin after he or she has settled in. Introductions should be the first order of business and can be made during an informal tour of the department.

The coding manager or designee overseeing the orientation to the department should have a checklist of items to be discussed and information to be disseminated (table 4.2). The facility may use a generic form with space included for departmental specifics. Current JCAHO

Table 4.2.   **Sample checklist for orientation to the department and to functions of the job**

Departmental Orientation	Trainer Initials	Employee Initials	Date
General:			
Workstation location			
Policies regarding workstation appearance			
Work hours			
Sign-in procedures			
Sick day procedures			
Vacation day procedures			
Introduction to staff			
Departmental grievance procedures			
Functional:			
Job description			
Performance measurement			
Work distribution			
Computer training			
Telephone training			
Daily tasks			
Weekly tasks			
Other periodic tasks			
Physician query procedures			
Problem chart procedures			
Missing information procedures			
Coding guidelines			
Coding resources			
Coding question procedures			
Subsequent work flow			
Departmental work flow			

standards can be used to ensure that the checklist includes all the requirements of continued employment, such as verification that the employee has read and understood the organizational mission statement and confidentiality policy.

The policy and procedure manual and the HIM department's table of organization also should be reviewed and discussed. Sections that do not necessarily pertain to the employee's immediate job function may be included to provide an overall picture of the department's functions and responsibilities. The department also may have the new staff member rotate through all or most of the job functions. Actually seeing the functions in action helps to clarify the department's role within the healthcare facility.

The new employee should sign off on the checklist to indicate that the orientation process has been completed. The checklist then should be signed and dated by the HIM manager or a supervisor. It may be kept in the HR department or in the employee's file within the HIM department. In addition, a confidentiality statement should be signed with the signature witnessed and dated. The confidentiality statement should then be reviewed annually or according to organizational policy. Any employee-specific confidential information, such as computer passwords, must be kept in a secure location.

Orientation to the Functions of the Job

The next part of the new employee's orientation is to address the specific functions of the job. To be fully functional in, and comfortable with, the new position, the new coder must first be instructed on the department's operations. For example:

- How is work distributed?

- What tasks are to be performed in addition to coding?

- What happens to the health record after it is coded?

These and other functional orientation questions are listed in table 4.2. One important reason for formalizing this review is to document that it occurred. This ensures that a lack of knowledge of job functions cannot be used as an excuse for incomplete work.

Orientation to the functions of the job also should:

- Review the regulatory requirements that affect the position

- Determine the need for training

- Clarify the standards used to measure the employee's progress

- Explain the probationary period

- Discuss the job productivity expectations

Regulatory Requirements

Healthcare facilities and their employees must meet numerous regulatory and accreditation standards. The coding manager should review the facility's corporate compliance, coding compliance, and performance improvement programs with the new coder.

Often the arrival of a new employee gives the HIM department the opportunity to involve the entire coding staff in a formal review of the facility's regulatory and compliance programs.

Need for Training

A new employee's need for training can be based on the areas of weakness identified from the coding test taken during the interviewing process. The coding manager should schedule education and training in these areas before the coder begins the actual work of coding.

The coding manager should discuss all identified coding errors with new employees. Occasionally, the reviewer is wrong. Unless the error is clear, new employees should be given the opportunity to defend their coding with authoritative references. This process enables them to develop a collaborative relationship with the coding supervisor and with coworkers that will have long-term benefits.

Standards of Measurement

One goal of the functional orientation is to ensure that the new coder understands the standards that will be used to measure his or her job performance. For example:

- How often is the performance reviewed?

- Who performs the review?

- How will errors be handled?

All employees should be given routine, collaborative, and educational feedback. This feedback is particularly important for new coders, who find it unproductive and stressful to wonder for weeks or months how well they are doing.

Probationary Period

An employee hired to fill an open position generally serves a period of probation. The intent of the **probationary period** is to give the employee the opportunity to demonstrate his or her ability to perform the duties of the position.

Most states specify the duration of the probationary period, which typically is three months. The probationary period is the last opportunity the employer has to rectify a hiring error with minimal effort. Probationary periods typically can be extended at weekly or monthly intervals for any length of time, although usually no more than six months.

If the new employee's work during the probationary period is unsatisfactory, the coding manager should identify the specific areas that need improvement and then discuss possible remedies with the probationary coder. Ideally, the new employee will demonstrate steady progress throughout this period. When he or she has done so (even though not meeting every expectation), the coding manager must decide whether to extend the probationary period or remove the coder from probationary status.

During the probationary period, healthcare facilities often compensate an employee at less than full pay and withhold certain benefits, such as health insurance. The purpose of the probationary period is to ensure that the potential coder is qualified for the position, not to "buy time" to interview other candidates. The coding manager should not "string along" an individual for an extended period of time without making a decision. Organizations that engage in such unfair and unethical hiring practices will soon become known in the coding community and begin to experience hiring difficulties.

Terminating an employee after he or she has been taken off probation can be difficult and stressful. Thus, to avoid difficulties, the coding manager should be aware of all written policies, legalities, and union agreements regarding probationary periods and the hiring and firing of staff.

Productivity Expectations

The productivity expectations of the position should be clearly stated. An employee's failure to meet productivity standards can be grounds for dismissal. The coding manager who treats productivity expectations lightly is likely to end up with unproductive employees.

As indicated earlier, two indicators of a coder's skill are the types of errors he or she makes and the speed at which he or she can work. For example, coders who achieve 100 percent accuracy in assigning principal diagnoses and DRG groupings but occasionally miss an additional diagnosis are more accurate than those who make mistakes selecting principal diagnoses and DRGs but correctly code everything else. All coding is important, but correct coding of principal diagnoses and DRGs produces the most benefits and the least need for recoding after quality audits.

However, the coder who completes only one health record per day with 100 percent accuracy is clearly not productive. The speed at which a coder can work depends on a number of factors, including the quality of the documentation in the health record and the extent of his or her responsibilities. Coders can code more health records in a day when they do not also have to abstract and to enter data. On the other hand, coders who enter their own data have the opportunity to review the results and correct errors at the time of entry.

Choosing Alternatives to Full-Time Staffing

The past twenty years have seen the emergence of a number of viable alternatives to the hiring of full-time, permanent employees. These include job sharing, telecommuting, and outsourcing.

Job Sharing

Employee morale and productivity often suffer when staff have to share the workload left by an unfilled position. Basically, job sharing refers to the situation in which two or more individuals share the tasks of one job or of one full-time equivalent (FTE) position. Typically, the employees occupy one work space and are rarely in the office at the same time.

Advantages of Job Sharing

Job sharing is a good alternative when the position calls for a full-time coder, but the pool of qualified candidates consists exclusively of part-time workers. Moreover, cost savings can occur if no benefits are paid in a job-sharing arrangement.

The major advantage to job sharing is that the work can still be done even though the position has not been filled. Often a job-sharing position can be retained as a full-time position rather than converted to two part-time positions.

Disadvantages of Job Sharing

However, job sharing also has disadvantages. For example:

- The resignation of one of the individuals sharing the job can create replacement problems.
- Performance evaluation may be problematic depending on how the job is shared (which is often left up to the employees). Although actual coding tasks can be reviewed, non-

coding activities such as customer relations and collaboration with other departments may be difficult to assess. For example, one person sharing the job may leave a telephone message and the other may take the return call and complete the task. Moreover, if a performance problem occurs, the supervisor may be unable to determine where it originated.

- Because the employees sharing the job must work as a team to complete the job function, the coding manager may need to spend extra time monitoring their working relationship and to pay close attention to any reported issues of miscommunication or evidence of incomplete tasks.

Using Current Staff in Job Sharing

When job sharing is not feasible, other staff may be cross-trained to assume the clerical tasks of the coding position. One part-time employee could then perform coding tasks.

Overtime hours and pay may be an attractive incentive for staff to participate in job sharing in the short term, particularly during holidays and/or summer vacation time. However, staff often begin to question the fairness of the compensation when required to do additional work over the long term.

Telecommuting

Telecommuting is an arrangement in which an employee works at home and communicates with the office via electronic means. It allows employees to be hired who are not in routine commuting distance from the facility.

Technically, many consultant coders are types of telecommuters. They work for a coding service vendor but perform services at the healthcare facility. They submit time sheets and expense reports to the vendor and receive instructions and assignments electronically from the vendor. Indeed, many consultant coders have never set foot in their actual employer's office.

Some employees combine working at home and in the office. This is most common when they live within commuting distance from the office. However, a growing number of employers are willing to periodically fund the transportation of employees from distant sites.

In the main, telecommuting attracts individuals who prefer either to work at home or not to relocate. Without question, a healthcare facility's ability and willingness to allow telecommuting increases the pool of potential candidates. In addition, the use of telecommuters can decrease the physical work space allocated to a position.

Telecommuting is a viable alternative, however, only if all technical, confidentiality, and access issues can be resolved. The fact that communication with telecommuters is largely electronic makes supervision of their work challenging. Moreover, technical support can be difficult, particularly if the employee is located outside the normal commuting range. The same is true with regard to ensuring confidentiality.

Work-at-home coders must employ consistently high professional standards to counteract negative stereotypes, such as the perception that patient records are visible at a coder's kitchen table while the neighbors are sitting around drinking coffee. Telecommuters are sometimes perceived by in-house staff as doing less work, being elitist, and placing a burden on the facility. One drawback of telecommuting is that the bonding among employees that facilitates collaboration may be lacking. Thus, coding managers should orient new telecommuters on-site and encourage networking among the coding staff via e-mail. Thanks to videoconferencing, telecommuters can participate in staff meetings and informal discussions as readily as if they were on-site.

Outsourcing

Outsourcing of the coding function from consulting firms can be a long- or short-term alternative when a shortage of qualified candidates makes hiring difficult or when the HIM department has insufficient resources to train in-house staff. Consulting firms tend to attract talented coders with high productivity levels.

As a long-term alternative, a healthcare facility can cover its coding function by using a combination of in-house employees and consultants. This strategy is typically used in a job market with a shortage of qualified coders.

The outsourcing of coding tasks offers several advantages, including:

- Consultant coders who perform unsatisfactorily are more easily replaced than in-house coders who perform unsatisfactorily.

- Consultant coders may be more experienced and productive than full-time in-house coders.

- The facility can use consultants to fill temporary needs caused by vacations and illness.

- Consultant coders may be willing to work outside regular business hours.

The disadvantages to outsourcing include:

- Coding managers or department supervisors have little control over consultants beyond monitoring the quality of their work.

- Nothing prevents consultants from leaving the facility when their productivity requirement has been met for the day or if a better job placement comes along.

- Generally, consultant coders are not assigned noncoding tasks and cannot be expected to "pitch in" when an in-house employee is absent. The consultant coder may have gone into consulting partly to get away from that type of burden, which also helps to explain consultants' generally high levels of productivity.

- In-house coders sometimes resent what they perceive to be the elitist attitude of contract coders. The coding manager should not minimize or ignore the potential impact of this issue on regular coding employees.

Using Coding Vendors

The decision to use coding vendors involves finding potential candidates, writing requests for proposals (RFPs), evaluating the proposals submitted, and contracting with the selected vendor. Several levels of vendors provide coding services: independent consultants, coding contractors with multiple employees, and multiservice contractors for whom coding is one part of the business. Each type of vendor has advantages and disadvantages.

Independent Consultants

Independent consultants perform coding services either as solely independent contractors or to supplement their regular employment. Because of low overhead, they tend to be relatively inexpensive compared to coding companies. Independent consultants often have a wealth of knowledge and can provide excellent advice about processing procedures, productivity issues, and physician relations. Sometimes they can become engaged in departmental affairs, even to the point of attending staff meetings and office parties. The Internal Revenue

Service (IRS) has very clear guidelines about what constitutes an independent contractor. Any independent consultant contract should include a standard independent contractor clause. An independent contractor who has only one organization as a client for a significant period of time looks, to the IRS, like an employee and probably should be put on the organization's payroll.

Multiservice Contractors

Multiservice contractors are generally small, local companies that provide coding services, as well as coding-related services such as DRG audits. Some of these companies are actually sole proprietorships or independent contractors who subcontract other independent contractors or other coding companies. Thus, coding managers may encounter coders who have been in their department under different organizational umbrellas at different times. Some inherent risk may be attached to the hiring of such coders because the burden of responsibility in the event of error may be unclear.

Coding Contractors with Multiple Employees

Other coding contractors actually hire coders, some of which are trainees. These coding companies have the resources to maintain stable training schedules and are in a better position to hire trainees than healthcare facilities might be. Coding managers should know, however, whether the contract coder is a trainee, how long he or she has been or will be in training, and what, if any, burden this will place on the HIM department. Coding quality is the coding manager's top priority and, as such, should be the key issue in contracting.

Writing the Request for Proposal

A **request for proposal (RFP)** is the means used by facilities to solicit information in writing from vendors about specific services and their costs. The RFP should be simple and clear and should specify a predetermined format for responses, particularly for pricing and productivity. Some vendors charge by the health record; others, by the hour. To compare rates, the RFP can require all the vendors to standardize their pricing and to give a per-health record rate based on their hourly rate and on standard productivity requirements.

The following issues should be addressed in every RFP for coding services:

- Coding quality

- Price

- Volume productivity

- Noncoding tasks

Coding Quality

Because the facility is contracting with a vendor as opposed to hiring an employee, it should determine how the vendor plans to ensure the quality of the services it is providing. Answers to the following questions can help the coding manager determine whether the vendor's quality program is in line with the HIM department's coding compliance concerns:

- Does the vendor have a quality assurance (QA) plan, in-service training program, and/or some other continuing education plan?

- Will the vendor audit the quality of its work?

- How does the vendor determine coding quality?

Price

Obviously, the price of services is important, but coding managers should avoid simply hiring the vendor who offers the cheapest price without examining its proposal for add-ons. For example, $10 per health record may look less expensive than $11 per health record, but when the $10 proposal includes a surcharge for any length of stay (LOS) of more than six days and the facility's average LOS is five days, the actual fees may regularly exceed $11 per health record. Thus, the price and any variations mentioned must be fully considered in evaluating which vendor's pricing is best.

Volume Productivity

Although the vendor's volume productivity requirements are generally nonnegotiable, the coding manager also should definitely examine the vendor's employee policies regarding productivity. For example, if the HIM department has 100 health records available to code and the consultant coder's productivity requirement is 50 health records per day, will the coding manager have the opportunity to give the consultant additional work? A contract provision that allows the coding manager to request, say, three to five health records in addition to standard productivity specifications may enable the HIM department to complete a full discharge day of work or to code an extra record with high unbilled charges.

Noncoding Tasks

The HIM department should not assume that a consultant coder will perform noncoding tasks such as filing loose sheets, entering data, calling other departments for reports, contacting physicians, or answering the telephone. Although these tasks are included in the normal operating procedures for employee coders, consultant coders are not required to perform them unless the contract so specifies. Thus, if the consultant coder is expected to perform noncoding tasks, the HIM department should specify them, along with detailed procedures, in the RFP so that they can be factored into the overall price of the service.

Evaluating Vendor Responses

Before responding to an RFP, a vendor may request a meeting to discuss the requirements of the job and the case mix. In this way, the vendor can observe the state of the HIM department's records at the time of coding and become acquainted with all the quirks of the department's processing. Many outsourcing contracts end disastrously when this kind of information is not requested or conveyed up front. Indeed, coding managers should be wary of a vendor whose quote for coding services falls well below the quotes of the other bidders. Such a vendor probably has not taken into consideration the case mix, the difficulty of the health records, or the unique processing requirements, or noncoding tasks, of the system.

An objective review of the proposals is essential for making a sound hiring decision. The review should be based on specific criteria that are defined in advance, including:

- Qualities

- Characteristics

- Skills

- Experience

- Price

When a vendor does not respond as requested, the coding manager must decide whether to ask for clarification or to eliminate the vendor from consideration. Generally speaking, it is safe to assume that a vendor whose RFP response does not conform to requirements will be similarly negligent in dealing with processing requests.

The coding manager should rank his or her priorities and weight the responses in a decision matrix. (See table 4.3.) This method of analysis helps to focus on the vendors who most closely meet the organization's needs. Each vendor's weighted score is the sum of the criterion scores times the criterion's rank. In table 4.3, for example, vendor 1 is $(3 \times 3) + (5 \times 2) + (5 \times 1) = 24$.

The rankings of priorities can be more complex. For example, if quality assurance is significantly more important to the facility than cost, its weight (rank) might be 4 instead of 3. To ensure an objective evaluation, the HIM department should develop criteria priorities and measures for scoring in advance of reviewing the RFP.

Avoiding Common Pitfalls

Both in-house employees and outsource personnel sometimes have perceptions about issues such as customer service, staffing, productivity, and work flow that can negatively affect the HIM department's relationship with its vendor. If the vendor's contract does not address these issues, the parties should consider an addendum.

Customer Service Issues

The customer service relationship between the HIM department and the coding vendor is very important. The contract should address how problems in this area will be resolved and by whom. For example:

- Will vendor personnel be required to interact with noncoding personnel and physicians?

- How will the consultant coder's physician queries be handled?

- How will coder errors be handled?

This last question is particularly important. Even though the vendor may have a quality assurance plan, the healthcare facility is ultimately responsible for ensuring the quality of its coding. Thus, the work of consultant coders should be included in the HIM department's routine quality audits. However, the department should follow its protocols at all times. Like employee coders, consultants must be afforded the opportunity to review and defend their work.

Table 4.3.   Sample decision matrix for vendor selection

Rank	Criteria	Vendor 1	Score	Vendor 2	Score	Vendor 3	Score
3	Quality assurance	Limited	3	Full Program	5	Full Program	5
2	Continuous coverage guaranteed	Yes	5	Yes	5	No	1
1	Cost per chart	$7	5	$13	1	$10	3
	Weighted score		24		26		20

Scores range from 1 to 5, with 5 being the highest and 1 the lowest.

Staffing Issues

The vendor's contract may call for the coding of a certain number of health records during a period of time but not address how to achieve that productivity level. If the vendor sends a different contract coder every week, the work flow in the HIM department is disrupted. Even new contract coders must be oriented and their work reviewed. Therefore, if "revolving door" staffing is problematic for the HIM department, it should be prohibited in the contract.

Productivity Issues

As mentioned previously, the productivity quantity standards for employee staff and consultant staff may differ significantly. For example, it is not unusual for employees to code twenty-five to thirty health records per day, compared to a consultant's rate of fifty to sixty health records per day.

Productivity standards for consultant staff should be stated in the contract. When no quality issues exist, it is absolutely inappropriate for the coding manager to ask the consultant to slow down to match the employee rate. Rather, the coding manager should explain the differences in the requirements and point out to the regular staff that they may be performing non-coding duties that contribute to those differences. Indeed, the coding manager may find it more difficult to explain the differences in productivity rates to his or her administrative superiors who are unfamiliar with departmental processing issues. He or she must be prepared to defend the department's internal productivity requirements or to reevaluate them as needed.

Without question, consultant coders are an expensive line item in the HIM department's budget. Some departments attempt to justify the cost by having the consultant code the most difficult records. If this is the plan, the coding manager should explain it up front so that the vendor can determine an appropriate price. If the coding manager agrees to a normal case mix and does not provide it, the HIM department can expect to lose the consultant or to face a significant rate hike as soon as the contract permits.

Work-Flow Issues

Problematic work-flow issues include loose paperwork, available paperwork, and analysis. Optimally, the consultant coder should be provided with an agreed-on number of records that have been preassembled and analyzed (although production delays may occasionally present challenges). If the production cycle places coding before analysis, this should be specified up front to bring the price quotes in line with reality and to prevent problems down the road.

Amending the Proposal

The vendor's response to the RFP is a proposal, not a legal contract. Thus, the coding manager should not hesitate to require the amendment of any item in the vendor's response that does not meet the HIM department's requirements. However, it should be noted that amendments to the proposed terms will likely result in a change in the quoted price for services.

During the contract negotiation or amendment process, some of the previously discussed issues may come to light. For example, the RFP may have asked for a proposal to code 100 health records per week but not have specified the hours the department would be open to the consultant, with the result that the vendor quoted a price based on regular business hours. During the amendment process, the vendor discovers that the facility is willing to allow the consultant to work evening and Saturday hours. Such clarification may provide more choices in terms of the consultants who are available to fulfill the contract.

Finalizing the Contract

If the coding manager does not have authority to sign the vendor contract, it may have to pass through administrative, purchasing, and legal reviews. If this occurs, parties from those areas should be involved in the final selection and negotiation process to avoid delays in executing the contract. (See table 4.4 for a summary of key contract issues.)

The coding manager would be wise to have the facility's corporate counsel review the contract in its preliminary stages so that any legal concerns can be addressed in the negotiation stage. Involving legal counsel at the negotiation stage will enable the final contract to be reviewed and executed on a timely basis. Legal review also will ensure the protection of both the coding manager and the healthcare facility.

Designing Retention Strategies

Like organizations in other industries, healthcare facilities often use financial and other incentives to maintain staff loyalty in a competitive marketplace. HIM departments might use various strategies such as bonuses, job enrichment, promotions, and training to ensure the retention of coding staff.

Table 4.4.   **Key vendor contract issues**

Issue	Questions	Comments
Productivity	What are the productivity measures and requirements?	Understanding the "available work" requirements (How many records need to be ready to code?)
	How will they be enforced?	Important for keeping current with the coding function
	Are there any "minimum available work" requirements?	Understanding the vendor's policies and procedures if work is unavailable
Quality control	How will coding quality be measured and reported?	Not only what the vendor's standards are, but also how to go about resolving differences
	How will necessary quality interventions be conducted?	How to handle identified errors and other quality issues
Employee relations	Who will actually be doing the coding?	Understanding the relationship between the vendor and the workers that it provides
	How will unsatisfactory workers be handled?	How easy will it be to replace an unsatisfactory worker?
	Is coverage guaranteed if a scheduled worker is not available?	Exploring depth of the vendor's coding staff
Department interaction	Exactly what tasks will the consultant coder be expected to perform?	Ensuring that the vendor is aware of all information
	Who will provide training for those tasks?	Fully discussing whether trainee coders will be used
Cost variances	How is payment for services rendered calculated?	Ensuring the validation of invoices
	What, if any, variances in payment are expected, and how are they calculated?	Length-of-stay variances, case-mix variances
Confidentiality	What confidentiality policies and procedures are in place?	Particularly in reference to distance coding, how is compliance assured?
	Who will sign the facility's confidentiality agreement?	HIPAA privacy regulations will require a formal agreement.

Bonuses

Most healthcare facilities offer annual wage increases, merit increases, or both. However, when these prove inadequate, the coding manager may find it necessary to offer bonuses.

Service Bonus

A **service bonus** is a monetary reward given to long-term staff in recognition of their skills and commitment to the facility. Working with the HR department, the coding manager should determine whether other departments in the facility, such as critical care nursing or physical therapy, have service bonuses in place. If so, he or she should review the process used by these departments to determine service bonuses. However, if no written policy and procedure is in place for service bonuses, the coding manager should work with the HR department to draft a generic policy that would apply equally to all positions in the facility. Documentation to support service bonuses should include the costs of recruitment, training, and vacancy coverage. Service bonuses may be awarded on a yearly basis and designed to be more financially attractive than the sign-on bonuses mentioned earlier. No criteria other than successful passing of the yearly performance review may be needed to receive a service bonus.

The cost of low morale is difficult to assess. Unproductive hours, absenteeism, and feelings of underappreciation, however, are legitimate factors to consider when the facility's goals include the retention of qualified staff. Service bonuses acknowledge and reward long-term staff through employer recognition of their skills and commitment.

Productivity Bonus

Healthcare organizations also may use **productivity bonuses** to reward exceptional performance or to motivate improvements in performance. For example, productivity bonuses might be considered for:

- Coders who consistently perform above and beyond established productivity standards: These are the employees that the facility most wishes to retain, but the most likely to be offered financial rewards by competitors.

- Coders who, for various reasons, slow down or stop coding when they have met the usual quantity standard: These individuals might be inspired to maintain high performance if financial rewards for increased productivity were in place.

- Coders who consistently produce more than others in the department: These individuals may eventually become resentful if they perceive that they are being compensated the same as less-productive staff.

Before offering productivity bonuses, however, the coding manager must determine whether current productivity standards are realistic and a fair exchange for present compensation. Bonuses should be offered only when the normal standards are far exceeded. If the standards are properly designed, this should not occur on a daily basis.

For example, when the quantity standard is twenty-five health records coded daily, coders will qualify for a bonus only when they exceed thirty or thirty-five health records with acceptable accuracy. If coders consistently code thirty to thirty-five records per day, the quantity standard may have been set too low. However, raising the quantity standard after the productivity bonus program is in place could make the facility appear insincere in its intent to reward productivity—the reward will seem perpetually out of reach and lose its meaning as an incentive. Conversely, if the bonus is too easy to get, staff may wonder why it is not simply included in their usual wages or may come to believe their usual wages are inadequate.

In addition to volume productivity, it is important to maintain coding accuracy. Records must be distributed in such a way that each coder is given a similar mix of easy-to-difficult cases. Coders should never be rewarded for quantity in the absence of meeting quality standards.

Job Enrichment

Money is not the only motivator that retains employees. Location, environment, and self-actualization can be equally important. Thus, an important part of the coder's annual review is to determine whether he or she has any personal or professional goals that the organization can help to satisfy. For example, the coder may want to become involved with quality audits. Rather than ignore this goal and risk losing the employee, the coding manager could assign new duties that will satisfy the coder's desires and interests. Table 4.5 offers a list of possible enrichment activities.

It is not always possible to achieve job enrichment for every employee. In addition, the desires of individual coders must be balanced with the needs of the department. In any event, whenever a coder is asked to perform additional tasks, the HIM department must provide appropriate training.

Promotion

It is impossible to promote every employee who wants to be promoted. Likewise, not every employee who wants to supervise has the temperament, talent, or training to be a supervisor. However, not every promotion leads to supervisory responsibilities. Several levels of coding staff can be defined. The following job titles represent potentially nonsupervisory positions with progressively more responsibility:

- Trainee
- Outpatient coder
- Inpatient coder
- Coding specialist
- Lead coder
- Head coder

Table 4.5. Possible job enrichment activities

Quality assurance activities	• Qualitative analysis screening • Coding audit activities
Interdepartmental reporting	• Routine medical staff activity reporting • Analysis of procedure index versus ancillary department activity
Staff development	• Continuing education
Physician interaction/liaison	• Physician query process coordination • Physician education

Table 4.6 describes possible criteria for these levels.

One problem with this approach is that both employees and the HR department may assume that the highest-level coder in the progression should be next in line for promotion to coding supervisor. However, many coders do not want the responsibilities of the supervisory role. The coding manager must ensure that the appropriate person is being groomed for the supervisory position. Only by talking to employees on a regular basis can the coding manager determine their needs and professional goals.

Continuing Education

Credentialed coders require continuing education to maintain their credentials. Regardless of the specific credential, maintenance of coding skills should be a job requirement. Thus, the job description should reflect the mandatory nature of continuing education and describe the measures required to satisfy it.

Beyond the maintenance of credentials, some coders regard continuing education opportunities as a route toward career advancement. It is the HIM department's responsibility to provide support to such coders. Coding managers should have input into the process of continuing education to ensure that coders are both maintaining and developing their professional skills.

Conclusion

To ensure effective recruitment of coding staff, managers must know the needs of the facility and understand the needs of coders. Performing a needs assessment through job analysis, productivity review, analysis of staff complement, and salary survey helps the manager improve his or her recruiting efforts.

Effective advertising focuses on the appropriate medium and ensures that the recruitment language is correct and clear. Interviewing should be consistent among applicants, with attention paid to resume specifics and courtesy to the applicants. If testing is to take place, it must reflect the actual work that the applicant would be expected to do.

Table 4.6.   Coding positions with increasing levels of responsibility

Level	Title	Responsibilities
1	Coder trainee	Abstracting, data entry, filing loose sheets, coding of a limited case mix with 100% review.
2	Outpatient coder	Abstracting, data entry, filing loose sheets, coding of emergency and clinic records; 100% review until accuracy productivity benchmarks are met
3	Inpatient coder	Abstracting, data entry, filing loose sheets, coding of inpatient and ambulatory surgery records; 100% review until accuracy productivity benchmarks are met
4	Coding specialist	Abstracting, data entry, filing loose sheets, coding of a wide variety of records; performs coding accuracy reviews under the direction of the coding supervisor and researches coding questions
5	Lead coder	Abstracting, data entry, filing loose sheets, coding of a wide variety of records; performs coding accuracy reviews under the direction of the coding supervisor, researches coding questions, compiles and prepares productivity reports, compiles and prepares ad hoc reports based on diagnosis, DRG, physician, and/or service

Orientation to the facility, the department, and the specific job responsibilities should be standardized and documented. Training must continue through the probationary period with clearly defined productivity expectations. Employee retention may be improved with the effective use of productivity bonuses.

Alternatives to full-time staff include part-time staff and job sharing. Telecommuting and outsourcing are alternatives when the existing applicant pool is not adequate. The effective coding manager will carefully address productivity, work flow, and cost issues when recruiting staff for traditional and alternative coding positions.

References and Bibliography

Bienborn, J. 1999. Automated coding: The next step? *Journal of the American Health Information Management Association* 70(7): 38–42.

Dunn, R. 2001. Developing facility-specific productivity measures. *Journal of the American Health Information Management Association* 72(4): 73–74.

Dunn, R., and C. Mainord. 2001. The latest look at coding trends. *Journal of the American Health Information Management Association* 72(7): 94–96.

Occupational Safety and Health Administration. 1998. *Act of 1970 (29CFR1607.5)* (amended). Washington, D.C.: U.S. Department of Labor.

Picard, A. 1999. Job hunting in the electronic age. *Journal of the American Health Information Management Association* 70(7): 78–80.

_____. 1999. Using electronic resources to recruit and hire employees. *Journal of the American Health Information Management Association* 70(8): 80–83.

Chapter 5

The Charge Description Master

Vickie L. Rogers, MS, RHIA

The **charge description master (CDM)** is known by various names, including:

- Chargemaster

- Charge compendium

- Service master

- Price compendium

- Service item master

- Charge list

Basically, the CDM is a translation table that puts the appropriate codes on the UB-92 (HCFA-1450) billing form and that categorizes services and supplies for accounting purposes. The following statement explains the importance of the CDM for reimbursement:

> The various supplies and services listed on the chargemaster for the average facility drives reimbursement for approximately 73 percent of the UB-92 claims for outpatient services alone. . . . A current and accurate chargemaster is vital to any healthcare provider seeking proper reimbursement. Without it, the facility would not receive proper reimbursement. Among the negative impacts that may result from an inaccurate chargemaster are:
>
> - Overpayment
>
> - Underpayment
>
> - Undercharging for services
>
> - Claims rejections
>
> - Fines
>
> - Penalties

Because a chargemaster is an automated process that results in billing numerous services for a high volume of patients—often without human intervention—there is a high risk that a single coding or mapping error could spawn error after error before it is identified and corrected (AHIMA 1999).

What Is the Charge Description Master?

The charge description master (CDM) is a list of supplies and services with corresponding charges for each of those items. Usually, items are grouped together by the departments and nursing units of the healthcare facility. The patient accounting department and each of the other departments generally maintain those items that apply to charges generated by their departments. In some institutions, the HIM department assists with assigning the correct CPT/HCPCS codes to items on the CDM.

Purposes of the CDM

The principal purpose of the CDM is to allow the healthcare facility to efficiently charge routine services and supplies to the patient's bill. In addition, the CDM provides:

- Departmental workload statistics
- CPT/HCPCS codes for repetitive high-volume services and supplies
- Methods to group services

Department Workload Statistics

Department managers frequently use the CDM as a tool to accumulate workload statistics and to track resources. Workload statistics can assist managers with the tasks of monitoring productivity and forecasting budgets. The statistics can provide data regarding resources used, such as equipment, personnel, services, supplies, and so on.

Hard Coding of CPT/HCPCS Codes

The CDM relieves the HIM department of repetitive coding that does not require documentation analysis. For frequently performed procedures, CPT/HCPCS codes may be hard coded into the CDM to be included automatically on the UB-92. **Hard coding** is the process of attaching a HCPCS code to a procedure so that the code will automatically be included on the patient's bill. For example, a complete blood count is one of the tests most frequently performed by healthcare laboratories. Hard coding assures that the code will be reproduced accurately each time that test is ordered. Other areas of the healthcare facility that have tests or services hard coded into the CDM include:

- Radiology
- EKG and other cardiology services
- EEG
- Respiratory therapy and pulmonary function
- Rehabilitation services (including physical therapy, occupational therapy, audiology, and speech therapy)
- Emergency department

Radiology services, cardiac catheterizations, and endoscopic procedures may either be hard coded into the CDM or manually coded by the HIM department staff. This is a joint decision that must be made between the HIM department and the patient accounting department based on the quality, workload, and productivity of the facility's outpatient coders. In some instances, it may be appropriate to have technicians in various areas assist with coding at the point of service. For example, radiology special procedure technicians have in-depth knowledge regarding interventional radiology procedures and the accompanying injection procedures.

Grouping Items on the CDM

The CDM can also provide a method for grouping items that are frequently reported together. Items that must be reported separately but that are used together, such as interventional radiology imaging and injection procedures, are called **exploding charges.** When grouped together, those items will be included automatically on the bill. This happens because the CDM uses a **pointer**—an item that has no dollar value and no code attached and that is mapped to two or more items with separate charges. When this pointer is charged, the grouped charges are added to the bill.

Each software program uses different terminology. Other names for pointers and exploding charges are:

- **Drivers and passengers**—The driver is the item that will explode into other items.

- **Parents and children**—The parent is the item that explodes into other items.

In the following example, codes 76932 and 93505 are automatically added to the bill when the charge for an ultrasonic endomyocardial biopsy is entered into the CDM:

Pointer	**Ultrasonic endomyocardial biopsy**
Driver	
Parent	
Exploding charge 1	76932 Ultrasonic guidance for endomyocardial biopsy
Passenger	
Child	
Exploding charge 2	93505 Endomyocardial biopsy
Passenger	
Child	

Elements of the CDM

Each item (service or supply) on the CDM has the following seven elements, as shown in figure 5.1:

- Charge code

- Item description

- General ledger (G/L) key

- Revenue code

- Insurance code mapping

- Charge

- Activity date/status

Figure 5.1.   Sample CDM

Charge Code	Item Description	CPT/HCPCS Code INS CODE A	INS CODE B	INS CODE C	Revenue Code	G/L Key	Activity Date
2110410000	ECHO ENCEPHALOGRAM	76506	76506	Y7030	320	15	12/2/1999
2110410090	F/U ECHO ENCEPHALOGRAM	76506	76506	Y7040	320	15	12/2/1999
2110413000	PORT US ECHO ENCEPHALOGRAM	76506	76506	Y7050	320	15	12/2/1999
2120411000	ULTRASOUND SPINAL CONTENTS	76800	76800	Y7060	320	15	12/2/1999
2130401000	THYROID SONOGRAM	76536	76536	Y7070	320	15	1/1/2001
2151111000	TM JOINTS BILATERAL	70330	70330	Y7080	320	15	8/12/2000
2161111000	NECK LAT ONLY	70360	70360	Y7090	320	15	10/1/1999
2162111000	LARYNX AP & LATERAL	70360	70360	Y7100	320	15	10/1/1999
2201111000	LONG BONE CHLD AP	76061	76061	Y7110	320	15	8/12/2000
2201401000	NON-VASCULAR EXTREM SONO	76880	76880	Y7120	320	15	10/1/1999
2210111000	SKULL 1 VIEW	70250	70250	Y7130	320	15	1/1/2001
2210112000	SKULL 2 VIEWS	70250	70250	Y7140	320	15	8/12/2000
2210114000	SKULL 4 VIEWS	70260	70260	Y7150	320	15	8/12/2000
2211111000	MASTOIDS	70130	70130	Y7160	320	15	1/1/2001
2212111000	MANDIBLE	70110	70110	Y7170	320	15	12/2/1999
2213111000	FACIAL BONES	70140	70140	Y7180	320	15	12/2/1999
2213114000	FACIAL BONES MIN 4	70150	70150	Y7190	320	15	12/2/1999
2214111000	NASAL BONES	70160	70160	Y7200	320	15	1/1/2001
2215111000	ORBITS	70200	70200	Y7210	320	15	1/1/2001
2217711000	PARANASAL SINUSES	70220	70220	Y7220	320	15	1/1/2001

Charge Code

The **charge code** is the numerical identification of the service or supply. Each item has a unique number with a prefix that indicates the department or revenue center in which the service or supply is provided. The charge code links the item to a particular department for revenue tracking, budget analysis, and cost-accounting reasons. Charge codes are issued in numerical order per department or nursing unit. As activity is posted to the item, the service department and the finance department accumulate data on services and supplies on a monthly, quarterly, and annual basis. As a general rule, if an item has had no activity within the recent fiscal year, it should be considered for deletion or inactivation.

The Item Description

The **item description** is the actual name of the service or supply. Because space is limited on the CDM, only a certain number of characters can be used to describe each item. The department or nursing unit chooses the item description. When describing a service or supply, the department or nursing unit should remember that this description appears on the patient's detailed bill. Within the constraints of space, the item description should be as clear as possible. In that way, the patient will understand what the charge represents. When linked to a CPT code, the item description should match the CPT code descriptor as closely as possible.

The General Ledger Key

The **general ledger (G/L) key** is the two- or three-digit number that assigns each item to a particular section of the general ledger in the healthcare facility's accounting section. Each time the item is chosen, it is tracked into the accounting system. Financial reporting on departmental activities is then possible at the end of each month, quarter, or year.

The Revenue Code

The **revenue code** is the three-digit number used for Medicare billing. It totals all items and their charges for printing on the UB-92. A complete list of revenue codes appears in appendix 5.1 at the end of this chapter. Medicare regulations require that items billed to the federal program be identified with a revenue code and, in some instances, with a specific CPT/HCPCS code. (See appendix 5.2 for revenue codes identified with specific CPT/HCPCS codes.)

The revenue code also tracks Medicare costs by revenue centers for the Medicare cost report. In most healthcare facilities, the entire billing process is electronic and an actual hard copy of the bill is not issued. The electronic version of the UB-92 should contain the same information that a hard copy of the UB-92 would contain. Figure 1.1 shows an example of an electronic UB-92 form.

Insurance Code Mapping

Insurance code mapping allows a healthcare facility to hold more than one CPT/HCPCS code per CDM item. As many as five columns may be available for mapping specific codes to one item. Typically, CPT codes are listed in the first column because most payers accept one CPT/HCPCS code. However, some state Medicaid programs—such as those in Michigan, New York, Ohio, Pennsylvania, and California—use different HCPCS codes than Medicare does. In those states, healthcare facilities might have one column for Medicare, a second column for Medicaid, and a third column for certain Blue Cross/Blue Shield programs, if the state requires multiple codes for the same item on the CDM.

Code selection is based on the patient's financial class, which is verified when a patient presents for admission or for an encounter for outpatient services. The Health Insurance Portability and Accountability Act (HIPAA) requirements are expected to standardize coded transactions so that coding by financial class of the patient will no longer be required.

Charges

Charges represent the dollar amounts owed by patients to the healthcare facility for specific services or supplies. The charges are set by the facility based on fee schedules, on contractual arrangements with healthcare plans, or on the organization's cost-accounting system. Each budget year, charges are adjusted based on available information. Each facility determines the method of increasing its charges—a flat dollar amount increase, a percentage across-the-board increase, or an increase based on contracts.

Typically, each item has only one charge. However, the charge is adjusted based on contractual arrangements with certain payers or groups of payers.

Activity Date/Status

The **activity date/status** element indicates the most recent activity of an item. This may be coded or given a date of activity. Different accounting systems use the activity date to denote a variety of activities. It can indicate whether an item is active or not. Many accounting systems never delete items; they just inactivate them.

The activity date can also indicate whether an item has had any charges made or whether there has been any activity in the current fiscal year. For budgetary reasons, if an item has had activity during the current fiscal year, it is better to "turn it off" rather than to delete the item. The activity then can be reactivated and used in the budget and workload indicator process.

Type of Coding Required for the CDM

For Medicare reporting, Levels I, II, and III of HCPCS codes are used on the CDM. (See chapter 1 for discussion of the three levels of CPT codes.) The CDM should have the capability of holding more than one CPT/HCPCS code per item. It is possible that the same item may appear in more than one department on the CDM. For example, the code for venipuncture may appear in the laboratory, clinic, and emergency department sections of the CDM.

Transferring Items on the CDM to Charges on a UB-92

The completion of a UB-92 claim form begins with the registration process for an inpatient admission or for an outpatient encounter. At the time of registration, the patient provides basic demographic information as well as insurance information. At or before the time of admission, the insurance information is verified and an insurance code is assigned. This code indicates how the items charged to the patient during the stay will be categorized.

Posting Charges to the Patient's Account

As services and supplies are used for the patient, charges are posted to the patient's account by CDM item number, using a variety of methods. In an electronic system, when the item number is entered into the order-entry software, several actions take place. The department involved with the service or supply receives notification that an order has been placed. At the same time, the accounting system is notified that a particular order has been placed. With order-entry software, electronic charges are posted to the account as soon as the item is ordered. Tests are added to the account at the time service is provided or at the time of order. Charges may be grouped together (batched) and transferred from the order-entry system to the accounting system at a designated time, such as midnight, to capture the correct date the service or supply was ordered or provided.

If the facility does not have order-entry software, the charges may be posted by hand each night at midnight. Departments complete manual "charge tickets" for each patient seen during the course of the day. At the end of the business day, the charge tickets are forwarded for data entry into the accounting system.

For outpatient services and supplies, charges are posted at the time of the order. The coding manager must make sure that posted items were actually provided and that items actually provided are posted to the correct account.

Preparing the Preliminary Bill

When a patient is discharged, the accounting system is notified of the patient's discharge status and the preliminary bill is prepared. The actual process of submitting a claim to the payer may be delayed for the bill hold period of three-to-five days for inpatients; seven-to-ten days for outpatients. The **bill hold period** is the time that a bill is suspended in the billing system awaiting late charges, diagnosis/procedure codes, insurance verification, and so on.

Under the ambulatory payment classification (APC) system, Medicare does not accept separate bills for late charges. As a result, many healthcare facilities experience a rise in outpatient accounts receivable balances because late charges must be processed with the rest of the patient's bill or an adjusted claim must be filed. Those actions delay payment and create extra work.

Inpatients' Bills

No CPT/HCPCS codes are required by Medicare on bills for inpatients. Charges are accumulated and posted on the UB-92 by revenue codes only. For inpatients, separate charges for certain departments do not have to be reported on a line-item basis. The charges are accumulated according to the nursing units and other services provided to the patient, as shown in figure 5.2.

Outpatients' Bills

The UB-92 requires that CPT/HCPCS codes be printed in field locator 44 on bills for outpatients. In addition, ancillary departments must identify charges separately with the appropriate CPT/HCPCS codes. Many of those codes, with the exception of surgical CPT codes, come from the CDM. Those codes are assigned by the HIM department and entered into the billing software. The codes then appear on the UB-92, as shown in figure 5.3.

Coding and the CDM

The process for attaching specific codes to items on the CDM can be accomplished in the following ways:

Figure 5.2.   Partial UB-92 form for an inpatient

	42 REV. CD.	43 DESCRIPTION	44 HCPCS / RATES	45 SERV. DATE	46 SERV. UNITS	47 TOTAL CHARGES	48 NON-COVERED CHARGES	49	
1	121	MED-SUR-	914.10	021599	8	7312 80			1
2	250	PHARMACY		021599		942 95			2
3	260	IV THERAPY		022399		47 38			3
4	279	SUPPLY/OTHER		021899		31 82			4
5	301	LAB/CHEMISTRY		021699		417 65			5
6	305	LAB/HEMATOLOGY		021699		60 05			6
7	309	LAB/OTHER		022399		50 99			7
8	340	NUCLEAR MEDICINE		021699		1350 80			8
9	410	RESPIRATORY SVC		022299		25 64			9
10	421	PHYS THERP/VISIT		021899		348 60			10
11	481	CARDIAC CATH LAB		021799		182 05			11
12	636	DRUG/DETAIL CODE		021699		240 00			12
13	730	EKG/ECG		021999		39 32			13
14	803	DIALY/INPT/CAPD		021899	6	578 40			14
15	921	PERI VASCUL LAB		022299		598 70			15
16	001	TOTAL CHARGES			14	12227 15			16
17									17
18									18
19									19
20									20
21									21
22									22
23									23

Figure 5.3.   Partial UB-92 form for an outpatient

	42 REV. CD.	43 DESCRIPTION	44 HCPCS / RATES	45 SERV. DATE	46 SERV. UNITS	47 TOTAL CHARGES	48 NON-COVERED CHARGES	49	
1	250	PHARMACY		110700	2	5 28			1
2	320	DX XRAY	76506	110700	2	264 50			2
3	740	EEG	95819	110700	1	355 00			3
4	761	TREATMENT ROOM	99142	110700	1	126 00			4
5									5
6									6
7									7
8									8
9									9
10									10
11									11
12									12
13									13
14									14
15									15
16	001	TOTAL CHARGES			6	750 78			16
17									17
18									18
19									19
20									20
21									21
22									22
23									23

- Department managers may identify codes and attach them to the services or supplies.

- A designated individual, committee, or workgroup within the department also may identify and attach the codes.

- A particular facility employee may be responsible for coding and maintaining the CDM that attaches the code. (See chapter 2 for a detailed description of the chargemaster coordinator's role.)

- A consulting firm may be used to review and update the codes for each item in the CDM when the required skills are not available within the staff.

Revenue Codes and the APC System

Recent requirements for the APC system indicate that the service or supply should be assigned the revenue code for the department in which the service or supply is provided. However, in some instances, specific revenue codes are assigned to specific CPT/HCPCS codes. Appendix 5.2 lists specific revenue code and CPT/HCPCS requirements.

Under the APC system, certain revenue codes have been packaged into the procedure code. That is, when charges for items using the packaged revenue codes appear on a Medicare bill, they will not be paid separately. For example, the following revenue codes are packaged into an APC procedure (*Federal Register* 2000):

250	Pharmacy
258	IV Solutions
370	Anesthesia
710	Recovery Room
762	Observation Room

The complete list of packaged revenue codes is given on page 18484 of the April 7, 2000, *Federal Register*. They may also be obtained through the healthcare facility's fiscal intermediary (FI).

Assigning the Most Specific Revenue Code

Medicare requires providers to assign the most specific revenue code for their services. For example, providers have the following CT scan revenue codes to choose from:

CT Scan—General	350
CT Scan—Head Scan	351
CT Scan—Body Scan	352
CT Scan—Other CT Scans	359

For CPT code 70450, Computerized axial tomography, head or brain; without contrast material, the appropriate revenue code is 351, CT Scan—Head Scan. That code is the specific revenue code required by Medicare, as opposed to 350, CT Scan—General, the generic revenue code. Revenue code 359, CT Scan—Other CT Scans, is not used by Medicare but is reserved for state use in local billing requirements.

Use of revenue codes ending in "0" (General) and "9" (Other) may cause delays in payment from Medicare. In the event that a specific revenue code is not available, Medicare will accept the general revenue code. For example, Pulmonary Function has only two revenue codes, 460 and 469. In that instance, 460 would be the only acceptable code to use on a UB-92 for Medicare claims filed for Medicare beneficiaries.

Editing Programs for Revenue Codes

A healthcare facility's computer system should have an editing program that reviews revenue codes and any CPT/HCPCS code assignments prior to issuing the UB-92 to Medicare. The latest version of the Medicare outpatient code editor (OCE) should be installed to review claims prior to releasing information to the Medicare program. OCE software contains the National Correct Coding Initiative (NCCI) edits for CPT. The NCCI edits evaluate the relationships between CPT codes on the bill. They also identify component codes that were used instead of the appropriate comprehensive code, as well as other types of coding errors.

Keeping Current with Federal Requirements

With increased federal requirements for information on hospital outpatient services, the CDM has become a major communication tool not only with federal programs but also with commercial insurance payers. Keeping this communication tool current is a challenging task.

To keep current with federal programs, Web sites and intermediary bulletins serve as the best resources. The Annotated List of Additional References at the end of this chapter includes federal government Web sites with information about changes in HCPCS Level II codes, revenue code requirements, and so on. Coding managers should consult those Web sites on a regular basis.

CDM Data Quality and Reimbursement

The CDM provides a database for chargeable services within healthcare facilities. As departmental activity is accumulated, a database of information becomes available. When department managers begin to accumulate information about current charges, management reports from the CDM system will be useful. Some reports that may be available include:

- Charge activity report—Summarizes volume activity for each item in the department CDM

- CDM budget report—Identifies summary charge and reimbursement by CDM item

- Inactive charges report—Lists items currently considered inactive

- CDM zero activity report—Identifies items with no activity for the current fiscal year and provides the department manager with information for inactivating/deleting items

For compliance purposes, it is important to track all changes made to the CDM over time. It is recommended that a copy of the CDM be printed or that a file be maintained electronically with all major changes listed in chronological order. If there is a need to establish which charges were in effect during a specific time period, the documentation is then available for reference.

Systems of Reimbursement

The systems of reimbursement for inpatients and outpatients differ between Medicare and Medicaid. Other insurance plans reimburse for inpatients based on the terms of contracts signed with a healthcare facility. They reimburse for outpatients on the basis of fee schedules or percentage of charges.

Medicare and Medicaid Inpatient Bills

On Medicare inpatient bills, most items included in the CDM are reimbursed through the diagnostic-related group (DRG) system.

Medicaid reimbursement varies from state to state. In some states, Medicaid payments are made through a DRG system. In other states, Medicaid pays on a per diem rate based on the patient's length of stay.

Medicare and Medicaid Outpatient Bills

Reimbursement for Medicare outpatients depends on the type of item on the CDM: service, procedure, or supply. If the item is a supply, it will be either packaged as part of the APC reimbursement or identified on the pass-through list with a separate reimbursement based on the pass-through codes or categories. (See chapter 1 for a discussion of pass-through lists and codes.) If the item is a service or procedure in one of the following areas, it will be paid based on a fee schedule:

- Laboratory
- Occupational therapy
- Physical therapy
- Speech therapy

The remaining diagnostic and therapeutic procedures identified on the CDM are paid under the APC system.

Medicaid pays for outpatient diagnostic testing on a fee-schedule basis. It pays for outpatient surgical procedures on the basis of an APC type of system or by CPT code on a fee-schedule basis.

The Reimbursement Process

The reimbursement process begins upon the payer's receipt of an electronic or paper UB-92 claims form. If all of the information on the UB-92 is correct, payment is issued for the services covered under the patient's policy or program.

Frequently, the payment (check) is returned to the provider in a batch format with an explanation of payment called a remittance advice. The check to the provider represents the total payment for all the patients processed on a given remittance advice.

The level of detail on the remittance advice varies from payer to payer. Some payers provide CPT/HCPCS code-level detail and identify each payment for each item. Other payers just list the patients' names with payment amounts. In either case, the patient accounting department enters the payment information into the accounting system and adjusts the balance for each patient's visit or encounter. If a balance remains, it is written off completely resulting in a zero balance, or the patient is billed for the remaining amount due. (See chapter 10 for a discussion of write-offs.)

Detailed Medicare reimbursement information can be found on the Medicare Reimbursement Reference Grid Web site. (See the Annotated List of Additional References at the end of this chapter.)

CDM Maintenance

Although the principal owner of the CDM is the finance department in most instances, maintaining the CDM is a joint responsibility. Ideally, updating and maintaining the CDM is the work of a team, or committee, that includes members from the finance, patient accounting, information systems, and HIM departments. Managers of clinical departments, such as laboratory or radiology, should serve on the CDM maintenance committee on a rotating basis. The interdepartmental approach exposes the clinical departments to the issues faced by the nonclinical departments. This approach also promotes a greater understanding throughout the facility about the reporting and reimbursement process.

Adding a New Item to the CDM

The process for adding a new item to the CDM is as follows:

1. A request to add a new item (service, procedure, or supply) to the CDM originates in the department requesting the change. The department should use a form similar to the one in figure 5.4 to request a new item.

2. The request should then be circulated to the CDM maintenance committee for review. Committee members from the finance department or the patient accounting department review the request to evaluate any potential financial impact and to assign the new item's revenue code, insurance code, and charge number. A committee member from the information system department might also be responsible for those tasks.

3. A qualified coder should review the suggested CPT/HCPCS code to ensure the accuracy of the new item's description.

4. The committee should exercise caution if the new item represents new technology or new services. Items covered by Medicare must have FDA approval for use with Medicare patients.

5. When the item is a supply, it may qualify for pass-through payment on APC claims.

6. When the supply is accompanied by a manufacturer-recommended CPT/HCPCS code, the code should be reviewed for appropriateness.

7. Once the item has received all the appropriate approvals, the requesting department is notified of the new item information—charge number, item description, charge, CPT/HCPCS codes, revenue code, and insurance code. The item is then made available for use by the department. (See figure 5.5 for an example of the process for requesting a new item on the CDM.)

Figure 5.4.   New charge request form

New Charge Form	
Routing Dates	
TBS Date	07/26/2000
TDS Date	07/28/2000
CDM Date	07/31/2000
S/M Date	08/01/2000

CDM Data	
Charge Number	401-9917-9
Description (30 char. max)	GUIDE WIRE 292.40
CPT/HCPCS Codes	A B C D M N O S W Z
Item Type	N
Charge Price	$76.50
Ins. Code	27
UB-92 Rev. Code	A 272 B 272 C 272 D 272 M 272 N O S W 272 Z

Comments	

Requestor Info	
Contact Person (Requestor)	Janice X. Jones
Phone Number	14714

Figure 5.5.   New charge request process

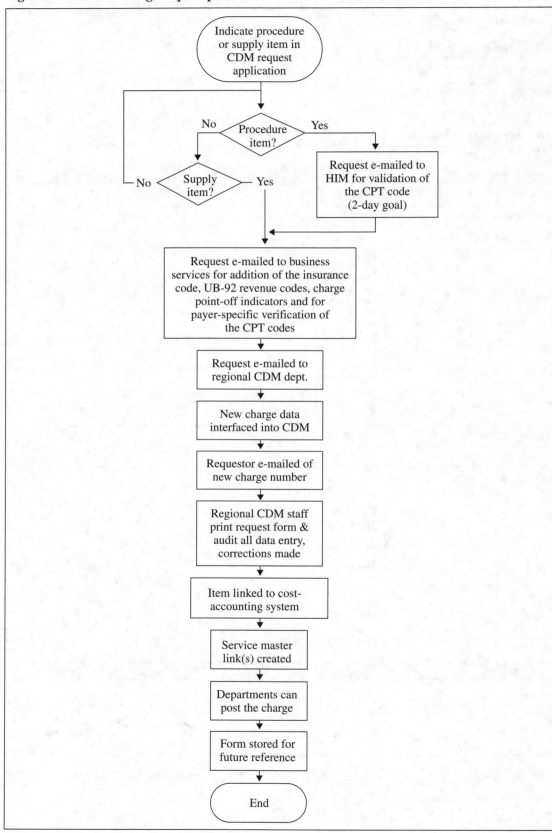

Changing an Existing Item on the CDM

Requests for changes to existing items on the CDM should follow a process similar to that of adding a new item to the CDM. If the change is a different CPT/HCPCS code, the HIM department member of the CDM maintenance committee should verify the correctness of the change.

Conclusion

Effective CDM management requires a team effort among many departments of the healthcare facility. The various medical departments, the nursing units, and the financial department all depend on the coding expertise of HIM professionals to avoid incorrect coding and potential compliance issues. Only through the use of a variety of experts can healthcare organizations master the complexities and reap the benefits of chargemaster technology.

References and Bibliography

AHIMA. 1999. Practice Brief: The care and maintenance of charge masters. *Journal of the American Health Information Management Association* 70(7) (Aug.).

Federal Register. 2000. Final rule for the outpatient prospective payment system. 65(68): 18484.

Annotated List of Additional References

To locate your local intermediary, go to www.hcfa.gov and follow the instructions for Medicare intermediaries. Most fiscal intermediaries have bulletins available at their web site that can be downloaded. Some state Medicaid programs have web sites that will provide access to state manuals, as well as Medicaid bulletins that have coding guidance for the Medicaid program in that state.

Web site address for program transmittals: <http://www.hcfa.gov/pubforms/transmit/memos>.

Web site address for frequently asked questions regarding OPPS: <http://www.hcfa.gov/medlearn/faqclaim.htm>.

Web site address for OPPS quick reference guide: <http://www.hcfa.gov/Medlearn/opps73.doc>.

Medicare reimbursement reference grid: <http://www.ahima.org/infocenter/rgrid_nav.html>.

Appendix 5.1

List of Medicare Revenue Codes (Medicare Hospital Manual [Pub 10, Section 443])

Field Locator (FL) 42 Revenue Codes for Outpatient Ancillary Services

Pharmacy   25X

Pharmacy—General	250
Pharmacy—Generic Drugs	251
Pharmacy—Nongeneric Drugs	252
Pharmacy—Take-Home Drugs	253
Pharmacy—Drugs Incident to Other Diagnostic Services	254
Pharmacy—Drugs Incident to Radiology	255
Pharmacy—Experimental Drugs	256
Pharmacy—Nonprescription	257
Pharmacy—IV Solutions	258
Pharmacy—Other Pharmacy	259

IV Therapy   26X

IV Therapy—General	260
IV Therapy—Infusion Pump	261
IV Therapy—IV Therapy/Pharmacy Services	262
IV Therapy—IV Therapy/Drug/Supply Delivery	263
IV Therapy—IV Therapy/Supplies	264
IV Therapy—Other IV Therapy	269

Medical/Surgical Supplies and Devices   27X

Medical/Surgical Supplies and Devices—General	270
Medical/Surgical Supplies and Devices—Nonsterile Supply	271
Medical/Surgical Supplies and Devices—Sterile Supply	272
Medical/Surgical Supplies and Devices—Take-Home Supplies	273
Medical/Surgical Supplies and Devices—Prosthetic/Orthotic Devices	274
Medical/Surgical Supplies and Devices—Pacemaker	275
Medical/Surgical Supplies and Devices—Intraocular Lens	276
Medical/Surgical Supplies and Devices—Oxygen Take-Home	277
Medical/Surgical Supplies and Devices—Other Implants	278
Medical/Surgical Supplies and Devices—Other Supplies/Devices	279

Oncology   28X

Oncology—General	280
Oncology—Other	289

Durable Medical Equipment (Other than Renal)   29X

DME (Other than Renal)—General	290
DME (Other than Renal)—Rental	291
DME (Other than Renal)—Purchase of New DME	292
DME (Other than Renal)—Purchase of Used DME	293
DME (Other than Renal)—Supplies/Drugs for DME Effectiveness (HHAs Only)	294
DME (Other than Renal)—Other Equipment	299

Laboratory   30X

Laboratory—General	300
Laboratory—Chemistry	301
Laboratory—Immunology	302
Laboratory—Renal Patient (Home)	303
Laboratory—Nonroutine Dialysis	304
Laboratory—Hematology	305
Laboratory—Bacteriology and Microbiology	306
Laboratory—Urology	307
Laboratory—Other Laboratory	309

Laboratory Pathological   31X

Laboratory Pathological—General	310
Laboratory Pathological—Cytology	311
Laboratory Pathological—Histology	312
Laboratory Pathological—Biopsy	314
Laboratory Pathological—Other	319

Radiology—Diagnostic   32X

Radiology—Diagnostic—General	320
Radiology—Diagnostic—Angiocardiography	321
Radiology—Diagnostic—Arthrography	322
Radiology—Diagnostic—Arteriography	323
Radiology—Diagnostic—Chest X-ray	324
Radiology—Diagnostic—Other	329

Radiology—Therapeutic   33X

Radiology—Therapeutic—General	330
Radiology—Therapeutic—Chemotherapy—Injected	331
Radiology—Therapeutic—Chemotherapy—Oral	332

Other Imaging Services   40X

    Other Imaging Services—General   400
    Other Imaging Services—Diagnostic Mammography   401
    Other Imaging Services—Ultrasound   402
    Other Imaging Services—Screening Mammography   403
    Other Imaging Services—Positron Emission Tomography   404
    Other Imaging Services—Other Imaging Services   409

Respiratory Services   41X

    Respiratory Services—General   410
    Respiratory Services—Inhalation Services   412
    Respiratory Services—Hyperbaric Oxygen Therapy   413
    Respiratory Services—Other Respiratory Services   419

Physical Therapy   42X

    Physical Therapy—General   420
    Physical Therapy—Visit Charge   421
    Physical Therapy—Hourly Charge   422
    Physical Therapy—Group Rate   423
    Physical Therapy—Evaluation or Reevaluation   424
    Physical Therapy—Other Physical Therapy   429

Occupational Therapy   43X

    Occupational Therapy—General   430
    Occupational Therapy—Visit Charge   431
    Occupational Therapy—Hourly Charge   432
    Occupational Therapy—Group Rate   433
    Occupational Therapy—Evaluation or Reevaluation   434
    Occupational Therapy—Other Occupational Therapy   439

Speech-Language Pathology   44X

    Speech-Language Pathology—General   440
    Speech-Language Pathology—Visit Charge   441
    Speech-Language Pathology—Hourly Charge   442
    Speech-Language Pathology—Group Rate   443
    Speech-Language Pathology—Evaluation or Reevaluation   444
    Speech-Language Pathology—Other Speech-Language Pathology   449

Emergency Room   45X

    Emergency Room—General   450
    Emergency Room—EMTALA Emergency Medical Screening Services   451
    Emergency Room—ER Beyond EMTALA Screening   452
    Emergency Room—Urgent Care   456
    Emergency Room—Other Emergency Room   459

Pulmonary Function   46X

    Pulmonary Function—General   460
    Pulmonary Function—Other Pulmonary Function   469

Audiology   47X

Cardiology   48X

Ambulatory Surgical Care   49X

Outpatient Services   50X

Clinic   51X

Freestanding Clinic   52X

Osteopathic Services   53X

Ambulance   54X

EKG/ECG (Electrocardiogram)   73X

EEG (Electroencephalogram)   74X

Gastrointestinal Services   75X

Treatment or Observation Room   76X

Preventive Care Services   77X

Lithotripsy   79X

Organ Acquisition   81X

Hemodialysis—Outpatient or Home   82X

Peritoneal Dialysis—Outpatient or Home   83X

    Peritoneal Dialysis—Outpatient or Home—General   830
    Peritoneal Dialysis—Outpatient or Home—
        Peritoneal/Composite or Other Rate   831
    Peritoneal Dialysis—Outpatient or Home—Home Supplies   831
    Peritoneal Dialysis—Outpatient or Home—Home Equipment   833
    Peritoneal Dialysis—Outpatient or Home—Maintenance/100%   834
    Peritoneal Dialysis—Outpatient or Home—Support Services   835
    Peritoneal Dialysis—Outpatient or Home—Other Outpatient Peritoneal
        Dialysis   839

CAPD (Dialysis)—Outpatient or Home   84X

    CAPD (Dialysis)—Outpatient or Home—General   840
    CAPD (Dialysis)—Outpatient or Home—CAPD/Composite or Other Rate   841
    CAPD (Dialysis)—Outpatient or Home—Home Supplies   842
    CAPD (Dialysis)—Outpatient or Home—Home Equipment   843
    CAPD (Dialysis)—Outpatient or Home—Maintenance/100%   844
    CAPD (Dialysis)—Outpatient or Home—Support Services   845
    CAPD (Dialysis)—Outpatient or Home—Other Outpatient CAPD   849

CCPD (Dialysis)—Outpatient or Home   5X

    CCPD (Dialysis)—Outpatient or Home—General   850
    CCPD (Dialysis)—Outpatient or Home—CCPD/Composite or Other Rate   851
    CCPD (Dialysis)—Outpatient or Home—Home Supplies   852
    CCPD (Dialysis)—Outpatient or Home—Home Equipment   853
    CCPD (Dialysis)—Outpatient or Home—Maintenance/100%   854
    CCPD (Dialysis)—Outpatient or Home—Support Services   855
    CCPD (Dialysis)—Outpatient or Home—Other Outpatient CCPD   859

Reserved for Dialysis (National Assignment)   86X

Reserved for Dialysis (National Assignment)   87X

Miscellaneous Dialysis   88X

    Miscellaneous Dialysis—General   880
    Miscellaneous Dialysis—Ultrafiltration   881
    Miscellaneous Dialysis—Home Dialysis Aid Visit   882
    Miscellaneous Dialysis—Other Miscellaneous Dialysis   889

Reserved for National Assignment   89X

Psychiatric/Psychological Treatments   90X

    Psychiatric/Psychological Treatments—General   900
    Psychiatric/Psychological Treatments—Electroshock Treatment   901
    Psychiatric/Psychological Treatments—Milieu Therapy   902
    Psychiatric/Psychological Treatments—Play Therapy   903
    Psychiatric/Psychological Treatments—Activity Therapy   904
    Psychiatric/Psychological Treatments—Other   909

Psychiatric/Psychological Services   91X

Psychiatric/Psychological Services—General	910
Psychiatric/Psychological Services—Rehabilitation	911
Psychiatric/Psychological Services—Partial Hospitalization—Less Intensive	912
Psychiatric/Psychological Services—Partial Hospitalization—Intensive	913
Psychiatric/Psychological Services—Individual Therapy	914
Psychiatric/Psychological Services—Group Therapy	915
Psychiatric/Psychological Services—Family Therapy	916
Psychiatric/Psychological Services—Biofeedback	917
Psychiatric/Psychological Services—Testing	918
Psychiatric/Psychological Services—Other	919

Other Diagnostic Services   92X

Other Diagnostic Services—General	920
Other Diagnostic Services—Peripheral Vascular Lab	921
Other Diagnostic Services—Electromyelogram	922
Other Diagnostic Services—Pap Smear	923
Other Diagnostic Services—Allergy Test	924
Other Diagnostic Services—Pregnancy Test	925
Other Diagnostic Services—Other Diagnostic Service	929

Not Assigned   93X

Other Therapeutic Services   94X

Other Therapeutic Services—General	940
Other Therapeutic Services—Recreational Therapy	941
Other Therapeutic Services—Education/Training	942
Other Therapeutic Services—Cardiac Rehabilitation	943
Other Therapeutic Services—Drug Rehabilitation	944
Other Therapeutic Services—Alcohol Rehabilitation	945
Other Therapeutic Services—Complex Medical Equipment—Routine	946
Other Therapeutic Services—Complex Medical Equipment—Ancillary	947
Other Therapeutic Services—Other Therapeutic Services	949

Other Therapeutic Services (extension of 94X)   95X

Professional Fees   96X

Professional Fees—General	960
Professional Fees—Psychiatric	961
Professional Fees—Ophthalmology	962
Professional Fees—Anesthesiologist (MD)	963
Professional Fees—Anesthetist (CRNA)	964
Professional Fees—Other Professional Fees	969

Professional Fees (extension of 96X)   97X

Professional Fees—Laboratory	971
Professional Fees—Radiology—Diagnostic	972

Professional Fees—Radiology—Therapeutic	973
Professional Fees—Radiology—Nuclear Medicine	974
Professional Fees—Operating Room	975
Professional Fees—Respiratory Therapy	976
Professional Fees—Physical Therapy	977
Professional Fees—Occupational Therapy	978
Professional Fees—Speech Pathology	979

Professional Fees (extension of 96X and 97X)   98X

Professional Fees—Emergency Room	981
Professional Fees—Outpatient Services	982
Professional Fees—Clinic	983
Professional Fees—Medical Social Services	984
Professional Fees—EKG	985
Professional Fees—EEG	986
Professional Fees—Hospital Visit	987
Professional Fees—Consultation	988
Professional Fees—Private-Duty Nurse	989

Patient Convenience Items   99X

Patient Convenience Items—General	990
Patient Convenience Items—Cafeteria/Guest Tray	991
Patient Convenience Items—Private Linen Service	992
Patient Convenience Items—Telephone/Telegraph	993
Patient Convenience Items—TV/Radio	994
Patient Convenience Items—Nonpatient Room Rentals	995
Patient Convenience Items—Late Discharge Charge	996
Patient Convenience Items—Admission Kits	997
Patient Convenience Items—Beauty Shop/Barber	998
Patient Convenience Items—Other Patient Convenience Items	999

Appendix 5.2

HCPCS Revenue Code Chart

The following chart reflects HCPCS coding required to be reported under OPPS by hospital outpatient departments. This chart supersedes coding instructions and edit requirements for outpatient surgery, diagnostic and medical services, and radiology services represented in §§3626.4, 3627.9 and 3631 of the Medicare Intermediary Manual. It is intended to be used as a guide by hospitals to assist them in reporting services rendered. Note that this chart does not represent all HCPCS coding subject to OPPS but will be expanded at a later date.

Revenue Code	HCPCS Code	Description
*	10040–69990	Surgical Procedure
*	92950–92961	Cardiovascular
*	96570, 96571	Photodynamic Therapy
*	99170, 99185, 99186	Other Services and Procedures
*	99291–99292	Critical Care
*	99440	Newborn Care
*	90782–90799	Therapeutic or Diagnostic Injections
*	D0150, D0240–D0274, D0277, D0460, D0472–D0999, D1510–D1550, D2970, D2999, D3460, D3999, D4260–D4264, D4270–D4273, D4355–D4381, D5911–D5912, D5983–D5985, D5987, D6920, D7110–D7260, D7291, D7940, D9630, D9930, D9940, D9950–D9952	Dental Services
*	92502–92596, 92599	Otorhinolaryngologic Services (ENT)
278	E0749, E0782, E0783, E0785	Implanted Durable Medical Equipment
278	E0751, E0753, L8600, L8603, L8610, L8612, L8614, L8619, L8630, L8641, L8642, L8658, L8670, L8699	Implanted Prosthetic Devices
302	86485–86586	Immunology
305	85060–85102, 86077–86079	Hematology
31X	80500–80502	Pathology—Lab
310	88300–88365, 88399	Surgical Pathology
311	88104–88125, 88160–88199	Cytopathology
32X	70010–76999	Diagnostic Radiology
333	77261–77799	Radiation Oncology
34X	78000–79999	Nuclear Medicine
37X	99141–99142	Anesthesia

413	99183	Other Services and Procedures
45X	99281–99285	Emergency
46X	94010–94799	Pulmonary Function
480	93600–93790, 93799, G0166	Intra Electrophysiological Procedures and Other Vascular Studies
481	93501–93571	Cardiac Catheterization
482	93015–93024	Stress Test
483	93303–93350	Echocardiography
51X	92002–92499	Ophthalmological Services
51X	99201, 99215, 99241–99245, 99271–99275	Clinic Visit
510, 517, 519	95144–95149, 95163, 95170, 95180, 95199	Allergen Immunotherapy
519	95805–95811	Sleep Testing
530	98925–98929	Osteopathic Manipulative Procedures
636	A4642, A9500, A9605	Radionclides
636	90296–90379, 90385, 90389–90396	Immune Globulins
636	90476–90665, 90675–90749	Vaccines, Toxoids
73X	G0004–G0006, G0015	Event Recording ECG
730	93005–93014, 93040–93224, 93278	Electrocardiograms (ECGs)
731	93225–93272	Holter Monitor
75X	95812–95827, 95950–95962	Electroencephalogram (EEG)
762	99217–99220	Observation
771	G0008–G0010	Vaccine Administration
88X	90935–90999	Non-ESRD Dialysis
901	90870, 90871	Psychiatry
903	90910, 90911, 90812–90815, 90823, 90824, 90826–90829	Psychiatry
909	90880	Psychiatry
910	90801, 90802, 90865, 90899	Psychiatry
914	90804–90809, 90816–90819, 90821, 90822, 90845, 90862	Psychiatry
915	90853, 90857	Psychiatry
916	90846, 90847, 90849	Psychiatry
917	90901–90911	Biofeedback
918	96100–96117	Central Nervous System Assessments/Tests
92X	95829–95857, 95900–95937, 95970–95999	Miscellaneous Neurological Procedures

920, 929	93875–93990	Non Invasive Vascular Diagnosis Studies
922	95858–95875	Electromyography (EMG)
924	95004–95078	Allergy Test
940	96900–96999	Special Dermatological Procedures
940	98940–98942	Chiropractic Manipulative Treatment
940	99195	Other Services and Procedures
943	93797–93798	Cardiac Rehabilitation

*Revenue codes have not been identified for these procedures, as they can be performed in a number of revenue centers within a hospital, such as emergency room (450), operating room (360), or clinic (510). Instruct your hospitals to report these HCPCS codes under the revenue center where they were performed.

NOTE: The listing of HCPCS codes contained in the above chart does not assure coverage of the specific service. Current coverage criteria apply.

Part II

Monitoring for Excellence of Service Delivery

Chapter 6

Performance Management and Process Improvement

Anita Orenstein, RHIT, CCS, CCS-P

Effective management of processes in the coding department includes analyzing those processes and improving them to be efficient and adaptable. To be efficient, the coding function must be completed with the lowest possible use of resources. To be adaptable, it must respond to customers' changing requirements. Coding managers should ask themselves the following questions:

- Am I utilizing the coding staff's expertise to the fullest?

- Am I meeting the needs of the facility's customers?

This chapter will help to answer those questions and will provide the tools necessary to evaluate and improve current coding processes.

Process Improvement: Thinking out of the Box

"Out-of-the-box thinking" is an expression heard frequently in business situations. Often coding managers think that their current processes are the best way or the only way to perform functions because they are the way things have "always been done." Using out-of-the-box thinking, or changing the paradigm, in relation to those processes may result in a more efficient way of doing things.

Over the years, many changes have occurred in the way HIM departments carry out processes. The following examples illustrate some of these changes:

- HIM departments have gone from handwriting **master patient index (MPI)** information on index cards to using computerized MPI systems to using the enterprisewide MPI. The MPI is the link tracking patient, person, or member activity within an organization or enterprise and across patient care settings. The MPI identifies all patients who have been treated in a facility or enterprise and lists the health record or identification number associated with the name.

- The person responsible for reporting daily, monthly, and/or quarterly statistics once maintained those statistics in manual logs and calculated them by applying various formulas. Today, most facilities maintain statistics through automated system logs from which a detailed report of the statistics, along with graphic illustrations, results.

- In the past, the coder reviewed the face sheet of a health record and assigned codes based on the final diagnoses and procedures listed there by the physician. Now, coders analyze the entire health record and assign ICD-9-CM and CPT codes based on physician documentation and application of official coding guidelines.

Change is all about process improvement: how to complete required tasks more efficiently and with the greatest accuracy possible. The three changes just mentioned, as well as many others, were made because coding professionals changed their paradigms by thinking out of the box.

Managing Change

Change can be a difficult concept for some people because they have a comfort level in their daily routines. For example, most people have a regular morning routine. It might consist of turning off the alarm, getting out of bed, showering, brushing their teeth, dressing, having breakfast, and driving to work. If that routine is suddenly interrupted because the car is no longer available, a person must make a change and take the bus to work. To save time, that person takes a mug of coffee and something to eat on the bus. At first, this change in routine does not feel comfortable. Over time, however, the change becomes a new routine. In fact, the person might even enjoy reading the newspaper or a book on the bus ride to work!

Change versus Transition

The terms *change* and *transition* are sometimes used interchangeably, although these terms have different meanings. Understanding the differences will help those involved in process improvement to move forward with a more positive attitude. Change occurs when something starts or stops, or when something that was done one way is now done in another way. Change can occur all at once or in phases. Transition is more a psychological process that extends over a period of time. The following three phases take place in any transition process:

- Phase one: Letting go
- Phase two: The "neutral zone"
- Phase three: A new beginning

Phase One: Letting Go

In phase one, staff members have to let go of the old situation and of the old identity that went with it. However, they often have difficulty letting go of responsibilities for which they once took ownership. In phase one, people have several feelings. Table 6.1 illustrates some feelings of loss, as well as possible solutions.

Sometimes people seem to be resisting change when in reality, they are struggling with phase one of transition. It can help to identify continuities that balance the losses and to reemphasize new connections to new processes. While people are in mourning over the old process, certain behaviors, such as denial, anger, bargaining, grief, and despair, should be expected. Those behaviors usually take place before final acceptance of the change.

Phase Two: The Neutral Zone

Phase two, referred to as the "neutral zone," is considered the heart of transition. This phase is a time of reorientation. Staff still experience feelings of "loss" and may be unclear about the new process. Feelings fluctuate between hopefulness and frustration. Staff may sometimes seem to be just going through the motions of the new process.

Table 6.1.   **Issues of loss and possible solutions**

Loss Issue	Possible Solutions
Loss of turf	Emphasize "interest-based" rather than "position-based" status so that staff members feel they are equal
Loss of attachments	Reattach staff through a process of team building
Loss of meaning in an issue	Convert this to an information-based issue by confronting the problem rather than by simply explaining the solution
Loss of a competence-based identity	Train staff in new competencies
Loss of control	Involve staff in creating the new process to compensate for the loss

The neutral zone can be converted to an opportunity if staff are given assistance in redefining themselves and their future direction. Coding managers should provide training to enhance staff members' current positions and to provide opportunities for career advancement.

Phase Three: A New Beginning

In phase three, staff may be involved in the following activities:

- Developing new competencies

- Establishing new relationships

- Becoming comfortable with new policies and procedures

- Constructing plans for the future

- Learning to think in new paradigms

Process Analysis: Work Imaging

Before starting a process analysis, coding managers should have a complete understanding of current coding processes. They should ask themselves the following questions:

- Can improvements be made to better utilize the existing staff?

- What noncoding functions does the coding staff complete?

- Is there a way to simplify the process and work "smarter" by eliminating and/or reassigning noncoding functions?

Once the process has been defined, coding managers can establish productivity standards. They also can make a true analysis of the coding time required of full-time equivalent employees (FTEs) through a work-imaging study. A **work-imaging study** can be described in the following way:

- It is a snapshot of the current process that identifies potential areas for change in the process.

- It quantifies opportunities to improve the healthcare organization's structure.

- It shows where to consolidate functions and responsibilities.

Design and Documentation of a Work-Imaging Study

Designing a work-imaging study need not take a great deal of time or planning. Coding managers simply create a comprehensive list of functions that the current coding staff completes. Once they have created the list, they develop a worksheet (table 6.2) that documents the "imaging" of each coder's workday.

Each coder then completes a worksheet. The coders document the time they spend each day on functions as shown in table 6.2. Documentation of functions for one to two weeks provides a solid foundation for the study.

Analyzing the Work-Imaging Study

When the coders have completed their worksheets, the coding manager calculates the percentage of time spent on each function listed on the worksheets. In the example shown in figure 6.1, only 44 percent of the coders' time was spent on actual coding and abstracting functions. The other functions may be viewed as barriers to the coding process.

The Process Redesign/Improvement Team

The coding team should be involved in process redesign. Because coders have fundamental knowledge of the coding process, they are vital to the success of process redesign activities. It is important to empower staff members to change processes and then to recognize them for their part in those improvements. In addition, staff members accept change much easier when they have been part of the decision-making process for change. By being part of the process redesign team, the coding staff also will more easily go through the early phases of the transition period.

The first step in process improvement is to assemble the team. Table 6.3 lists the members of the process improvement team and their respective functions.

Table 6.2. Work-imaging worksheet

Activity	Monday	Tuesday	Wednesday	Thursday	Friday
Coding and abstracting					
Filing records					
Retrieving records					
Assisting physicians					
Assisting department "walk-ins"					
Locating documentation					
Attending meetings					
Responding to business office questions and issues					
Communicating with physicians					
Attending training					
Performing quality reviews					
Other (specify)					

Figure 6.1.   Breakdown of coder's time

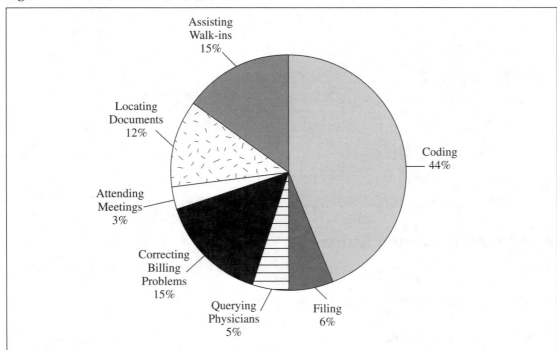

Table 6.3.   The process improvement team

Team Member	Responsibility
Facilitator Does not need the fundamental knowledge of the team members; may be from another department but needs to know performance improvement processes with training and/or experience in facilitating teams in the past	Trains team on performance improvement Remains neutral Is a nonvoting member Makes suggestions Coaches and is a motivator Recognizes team/individual achievements Keeps team on track

Team Leader
Recognized as leader and organizer of the group
	Works with facilitator and guides team to plan and coordinate the work of the team
	    Provides direction
	    Initiates activities
	    Encourages members
	    Contributes ideas
	    Interprets data
	    Makes assignments
	    Schedules meetings
	    Creates the agenda

Team Members Associated together in their work activity with a fundamental knowledge of the work and process	Identifies current processes and barriers Participates in decision making Identifies opportunities for improvement
Timekeeper	Keeps track of and calls time remaining on each agenda item
Recorder	Responsible for taking minutes

The success of the process improvement team depends on the following seven key elements:

- Establishing ground rules

- Stating the purpose/mission of the team

- Identifying customers and their requirements

- Documenting current processes and identifying barriers

- Collecting and analyzing data

- Identifying possible solutions by brainstorming

- Making recommendations for changes in the coding process

Establishing Ground Rules

Ground rules must be agreed upon at the very beginning. All members of the team should have input into the ground rules. They should agree to abide by them for the sake of the team's success. Some ground rules that team members should consider are:

- Arrive on time for meetings

- Complete and present the results of assignments from the previous meeting

- Respect the opinions of all team members

- Listen to other team members' points of view without criticism

- Stick by decisions that are made by the team

Stating the Purpose or Mission of the Team

The team must answer this question: Why has this team been formed? The team must define its mission in order to create a "map" or plan. For the team in this example, the purpose may be stated as: To meet customers' needs by improving the coding process through better use of the skills, expertise, and time of HIM coders.

Identifying Customers and Their Requirements

The process improvement team must identify the customers associated with the coding process. Such a customer is anyone who uses coded data, for whatever purpose. Customers are both internal, such as the facility's business office, and external, such as third-party payers. The process improvement team identifies all these customers and what their requirements are.

Having identified its customers, the team works toward modifying the coding process to meet the customers' requirements. Table 6.4 identifies possible internal and external customers and their requirements that relate to coding functions.

Documenting Current Processes and Identifying Barriers

The process improvement team works together to discuss and document current coding processes. For this step, the team's knowledge is vital because members must answer the following questions:

Table 6.4. Customers of the coding process and their requirements

Internal Customers	Requirements
Business office	Timely and accurate billing
	Timely responses to queries regarding billing issues
Physicians	Availability of chart for completion as soon as possible after discharge, including any necessary coding query forms
	Accurate coded data
External Customers	**Requirements**
Third-party payers	Timely and accurate bills
HIM department	Procedure that will not disrupt the record completion processes
Administration/finance	Discharge to coding within four days
	Accurately coded data

- What is the current coding process?

- Where are the starting and ending points of the process?

- What are the barriers to the coding process?

A diagram of a typical coding process with its barriers is shown in figure 6.2.

The team must also consider other functions that affect the coding process. Team members should include the following questions in their evaluation:

- When does the health record arrive in the HIM department after the patient is discharged?

- How is the health record brought to the HIM department?

- What mechanism is in place to ensure that all discharges are sent daily to the HIM department?

- Who in the HIM department is responsible for ensuring that all discharges have been received?

- How soon are health records assembled?

- How soon are they analyzed?

- At what point are health records available for the coders?

- How are the health records made available for the coders?

- When coders have questions for physicians, is there a procedure in place for the health record to be routed back to the coders for completion?

- Who is responsible for locating documentation in the health record that is missing and needed for coding, such as laboratory results and dictation?

- Do coders have access to the electronic health record?

- What is the turnaround time for transcription?

- Do coders have access to dictation prior to its being transcribed?

- When coding is complete, what is the process for routing the health records back to the HIM department for completion?
- Is concurrent coding performed? If so, what is that process?

Collecting and Analyzing Data

Earlier in this chapter, a sample analysis of the coding process began with collecting data from a work-imaging study. The sample study identified barriers to the coding process. When the barriers are identified and the coding process is changed, data can then be recalculated to show

Figure 6.2.   A typical coding process

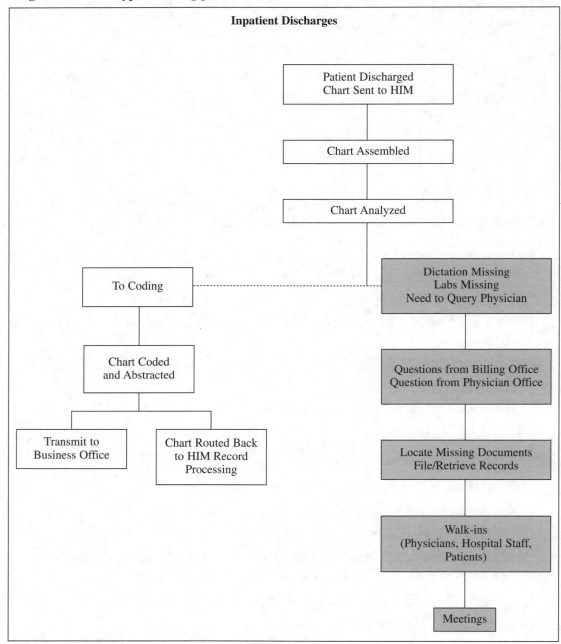

Note: Grey shading incidates barriers to the coding process.

a true picture of how much time will be available to coders for coding. Additional data can be acquired through benchmarking and productivity studies, which will be discussed later in this chapter.

The sample work-imaging study indicated that coders spent a significant percentage of time on noncoding functions. The process improvement team should consider assigning those noncoding functions to other HIM department staff. At this point in the process, the team should request that a member of the HIM clerical staff join the team. The clerical staff member's perspective and knowledge will be helpful in reassigning noncoding functions.

The noncoding functions can often be integrated into the existing clerical functions without the hiring of additional staff. In the event that additional staff is required, a clerical position is easier to fill, is less costly, and requires less training than a coding position.

When the noncoding functions are allocated to the clerical staff, the percentage of time that coders spend on coding functions should increase, as illustrated in figure 6.3. The data on the graph in figure 6.3 represent a 33 percent increase in time spent on coding.

Identifying Possible Solutions by Brainstorming

Brainstorming is a useful technique that promotes creative thinking as team members identify possible solutions for process improvement. During brainstorming, the team generates new, potentially useful ideas. Brainstorming requires team members to follow four basic ground rules:

- Welcome all ideas. During brainstorming, no judgments are made about ideas presented—there are no wrong or ridiculous proposals.

- Be creative in contributions—think out of the box! Because change involves risk taking, it is important to be open to new ideas. Every person's point of view is valuable. Team members should be encouraged to say whatever occurs to them as a solution, no matter how far-fetched it may seem. Far-fetched ideas may trigger more practical ones, and in some cases present valid solutions.

Figure 6.3.   **Use of coders' time after allocating noncoding functions to clerical staff**

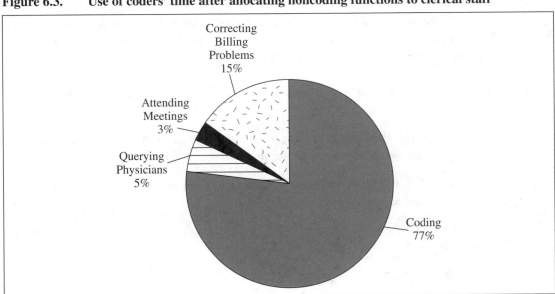

- Attempt to contribute a large quantity of ideas in a short amount of time. The more ideas there are, the more likely it is that there will be several useful ones.

- "Piggyback" on one another's ideas. Team members should feel free to combine ideas and to add to or to build on the ideas of others to create combinations, improvements, or variations.

Making Recommendations for Process Change

The process improvement team is responsible for putting together in a report format the outcome of its work, as well as recommendations for improving the coding process. The recommendations are finalized after all data have been received and analyzed. These data include findings from the benchmarking study (see the next section of this chapter), as well as from productivity measurements. The recommendations should take into account anything that might have an impact on the organization, such as:

- Utilization of staff

- Effect on the budget

- Change in productivity

- Number of days in accounts receivable

- Effects on customer requirements

Benchmarking

The goal of benchmarking is to increase performance by identifying best practices, measuring and comparing a selected work process, and conducting interviews with the benchmark organization or organizations. Opportunities for process improvement can be identified where best practice has been applied in other organizations. A benchmark organization is usually a competitor of similar size.

Before embarking on a benchmarking project, coding managers should determine the criteria or indicators for the benchmark comparison. Some areas they should consider and questions they should ask the benchmark organizations are:

- How many coder hours, not including overtime hours, does each of the facilities budget for full-time employees (FTEs)?

- What is the average number of health records coded per day or per hour by patient type, such as inpatient, outpatient surgical, ancillary, and emergency department?

- What standards does the facility expect coders to meet for both productivity (health records per day) and quality (percentage of accuracy)?

- Is the coding staff credentialed? If so, what type of credentials are represented—RHIT, RHIA, CCS, CCS-P, CPC, CPC-H, or other?

- Does the organization have a coding incentive plan?

- What is the compensation rate for coding professionals?

- Does the organization use contracted services for coding?

- Are coders abstracting as well as coding, or are those functions performed separately? If they are performed separately, who performs them?

- Who performs quality monitoring? Does the coding supervisor conduct this, or are auditors/quality monitors applied by external reviewers? What are their responsibilities? How frequent are the reviews?

- How many lead coders does the facility have? What are their responsibilities?

- Do coders have clerical support? If so, for what functions?

- What is the facility's case-mix index (CMI)? In benchmarking, knowing the CMI is essential because it is the closest measure for comparing like facilities. CMI is used as a measurement for inpatients. The CMI is the sum of all patient encounters' relative weight, based on DRGs divided by the number of all encounters. The higher the CMI, the more complex the records; therefore, the higher the CMI, the lower the expected productivity. (See chapter 11, Case-Mix Management, for a detailed discussion of the CMI.)

Coding managers can request this information from hospitals of similar size to their own. After the information has been returned, coding managers can compare and analyze the data. Figures 6.4 through 6.8 show graphic representations of an example of benchmark results. Hospital A, Hospital B, and Hospital C represent the benchmark organizations. The Home Hospital is the facility conducting the study.

Figure 6.4.   Number of clerks (noncoding functions)

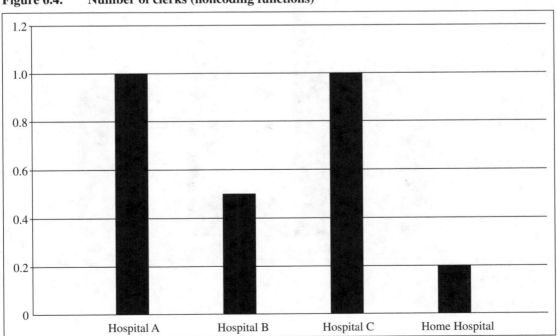

Figure 6.5.   **Inpatient coding standard: health records per day**

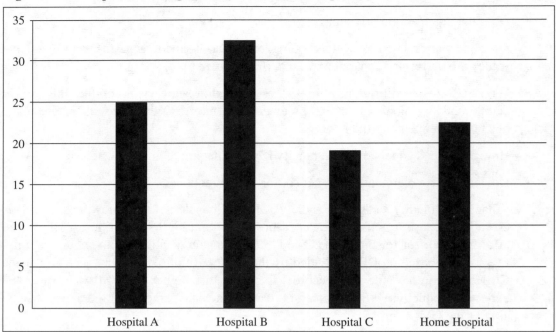

Figure 6.6.   **Medicare case-mix index (CMI)**

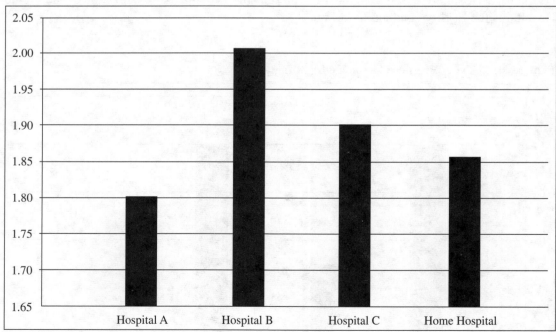

Figure 6.7. Non-Medicare (all-payer) case-mix index (CMI)

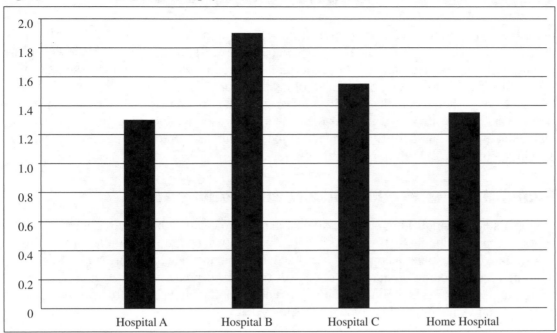

Figure 6.8. Number of coding supervisors/auditors

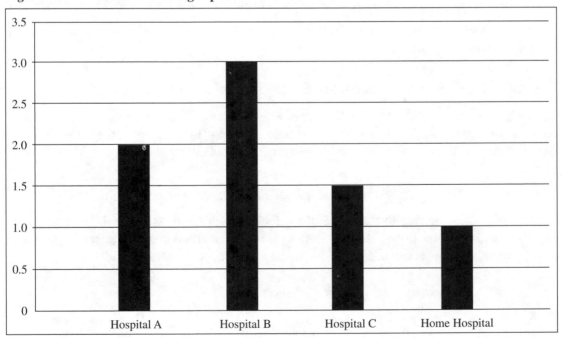

Establishing Productivity Standards

Once the coding process has been refined, the process improvement team can establish productivity standards. As in the analysis of the coding process, the current productivity of the coding staff must be determined. The team can use a productivity measurement worksheet, as shown in table 6.5, to capture the number of health records coded per day.

Each coder should complete a daily worksheet, such as the one in table 6.5, for a specified time period (one or two weeks). After the coders have recorded those data, the team can calculate the average number of health records coded per hour by record type. This calculation provides a baseline of current productivity levels.

Evaluating the Productivity of the Coding Staff

The next step in establishing productivity standards is to evaluate how the productivity of the Home Hospital's coding staff compares with that of other facilities of similar size and case mix. Figure 6.9 illustrates a comparison of standards from the benchmarking study (figure 6.5) with the average coding productivity of each of the four hospitals.

Figure 6.10 presents a comparison of the coding productivity standard with the CMI of each hospital. A review of this comparison shows that:

- Hospital A has the lowest CMI with the highest productivity. This makes sense because the lower the case mix, the less complicated the records should be.

- Hospital B does not meet its productivity standard and has the highest CMI in the benchmark study. This may indicate that Hospital B's standards should be reevaluated.

- Hospital C exceeds its standard; but in relationship to its CMI, the standard may be too low.

Using the CMI to Establish Standards

The coding manager of the Home Hospital now must establish its standards. For purposes of an example, the average productivity for inpatient coders at Home Hospital is twenty-four (24) health records per day. One method of calculating the productivity standard uses the following formula:

$$CMI \times 12.5 = lower\text{-}limit\ productivity\ rate\ from\ which\ to\ build$$

For example, referring to figure 6.5, the calculation for the health records per hour based on this calculation would be reflected in table 6.6. This methodology is especially useful in multisystem hospitals because using the CMI formula "levels the playing field."

Table 6.5.   Productivity measurement worksheet

Date:	Number Coded	Time Spent Coding (hours/minutes)
Inpatient Records		
Outpatient Surgical Records		
Emergency Department Records		
Ancillary Records		

Figure 6.9. **Coding standard compared with average productivity**

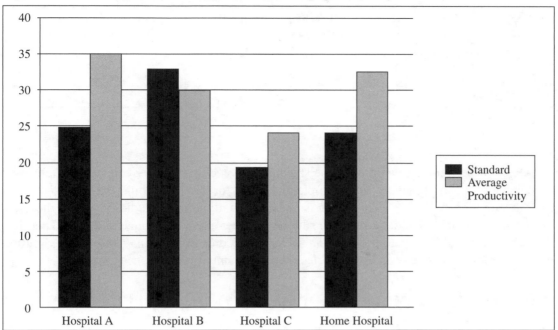

Figure 6.10. **CMI compared with productivity standard**

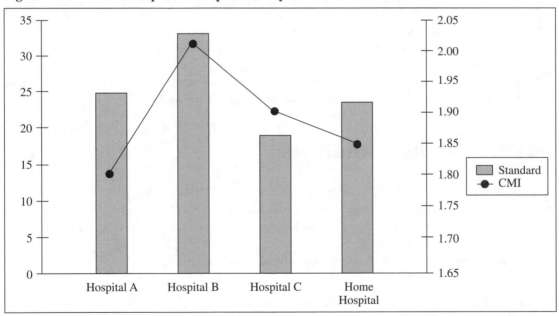

Table 6.6.   Comparison of productivity standards by hospital

Hospital	Benchmark Standard (Health Records per Day)	CMI-Adjusted Standard (Health Records per Day)
Hospital A	25	22.5
Hospital B	33	25.12
Hospital C	19	23.75
Home Hospital	Not Established	23.25

Using these figures as a base for the standard, the coding manager can create a range for acceptable productivity levels. For example, the range for Home Hospital may be from 23.25 to 26 health records per day. This range is consistent with national studies in which the average standard for inpatient coders is 31 health records per day with a range of 20 to 60 per day. An average productivity rate greater than 26 health records per day may warrant recognition in the form of an incentive and/or be reflected on the annual performance appraisal.

Considerations Other Than CMI

The CMI is not the only factor the coding manager must consider when establishing a productivity standard for coders. For example, if coders do not abstract the health record, the coding manager would have to adjust the formula to allow for that. The same would be true if the facility had an extensive database that required considerable abstracting. In that case, the CMI would be multiplied by a smaller number.

The CMI cannot be utilized for same-day surgical, emergency department, or ancillary records. In those cases, coding managers use the averages from the benchmarking study to compare their own hospital's productivity with that of hospitals of the same size and case mix. In this context, case mix would indicate the probability of similar patient encounters. For example, if the average range for same-day surgical records were 21 to 80 records per day, a coding manager might determine that coders should maintain a range of 40 to 55 records per day.

Coding Volume Analysis

After the analysis of the current coding process has been conducted and its redesign has taken place, the coding manager must ask this question: How many coders does the HIM department need? Coding managers often respond to increases in accounts receivable days by hiring additional coders or outsourcing work. Either of those responses is an easy way to solve the problem; however, neither may be the most cost-effective solution.

Calculating Required Coding Hours

The first step in determining the number of coders needed is to calculate the HIM department's needs based on volume. The formula in figure 6.11 calculates the required coding hours per day for 28,000 inpatient discharges per year when the facility's standard is 3.77 inpatient health records per hour.

The same formula can be applied to each patient type using the number of discharges per year and the number of health records per hour.

Figure 6.11.   Required coding hours per day based on volume

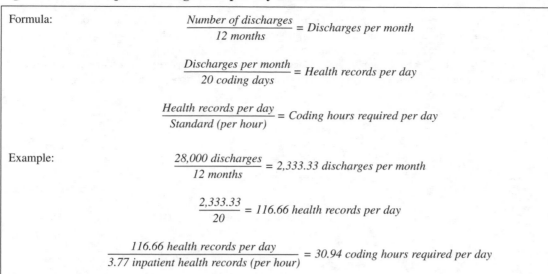

Formula:

$$\frac{Number\ of\ discharges}{12\ months} = Discharges\ per\ month$$

$$\frac{Discharges\ per\ month}{20\ coding\ days} = Health\ records\ per\ day$$

$$\frac{Health\ records\ per\ day}{Standard\ (per\ hour)} = Coding\ hours\ required\ per\ day$$

Example:

$$\frac{28,000\ discharges}{12\ months} = 2,333.33\ discharges\ per\ month$$

$$\frac{2,333.33}{20} = 116.66\ health\ records\ per\ day$$

$$\frac{116.66\ health\ records\ per\ day}{3.77\ inpatient\ health\ records\ (per\ hour)} = 30.94\ coding\ hours\ required\ per\ day$$

Calculating Required Number of Coders

When calculating the number of coders needed to meet the required coding hours per day, the coding manager uses the number of annual budgeted hours per coder minus the number of hours per year that each coder accrues for vacation, sick leave, and training. The coding manager should also use the data gained from the work image during the process redesign.

The data in figure 6.3 showed that after the coding process was redesigned, coders spent an average of 77 percent of their time coding. This equals 6.16 coding hours per day per coder. If the coding manager divides the 23.5 health records per day (table 6.6) by 6.16 hours, the result is 3.77 health records coded per hour per coder.

Figure 6.12 illustrates a formula for calculating the number of coder hours per day available for coders who spend 77 percent of their time on coding functions. The example is based on five full-time coders, each eligible for 600 hours of vacation/sick leave and 40 hours of training.

Figure 6.11 illustrates that the required coding hours required per day is 30.94 hours; figure 6.12 shows that 30.8 coder hours are available per day. In this example, the HIM department has an adequate number of coders to meet its coding volume requirements.

How did redesigning the coding process help the department meet its volume requirements? In the work-imaging study, only 44 percent of coders' time was spent on coding and abstracting. In figure 6.13, the formula from figure 6.12 is applied to calculate the number of coder hours available at 44 percent productivity. If process improvement had not taken place, the HIM department would have been short by 13.2 hours a day, or more than one full-time coder!

Staff Development

Staff development means more than just training. True staff development emphasizes personal growth and improvement of employees' potential. It maximizes their contributions, improves performance, provides motivation, and improves morale. Training opportunities abound for coding staff. Education is a fundamental element for developing excellent coders.

Figure 6.12.   **Required number of coders per day**

Formula: This calculation involves multiplying the annual hours per coder (a) by the number of FTEs (b) in the department to arrive at total annual hours (x) for the staff as a whole. From this number, vacation and sick hours (c) and training hours (d) are subtracted to arrive at the total available hours per year (y). This number is then multiplied by the applicable productivity rate as a percentage (e) to determine the number of productive coding hours for the staff (z), and the calculation is reduced from an annual to a daily figure to arrive at coder hours available per day.

$$a \times b = x$$

$$(x - c) - d = y$$

$$\frac{y \times e}{12 \ months} = z$$

$$\frac{z}{20 \ coding \ days} = Coder \ hours \ available \ per \ day$$

Example:

$$a = 2{,}080, \ b = 5, \ c = 600, \ d = 200, \ e = 77\%$$

$$2{,}080 \times 5 = 10{,}400$$

$$10{,}400 - 600 - 200 = 9{,}600$$

$$\frac{9{,}600 \times 77\%}{12} = 616$$

$$\frac{616}{20} = 30.8 \ coder \ hours \ available \ per \ day$$

Figure 6.13.   **Coder hours available based on 44 percent of time spent on coding functions**

$$a = 2{,}080, \ b = 5, \ c = 600, \ d = 200, \ e = 44\%$$

$$2{,}080 \times 5 = 10{,}400$$

$$10{,}400 - 600 - 200 = 9{,}600$$

$$\frac{9{,}600 \times 44\%}{12} = 352$$

$$\frac{352}{20} = 17.6 \ coder \ hours \ available \ per \ day$$

When determining productivity standards and staffing requirements, coding managers should add time for educational opportunities to the equation. Too often, managers feel that training/education takes too much time or is not covered in the budget. Astute HIM managers realize that they cannot afford not to provide continuing training for their coders.

Benefits of Continued Education/Training

A well-trained coding staff helps to ensure complete and accurate coding, which is essential for the integrity of the data collected. Precise coding helps to ensure compliance with regulatory requirements (see chapter 8, Compliance Issues) and helps to facilitate consistency of coding in the healthcare facility or organization.

In addition, coders consider training as an enhancement to their job. Coding professionals take pride in their work and welcome the opportunity to gain knowledge and skill. Organizations that provide continuing education take an additional step in retaining qualified coders.

In-House Training

In-house training programs presented by physicians or clinical department staff on complicated diagnoses, disease processes, and surgical procedures help coders learn to assign the most accurate codes. In addition, the interaction between the clinical staff and coders helps cultivate a relationship for better communications. It also affords physicians the opportunity to learn about coding guidelines and regulatory requirements. In-house training is also an ideal way to communicate to physicians how documentation plays a role in code assignment, the payment process, and compliance issues.

How does a coding manager determine the kind of training to present to the coding staff? Much depends on the findings of quality reviews (see chapter 7, Quality Control Issues). Managers can use quality review findings to identify trends and issues that could be addressed in training, such as:

- Complex DRGs

- Disease processes

- Surgical procedures

- Prospective payment systems

- Coding criteria and guidelines

- Laboratory values

- Compliance requirements and regulatory issues

Complex DRGs

Presentations on complex DRGs should include the etiology and manifestations of conditions, along with related complications. For example, a presentation on complex DRG 416, Septicemia, age 18 or older, could include the difference between septicemia, urosepsis, and a urinary tract infection. That presentation would also include the etiology and manifestations for septicemia, abnormal laboratory values, and treatment options.

Coders must also be aware of the coding guidelines related to assigning complex diagnosis codes. An in-house training presentation for the DRGs related to pneumonia could include the following information:

- The etiology, manifestations, and complications of pneumonia, such as respiratory failure

- The diagnosis and treatment of pneumonia

- Official coding guidelines related to pneumonia and complications of pneumonia

- The differences between DRG 089, Simple pneumonia, and DRG 079, Respiratory infections and inflammations, age 18 or older, with CC

- Common errors in assigning DRG 079, including inappropriately assigning "other specified" bacterial pneumonia

Disease Processes

For coders to have a complete understanding of a disease process, reviews should include the following:

- The etiology, manifestations, and therapeutic and surgical treatments

- Examples of surgical cases for coding

- The ICD-9-CM and CPT coding guidelines for both diagnoses and procedures

Surgical Procedures

Surgical procedures, especially those that are difficult to code, should be reviewed in detail. For example, in coding sinus surgery, a review of the anatomy, physiology, and pathophysiology of the sinuses is valuable in understanding the operative procedures.

Prospective Payment Systems

How prospective payment systems affect coding is another important topic for in-house training. HIM department coders need a thorough understanding of how DRG results are reported and how they affect the CMI. The accuracy of coding and sequencing absolutely affects DRGs and the CMI and has a far-reaching impact on healthcare organizations.

Training regarding the CMI should include the following information:

- Finance departments use the CMI for many purposes, such as budgeting for staff and capital expenses, internal and external reporting, planning, clinical programs, and numerous other resources.

- The CMI can also influence coding productivity. That is, an increase in CMI may be indicative of more complicated health records that require more time for complete and accurate coding.

Training for outpatient prospective payment systems (OPPS) could include the following information:

- Ambulatory payment classifications (APCs), the OPPS for Medicare, were implemented in August 2000.

- Outpatient encounters are put into APC groups that, like DRG groupings, are based on the amount of resources they are likely to require.

- Unlike DRGs, multiple APCs can be assigned during a single encounter.

- Comprehensive knowledge of CPT codes, hospital-approved modifiers, and the application of Correct Coding Initiative (CCI) edits are essential for appropriate APC assignment.

Coding Criteria and Guidelines

To ensure consistency of coding, coding managers must make sure that all coders receive up-to-date coding criteria and guidelines. This is especially true for guidelines that are not published in the official coding guidelines or as supplements to the official guidelines but that are requested by payers or other parties.

Physicians should also be involved in the development of criteria for assigning codes to clinical information. In-house training presentations should include demonstrations on the appropriate use of approved physician query forms.

Having skilled coding professionals highly involved in the process of developing and maintaining coding criteria greatly optimizes the opportunity for covering all significant coding areas. If a hospital is part of a multihospital system, the coding manager should organize a committee that develops or reviews such criteria to facilitate consistency among the entities. Both single-hospital and multihospital systems should be sure that all coders receive information consistently so that each coder has the same understanding of how to apply the criteria.

Laboratory Values

Understanding laboratory values helps coders arrive at the most accurate diagnosis code. However, it is inappropriate to code directly from any laboratory report. Instead, an abnormal report may indicate the need to query the physician for clarification or further documentation.

To help coders, in-house training on laboratory values could include the following information:

- Differences between pathogens and contaminants on cultures

- Abnormal chemistry values and what they may indicate, along with the associated clinical signs or symptoms documented in the health record

For example, abnormal liver enzymes could indicate a common bile duct stone, biliary tree fibrosis, biliary tree cirrhosis, infiltration of the biliary tree by pancreatic carcinoma, inflammation of the biliary tree due to infection, or inflammation of the biliary tree secondary to pancreatitis.

Using the example of pancreatitis, coders could further learn that:

- Symptoms of pancreatitis are pain, nausea, and vomiting.

- A diagnosis is made by an assessment of the symptoms, amylase and lipase laboratory values, and CT scan.

- Complications may include shock, sepsis, respiratory failure, infection, or pseudocyst.

Although a coder cannot make a "diagnosis" from those findings in the health record, the coder can better understand the implications of abnormal values and know when a physician's review is warranted based on the documentation in the health record.

Compliance Requirements and Regulatory Issues

In-house training should also focus on compliance requirements and regulatory issues that involve code reporting. The coding staff should be updated at least annually on compliance requirements. This ensures that coders understand the healthcare organization's compliance program, as well as the current Office of Inspector General (OIG) work plan. Training related to the OIG work plan should emphasize coding and related topics, such as disposition assignment, APCs, and DRGs.

Less Formal In-House Training

Coding managers should also offer less formal in-house training on a regular basis. One way of doing this is to meet with coders and discuss appropriate coding for problem health records. Coding is sometimes more an art than a science so such discussions benefit the entire coding team.

Publications for Training

Another method of less formal training is to make publications containing articles on coding, clinical information, and billing compliance easily accessible to staff. Coders can read the articles and then discuss the topics as a group so that everyone has the same understanding of the information.

The AHA's *Coding Clinic,* published quarterly, should be readily available to all coders. In addition to providing a basis for group discussions, *Coding Clinic* provides two continuing education quizzes each year and is an excellent source for continuing education credits. The AHA's new publication, *Coding Clinic on HCPCS,* and the AMA's *CPT Assistant,* published monthly, can also be used as training tools.

In-House Published Newsletters

Newsletters published by the HIM department are excellent tools for communicating both to coders and to physicians. Newsletters for physicians should be kept to one page and should focus on documentation requirements and coding guidelines. Newsletters for coders may include the following:

- Regulatory updates
- Operative techniques
- Coding tips
- Anatomy and physiology notes
- Clinical topics

Newsletters can help coordinate training provided to coders and physicians. For example, training might be presented to coders on the differences in coding septicemia versus urosepsis. A corresponding newsletter could be created for physicians in which the coding guidelines for septicemia versus urosepsis are specified. The newsletter could also provide examples of appropriate and inappropriate documentation.

Training in a Multihospital System

If a facility is part of a multihospital system, the HIM departments should bring coders from the different facilities together for training. Such training is beneficial in the following ways:

- It facilitates a forum for networking among the coders and gives them an opportunity to discuss concerns with other coders. Coding managers may find it advantageous to ask that questions or "hot issues" be submitted ahead of time.
- It promotes consistency in the hospital system by providing a more accurate database that includes codes for clinical data management.

Training New Staff Members

The HIM department should have a policy and procedure for training and monitoring new coding staff. New employees may have just completed a coding certificate program to earn their RHIA or RHIT credentials, or they may be experienced coding professionals new to the healthcare facility. In any case, some training is necessary. Newly certified coders take at least a year to become proficient.

With newly hired coders, managers should focus on the quality of the coding, not on productivity. HIM departments should have quality standards established for the new coders' first 30, 60, and 120 days. These standards should be achievable and comparable to those expected of the experienced coding staff. However, lower quality might be expected for a new coder who is not familiar with individual physicians' documentation styles or with the facility's health record format.

Coding managers should see that close monitoring of, and concurrent training for, new coders is provided. When possible, coding managers should have one person responsible for training new coders. This helps ensure consistency. When the trainer and coder feel comfortable with the quality of coding, less monitoring is necessary. The goal, of course, is to have all coders, including new staff, meet the established quality and productivity standards.

Educational Opportunities outside the Facility

Seminars and conferences held outside the facility are a budget expense for the HIM department. As such, plans for them should be made ahead of time when possible.

The Society for Clinical Coding, private consulting companies, state HIM associations, and AHIMA are all good sources for outside seminars. Audio teleconferences, Web seminars, and videotapes of off-site seminars and conferences are other excellent choices. They enable multiple coders to take part in the seminar for one low registration fee.

Quality Standards

A balance must be struck between increasing productivity and maintaining quality results. High output (productivity) is useless without quality data. Although 100 percent code assignment accuracy would be ideal, it is not realistic—many variables are part of the process.

Minimum Quality Standards

Quality standards should be high enough to validate the data, but achievable with some room for error. Each organization should determine the threshold for its minimum quality standards.

Figure 6.14 illustrates quality standards for inpatient coding compared with the current quality of coding. In this graph, a minimum of 95 percent accuracy is required for each category of coding. The desired accuracy rates vary from category to category. Between the minimum standard and the desired accuracy lies the range of acceptable quality for each category.

Meeting Desired Accuracy

The appropriate assignment of the principal diagnosis code is critical. This is especially true for inpatient coding because the principal diagnosis code usually drives the DRG and, in

Figure 6.14.   **Current coding quality compared to standards**

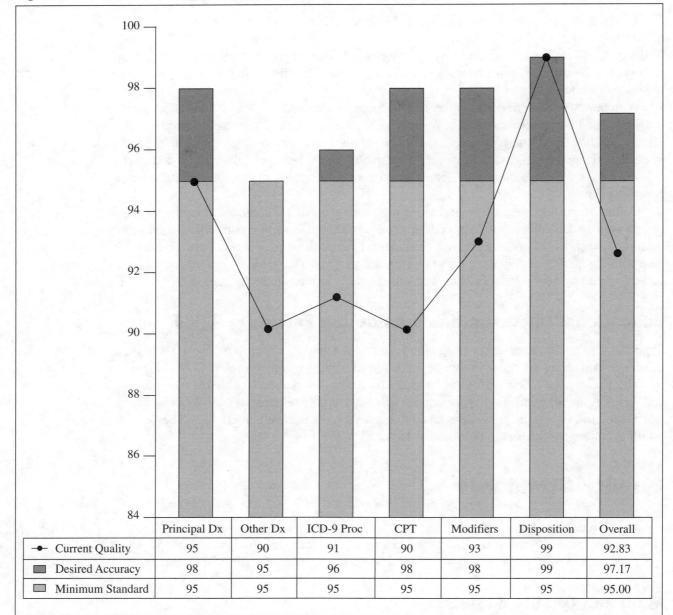

	Principal Dx	Other Dx	ICD-9 Proc	CPT	Modifiers	Disposition	Overall
Current Quality	95	90	91	90	93	99	92.83
Desired Accuracy	98	95	96	98	98	99	97.17
Minimum Standard	95	95	95	95	95	95	95.00

many cases, the corresponding payment. For this reason, the percentage of accuracy for coding principal diagnoses should be as close to 100 percent as possible. The graph in figure 6.14 shows a desired accuracy of 98 percent for coding principal diagnoses.

Other diagnosis codes are equally important, but they do not have the impact on payment or compliance that the principal diagnosis code has. When considering other or secondary diagnoses, coders must realize that the evaluation of complication and comorbidity (CC) is critical, as well as those conditions that do not affect DRG payment. Other diagnoses may be categorized as being "weighted" because some codes are more crucial to capture than others. The quality standard for other diagnoses may therefore be lower than that of the principal diagnosis.

Phase-in Period for Quality Standards

When implementing quality standards, coding managers should phase in the accuracy requirement. They could establish small increments at thirty-day intervals until each standard is met. During the phase-in period, coders should receive any training necessary to meet the accuracy requirements.

If the current accuracy rates are significantly lower than the minimum standard, coding managers must allow a long enough phase-in period for coders to meet the requirements. Similar to the program for training new coders, continuous monitoring may be required until coders meet the desired accuracy requirements

Conclusion

Coding professionals hold a unique position in today's healthcare systems. Healthcare facilities rely on coded data for a variety of statistical uses in addition to reporting codes for payment purposes. A fine balance exists between coding quality and coding productivity. How to maintain this balance has always been a subject of controversy and concern.

Members of a coding staff possess the fundamental knowledge to work together as a team to measure, analyze, and redesign current coding processes. Their involvement helps them to appreciate the benefits that process improvement can bring to them as well as to the healthcare organization.

In managing the coding process, it is possible both to maximize coder resources and to maintain optimal quality. Coding productivity is an important issue for the efficiency and profitability of a healthcare facility. Establishing quality standards is essential for adequately maintaining a coding staff that meets the needs of the facility's customers.

References

Bridges, W. 1991. *Managing Transitions: Making the Most of Change.* Boston, Mass.: Addison-Wesley Publishing Company.

Dunn, R. 1996. HIM issues: A survey of professionals. *Journal of the American Health Information Management Association* 67(5): 61–66.

_____. 2001. Developing facility-specific productivity measures. *Journal of the American Health Information Management Association* 72(4): 73–74.

Elliot, C., P. Shaw, P. Isaacson, and E. Murphy. 2000. *Performance Improvement in Healthcare: A Tool for Programmed Learning.* Chicago: American Health Information Management Association.

Medical Educational Services, Inc. 1996. *Understanding and Interpreting Frequently Ordered Laboratory Tests.* Altoona, Wis.: Medical Educational Services, Inc.

Acknowledgments

The author wishes to thank Mary Staub, RHIA, Intermountain Health Care, for her assistance in the development of formulas for establishing productivity standards and staffing requirements.

Chapter 7

Quality Control Issues

Vickie L. Rogers, MS, RHIA

Since the implementation of the inpatient and outpatient prospective payment systems (PPSs), the need for clinical information in the form of coded data has been magnified dramatically. The following entities base financial decisions on the information provided by coding professionals:

- Private audit/review organizations

- Third-party administrators

- Employers

- Fiscal intermediaries (FIs) for Medicare and selected other health plans

- Commercial insurance groups

The need for accurate and complete information has resulted in a close examination of the coding process within HIM departments. Practices, policies, staff qualifications, training, and types of quality control programs are critical elements in the data quality review process. In relation to coded data, **data quality reviews** are an examination of health records to determine the level of coding accuracy and to identify areas of coding problems.

As coding professionals face a transition in the reimbursement system of government programs, an accurate database for planning is critical. The data that coding professionals provide today will have a profound impact on future reimbursement. By completely and accurately describing the resources used for patients, coding professionals assure themselves that the database for reimbursement decisions is as detailed as possible. (See appendix 7.1 for an AHIMA practice brief on data quality.)

Additionally, health information professionals must meet the pressures of deadlines and of outside audit/review organizations. In doing so, they realize the critical need for adopting ethical practice standards. Recognizing that responsibility, the AHIMA board of directors approved standards of ethical coding in 1991 and revised them in December 1999. (See appendix 7.2 for the current coding standards.)

Ongoing Data Quality Improvement

Quality, as it applies to coded data, means that the performance of the coding function within an HIM department is accomplished at the highest level of accuracy and of efficiency possible. Likewise, data quality is most appropriately expressed in terms of the following needs of customers:

- Appropriate reimbursement to hospitals

- Accurate reporting of patients' illnesses and related treatments

- Ability of payers to identify all resources required to treat beneficiaries

Goals of a Data Quality Improvement Program

The design and implementation of a data quality improvement program begin with setting the following goals:

- To establish an ongoing monitor for identifying problems or opportunities to improve the quality of coded data for inpatient and outpatient cases

- To determine the cause and scope of identified problems

- To set priorities for resolving identified problems

- To implement mechanisms for problem solving through the approval of corrective action plans

- To ensure that corrective action is taken by following up on problems with appropriate monitors

Methods for Monitoring and Evaluating a Data Quality Improvement Program

The methods to be used for monitoring and for evaluation should be clarified in the data quality improvement program. Coding managers should share the findings from data quality evaluations and reviews in the following ways:

- Discuss the specific findings from each evaluation and review with the coding staff

- Incorporate specific findings pertinent to individual coders into their employee performance evaluations

- Submit overall findings to the quality improvement committee or its counterpart for further study, if necessary

Staff Responsibilities in the Data Quality Review Process

The HIM department should schedule data quality reviews on a regular and ongoing basis. The review schedule will depend on the number of coders and the identified coding problems. If the coding staff consists of several clinical coding specialists, a rotating schedule should be established to review all coders on an annual basis. If the coding staff consists of one or two clinical coding specialists with no supervisor, the HIM department has the following choices for conducting reviews:

- Coders review each other's work.

- The HIM department manager reviews the coders' work.

- An external consulting firm is contracted to conduct the review.

The initial review should be conducted using a representative sample of both coding staff and common diagnoses and procedures. This review will serve as a baseline for future comparisons. After analyzing the results of the review, the appropriate supervisor will identify problems that relate to coding and abstracting issues.

Coding Managers' Responsibilities in the Data Quality Review Process

Coding managers also play an important part in the data quality review process. They are responsible for the following types of activities:

- Preparing specific coding criteria

- Planning educational sessions for coders

- Evaluating and monitoring education action plans for individual coders

- Monitoring ethical coding practices

- Evaluating and monitoring coding and abstracting quality

- Preparing performance evaluations

Data Quality Reviews and Compliance

The design of any data quality review program should address the compliance initiatives in effect throughout the healthcare organization and within the HIM department. When the analysis of the review is complete, the HIM department should communicate the review's findings to the compliance department. (See chapter 8, Compliance Issues, for a discussion of the relation of compliance requirements to the coding function.)

Reviewing Inpatient Coding

The HIM department should consider auditing or reviewing health records after coding but before billing, rather than performing a retrospective audit after claims have been submitted for payment. This issue should be settled with the compliance department during the planning stage of the data quality improvement program.

Selecting the Sample for an Inpatient Review

Health records for inpatient review can be pulled using the inpatient database from the HIM system abstracts. The sample size will vary depending on the type of review, the size of the hospital, the number of coders to be included, compliance requirements for sampling, and the number of inpatient discharges. (See chapter 8, Compliance Issues, on sampling for corporate compliance.)

For an initial baseline review, the HIM manager could do sample selection. The best method of sample selection might be to pull a random sample of health records by volume and average charges. For a focused review, the HIM manager might have to develop specific reports. To understand how the codes were reported, code assignment should include the end result, which is generally the UB-92 claim form.

Focused Inpatient Reviews

The HIM department can plan focused reviews based on specific problem areas after the initial baseline review has been completed. Some potential problem coding areas for focused reviews include the following:

- Surgical complications

- Obstetrical complications

- DRG 468 or other DRG code assignments that occur infrequently

- Neoplasm

- Diabetes mellitus

- Dehydration as the principal diagnosis

- Gastrointestinal bleeding

Topics for focused reviews may also be based on:

- Controversial issues identified in *Coding Clinic*

- Recent data quality issues identified by external review agencies

- Discussions of inpatient coding issues presented in journals

Using published statistical reports for comparisons is another approach for conducting focused reviews. For example, the Office of the Inspector General (OIG) publishes an annual report of focused DRG pairs. By using this information, the health information manager might be able to identify other topics for comparisons.

Forms Used in the Inpatient Review

In the inpatient review, forms are used to track cases, to identify individual variations, and to monitor the type of variations made by individual coders. A form should be completed for each health record included in the sample. Examples of some suggested forms are provided in figures 7.1 through 7.4 and in appendix 7.3.

How Each Inpatient Health Record Is Reviewed

To begin the review, the coding supervisor checks the inpatient health record to ensure that the diagnosis billed as principal meets the official Uniform Hospital Discharge Data Set (UHDDS) definition for principal diagnosis. The **principal diagnosis** must have been present on admission, been a principal reason for admission, and received treatment or evaluation during the stay. If several diagnoses meet all those requirements, the principal diagnosis could be any one that meets the above requirements.

If the principal diagnosis was chosen incorrectly, the reviewer determines the correct diagnosis. If this can be determined using coding conventions and guidelines, the reviewer need not consult the attending physician. If the documentation in the health record is unclear, the reviewer should consult the attending physician. When a physician clarifies the documentation, the clarification should support the code selection and be in the form of an addendum to the

Figure 7.1.   **Coding compliance review/inpatient summary**

Name:_____   Age: _____   ADM:_____

MR #:_____   Sex: _____   DISCH: _____

ACCT #: _____   MD: _____   Facility: _____

HIC #: _____   LOS: _____   Payor:_____

Original Description and Codes   Revised Description and Codes

Diagnosis   DRG _____   Diagnosis   DRG _____

1. _____   1. _____   *Variance Type:*
                                                                PrDx Chg   /___/
2. _____   2. _____   ReSeq PrDx   /___/
3. _____   3. _____   Add 2nd Dx   /___/
                                                                Chg 2nd Dx   /___/
4. _____   4. _____   PrProc Chg   /___/
5. _____   5. _____   Chg 2nd Proc   /___/
                                                                Add Proc   /___/
6. _____   6. _____   Other   /___/
7. _____   7. _____

8. _____   8. _____

9. _____   9. _____

10. _____   10. _____

Operative Description and Codes   Operative Description and Codes

1. _____   1. _____

2. _____   2. _____

3. _____   3. _____

4. _____   4. _____

5. _____   5. _____

6. _____   6. _____

Disposition Code: _____   Disposition Code: _____

Summary Findings: _____

_____

_____

Recommendations: _____

_____

_____

_____

Date Reviewed: _____   Date sent to Rebill HIM for: _____

Reviewer: _____   Revised DRG Wt._____

Orig. DRG Wt. _____   Pmt. _____

Pmt: _____   Diff. _____

From Sue Prophet. 1999. *Health Information Management Compliance.* Chicago: American Health Information Management Association.

Figure 7.2.   Inpatient review: Variations by coder

Date of Review: _____	
Variation Type	
Inaccurate sequencing or specificity prin dx, affect DRG	_____
Inaccurate sequencing or specificity prin dx, no affect DRG	_____
Omission CC, affect DRG	_____
Omission CC, no affect DRG	_____
Inaccurate prin procedure, affect DRG	_____
Omission procedure, affect DRG	_____
More specific coding of dx or proc, no affect DRG	_____
Inaccurate coding	_____

From Sue Prophet. 1999. *Health Information Management Compliance.* Chicago: American Health Information Management Association.

health record. If any changes to documentation affect the DRG, the case must be rebilled. Ultimately, the coding supervisor should identify the coding problem and its source and should implement a corrective action to prevent the same errors from recurring.

The following list gives the standard steps in the review process for coding supervisors/ reviewers:

1. Review the health record to determine if all secondary diagnoses, complications/ comorbidities, and procedures billed are supported and justified.

2. Review secondary diagnoses to determine if any are supported by the health record, but not reported, and if they affect the DRG assignment.

3. Review the health record to determine that all secondary diagnoses have been completely identified and coded according to guidelines for the addition of secondary diagnoses.

4. For coding procedures, make sure that the entire operative record is available.

5. Review progress notes for bedside procedures to identify any procedures, such as debridements, that might affect DRG assignments.

6. Refer questions to a physician as needed, and ensure that new information is documented in the health record.

7. Regroup and rebill or resubmit the claim accordingly.

8. Establish the cause of the coding problem.

9. Implement corrective action.

Calculating Errors from the Inpatient Review

When all health records in the sample have been reviewed, the results/errors must be summarized for all health records and for individual coders. The two most common methods of calculating errors are the record method and the code method.

Figure 7.3.   Rebilling log

Insurance: _____   Patient Type: _____

Facility/Hospital

Date Sent to Business Office: _____

Patient		DRG/ASC Chg		Date of		Received		Comments
Account #	Name	From	To	RA	Rebill	Amount	Date	

(This portion to be completed by reviewer)   (This portion to be completed by the Business Office)

From Sue Prophet. 1999. *Health Information Management Compliance.* Chicago: American Health Information Management Association.

Figure 7.4. Medicare coding compliance validation worksheet: DRG/ICD-9-CM coding

Patient: _____   Age/Sex: _____ Financial Class: ____
Medical Record No.: _____   Facility: _____
Account No.: _____   Adm. Date: _____
Disch. Date: _____
Dr. Name: _____
Date Reviewed: _____

Disposition: _____   LOS: _____

FACILITY NARRATIVE	FACILITY CODE	REVIEWER NARRATIVE
1		1
2		2
3		3
4		4
5		5
6		6
7		7
8		8
9		9

1		1
2		2
3		3
4		4
5		5
6		6
7		7
8		8
9		9
10		10

DRG VARIANCES   Rationale for Change: _____
_____
_____
_____
_____

Hospital DRG _____
Relative Weight _____
Reimbursement _____

Reviewer DRG _____   Difference _____
Relative Weight _____
Reimbursement _____   Dictation: H&P: _____ D/C Summary: _____

From Sue Prophet. 1999. *Health Information Management Compliance.* Chicago: American Health Information Management Association.

The Record Method

The record method of calculating errors considers each health record coded incorrectly as one error. The advantages of the record method include that it:

- Allows for benchmarking with other hospitals that frequently use this method

- Permits the reviewer to track errors by case type

- Enables the reviewer to relate productivity with quality errors on a case-by-case basis

The disadvantages of this method include that it:

- Oversimplifies the type of health records coded by not identifying the coder's ability to identify codes that must be reported

- Does not identify the number of secondary diagnoses or procedures missed by the coder

The Code Method

The code method of calculating errors compares the total number of codes identified by the coder with the total number of possible codes that should have been coded. The advantages of the code method include that it:

- Recognizes the coder's ability to identify all codes that require reporting

- Weighs by code the more resource-intensive cases

- Permits better diagnostic results in terms of the kinds of errors the coder is making, such as omission of secondary diagnoses, missed sequencing, and so on

The disadvantages of this method include that it:

- Is difficult to compare results with benchmarking activities of other organizations that do not use this method

- Does not identify the specific coding problems of individual coders, thus making it difficult to assess educational needs of coders

It is important that the HIM department compare the accuracy of coders as individuals and as a group, as well as comparing accuracy by type of case and DRG. These comparisons will assist the management team in identifying corrective actions to implement, such as:

- Education or training for the coding staff

- Information for the clinical staff to improve documentation

Reviewing of Abstracts and Bills

Abstracts and bills should also be included in the inpatient review when the corresponding health records are being reviewed for coding. The reviewer should print and attach a copy of the abstract to the coding review worksheet. Then, the reviewer should identify and correct abstracting errors.

Completing the Inpatient Review

When the inpatient audit or review has been completed to this point and a final UB-92 has been printed, the reviewer should compare all the diagnoses and procedures printed on the bill with the coded information in the health record system. This will identify whether the communication software between the health record system and the billing system is functioning correctly. The HIM department should share the results of this comparison with the patient accounting department.

When the inpatient audit has been completed, the manager of the management team should determine how the findings will be shared individually with each coder and with the group of coders. Findings may indicate that documentation issues, coding policy, and procedure changes should be made and that educational programs are needed for the coding staff. Individual audit results by coder should become part of the individual employee's performance evaluation.

Reviewing Outpatient Coding

The HIM department should consider reviewing or auditing health records after coding but before billing, rather than performing a retrospective review after claims have been submitted for payment. This issue should be settled with the compliance department during the planning stage of the data quality improvement program.

Selecting the Sample for an Outpatient Review

If a review or audit is being conducted following the provision of services, coding managers can pull health records for outpatient review by using the outpatient database from the HIM system abstracts. If random sampling is used, the coding manager should request that coders hold all cases for review and selection. If a list of patients is used, the coding manager should pull every fifth case (or some other number).

If an outpatient database is not available, the coding manager can develop a sample from a surgery schedule (for a prospective review) or from outpatient remittance advice listings (for a retrospective review). The sample size and its composition, such as ambulatory surgery, endoscopy, clinic visits, or emergency room, should be based on the percentage of business each component represents. For example, if 55 percent of outpatient business is through the ambulatory surgery department, then the sample selected should include 55 percent of ambulatory surgery cases.

The sample size will also vary depending on the type of review, the size of the hospital, the number of coders to be included, compliance requirements for the sampling, and the number and type of outpatient discharges. (See chapter 8, Compliance Issues, on sampling for corporate compliance.) For an initial baseline review, the HIM manager could do sample selection. The best method of sample selection might be to pull a random sample of cases by volume and average charges. For a focused review, the coding manager might have to develop specific reports. If all outpatient cases are in the abstracting system, the manager may select cases by using a CPT code range or specific groups of CPT codes.

Focused Outpatient Reviews

The HIM department can plan focused outpatient reviews based on specific problem areas after the initial baseline review has been completed. Some potential problem coding areas for focused outpatient reviews include the following:

- Modifier use

- Emergency room use of modifier -25

- Podiatry procedures

- Cardiac catheterizations

- The top twenty-five APC groups by volume and charges

- Procedure and diagnoses codes by surgery subsection of CPT

Topics for focused reviews may also be based on:

- Problematic coding issues identified in *CPT Assistant*

- Recent data quality issues identified by external review agencies

- Discussions of outpatient coding issues presented in journals or newsletters

Forms Used in the Outpatient Review

During the review, forms are used to track outpatient health records, to identify individual variations, and to monitor the types of variations made by individual coders. A form should be completed for each health record included in the sample. Examples of suggested forms are provided in figures 7.3 and 7.5.

How Each Outpatient Health Record Is Reviewed

To begin the review, the reviewer checks each outpatient health record for the types of ICD-9-CM diagnoses and procedures previously described in the subhead Focused Outpatient Reviews. As a reference, the reviewer should use outpatient coding guidelines. For operative procedures, the reviewer must review the entire operative report to ensure that all appropriate codes were identified and that modifiers were added as needed.

In addition, the reviewer should run, if available, the most recent version of the Medicare outpatient code editor (OCE) on a sample of the health records. In this way, National Correct Coding Initiative (NCCI) edits, revenue code errors, and modifier errors that may have been overlooked will be identified.

Calculating Errors from the Outpatient Review

When all health records in the sample have been reviewed, the results and errors must be summarized for all health records and for individual coders. As in inpatient reviews, the same two methods of calculating errors—the record method and the code method—are used in outpatient reviews.

It is important that the HIM department compare the accuracy of coders as individuals and as a group, as well as comparing accuracy by type of case and APC. These comparisons will assist the management team in identifying the following corrective actions to implement:

- Education or training for the coding staff

- Information for the clinical staff to improve documentation

Figure 7.5.   Rebilling summary/coding change

Name: _____   Age: _____   Adm: _____

MR #: _____   Sex: _____   Disch: _____

Acct #: _____   MD: _____   Facility: _____

HIC #: _____   Dispos: _____   LOS: _____

Original Codes — Diagnosis

1. _____
2. _____
3. _____
4. _____
5. _____
6. _____
7. _____
8. _____
9. _____
10. _____

Revised Codes — Diagnosis

1. _____
2. _____
3. _____
4. _____
5. _____
6. _____
7. _____
8. _____
9. _____
10. _____

Operative Codes

1. _____
2. _____
3. _____
4. _____
5. _____
6. _____

Operative Codes

1. _____
2. _____
3. _____
4. _____
5. _____
6. _____

Disposition Code: _____

CPT Codes

1. _____
2. _____
3. _____
4. _____
5. _____
6. _____

CPT Codes

1. _____
2. _____
3. _____
4. _____
5. _____
6. _____

The above account/record has been identified to have a coding change. Please rebill with the revised codes as soon as possible. If you have any questions please contact: A. ABCDEF@ 111-222-3333.

Date rebilled: _____

Return this form to the HIM Department once rebill has been processed. THANK YOU

From Sue Prophet. 1999. *Health Information Management Compliance.* Chicago: American Health Information Management Association.

Reviewing of Abstracts and Bills

Abstracts and bills should also be included in the outpatient review when the corresponding health records are being reviewed for coding. The reviewer should print and attach a copy of the abstract and the outpatient encounter form, if used, to the coding review worksheet. (See sample worksheets in figures 7.1 through 7.4.) Then, the reviewer should identify and correct abstracting errors.

Completing the Outpatient Review

When the outpatient review has been completed to this point and a final UB-92 has been printed, the reviewer should compare the diagnoses/procedures printed on the bill with the coded information in the health record system. This will identify whether the communication software between the health record system and the billing system is functioning correctly. The HIM department should share the results of this comparison with the patient accounting department.

When the outpatient audit has been completed, the manager of the management team should determine how the findings will be shared individually with each coder and with the group of coders. Findings may indicate that documentation issues, coding policy, and procedure changes should be made and that educational programs are needed for the coding staff. Individual audit results by coder should become part of the individual employee's performance evaluation.

The Payment Error Prevention Program

The Payment Error Prevention Program (PEPP) is an external involuntary monitoring program (TMF 2000). PEPP is an important part of a broad-based CMS initiative to reduce payment errors and to protect Medicare funds. CMS has charged state peer review organizations (PROs) with the responsibility of implementing PEPP. PEPP is being phased in nationwide to correspond with each PRO's contract period. There are three cycles of contract periods for PROs. Each cycle lasts three years.

PEPP's Purpose

The mission of PEPP is to reduce Medicare PPS inpatient hospital payment errors at the national and state levels. Medicare program audits in general indicate that payment errors occur for the following reasons:

- Lack of documentation to support diagnoses and treatments billed

- Coding inaccuracies

- Inappropriate care

- Care rendered in the wrong setting

PEPP will initially focus on several of these areas that contribute to payment errors, such as:

- Medically unnecessary admissions and procedures

- Prevalent DRG coding errors

- DRG upcoding

- Preadmissions due to incomplete care or premature discharge

- Inappropriate transfers

- Other billing errors that affect payment, such as billing to the wrong provider number

Since 1995, CMS has used two specialized contractors called clinical data abstraction centers (CDACs). These contractors validate DRGs on annual national samples of Medicare claims. As part of PEPP, the CDACs have been charged with the responsibility of initially screening a random sample of health records from every state. The CDACs are currently screening approximately 92 health records per month, or 1,100 records per year, for each state. The CDACs then forward health records that fail the screening criteria to the PRO for review.

The Role of PROs in PEPP

The PROs will conduct a full review of each health record that fails the initial CDAC review. If a fully reviewed health record shows a confirmed payment error, the PRO will notify the FI that will make the adjustment. Those adjustments will correct both overpayments and under-payments made to hospitals by Medicare. Based on PRO review results for the health records, a national baseline payment error rate and a baseline payment error rate for each state will be calculated.

To determine potential problem areas that occur at the local level, the PROs will also analyze their own state-specific discharge data. Each PRO will be responsible for the following activities:

- Profiling discharge data to identify problem areas and to target potential payment errors

- Selecting medical records for data collection/health record review to confirm suspected payment errors

- Requesting improvement plans from hospitals when error patterns are identified

- Monitoring the success of the plans through profiling and additional review as appropriate

PROs will also work to reduce payment errors on a statewide basis by providing educational programs on specific topics to solve problems that affect all hospitals.

Evaluating PEPP

CMS will evaluate the effectiveness of PEPP by remeasuring the payment error rate and by comparing the new error rate with baseline data both nationally and for each state. This evaluation will occur at specific intervals throughout the program. It should be emphasized that a PRO's performance will not be assessed on dollars saved. Rather, it will be based on reduction of payment errors—both overpayment errors and underpayment errors.

Findings from the PEPP reviews at the individual hospital level should be addressed through the corporate compliance department. Appeals for those findings should be handled according to corporate compliance policies and procedures. HIM departments can use the results of the national and state PEPP monitoring activities as benchmarks for ongoing internal data quality improvement.

Using External Coding Consultants as Independent Quality Review Resources

The decision to request an external data quality evaluation can be made within the HIM department by the facility's executives or by the finance department. Regardless of the source of the decision, the process of bringing in an external auditor or reviewer can sometimes be lengthy. However, using external coding consultants as reviewers can bring a fresh perspective to the facility's coding function.

Types of Coding Consultants

A variety of coding consultants is available to assist with the evaluation of both inpatient and outpatient coding. These consultants can come from one of the following types of firms:

- Small firms that provide specialized types of reviews
- Larger firms that offer full-service accounts receivable and HIM evaluations
- Certified public accounting firms that work closely with the finance department

The Advantages of Using External Consultants

Using external coding consultants to review inpatient and outpatient coding processes has the following advantages:

- They provide an independent opinion.
- They are often more up-to-date on coding regulations and guidelines than internal coding staff because they can devote the necessary time to those activities.
- They can verify that the quality of the facility's coded data is as high as possible.
- They do not feel the pressure that the coding staff does from the facility's finance department.
- They can critically evaluate the coding function and the quality of coded data because they are not involved in the facility's coding operation.
- The facility's coding staff can learn new techniques for evaluating data quality as a result of the external review.

Preparing a Request for Proposal

When a department in the healthcare facility has made the decision to conduct an external coding evaluation, the department manager must prepare a request for proposal (RFP). The RFP should define the facility's expectations, guide vendors in their responses, and clarify the facility's needs and objectives. An RFP has two major sections: a technical proposal section and a business proposal section.

The Technical Section of the RFP

The technical section of the RFP contains the following basic components:

- Cover letter, which introduces the facility, identifies its interest in procuring consulting services, and, in some instances, contains the entire technical proposal section

- Statement of the project's purpose, which identifies the exact nature of the project

- Definition of objectives, which specifically and clearly addresses the nature of the facility's needs

- Scope of work, which delineates the type of review that the facility wishes to have completed

- Delivery orders, which include the following information:

  —Profile of requesting facility, which provides a detailed description of the types of services offered by the facility and the details about which services are to be included in the work, volume statistics, and perhaps payer information by volume or percentage of services

  —Functional/technical requirements, including the type of encoder/grouper the facility may require the consultant to use

  —Training requirements needed by consultants to be eligible for consideration

  —Deliverables, or a listing of those products expected at the end of the evaluation

  —Request for references from previous clients with projects similar to the proposal

  —Conditions of bidding, which includes how bids will be accepted or conditions that will result in the bid being rejected, nondiscrimination clause, performance and default clauses, collusive bidding clauses, implementation team, and the closing date for bids

The Business Section of the RFP

The business section of the RFP includes the following components:

- The cost statement

- Limitations

- Contract terms for payment, liability insurance, confidentiality, and so on

Results from Using a Consultant

When the audit has been concluded, the hospital should expect a final report from the consultant or consulting firm that includes the following:

- The findings with statistics as appropriate to the type of audit performed

- Identification of specific results of the audit in a table or other organized format with variations shown on a case-by-case basis

- Recommendations for improving both coding and documentation

- The overall impact of the review and its implications for the organization

In addition, the consultants should:

- Provide a summary of the coding and documentation issues identified in the audit through educational sessions for the coding and clinical staffs

- Present an executive summary of the audit's major findings during an exit conference with the management team

Conclusion

The increased need for coded data in all areas of healthcare delivery and reimbursement has brought about a corresponding need for data quality monitoring and evaluation programs in healthcare organizations. Auditing and review activities are performed in both inpatient and outpatient settings to ensure the highest levels of coding accuracy and efficiency among coding staff. Ensuring the accuracy of coded data is a shared responsibility between HIM professionals and clinicians (AHIMA 1996).

With the implementation of PEPP, quality control of coded data is now a mandated effort through which the federal government intends to reduce payment errors and to protect Medicare funds. Maintaining data quality is an ongoing effort that affects many aspects of the current healthcare environment but that relies primarily on the commitment and the expertise of today's HIM professionals.

References and Bibliography

American Health Information Management Association. 1996. Practice Brief: Data quality. *Journal of the American Health Information Management Association* 67(2).

Texas Medical Foundation. 2000. *Payment Error Prevention Program (PEPP) Compliance Workbook*. Austin, Tex.: Texas Medical Foundation.

Appendix 7.1

Practice Brief: Data Quality

Background

Complete and accurate diagnostic and procedural coded data is necessary for research, epidemiology, outcomes and statistical analyses, financial and strategic planning, reimbursement, evaluation of quality of care, and communication to support the patient's treatment. Upon the implementation of an inpatient prospective payment system, Medicare and several other payers required physicians to attest to the accuracy of the diagnoses and procedures being reported on inpatient claims prior to billing. The administrative burden of this requirement was recently deemed far greater than its success in preventing fraud and abuse, and thus the attestation requirement was eliminated. However, the loss of this requirement does not mean the need for accurate coded data has diminished.

To the contrary, the quality of healthcare data is more critical than ever before. Adherence to approved coding principles that generate coded data of the highest quality remains important. In this new era of clinical data management, health information professionals must continue to meet the challenges of maintaining an accurate and meaningful database reflective of patient mix and resource use. As long as diagnostic and procedural coding serves as the basis for payment methodologies, the ethics of clinical coders will be challenged. Assuring accuracy of coded data is a shared responsibility between health information management professionals and clinicians. The HIM professional continues to have the unique responsibility of assessing and coding clinical data. Within their organizations, health information management professionals translate clinical information into coded data and then evaluate, analyze, and maintain its accuracy, validity, and meaningfulness. Health information professionals are responsible for the achievement and maintenance of data of the highest quality.

Clinical Collaboration

The Joint Commission on Accreditation of Healthcare Organizations and the Medicare Conditions of Participation require final diagnoses and procedures to be recorded in the medical record and authenticated by the responsible practitioner. Physician documentation, in its entirety, is the cornerstone of accurate coding. Meaningful diagnostic and procedural coded data originate from the collaboration between clinicians with extensive clinical experience and coding professionals with comprehensive classification systems expertise. Elimination of the attestation requirement does not mean the end to this collaboration, but rather a continued opportunity for dialogue and communication. Clinical documentation from which the coded data is derived continues to rely on information provided by healthcare practitioners. More than ever before, healthcare providers rely on coded clinical data for financial viability. Thus, the need for collaboration, cooperation, and communication between clinicians and coders continues to grow.

Clinical Database Evaluation

Ongoing evaluation of the clinical database may assure that ethical reporting of clinical information occurs. Regular evaluation of the quality of the database provides evidence that the clinical data remains consistent with standards of ethical coding practice. Evaluation can be conducted by diagnosis-related group (DRG), pertinent clinical issues, high dollar cases, high volume DRGs, or particular diagnoses or procedures. The diagnosis and procedure codes should be reviewed to ensure the accuracy of coding, appropriate sequencing, and clinical pertinence. Reporting review results to administration and the medical staff increases their awareness of coded data quality issues within the facility.

Recommendations

The coding professional should:

- Thoroughly review the entire medical record as part of the coding process in order to assign and report the most appropriate codes

- Adhere to all official coding guidelines as approved by the Cooperating Parties[1]

- Observe sequencing rules identified by the Cooperating Parties[1]

- Select the principal diagnosis and procedure according to UHDDS definitions[2]

- Assign and report codes, without physician consultation, to diagnoses and procedures not stated in the physician's final diagnosis only if these diagnoses and procedures are specifically documented by the physician in the body of the medical record and this documentation is clear and consistent

- Utilize medical record documentation to provide coding specificity without obtaining physician concurrence (such as utilizing the radiology report to identify the fracture site)

- Maintain a positive working relationship with physicians through ongoing communication and open dialogue

The coding professional should not:

- Add diagnosis codes solely based on test results

- Misrepresent the patient's clinical picture through incorrect coding or add diagnoses/ procedures unsupported by the documentation in order to maximize reimbursement or meet insurance policy coverage requirements

- Report diagnoses and procedures that the physician has specifically indicated he/she does not support

As the need for coded data of the highest quality continues to grow, HIM professionals need to build and develop their role as clinical data managers. In order to achieve this end, coder education in the areas of anatomy and physiology, medical terminology, disease pathology, pharmacology, and laboratory studies, as well as classification and reimbursement systems, should be encouraged. Dialogue between health information professionals and clinicians should also be encouraged, as it improves coder clinical competency and educates the clinician on documentation practice issues.

Additional Recommendations in the Absence of Physician Attestation

The coding professional should:

- Assess physician documentation to assure that it supports the diagnosis and procedure codes selected

- Consult the physician for clarification when conflicting or ambiguous documentation is present; ask the physician to add information to the record before assigning a code that is not supported by documentation

- Provide the physician the opportunity to review reported diagnoses and procedures on pre- or post-bill submission, via mechanisms such as:

  —providing a copy (via mail, fax, or electronic transmission) of the sequenced codes and their narrative descriptions

  —placing the diagnostic and procedural listing within the record and bringing it to the physician's attention

- Revise the codes if the physician disagrees with code selection

- Offer coding and classification system education to any and all clinicians (e.g., provide pertinent official coding guidelines)

- Develop institutional coding policies in the absence of official guidelines

Notes:

1. American Hospital Association; American Health Information Management Association; Health Care Financing Administration; National Center for Health Statistics.

2. Uniform Data Discharge Set.

Prepared by:
Coding Policy and Strategy Committee

Reviewed by:
Society for Clinical Coding

Appendix 7.2

Standards for Ethical Coding

The Standards for Ethical Coding were presented and approved at the April 1991 meeting of the AHIMA Board of Directors and revised in December 1999. These standards were developed by the Council on Coding and Classification to give health information coding professionals ethical guidelines for performing their task. A conscientious goal for coding and maintaining a quality database is accurate clinical and statistical data. The following standards of ethical coding, developed by AHIMA's Coding Policy and Strategy Committee and approved by AHIMA's Board of Directors, are offered to guide coding professionals in this process.

1. Coding professionals are expected to support the importance of accurate, complete, and consistent coding practices for the production of quality healthcare data.

2. Coding professionals in all healthcare settings should adhere to the ICD-9-CM (International Classification of Diseases, 9th revision, Clinical Modification) coding conventions, official coding guidelines approved by the Cooperating Parties,* the CPT (Current Procedural Terminology) rules established by the American Medical Association, and any other official coding rules and guidelines established for use with mandated standard code sets. Selection and sequencing of diagnoses and procedures must meet the definitions of required data sets for applicable healthcare settings.

3. Coding professionals should use their skills, their knowledge of currently mandated coding and classification systems, and official resources to select the appropriate diagnostic and procedural codes.

4. Coding professionals should only assign and report codes that are clearly and consistently supported by physician documentation in the health record.

5. Coding professionals should consult physicians for clarification and additional documentation prior to code assignment when there is conflicting or ambiguous data in the health record.

6. Coding professionals should not change codes or the narratives of codes on the billing abstract so that meanings are misrepresented. Diagnoses or procedures should not be inappropriately included or excluded because payment or insurance policy coverage requirements will be affected. When individual payer policies conflict with official coding rules and guidelines, these policies should be obtained in writing whenever possible. Reasonable efforts should be made to educate the payer on proper coding practices in order to influence a change in the payer's policy.

7. Coding professionals, as members of the healthcare team, should assist and educate physicians and other clinicians by advocating proper documentation practices, further specificity, and resequencing or inclusion of diagnoses or procedures when needed to more accurately reflect the acuity, severity, and the occurrence of events.

---

*The Cooperating Parties are the American Health Information Management Association, American Hospital Association, Health Care Financing Administration, and National Center for Health Statistics. All rights reserved. Reprint and quote only with proper reference to AHIMA's authorship.

8. Coding professionals should participate in the development of institutional coding policies and should ensure that coding policies complement, not conflict with, official coding rules and guidelines.

9. Coding professionals should maintain and continually enhance their coding skills, as they have a professional responsibility to stay abreast of changes in codes, coding guidelines, and regulations.

10. Coding professionals should strive for optimal payment to which the facility is legally entitled, remembering that it is unethical and illegal to maximize payment by means that contradict regulatory guidelines.

Revised 12/99

Appendix 7.3

PEPP Audit Tool for Coding

Preparation

1. Prior to reviewing a group of cases with similar diagnoses and procedures, review related coding conventions and guidelines.

2. Identify possible coding problems that can occur.

Record/Claim Review (Document findings below)

	Yes	No
1. Does the medical record:		
a. match the claim being reviewed (patient name/admission date);	___	___
b. contain an inpatient admission order for the date of admission and the level of care billed; and	___	___
c. match the provider and number billed, e.g., PPS versus non-PPS?	___	___
2. Is medical record documentation present to substantiate the principal diagnosis as:		
a. present on admission	___	___
b. a principal reason for admission; and	___	___
c. treated or evaluated during the stay?	___	___
3. Is medical record documentation present to support diagnoses and complications/comorbidities billed?	___	___
4. Are there any secondary diagnoses or complications/comorbidities that are supported by medical record documentation and affect the DRG but were not billed?	___	___
5. Is medical record documentation present to support procedures billed?	___	___
6. Are there any procedures that are supported by medical record documentation and affect the DRG but were not billed?	___	___
7. Is medical record documentation present to support the patient's age and discharge status?	___	___
8. Are there any other coding errors? Note problem area below:	___	___

  a. _____ Code does not match diagnosis/procedure

  b. _____ Code lacks specificity

  c. _____ Sequencing is incorrect

  d. _____ Coding does not follow ICD-9-CM coding conventions

  e. _____ Coding does not follow *Coding Clinic* guidelines

Findings

Billed Diagnostic Codes	Supported by Medical Record (X if yes)	Not Supported by Medical Record (X if no)	Coded Correctly Yes/No	If Not Supported Note Problems
Principal			/	
Secondary			/	
			/	
			/	
			/	
			/	
			/	
			/	
			/	
			/	
Billed Procedure Codes			/	
			/	
			/	
			/	
			/	
			/	
			/	
Billed Discharge Status			/	

DRG: _____

Review of Possible Problems/Regrouping Codes

1. When necessary, refer to the physician for clarification.

2. Code and regroup to determine if changes affect the DRG. Note discharge date _____ / age _____ / gender _____.

Revised Diagnosis Codes Principal	Narrative
Secondary	
Revised Procedure Codes	
Discharge Status	

DRG: _____

3.   Does coding affect the DRG?   Yes _____   No _____

4.   Identify the cause of any DRG change.

   _____ Principal diagnosis not present at admission
   _____ Principal diagnosis not treated/evaluated during stay
   _____ Principal diagnosis not principal reason for hospitalization
   _____ Secondary diagnosis or complication/comorbidity billed but not substantiated
   _____ Secondary diagnosis or complication/comorbidity substantiated in record but not
            billed and it changes the DRG
   _____ Procedure omitted from claim
   _____ Procedure billed but not substantiated in record
   _____ Procedure determined to be medically unnecessary and must be removed from
            the DRG
   _____ Disposition status is incorrect and it changes the DRG
   _____ Patient's age is incorrect and it changes the DRG
   _____ Correct diagnosis or procedure is incorrectly coded
   _____ Other _____

5.   If a DRG change occurred, note the following:

Original DRG   _____   Revised DRG   _____

Reimbursement _____   Reimbursement _____

Problems Identified

_____
_____
_____
_____
_____
_____
_____
_____

Recommendations

_____
_____
_____
_____
_____
_____
_____
_____
_____

Auditor _____   Date _____

Chapter 8

Compliance Issues

Cheryl L. Hammen, RHIT

In 1995, the federal government began intensive efforts to identify abusive and fraudulent healthcare claims through various initiatives. As it became evident that healthcare compliance was here to stay, healthcare providers began implementing internal compliance programs with a major focus on coding and billing activities. These programs were developed based on *Compliance Program Guidance* issued by the Office of Inspector General (OIG) of the Department of Health and Human Services (DHHS).

Health information managers responsible for coding functions recognized an opportunity to become a resource for their facilities. They took the lead in identifying areas of compliance risk that are associated with billing, monitoring these areas and implementing corrective action when necessary. The development of HIM compliance programs to support the facility's compliance program became the norm in hospitals across the country. Steps taken by these innovative leaders are presented in this chapter to provide guidance in ensuring an efficient and effective compliance program.

Healthcare Fraud and Abuse

Healthcare fraud is a deception or misrepresentation by a provider, or by a representative of a provider, that may result in a false or fictitious claim for inappropriate payment by Medicare or other insurers for items or services either not rendered or rendered to a lesser extent than that described in the claim. In other words, healthcare fraud is the submission of a claim for payment of items or services that the person knew, or should have known, were not provided.

Healthcare abuse consists of practices that are inconsistent with generally accepted fiscal, business, or professional practices. Such unacceptable practices result in unnecessary costs to Medicare or to other third-party payers because they are not considered medically necessary, or they fail to meet recognized medical standards of care.

Optimization of Coding

Optimization generally refers to the procedure or procedures used to make a system or design as effective or functional as possible. When coders "optimize" the coding process, they attempt to make coding for reimbursement as accurate as possible. In this way, the healthcare facility can obtain the highest dollar amount justified within the terms of the government program or the insurance policy involved.

Methods for optimization of coding and subsequent reimbursement began appearing shortly after the implementation of DRGs because hospitals wanted to make sure they obtained the highest possible reimbursement for each inpatient case. Hospitals wanted to ensure that not only all applicable codes, but also the codes providing the best payment appeared on claim forms. A number of optimization tools were developed by hospitals and vendors to meet that objective. These tools include tips in reviewing specific DRGs provided in book form, as well as software programs that "alert" coders to potential optimization opportunities.

Some software programs prompt coding staff or physicians to consider codes that might apply and point out those codes that might pay better. These programs are misused when code selection is based solely upon which code pays the most, rather than which code or codes most accurately reflect the services delivered. The express intent of most optimization tools, however, is not to cheat insurance plans out of benefits. A valid optimization tool provides the information required to ensure accurate and complete coding. It also provides the user with assistance in selecting the best codes to reflect the clinical circumstances.

Legitimate optimization is achieved through several methods:

- Improving documentation or access to documentation for better coding

- Providing educational programs for coders, clinicians, billers, and claims processing personnel to improve awareness of coding guidelines

- Making use of computer software edits, reminders, and automated assistance

- Reviewing claims to ensure appropriate coding for deserved payments

Clinical coding directly affects the amount of payment a facility receives from a payer. Individual coders sometimes tend to take an overly conservative approach to coding because they fear allegations of fraudulent or abusive billing practices by the government or others. Entire organizations have sometimes taken this route as a matter of policy. However, neither overly aggressive coding nor overly conservative coding ultimately benefits the organization, either from a financial perspective or from a compliance perspective.

Government Legislation and Initiatives

Since 1995, several federal initiatives and pieces of legislation related to investigating, identifying, and preventing healthcare fraud and abuse have been passed. The more notable ones are described in the following subheads. They provide background material for understanding the magnitude of fraud and abuse in the mid-1990s and the necessary steps taken to ensure reclamation of inappropriate funds to assist in the continuation of Medicare and Medicaid.

Civil False Claims Act

The Civil False Claims Act was passed during the Civil War. It was an effort to avoid false claims by government contractors for services billed but not provided and for items misrepresented in billing. The act was updated in 1986. Later, it was reinforced through the passage of the Health Insurance Portability and Accountability Act (HIPAA) in 1996 and by the Balanced Budget Act of 1997.

Qui tam, or whistle-blowing, legislation has been widely used in the application of the Civil False Claims Act in battling healthcare fraud and abuse. Qui tam legislation refers to a person acting on behalf of the government, although benefiting individually from a successful action. Anyone—a healthcare employee, a competitor, or a patient—may file a lawsuit alleging that there has been a violation of the Civil False Claims Act through the submission of false claims to Medicare, Medicaid, or other federally funded programs.

Successful false claims actions may result in the whistle-blower receiving an award of 15 to 30 percent of the monies recovered. However, seldom does a successful action result in a significant seven-figure award.

Health Insurance Portability and Accountability Act

A major portion of the Health Insurance Portability and Accountability Act (HIPAA), passed in 1996, focused on identifying healthcare fraud and abuse. Areas such as medically unnecessary services, upcoding, unbundling, and billing for services not provided were targeted.

Upcoding is the practice of using a code that results in a higher payment to the provider than the code that actually reflects the service or item provided. **Unbundling** is the practice of using multiple codes that describe individual steps of a procedure rather than an appropriate single code that describes all steps of the comprehensive procedure performed.

Title II of HIPAA mandated the establishment of fraud and abuse control programs to battle healthcare fraud and abuse. Monies were appropriated to fund those programs, and agencies were identified to participate in the government's efforts. Additionally, the Medicare Integrity Program was established. This program was charged with the following responsibilities, among others:

- Review of provider activities for potential fraudulent activity

- Audit of cost reports

- Payment determinations

- Education of providers and beneficiaries on healthcare fraud and abuse issues

Beneficiary incentive programs also were implemented. Those programs encourage Medicare beneficiaries to review their providers' bills carefully and to report any discrepancies to the secretary of DHHS. Beneficiaries also were encouraged to provide suggestions on improving the efficiency of the Medicare program.

HIPAA clarified the application of healthcare fraud and abuse sanctions to include all federal healthcare programs. The act provided guidance on the use of these sanctions, including criteria for modifying or establishing safe harbors and for the issuance of advisory opinions and special fraud alerts. Also included in the act were revisions to previous sanctions related to:

- Mandatory exclusion from Medicare

- Length of exclusion

- Failure to comply with statutory obligations

- Antikickback penalties

- Penalties for disposing of assets in order to gain Medicaid benefits

In response to a HIPAA mandate, data are currently being collected on healthcare providers who have received final adverse actions as the result of fraud and abuse investigation. Data elements to be collected were defined as part of the act. This database continues to be updated on a monthly basis with exclusions and reinstatements.

As a result of this legislation, many agencies began "partnering" to investigate fraud and abuse in the healthcare environment. This included federal, state, and private-sector organizations. Various agencies responsible for investigating and prosecuting healthcare fraud and abuse, such as the Federal Bureau of Investigation (FBI), experienced significant staff increases.

In complying with HIPAA legislation, Congress budgeted $120 million in 1998 to the DHHS OIG, CMS, the FBI, the Department of Justice (DOJ), and State Medicaid Fraud Control Units. In addition, the Administration on Aging (AOA) provided funding through grants.

Balanced Budget Act of 1997

Title IV, Subtitle D, Chapters 1 and 2 of the Balanced Budget Act (BBA) of 1997 focused on healthcare fraud and abuse issues, especially as they related to penalties. The circumstances under which civil money penalties are applied were based on the BBA. Those circumstances include entities that contract with excluded individuals and persons involved with healthcare industry kickbacks.

As a part of the BBA, the following penalties were implemented and are applied to entities that receive monies from federal healthcare programs and are convicted of healthcare-related crimes:

- First offense—Five years

- Second offense—Minimum of ten years

- Third offense—Permanent exclusion

The right of the secretary of DHHS to refuse to enter into Medicare agreements with those entities convicted of a felony under federal or state law is included in the BBA. Medicare's right to refuse to enter into an agreement with a provider convicted of a felony was extended beyond the individual provider to include family members in control of the entity when ownership or controlling interest was transferred in anticipation of adverse government actions.

Initiatives resulting from mandates in the BBA to improve program integrity included:

- Notifying beneficiaries of their right to request copies of detailed bills for healthcare services received

- Advising beneficiaries to review explanations of benefit and detailed bills for errors and to report these errors to the secretary of DHHS

- Initiating the data collection program, as mandated in HIPAA, to collect information on healthcare fraud and abuse

- Implementing a toll-free fraud-and-abuse hotline by DHHS

Other mandates for improving program integrity included requirements for disclosure of specific information by certain providers wishing to obtain or maintain their participation in the Medicare program. These requirements include those for disclosure of information and the provision of surety bonds by durable medical equipment suppliers and home health agencies. Limited application of these requirements applies to comprehensive outpatient rehabilitation facilities (CORFs) and other rehabilitation agencies.

The use of advisory opinions by DHHS to provide information on the prohibition of certain referrals was explained, as was the replacement of reasonable charge methodology with the use of fee schedules for some services.

Requirements for diagnostic information from physicians and nonphysician practitioners to determine medical necessity for certain items and services provided by another entity can be found in Section 4317 (b) (an amendment to Section 1842 (p) of 42 USC 1395u(p) of the BBA), which states:

> In the case of an item or service defined in paragraph (3), (6), (8), or (9) of subsection 1861(s) ordered by a physician or a practitioner specified in subsection (b)(18)(C), but furnished by another entity, if the Secretary (or fiscal agent of the Secretary) requires the entity furnishing the item or service to provide diagnostic or other medical information in order for payment to be made to the entity, the physician or practitioner shall provide that information to the entity at the time that the item or service is ordered by the physician or practitioner.

This is an important amendment because it relates to HIM departments and their documentation efforts to obtain diagnoses for outpatient services prior to the performance of those services. This information has recently been clarified by CMS in Transmittal A-01-61, which can be accessed at the CMS Web site, <http://www.cms.gov>.

Operation Restore Trust

Operation Restore Trust began in 1995 as a joint effort of the DHHS OIG, CMS, and AOA to target fraud and abuse in healthcare services. The program initially began in five states (California, Illinois, Florida, New York, and Texas), representing one-third of the nation's Medicare and Medicaid population.

Interdisciplinary teams of federal, state, and private-sector representatives investigated and audited healthcare providers. These teams identified new approaches for conducting healthcare investigations and audits, including using statistical surveys, working with DOJ, and training state organizations to detect and report potential fraud for further investigation.

Eventually, Operation Restore Trust expanded to other states across the country. This program focused on identifying fraud and abuse related to home healthcare services, nursing home services, and the provision of durable medical equipment and supplies. These efforts led to the implementation of a national toll-free fraud-and-abuse hotline, which enabled tipsters to call and report potentially fraudulent activity on the part of healthcare providers. Operation Restore Trust also led to the implementation of another initiative—the Voluntary Disclosure Program—and to the use of special fraud alerts based on audit and investigative findings.

In its first two years, Operation Restore Trust spent only $7.9 million to identify $188 million in overpayments to providers—a 23-to-1 return on investment. The monies overpaid have been attributed to criminal restitution and fines; civil judgments, settlements, and fines; and inappropriately billed or medically unnecessary services.

OIG Compliance Program Guidance

Over the past several years, the OIG has published several site-of-service documents to help providers develop internal compliance programs that include the seven elements for ensuring compliance as outlined in the U.S. Sentencing Guidelines in 1991:

1. Written policies and procedures

2. Designation of a compliance officer

3. Education and training

4. Communication

5. Auditing and monitoring

6. Disciplinary action

7. Corrective action

Compliance Program Guidance for Clinical Laboratories

The first OIG site-of-service document, *Compliance Program Guidance for Clinical Laboratories,* addressed clinical laboratories. It was first released in February 1997, then again in August 1998 as a revision to reflect CMS policy and the format provided in *Compliance Program Guidance for Hospitals,* which was released in February 1998.

Billing activities in the policies and procedures section of this document are specific to documentation and coding issues. The document instructs laboratories to ensure that codes accurately reflect the services provided. It further instructs them to consider technical expert review to ensure accuracy. Information is provided related to the requirement for accompanying ICD-9-CM diagnosis codes to ensure medical necessity and, therefore, coverage for the procedure performed.

Compliance Program Guidance for Clinical Laboratories instructs clinical laboratories *not* to do the following:

- *Not* to use diagnostic information from earlier dates of service

- *Not* to use cheat sheets for assigning reimbursable codes

- *Not* to use computer programs that automatically insert diagnosis codes without documentation from the physician

- *Not* to make up diagnostic information for claims

Compliance Program Guidance instructs clinical laboratories *to do* the following:

- Contact the ordering physician if diagnostic documentation has not been obtained prior to the encounter

- Provide services and diagnostic information for standing orders in connection with an extended course of treatment

- Accurately translate narrative diagnoses into ICD-9-CM codes

It is preferred that physicians provide only a narrative diagnosis with the laboratory ensuring the appropriate diagnostic code assignment.

Compliance Program Guidance for Hospitals

Compliance Program Guidance for Hospitals was released by the OIG in February 1998. Many of the risk areas outlined in this document are related to coding issues, such as:

- Billing for items or services not actually rendered

- Upcoding

- Outpatient services rendered in connection with inpatient stays (72-hour window rule)

- Unbundling

- Billing for discharge instead of transfer

- DRG creep, assigning a code resulting in a DRG with a higher payment rate than that supported by the documentation in the health record

The presence of health record documentation plays a major role in ensuring complete and accurate coding for billing purposes based on the content of this document. The guidance provides for the creation of a mechanism to ensure communication between the coders/billers and the clinical staff to achieve complete and accurate documentation before coding or billing is completed. The Official Coding Guidelines are listed in the guidance as the applicable regulations for coding claims. The document also suggests the implementation of random retrospective auditing to test for accuracy. Special training sessions for coders and billers are recommended to ensure ongoing education and skill enhancement.

Other Compliance Program Guidance Documents

Many other documents related to *Compliance Program Guidance* have been released since those for clinical laboratories and hospitals. They are all similar in format, using the seven elements for compliance as their main components. The content may differ, however, depending on the site of service. The *Compliance Program Guidance* documents (in addition to those for clinical laboratories and for hospitals) currently available include those for:

- Third-party billers
- Hospices
- Durable medical equipment
- Home health agencies
- Medicare+Choice
- Physician practices
- Skilled nursing facilities

Copies of the OIG's *Compliance Program Guidance* documents may be obtained at the OIG's Web site, <http://www.dhhs.gov/oig>.

OIG Work Plans

Annually, the OIG issues its work plan for the following fiscal year. The plan is usually available by October 1 and includes CMS projects; Public Health Service Agency projects; Administrations for Children, Families, and Aging projects; and departmentwide projects within DHHS.

The work plan encompasses projects that will be performed under the auspices of the OIG by the Office of Audit Services, the Office of Evaluation and Inspections, the Office of Investigations, and the Office of Counsel to the Inspector General. Each of these agencies assists in the development of the OIG work plan, identifying those areas for which they are responsible. The actions that are performed relate to audit, inspection, investigation, and litigation.

Targets of OIG Work Plans

For CMS projects, the major targets of OIG work plans are identified under specific sites or types of service, such as hospitals, nursing homes, or physicians. Areas related to the coding function are frequently found in the work plan. Some coding projects that have appeared in work plans include:

- Pneumonia DRG upcoding project

- Project Bad Bundle

- Physicians at teaching hospitals (PATH)

- Critical care codes

- DRG 14

- Revenue centers without HCPCS codes

- Automated encoding systems for billing

Many targets appear in the work plan multiple years in a row. Given changes in priorities, a major target may move down the list, or it may be that the audit, inspection, or investigation is a lengthy process that requires more than one year to complete. The OIG's annual work plan can be obtained from the OIG's Web site, <http://www.dhhs.gov/oig>.

Uses of OIG Work Plans

OIG work plans are important from a coding management perspective because they can be used for the following purposes:

- To focus monitoring and auditing activities

- To identify problem areas

- To provide education

- To develop policies and procedures

Corporate Compliance and Health Information Management

Because so many compliance issues are related to coding and billing functions, HIM staff have the potential to provide expert advice to senior management, to the compliance officer, and to other hospital departments. To accomplish this, the health information manager must take the initiative and begin working with staff who are in need of information about compliance-related issues.

Working with the Compliance Committee and Compliance Officer

The HIM department director and the coding manager probably have close contact with the facility's compliance committee, the compliance officer, or both. Providing them with current information related to coding and compliance issues establishes the health information manager as a resource for the benefit of the facility as a whole.

In many cases, health information managers rise to the top because they have expertise in the areas of coding, billing, and compliance. It is not unusual for a health information manager to become a permanent member of a facility's compliance committee.

Working as a Team

In addition to working with the compliance committee and compliance officer, the HIM department works with other departments as part of a facilitywide team to ensure compliance.

As part of the compliance committee, the health information manager or coding manager works closely with all departments to provide compliance education. However, a team effort is needed in working with certain groups or departments to meet the goals of compliance, appropriate reimbursement, and accurate claims submission.

Working with Medical Staff for Compliance

The health information manager must continuously promote complete, accurate, and timely documentation to ensure appropriate coding, billing, and reimbursement. This requires a close working relationship with the medical staff, perhaps through the use of a physician champion.

Physician champions assist in educating medical staff members on documentation needed for accurate billing. They can demonstrate how improved documentation assists not only with hospital billing and reimbursement, but also with physician-office billing and reimbursement. The use of physician champions is not a new concept. They have been used successfully in hospitals across the country. Medical staff are more likely to listen to a peer than to a facility employee, especially when the topic is documentation needed to ensure appropriate reimbursement.

Working with the Business Office for Compliance

The health information manager must also work with the business office to achieve successes in compliance. Most billers are unaware of the rules that govern coding as described in federal regulations. Health information managers can enhance billers' knowledge of those requirements. In addition, managers can inform billers of the importance of contacting the HIM department before changing codes to meet the requirements of certain payers.

Additionally, by developing this relationship, the coding manager can work in concert with the business office on denials from Medicare or from other federally funded or private health insurance plans. A process for handling denials should be established that includes:

- Receipt of the denial by the business office

- Notification of the coding manager by the business office

- Audit of the health record by the HIM department to ensure accurate coding based on existing documentation

- Notification of the business office regarding accuracy of the denial

- Creation of a response to the denial by the coding manager and business office

By working as a team, an accurate and timely response to denials can become a routine process. During this process, team members might also identify trends that warrant education for quality improvement purposes.

Working with the Admitting Department for Compliance

The coding manager works closely with the admitting department to ensure the following:

- Accurate patient status

- Receipt of physician documentation with reason for encounter and orders for outpatient services

- Application of advanced beneficiary notices (ABNs)

- Education regarding local medical review policies (LMRPs), which outline those diagnoses considered medically necessary for specific procedures

In return, the coding manager provides the admitting department with the expertise needed to ensure compliance in admitting activities related to documentation, coding, and regulations.

Working with Ancillary Departments for Compliance

In most facilities, each ancillary department is responsible for updating its portion of the charge description master (CDM). Usually, staff members in the ancillary departments do not have the expertise in HCPCS coding to ensure accuracy and timeliness in the updating process. The coding manager should take the lead in providing this expertise to the various ancillary departments. Such action ensures compliance in the facility's charging process as it relates to HCPCS codes.

The Health Information Management Coding Compliance Plan

The coding manager faces unique challenges in ensuring coding compliance. Because coding usually determines a facility's reimbursement for services rendered, it is a high-risk area that should be continuously monitored to ensure compliance with all applicable regulations.

In an effort to provide structure and accountability to this important process, HIM departments have implemented coding compliance plans to demonstrate the steps being taken to ensure data quality.

The coding compliance plan should be based on the same principles as those of the corporate program. It should include the following elements outlined in OIG compliance guidance documents:

- Code of conduct

- Policies and procedures

- Education and training

- Oral communication

- Auditing

- Corrective action

- Reporting

Numerous benefits, including the following, can be realized as a result of the coding compliance plan:

- Improved physician documentation

- Improved coding accuracy

- A decrease in denials

- Relevant physician and coder education

- Proactive research into variations from benchmark data and their underlying causes

- Timely identification, correction, and prevention of potential coding compliance risks

Code of Conduct

The HIM team should demonstrate its commitment and the facility's commitment to ensuring a culture of compliance by developing a code of conduct. Responsibilities related to compliance, the reporting of potential problem areas, and possible disciplinary action should be included in such a code. The use of the corporate compliance hotline also should be included to ensure that employees understand how to report questionable practices without fear of retribution.

To further a culture of compliance, job descriptions for coding functions should include a requirement for adhering to the coding compliance plan. Each employee should be required to sign an acknowledgment indicating awareness of and agreement with the plan. The signed acknowledgment should be maintained in the employee's file in case it is needed in the future. If an employee refuses to sign the acknowledgment or to adhere to the plan, the human resources department should become involved. This could result in termination of the employee for refusing to comply with a term of employment.

Policies and Procedures

Policies and procedures that describe the coding functions, standards, and practices of the facility should be established and documented. These policies and procedures should be incorporated into the HIM coding compliance plan to demonstrate the efforts being made by the staff to ensure complete and accurate coding and billing for reimbursement.

Health Information Management Coding Compliance Manual

In order to achieve compliance that both models and mirrors the corporate compliance program, the HIM department should develop a departmental coding compliance manual. Because the HIM department is responsible for the coding function, which is so closely related to many of the facilitywide compliance initiatives, this manual should include coding policies, procedures, and standards that directly support the corporate compliance program.

Development of Coding Policies and Procedures

In some facilities, the HIM department is required to work with the human resources department or another designated department to obtain policy/procedure numbers and to seek organizational approval of proposed coding policies and procedures.

Coding policies should include the following components:

- AHIMA's Code of Ethics

- AHIMA's Standards of Ethical Coding

- Official Coding Guidelines

- Applicable federal and state regulations

- Internal documentation policies requiring the presence of physician documentation to support all coded diagnosis and procedure code assignments

Procedures related to the actual coding function should include a step-by-step description of the process, thus ensuring maximum accuracy and productivity.

Three Sample Procedures

When documentation is ambiguous, incomplete, or requires clarification of clinical findings, a procedure should be in place for requesting that the physician provide additional documentation in accordance with procedures for late entries or for addenda to the health record.

A second procedure should be developed that provides for a second coding review following the addition of documentation by a physician to the health record. A second review may be needed to ensure complete and accurate coding and billing.

A third procedure should also be in place to ensure that corrected cases are rebilled following a coding compliance audit. Both increases (if within sixty days of original billing) and decreases to reimbursement should be rebilled. The coding manager should consult the business office regarding this procedure. The coding manager and business office manager should write a policy and procedure to ensure that the process flows smoothly from the HIM department to the business office to the fiscal intermediary (FI) or carrier. Follow-up should be included in the procedure to ensure that the rebill actually occurred. (See appendix 8.4 for AHIMA's Practice Brief, Developing a Coding Compliance Policy Document.)

Coding Standards

Coding standards should not include numerical goals for case mix, complication and comorbidity (CC) percentage, or any other measurement that encourages payment maximization. However, standards should exist that promote coding accuracy and maximum productivity.

Internal Coding Guidelines

In those instances where no official coding guidelines exist, internal guidelines should be developed to ensure coding consistency and accuracy. These internal guidelines should not conflict with ICD-9-CM, CPT, or HCPCS rules; the Official Coding Guidelines; *Coding Clinic* advice; *CPT Assistant* advice; or federal or state regulations. Coding and sequencing instruction provided in the ICD-9-CM should take precedence over Official Coding Guidelines. Official Coding Guidelines, however, should take precedence over facility-specific guidelines.

When clarification of a confusing or new coding issue is necessary, an official source, such as the AHA, AHIMA, the AMA, CMS, or NCHS should be contacted. Copies of written requests for guidance and the responses received should be maintained to demonstrate the efforts in place to obtain official guidance in those instances where confusion exists. Until an official response is received, a temporary internal coding guideline should be implemented. A copy of the request for official advice should be attached to the temporary guideline to indicate that a request for official guidance has been made.

Evaluation of Existing Coding Policies, Procedures, Standards, and Internal Guidelines

On an annual basis, coding managers should review and update coding policies, procedures, and standards, as well as internal coding guidelines, to ensure compliance with current regulations. Policies, procedures, and standards for coding should be mandatory regardless of the source of payment.

Coder job descriptions should also be included in the annual review. This ensures that job descriptions truly reflect the functions currently being performed by coders, the credentials necessary for performing certain coding functions, and the level of education, as well as the number of continuing education hours, required for the coding position.

To ensure that policies are accurate, they should be compared to the release of any official coding guidance or regulations during the past year. Similarly, procedures should be reviewed to determine if any changes have been made that should be incorporated into a procedure's description.

Standards regarding accuracy and productivity levels should be reviewed annually to determine the achievability of the goals and how they compare with standard industry measurements.

Changes made to existing policies, procedures, standards, and internal coding guidelines should include a revision date and should follow the facility's procedure for updating these types of documents.

Education and Training

Appropriate and frequent education and training of staff are key factors to ensure ongoing success with the coding compliance program. A major contributor to potential coding compliance issues may be related to inconsistencies and misinterpretations that arise when coders do not receive ongoing educational opportunities. Coders want to do the right thing; however, without adequate continuing education, accurate coding becomes difficult.

Compliance Education

In conjunction with the corporate compliance officer, the health information manager should annually provide education and training related to the importance of complete and accurate coding, documentation, and billing. At this time, a review of the facility's corporate compliance plan, the coding compliance plan, fraud and abuse legislation, and the OIG's current work plan should be provided.

Employees should also be provided with acknowledgment forms for the corporate and coding compliance plans at this time. To ensure compliance, management should designate a time frame for signing and returning the forms.

Technical Education

Technical education for coders should be provided monthly, if possible. This education should include findings associated with data monitoring and ongoing coding audits. Trends identified through those functions should be addressed. A determination should be made prior to the education session whether the errors identified in the audit were due to a deficiency in coding knowledge or to a deficiency in clinical knowledge. It may prove useful to have a physician present clinical issues related to specific body systems, diagnoses, or procedures during the session.

Coders should be encouraged to bring difficult cases to the education program. Time should be allotted for coders to present those cases and for the staff to discuss appropriate code assignments.

Areas that should be covered in technical coding education sessions, depending upon the type of provider, include:

- OIG focus areas per current work plan

- Clinical information related to problematic body systems, diagnoses, and procedures

- Changes to the inpatient and outpatient prospective payment systems (PPSs)

- Changes to ICD-9-CM, effective annually in October 1

- Application of the Official Coding Guidelines

- Application of E & M (Evaluation and Management) Documentation Guidelines

- *Coding Clinic* for ICD-9-CM to ensure consistency in application of advice provided

- *CPT Assistant* to ensure consistency in application of advice provided

Documentation Education

A focused effort should be made to provide documentation education to the medical staff. The coding manager or a physician champion should present documentation issues identified during the audit process, such as incomplete documentation, conflicting documentation, or missing documentation. Many potential compliance issues are the result of inadequate documentation for coding purposes. Improving documentation by the medical staff will ensure coding compliance, as well as the accuracy of the health record.

General areas of concern regarding documentation should also be included. For example, information on inpatient documentation for coding purposes will help ensure that the appropriate documentation is present at the time of discharge. Additionally, education and training related to documentation of the reason for the encounter and of the order for the service should be provided to the physician and/or the physician's office staff. This will ensure appropriate documentation and medical necessity at the time of patient registration.

Documentation education should be provided monthly, bimonthly, or quarterly depending on the severity of the issues. The topics should be related to the underlying cause of errors identified during the audit process.

To improve the overall quality of the health record, ancillary department employees should be included in documentation education. Ancillary departments can often benefit from education related to the translation of clinical information into coded data. Once they understand the difficulty associated with that function, the ancillary departments are usually helpful in providing information needed for accurate coding.

Oral Communication

Communication between the coding manager and the coding staff is vital to ensure that coding staff are consistently applying policies, procedures, standards, and internal coding guidelines. If the coding manager provides only written copies of new or revised information to the staff with no oral communication, a high potential exists for individuals to interpret and to apply the information inconsistently. By orally communicating with the staff as a group, the coding manager can ensure that everyone has heard the same message and that they understand the appropriate application of the information.

The same principle applies when the coding manager passes out copies of new or revised federal and state regulations. Oral communication ensures that everyone has the same understanding of the intent and application of the regulations.

The coding manager should also reiterate on a regular basis the steps that coders should take to report potential compliance violations. When the coding manager repeats the information frequently, coders are less likely to become whistle-blowers. Instead, they are more likely to understand the appropriate action they should take to prompt an internal investigation and resolution—the preferred process.

Auditing

Auditing or reviewing coding and PPS classifications—whether inpatient or outpatient—has become an important component in the daily operation of the HIM department. In an effort to ensure compliance, coding managers are spending more time on quality review activities to ensure billing accuracy. This can be a time-consuming process for a manager who is already doing "more with less."

The following sections on data monitors, identification of risk areas, considerations in performing an audit, and focus areas for various types of reviews are meant to provide guidance in the manual performance of the auditing function. Information specific to how the audit or review should be performed can be found in chapter 7, Quality Control Issues.

Internal Data Monitors

Medicare Provider Analysis and Review (MedPAR) billing data may be utilized as an internal data monitor to determine differences between a hospital's billed Medicare inpatient data and a national average of billed Medicare inpatients. Variations identified during this process may indicate fraudulent or abusive coding and billing practices—or there may be a valid explanation for the differences. The point is: Because a variation exists, it does not necessarily mean that there is a compliance issue. It does, however, indicate that further analysis and an audit should be performed to validate the variations as appropriate for that particular facility.

DRG monitoring is an excellent method for determining high-risk areas compared with national, regional, or state data. When calculating averages for internal data monitors, it is important for the HIM professional to consider whether the calculation will include all payers, only Medicare, or only a specific third-party payer. Also, it is important to use the same period of time in determining the number of discharges (or encounters) for both the numerator and the denominator.

National data for comparison of high-risk DRGs may be found on the Society of Clinical Coding Web site, <http://www.SCCoding.org>, or on the CMS Web site, <http://www.cms.gov>. Data for physician offices and outpatients are also available from CMS through its public use files (PUFs). Additional sources for obtaining external data for comparison purposes can be found in appendix 8.1.

Areas of External Focus

Data monitors should be established for all areas under investigation by the government or other external reviewers. Those areas may include the following:

- Monitoring of case-mix index
- Percentage of cases that result in the assignment of a DRG with complication or comorbidity

- Audit findings of high-risk DRGs

- Certain problematic diagnoses or procedures

- Variations in length of stay (LOS)

- Variations in charges

Specifics regarding the establishment of data monitors for each of these areas are discussed in the subheads that follow. The HIM professional should remember that many of these areas are "moving targets" that should be evaluated and changed as needed. For example, DRG 14, Specific cerebrovascular disorders except TIA, and DRG 15, Transient ischemic attack and precerebral occlusions, might be under investigation one year, but not the next year.

If a facility has significant variations—even after the external focus no longer exists—the data monitor should remain in place. However, if no variation exists, the benefit of continued monitoring diminishes.

Tools to use in determining the current external focus include the OIG's annual work plan, identification of its current DRG focus, and knowledge of Payment Error Prevention Program (PEPP) initiatives.

Case-Mix Index

Case-mix index (CMI) is the average relative weight for a specified population of inpatients during a specified period of time. In other words, CMI is determined when the DRG relative weights of all discharges in the population for the specified period are added and then divided by the total number of patients in that population for that time period.

Senior management monitors CMI to determine the financial health of an institution. Monitoring should be performed to identify significant, unexplained variations in the CMI. Ongoing analysis should consist of a comparison of the same period of time (for example, a quarter) from one year to the next. A variation in the percentage of change in the CMI from national, regional, or state CMI averages should result in an investigation as to the cause of the variation.

To determine the percentage of change in the CMI, the following formula should be used:

$$\frac{Current\ year's\ CMI - Last\ year's\ CMI}{Last\ year's\ CMI} \times 100 = Percentage\ of\ change\ in\ CMI$$

The CMI may legitimately vary for the following reasons:

- The addition of services representative of high-weighted DRGs

- Shifts in volumes from low- to high-weighted DRGs

- A new local or regional competitor

- The addition of specialty physicians to the medical staff

- Changes in coding practices or guidelines

Responsibility for understanding these reasons for CMI variations should fall under the auspices of the health information manager. By analyzing the data proactively, the HIM professional may avoid crisis or reactive measures when called upon to explain the CMI variation. An analysis of the potential causes of a variation may reveal an appropriate explanation. This should then be documented and kept, along with supporting information, for future reference.

Complication/Comorbidity DRG Percentage

Diagnoses that affect certain DRG assignments, when listed as additional diagnoses, are referred to as complications and comorbidities (CCs) in the inpatient PPS. The CC designation indicates that DRGs with CCs have a higher resource intensity, a higher relative weight, and, therefore, a higher reimbursement. Currently, 117 pairs of DRGs split based on the presence or absence of a complicating or comorbid condition. For example, rectal resection splits into two DRGs: DRG 146 (Rectal resection with CC) and DRG 147 (Rectal resection without CC). DRG 146 has a higher relative weight and reimbursement.

A CC percentage with a variation significantly higher than the benchmark may be an indicator of overcoding. Using 1999 MedPAR data, the national average for CC DRG percentage was 79 percent (rounded down). During the mid-1990s in the early days of coding compliance, data indicated that some hospitals consistently showed a CC percentage of 100 percent month after month. Ultimately, many of those hospitals were investigated, and settlements were agreed upon based on the significant variation initially identified during the government's statistical analysis. (See appendix 8.2 for information related to 1999 MedPAR national averages for CC pairs—surgical, medical, and total CC pairs are listed separately.)

CC DRG percentages should be monitored on a monthly basis using the following formula (n = number of discharges). Only discharges for those DRGs that split based on the presence or absence of a CC in the denominator should be monitored.

$$\frac{n(CC\ DRGs)}{n(CC\ DRGs) + n(no\ CC\ DRGs)} \times 100 = Percentage\ of\ CC\ DRGs$$

An example of this calculation can be seen in the CC/no CC pair, DRG 148/149 (Major small and large bowel procedures). At City Hospital, there were 187 discharges assigned to DRG 148 during the period in question. There were 41 cases assigned to DRG 149 during the same period. The calculation for determining the CC percentage for this pair is as follows:

$$\frac{187}{187 + 41} = \frac{187}{228} = .82017 \times 100 = 82.017\%$$

Of the 228 cases that were assigned to DRG 148/149 during the period in question, 82 percent were assigned to the higher-weighted DRG 148, reflecting the presence of CCs.

To determine the national average, some hospitals must have a CC percentage greater than the national average, while other hospitals must have a CC percentage less than the national average. In other words, no "number" is correct for all hospitals. However, when a significant variation from the benchmark number is identified, it should be investigated. If an inappropriate coding practice is identified, a corrective action plan should be instituted.

Audit Findings of High-Risk DRGs

Internal or external coding audits may identify significant areas of variation in DRG assignments. When certain DRGs appear to be problematic for a facility, the HIM professional should establish data monitors. National, regional, or state averages may then be utilized for comparison. Those DRGs may or may not represent the current external investigative focus, but they do represent a high-risk area for the facility. To determine the percentage of a high-risk DRG pair, the following formula (n = number of discharges) should be used:

$$\frac{n(DRG\ X)}{n(DRG\ X) + n(DRG\ Z)} \times 100 = Percentage\ of\ cases\ in\ DRG\ X$$

For example, in monitoring the percentage of cases in DRG 14 as opposed to the high-risk DRG pair 14/15, the following formula should be used (n = number of discharges):

$$\frac{n(DRG\ 14)}{n(DRG\ 14)\ +\ n(DRG\ 15)} \times 100 = Percentage\ of\ cases\ in\ DRG\ 14$$

The following example indicates the percentage of cases that fall into DRG 316, Renal failure, as opposed to DRG 316 and DRG 296/297, Nutritional & miscellaneous metabolic disorders age >17 (dehydration):

$$\frac{n(DRG\ 316)}{n(DRG\ 316)\ +\ n(DRG\ 296\ +\ DRG\ 297)} \times 100 = Percentage\ of\ cases\ in\ DRG\ 316$$

Appendix 8.3 contains information related to 1999 MedPAR national averages for high-risk DRG pairs. These high-risk pairs may or may not represent the OIG's current investigative focus.

Twenty Highest-Volume DRGs

By monitoring the twenty highest-volume DRGs at a hospital, the HIM department can determine significant changes that may occur in patient volumes, as well as shifts in the volumes.

For example, a high-weighted DRG not previously one of the top twenty in volume begins to appear consistently on the top-twenty list month after month. The HIM department should perform additional analysis and audit to determine the underlying cause of the sustained increase. The increase may be legitimately due to the addition of services or of specialty physicians. However, the cause must be determined and corrective action taken if the increase was the result of inappropriate coding practices.

Using 1999 MedPAR data, almost one-half of all Medicare discharges fell into one of the DRGs shown in table 8.1. These DRGs represent the twenty highest-volume Medicare DRGs that occurred nationally in 1999.

Table 8.1.   Twenty highest-volume DRGs nationally

DRG	Volume (percent)
127	5.884%
089	4.529%
088	3.493%
209	2.956%
014	2.871%
116	2.664%
430	2.641%
462	2.125%
174	2.045%
296	2.016%
182	2.016%
416	1.696%
138	1.656%
143	1.610%
079	1.581%
320	1.573%
121	1.412%
132	1.325%
015	1.208%
124	1.166%
Percent of Total Discharge	46.466%

Problematic Diagnoses

Data monitors for problematic diagnoses should be instituted if a specific diagnosis is under investigation within a high-risk DRG. At that point, the HIM professional may want to determine the frequency of those diagnoses within the DRG.

For example, DRG 79, Respiratory infections age >17 with CC, represents a significant variation in the percent of pneumonia cases. Perhaps the assignment of aspiration pneumonia (507.0) as the principal diagnosis was inappropriate. However, by benchmarking and comparing the percentage of cases with aspiration pneumonia as the principal diagnosis versus other principal diagnoses in DRG 79, the need for further audit and investigation may be determined. The calculation would be performed as follows (n = number of discharges):

$$\frac{n(PDX\ 507.0)}{n(DRG\ 79)} \times 100 = \text{Percentage of cases in DRG 79 with a principal diagnosis of 507.0}$$

Another example would include monitoring DRG 296 for the percentage of cases with a principal diagnosis of dehydration (276.5).

$$\frac{n(PDX\ 276.5)}{n(DRG\ 296)} \times 100 = \text{Percentage of cases in DRG 296 with a principal diagnosis of 276.5}$$

Problematic Procedures

In monitoring for inpatient compliance, it may prove useful to monitor the occurrence of certain problematic procedures within a category or subcategory of the ICD-9-CM. The difference of one digit in a four-digit procedure code can affect the DRG assignment when it is considered a valid operating room procedure. By monitoring and auditing these high-risk categories, the HIM manager can identify variations from internal benchmarks and institute education and training where necessary.

Depending on the procedure code assignment from category 38, Incision, excision and occlusion of vessels, the following DRGs may result:

- DRG 1/2   Craniotomy

- DRG 5   Extracranial vascular procedures

- DRG 7/8   Peripheral, cranial, and other nervous system procedures

- DRG 110/111   Major cardiovascular procedure

- DRG 478/489   Other vascular procedures

The relative weights and, therefore, the reimbursement for these DRGs differ significantly. If one incorrect digit is consistently assigned for a procedure that is frequently performed at a facility, it could result in a pattern of abuse that could capture the attention of external investigators.

For instance, the HIM manager may want to monitor the occurrence of procedure code 38.31, Intracranial vessel resection and anastomosis, as compared to code 38.32, Head and neck vessel resection and anastomosis. The calculation would be performed as follows (n = number of discharges):

$$\frac{n(PX\ 38.31)}{n(PX\ 38.31) + n(PX\ 38.32)} \times 100 = \text{Percentage of cases assigned to code 38.31}$$

The result indicates the percentage of cases assigned to code 38.31 (DRGs 1 or 2) rather than to code 38.32 (DRG 5).

Variations in Length of Stay and in Charges

Variations in length of stay (LOS) should be monitored to determine those cases within a DRG that have a LOS significantly less than the average LOS for other discharges assigned to the same DRG. Potentially, if the LOS is significantly shorter, there is a chance that DRG creep has occurred.

Variations in charges should be monitored for the same reason. As a benchmark, the charges for each Medicare DRG for the facility are averaged. These averages are used when actual charges are compared to determine variations.

When variations occur either in LOS or in charges, those particular cases that fall out should be audited to validate appropriate coding and DRG assignment.

Other Data Monitors

Although inpatient data monitors have been previously described, data monitors may be established for all patient care settings. Some of those not mentioned include:

- The occurrence of component code assignments as a percentage of the comprehensive code assigned to the same encounter

- The twenty highest-volume ambulatory payment classifications (APCs) within the organization for significant changes over time

- A bell curve analysis of E & M code assignments with comparison to physician

- The occurrence of certain modifiers (-59, Distinct procedural services) as a percentage of all outpatient/physician-office encounters

The Next Step

Data monitors should then be utilized to determine the next step in the process. If significant variations exist, the coding manager should drill down, or look at a greater level of detail, in the data to identify those specific cases that should be reviewed. The data should be provided in the form of a report representing case-specific information (health record number, account number, diagnosis codes, procedure codes, LOS, charges, and so on).

The coding manager should review the data to determine the cases to be included in the focused audit. Those cases that appear "different" from other cases in the report should be included in the actual audit.

Identification of Risk Areas

Many coding risk areas exist that vary upon the site of service. Some of these risk areas are discussed in the following sections.

DRG Coding Accuracy

ICD-9-CM coding for Medicare DRG assignment has been a major focus of the OIG's fraud and abuse efforts. Hospitals across the country have been subpoenaed for health records. Those records are then audited to ensure that the coding matches both clinical and physician documentation within the health record.

The criteria for evaluating health records for potentially inappropriate coding or DRG assignments are based on the premise that all coding must be supported by a physician's documentation of the diagnosis or of the procedure in the body of the health record. In addition to blatant violations of coding rules, such as upcoding, it was determined that many violations were caused by poor training or lack of facility-specific coding rules. **Assumption coding**—assigning codes based on clinical signs, symptoms, test findings, or treatment without supporting physician documentation—was also found to be a significant problem.

Appropriate application of the Official Coding and Reporting Guidelines, as well as of other federal rules and regulations, is also reviewed as a requirement of coding accuracy in all care settings.

The initial DRG efforts of the OIG included a comparison of the percentage of cases assigned to DRGs with CCs as opposed to those with and without CCs, and the DRG pair of complex versus simple pneumonia. In investigating CC percentages, the OIG determined that some hospitals were reporting 100 percent of their cases in DRGs with CCs month after month. At the time those investigations began, the national CC percentage was in the 83 to 85 percent range.

The OIG began its investigation of DRG pairs by comparing the national average for complex versus simple pneumonia to the average for individual hospitals to determine the potential for fraudulent or abusive coding patterns. Since 1998 when the pneumonia project began, the OIG has expanded its DRG investigations to include more than twenty pairs of DRGs. The OIG has also employed a more sophisticated statistical methodology for identifying aberrations in hospitals across the country. Currently, DRG pair 14, Specific cerebrovascular disorders except TIA, and 15, Transient ischemic attack and precerebral occlusions, are under scrutiny by the OIG.

When monitoring these averages, health information managers must remember this: If a variation exists, it does not necessarily mean there is a compliance problem. It does indicate, however, that the variation should be investigated to determine why it exists. In arriving at a national average, some hospitals will have percentages higher than the average and others will have percentages lower than the average.

Case-Mix Index

The OIG investigates variations in CMI over time for individual hospitals to determine trends that have occurred and to determine if such trends resulted from upcoding. Those investigations also include identifying any DRG that significantly influenced national trends in the CMI over time.

Changes in CMI may be attributed to any of the following factors:

- Changes in coding rules

- Changes in medical staff composition

- Changes in services offered

- Local competition

- Referrals

Health information management professionals should routinely monitor the CMI and determine the underlying causes of variations as part of their role in coding.

Discharge Status

Hospitals are now reimbursed using a transfer payment methodology when a patient receives post acute care (excluded hospitals, skilled nursing facilities, or home healthcare) within three days of inpatient discharge for DRGs 14, 113, 209, 210, 211, 236, 263, 264, 429, and 483. CMS is monitoring patients discharged with those ten DRGs to determine if post-acute services are received within the three-day postdischarge window. Hospitals stating "home, self-care" as the discharge disposition for those ten post-acute care DRGs may be reviewed by CMS to determine if billing practices are consistent with Medicare policy.

Prior to the passage of this Medicare rule, however, other issues related to discharge status were identified as compliance concerns. Cases with a discharge status of "left against medical advice" or "home, self-care" that are found, in fact, to have been transferred to another acute care facility represent compliance issues. Had they been appropriately classified to "transfer to another acute care facility," reimbursement would have been paid at a per diem rate based on LOS rather than at the full DRG rate. When an inappropriate discharge disposition is coded, there is potential for the occurrence of an honest mistake or for fraudulent or abusive coding. The government looks for patterns of abuse to assist in making this determination.

When hospitals merge, another area of potential fraud and abuse in the coding of discharge status occurs. Problems arise when a patient currently listed as an inpatient in Hospital A becomes a patient in Hospital B upon the merger or acquisition of Hospital A with or by Hospital B. The correct method of billing this patient is as a single admission under the provider number of the post-merger or acquiring hospital for a full DRG payment. However, in certain situations, such a patient might be billed for a transfer at the per diem rate based on LOS under the provider number of Hospital A (transferred to Hospital B on the date of the merger/acquisition) and for a full DRG payment under the provider number of Hospital B (admitted on the date of the merger). As with all the examples described in this chapter, the potential for an honest mistake occurring truly depends on the type and amount of training provided to those individuals responsible for ensuring appropriate coding and billing practices.

Services Provided under Arrangement

Services provided under arrangement with another healthcare facility have also been identified as a potential high-risk area for providers. When one facility is in a contractual relationship with another facility to perform services not currently offered at the first facility, the terms of the contractual relationship should be shared with the coding staff at both facilities to ensure complete and accurate coding.

For example, Hospital A does not provide cardiac catheterization; however, Hospital B down the street does. A patient is admitted to inpatient status in Hospital A, and the physician determines that a cardiac catheterization procedure is necessary during the current admission. The patient is then sent by ambulance to Hospital B for the cardiac catheterization and is returned to Hospital A following completion of the procedure.

The example just given illustrates an appropriate practice. The coding staff at the providing facility (Hospital B), however, needs to be aware that the inpatient facility (Hospital A) will code the procedure and will bill Medicare for the cardiac catheterization under the DRG system to avoid duplicate coding and billing. The service provider (Hospital B) will then bill the inpatient facility (Hospital A) for services provided to the patient.

Medicare rules must be followed in determining certain terms and conditions of the contract. This practice will not only affect Hospital A's DRG assignment, but also its cost reporting in terms of overhead and administrative costs. It is inappropriate for the billing facility to mark up procedures for these costs when they were not performed at that facility.

72-Hour Window

Medicare issued changes to the 72-hour window rule in the February 11, 1998, *Federal Register*. In summary, the changes included that:

- The following services are not subject to the 72-hour window rule and are excluded from the inpatient DRG payment:

    —Hospice, home health, or skilled nursing services covered under Medicare Part A and provided within 72 hours of inpatient admission

    —Ambulance services or maintenance renal dialysis services within 72 hours of admission

    —Nondiagnostic services unrelated to the admission

- The following services are subject to the 72-hour window rule for inclusion in the inpatient DRG payment:

    —All diagnostic services within 72 hours of admission

    —All nondiagnostic services related to the admission

CMS defines nondiagnostic-related services as having the same ICD-9-CM diagnosis code. This, however, is not a legal definition, only CMS's interpretation. If coders doubt whether the nondiagnostic service is related to the admission, they should query the physician.

Through the OIG's 1997 work plan, investigative efforts were begun related to the separate billing of those outpatient services when provided by the admitting hospital, by an entity wholly owned or operated by the admitting hospital, or by another entity under arrangement with the hospital.

Most coding departments are not responsible for determining the presence of outpatient services within 72 hours of inpatient admission. In many instances, this is determined in the business office. However, coders should be aware of the intent of the rules to ensure bundling of outpatient charges when appropriate.

DRG Payment Window

The OIG will continue investigating the billing of services provided to hospital inpatients by nonphysician providers. It appears that duplicate claims were made under Medicare Part B for services such as laboratory, radiology, and ambulance that should have been bundled into the Part A DRG payment to the hospital. In other words, an outpatient claim for the service was presented separately from that associated with the inpatient claim.

This continuing investigation of both hospital and Part B providers is the result of a settlement that noncompliant hospitals entered into after the Department of Justice recovered overpayments, penalties, and interest through the Civil False Claims Act.

Outpatient Prospective Payment System

The outpatient prospective payment system (OPPS) has become a focus to determine whether implementation has succeeded in ensuring adequate documentation, appropriate coding, and medical necessity for services provided in hospital outpatient departments. If hospitals have failed to install adequate controls to ensure accurate APC assignment, further investigation will be warranted to determine overpayments made to the hospital.

Medical Necessity

Medical necessity is a high-risk area in both the hospital and physician-office settings. According to the OIG's *Compliance Program Guidance for Clinical Laboratories* and LMRPs, the physician should provide the "reason for the encounter" prior to the performance of the service to ensure medical necessity and Medicare coverage. When the service is not considered medically necessary based on the "reason for the encounter," the patient should be provided with a waiver of liability—an advanced beneficiary notice (ABN)—indicating that Medicare will not pay and that the patient will be responsible for the entire charge.

A physician or hospital should be able to provide documentation of medical necessity for all outpatient services that are provided and that are billed to Medicare. When claims are submitted to Medicare that do not demonstrate medical necessity through documentation, an investigation that identifies a pattern may result in civil penalties.

Physicians at Teaching Hospitals

The OIG has been monitoring coding and documentation by physicians at teaching hospitals (PATH) for several years. The intent is to ensure that teaching physicians are in compliance with Medicare PATH regulations and that the appropriate level of service is being billed. Cases were identified during the initial phase of this investigation in which:

- Documentation did not support the presence of the teaching physician during the performance of significant procedures by residents.

- Teaching physicians were managing more residents than is allowed by a single teaching physician during a period of time.

- Health records did not contain sufficient documentation to support the level of service being billed.

Basically, a PATH investigation includes a review of the services being performed by residents, the supervision of the residents by teaching physicians, and the presence of appropriate documentation to support the level of service being billed. CMS's evaluation and management documentation guidelines are used to determine the correct E & M code and, thereby, the correct level of service for billing purposes.

Rules regarding PATH were issued by Medicare in December 1995 and were clarified in the *Medicare Carriers Manual* in July 1996.

Critical Care Codes

The OIG has been investigating the use of E & M critical care code 99291 (critical care evaluation and management of the critically ill or critically injured patient; first 30–74 minutes) and critical care code 99292 (each additional 30 minutes). To be appropriately assigned, these codes must be in accordance with the CPT guidelines surrounding these services and must be based on physician documentation.

Constant attention by a physician is necessary to care for a patient with a critical illness or injury in which a high probability of a life-threatening condition exists. Certain criteria, such as impairment of one or more vital organ systems, must be met before either of the codes previously listed can be appropriately assigned. The time attributed to critical care must be spent in work directly related to the patient's critical care—either at the bedside or elsewhere, as long as the physician is engaged in activities related to that patient's care.

Other Risk Areas: The CDM and the Superbill

The risk areas already described are by no means all-inclusive. Other risk areas for coding are just as important, depending upon the site of service. For example, codes that appear on a hospital's CDM should be audited on an annual basis to ensure that hard coding of certain procedures and services, supplies, drugs, and equipment is accurate. By neglecting to perform this function, a hospital or other provider could be at risk for inappropriate coding, APC assignment, and reimbursement.

Another area of concern is the superbill used in the physician-office or clinic setting. The superbill should also be audited on an annual basis prior to the implementation of updated CPT codes—that is, before January 1 of each year.

Coding Compliance Review Considerations

Prior to actually performing coding compliance reviews, the health information manager should consider certain aspects of the review process to ensure consistency and effectiveness. The specific criteria used in the audit process should be included in the HIM department's internal coding compliance plan.

Responsibility for Reviews

Responsibility for coding compliance reviews should be determined prior to implementing the review process in the HIM department. Responsibility for this function, as with any function, should be documented in the department's policy and procedure manual. The policy and procedure should then be included in the coding compliance plan. In most instances, the coding supervisor or the health information manager will be responsible for performing the reviews.

Staff members performing front-line coding should not be responsible for auditing their own work because this could be construed as a conflict of interest. In smaller hospitals or facilities, this may not be practical. Perhaps the hospital does not have a coding supervisor, and the health information manager is not skilled in coding. Other options should then be considered for performing the review, such as using a local coding consulting company. Perhaps the small hospital is part of a larger chain with other hospitals in the region. In such an instance, the smaller hospital could request that a coding supervisor from the larger facility in the chain come in to review its coding.

Internal and External Audits

In a larger hospital, coding compliance reviews may fall under the auspices of an internal audit department. The coding supervisor or the health information manager would then be responsible only for ensuring the availability of the records prior to the review. The internal auditors would perform the actual review. The results of the audit would be shared in accordance with guidelines set through the facilitywide compliance program.

Regardless of whether the coding supervisor, health information manager, or internal auditor reviews health records for compliance, an external review should be performed at least once a year. If problems have been identified in the past, an external audit should be performed twice a year to validate internal findings. To obtain an objective, third-party review of internal practices ensures that everyone—even those performing ongoing compliance reviews—is compliant with current rules and regulations related to the coding function.

Facilities, therefore, may choose to:

- Outsource coding compliance audit functions to an external auditing company

- Perform all coding compliance audits internally

- Use a combination of internal and external auditing

A combination of the two types of audits provides the best of both worlds: The facility can save money by performing the majority of the audits internally, using an external source only once or twice a year.

Prospective and Retrospective Reviews

Another consideration in developing policies and procedures for coding compliance reviews is determining the point in the flow of the health record at which the review will be performed. The question is: Should the record be reviewed for coding compliance prior to bill drop, prospective review, following bill drop, retrospective review? **Bill drop** indicates that the claim has been released as complete for submission to the insurer for payment.

By reviewing coding prospectively, or prior to bill drop, health information managers ensure that any errors identified during the review process are corrected and that the DRG is correct prior to bill drop. This will reduce the number of rebills that may occur over the course of a year, thereby reducing the hospital's risk. The drawback of a prospective review is that it cannot be focused on specific types of cases, whether referring to specific inpatient DRGs, specific outpatient APCs, or specific types of physician-office visits. When reviewing prospectively, reviewers have limited samples unless they are willing to review a few records every day until the sampling requirements are met.

In performing a retrospective review, the reviewer has the opportunity to focus on certain external or internal high-risk areas. This review can also include a review of the UB-92 for the appropriate transfer of codes. Specific numbers of health records per coder or per physician may be selected. However, if DRG inaccuracies are identified, rebilling must be performed—whether the correct DRG increases or decreases reimbursement. When a significant number of rebills have occurred, the FI may become interested in why so many claims are being rebilled. This could put the facility at risk for external investigation.

It is probably more prudent to conduct prospective reviews as a part of an ongoing internal coding compliance review process.

Frequency of Audits

The coding compliance audit policy should include parameters for the frequency of auditing—daily, weekly, or monthly audits may be considered. Establishing the frequency of audits will assist in ensuring that they are performed in a timely manner.

The frequency of coding compliance reviews depends on the individual facility. For example, a coding supervisor responsible for this function may only have four hours per week to devote to compliance activities. If that is the case, the sampling methodology would have to be determined to accommodate that type of schedule.

In another facility, perhaps the coding supervisor is able to schedule one week per quarter for coding compliance reviews. In that case, a much larger sampling can be reviewed and can include health records based on facility-specific selection criteria. The frequency of reviews may also depend on whether the reviews will be conducted prospectively or retrospectively.

Sampling Methodology

The policy for performing coding compliance audits should include information on selecting the samples for the audit. Various methodologies can be used, including the following:

- Specific number of health records by type of patient

- Certain percentage of health records by type of patient

- Number/percentage of health records by coder

- Statistically valid sampling formula

The sampling should include:

- Current areas of investigative focus

- Internal high-risk areas

- A random sampling of health records to determine overall accuracy

If established benchmarks are used to monitor coded data, the health information manager should include a review of any areas in which a significant variation from the benchmark has occurred.

Audit Worksheets

A separate audit worksheet is necessary for each type of patient audited because the type of data collected on each will vary to a certain degree. Data elements that should be collected may include:

- Type of patient

- Billing number/health record number

- Coder's name

- Physician's name

- Admission/discharge dates

- Length of stay

- Age

- Gender

- Original/audit discharge disposition

- Financial class

- Auditor's name

- Audit date

- Original/audit diagnosis and procedure codes

- Impact on case designation (that is, DRG or APC)

- Impact on reimbursement

- Root cause of coding error, such as documentation, coding error, Official Coding Guideline, coding convention, *Coding Clinic* advice, and so on

- Documentation present at final coding versus that present during audit

- Rationale for audit recommendations

Following the audit, the worksheets should be retained as specified in the facility's compliance program. Audit findings and trends identified on the worksheets should be summarized for individual and group education. Accuracy rates should be calculated for individual coders and the department as a whole, as well as for physicians regarding documentation issues.

Coding Compliance Reviews

Using specific criteria, each type of patient should be assessed to determine compliance with applicable regulations and the potential for risk. Current areas of investigative focus should be included in the assessment, as well as those areas in which previous reviews may have revealed problems. (See chapter 7 for techniques about reviewing inpatient and outpatient health records and how to determine errors.)

Reviewing Inpatient Health Records

Complete and accurate coding and DRG assignment of inpatient health records should be assessed to validate that physician and clinical documentation support it. Application of ICD-9-CM coding conventions and Official Coding Guidelines should be utilized in performing the review. The principal diagnosis, all additional diagnoses, and all significant procedures should be reviewed to determine not only upcoding, but also undercoding and total data quality. Timeliness of physician documentation should be reviewed because it can impact coding and billing from a time perspective, as well as from an availability perspective.

The sampling of records to be reviewed should be representative of current areas of investigative focus, including high-risk DRG pairs, CC percentage, and those DRGs with an LOS or charges significantly different from the hospital's average LOS or charges. If a significant variation in case mix exists, the twenty highest-volume DRGs should be reviewed to determine accuracy. Trended variations identified as the result of previous reviews should also be included in the review.

As part of the health record review, the accuracy of discharge status should be determined. For example, if a patient were transferred to another acute care hospital, the transferring hospital would receive only a portion of the DRG reimbursement—a per diem rate—as determined by the actual LOS. That is why the appropriate discharge disposition should be assigned based on health record documentation. If health record documentation provides conflicting information, the hospital should consider instituting a policy and procedure that assigns responsibility for appropriate documentation of discharge disposition to one discipline, such as discharge planners. This will improve discharge disposition accuracy for billing purposes. As a part of the review, the discharge disposition should also be reviewed to ensure that it has been transferred appropriately to the UB-92. Interface issues, however, may preclude the assignment of the intended discharge disposition.

Inpatient records should also be reviewed to ensure that coding of services provided under arrangement with another facility has been performed appropriately. The appropriate coding will depend on whether the facility is a provider or a receiver of services provided under arrangement. In instances in which this is unclear or when the HIM department is unaware of any contractual relationships, the business office director or chief financial officer should be queried.

If preadmission outpatient services provided within 72 hours of inpatient admission are identified during the review, the appropriate area, usually the business office, should be notified so that rebilling can occur. Ensuring compliance with the 72-hour window rule is usually not the responsibility of the HIM department. However, in instances in which errors are identified, it should be addressed.

Ambulatory Surgery and the Emergency Department

The HIM department should validate complete and accurate coding in accordance with ICD-9-CM coding conventions and the Diagnostic Coding and Reporting Guidelines for Outpatient Services (hospital-based and physician office). Additionally, the HIM department should validate CPT coding of procedures based on CPT guidelines and include a review for appropriate coding based on Correct Coding Initiative (CCI) and outpatient code editor (OCE) edits. Each procedure should have a correlating diagnosis to indicate the medical necessity of the procedure. Also, appropriate assignment of modifiers should be reviewed because these will affect APC assignment and, therefore, outpatient reimbursement.

The coding of the reason for the encounter, all additional diagnoses, and all significant procedures should be reviewed to determine data quality for ambulatory surgery and for emergency department coding. Timeliness of physician documentation should also be reviewed because dictation and transcription can affect the timeliness and accuracy of coding.

When the technology is available for reviewing all APC assignments at the point of quality review, APCs should be reviewed to validate appropriate transmission of HCPCS codes to the grouper and to the UB-92.

E & M codes assigned for emergency department facility charges should be reviewed using hospital-specific criteria to determine the appropriate levels. Although the coding for the facility charge may not be performed by the HIM coding staff, the codes should be reviewed to ensure accuracy and appropriateness.

When the hospital is also assigning E & M codes for physicians' billing, those codes should be validated based on CMS's E & M Documentation Guidelines.

Referred Outpatients

Only diagnosis codes need to be validated for referred outpatient coding because the procedures should be captured through the facility's charge description master. The HIM department should validate complete and accurate coding in accordance with ICD-9-CM coding conventions and the Diagnostic Coding and Reporting Guidelines for Outpatient Services (hospital-based and physician office). However, the presence of documentation indicating the reason for performing the service and the order for the service should also be verified.

Physician

E & M codes should be validated based on the presence of documentation to support the level of service provided by the physician and on the appropriate application of E & M Documentation Guidelines. In validating the E & M code assignment, close attention should be paid to E & M for day of discharge management services, critical care services, psychotherapy, and individual psychiatric testing for inpatients. These areas are or have been under investigation, thus warranting a continued close review for compliance with applicable regulations.

The HIM department should validate complete and accurate coding in accordance with ICD-9-CM coding conventions and the Diagnostic Coding and Reporting Guidelines for

Outpatient Services (hospital-based and physician office). Additionally, the department should validate CPT coding of procedures based on CPT guidelines and should include a review for appropriate coding based on Correct Coding Initiative (CCI) edits. Each procedure should have a correlating diagnosis to indicate the medical necessity of the procedure. Also, appropriate assignment of modifiers should be reviewed because they will affect physician reimbursement.

When reviewing records related to physicians at teaching hospitals, the HIM department should validate the existence of documentation to support the presence of the physician while residents provide services and supervision by the physician of residents providing services.

Corrective Action

Although corrective action is not the sole responsibility of the coding manager, many of the steps involved in the process will fall to the coding manager. The ultimate goal of corrective action is prevention of the same problem in the future. However, to reach that point in the corrective action process, many other steps must be performed.

When a compliance problem is identified in the form of a potential coding fraud or abuse issue, the coding manager should work within the steps provided in the corporate compliance program. Those steps probably include notification of the compliance officer. Once the compliance officer is involved, the coding manager may or may not be included in the investigation leading to corrective action.

Whether the coding manager is involved or not, the next steps are basically the same. An internal investigation is performed. It usually includes interviews with coding staff, coding management staff, and others who may be involved in the problem. The internal investigation also includes a review of data, policies, and previous educational efforts. This helps to identify the underlying cause of the problem. In other words: Is this truly a compliance issue, was it just an error, or was it a lack of knowledge?

Senior management, the compliance officer, and legal counsel then work through the details of reporting the issue and providing restitution for overpayments, penalties, and interest. The details of internal disciplinary action depend on the extent of the problem identified through the investigation and include input from the human resources department.

Based on the results of the audit, policies and procedures should be updated and/or revised to reflect the appropriate coding practice. Education should then be provided to the coding staff and other staff, as necessary, to ensure a thorough understanding of the appropriate coding practice and of future expectations.

At this point, ongoing auditing of the problem area should be instituted to ensure detection and prevention of the problem in the future. Ongoing auditing may be performed either internally or externally, depending on the circumstances surrounding the previously identified problem and on the procedure outlined in the corporate compliance program.

Reporting

All coding compliance activities should be performed, documented, and reported in accordance with direction provided by the corporate compliance program. If no specific guidance is provided, the compliance officer should be able to assist in determining the type of documentation required to demonstrate the compliance efforts of the HIM coding staff.

Usually, the documentation created should include:

- Trends identified
- Financial implications

- Corrective action taken

- Changes made to existing policies and procedures

- Education provided

- Report of findings to the compliance officer

- Dates and statistics for all coding compliance activities

Case-specific findings usually need not be included in the information provided to the compliance department. A summary of the findings including trends, financial implications, and corrective action are sufficient in reporting audit activities.

Departmental records of all coding compliance activities should be maintained in the HIM department. Retention of these records depends upon the regulations of the state in question and on guidance provided in the corporate compliance plan.

Tools and External Services Used in Coding Compliance

Coding managers make use of a variety of software products for coding, billing, and monitoring functions. Such tools can constitute an important part of the compliance review process.

Software

Encoder and quality review software are valuable tools for ensuring complete and accurate coding for billing purposes. However, inaccuracies and discrepancies in the software may result in compliance risks for the user. Before purchasing software, the HIM department should be sure that the software vendor provides the following services:

- A hotline for reporting errors and for requesting service

- Frequent updates reflecting corrections

- Regular updates to the coding systems and prospective payment systems

- A list of users for potential buyers to contact regarding their satisfaction with the software and services

Encoders

Inaccuracies in encoder software may result in a pattern of inappropriate coding that could send up "red flags" for possible investigations. If the ICD-9-CM codebooks, CPT codebook, *Coding Clinic,* or *CPT Assistant* indicate that another code is more appropriate than that provided through the encoder software, the coding supervisor should notify the vendor about the discrepancy. Corrections made as a result of communication between the vendor and the user ensures a better product from the vendor in future software updates.

The coding supervisor should keep a log that documents the following information regarding encoder errors:

- The date that the error was discovered

- The date that the vendor was notified

- The vendor's response to the discrepancy

- The date the software was corrected

The coding staff should be made aware of any encoder discrepancies so that they assign appropriate codes. The coding supervisor should stay informed about encoder errors so that, if needed, a study can be conducted of previously coded records to determine the potential financial impact of assigning inappropriate codes over time. If inappropriate codes have been used, rebilling may be necessary. When overpayment to a facility has occurred, the compliance officer should be notified.

Software for Quality Reviews

Software for quality reviews is available through several software companies. This software, through a series of internal edits, identifies accounts that may represent inaccurate or inappropriate coding.

Software for quality reviews can reduce the amount of time needed to perform data monitoring functions and to determine cases to review for a focused coding compliance audit. Although identification of specific accounts for review is not indicative of errors, it does reduce the amount of time the coding manager must spend in manually reviewing reports to determine those accounts that look "different" from similar accounts.

In the OIG's 1998 report *Using Software to Detect Upcoding of Hospital Bills* (OEI 01-97-00010), optimism was expressed regarding the use of such software. However, state-of-the-art software does not appear to provide the level of accuracy needed to ensure success using only software.

Software for quality reviews, therefore, must still be coupled with a manual review process to ensure accurate detection of potentially fraudulent or abusive coding practices. No current software package—in and of itself—can identify upcoding or undercoding without human intervention in the form of an actual health record review.

Consulting Firms

Time studies may reveal that the coding manager is unable to take on the additional task of conducting coding compliance reviews. As a result, many providers choose to contract with external coding compliance vendors. This is an appropriate solution as long as the vendor can meet certain criteria. External coding compliance companies should meet the following eleven criteria:

- Follow the Official Coding Guidelines approved by the Cooperating Parties (AMA, AHIMA, CMS, and NCHS). These guidelines are used in coding Medicare, Medicaid, and Civilian Health and Medical Program of Veterans Administration claims. They are also the guidelines that would be applied during an audit for a government investigation. The vendor's internal coding guidelines can be reviewed to ensure consistency with the Official Coding Guidelines.

   Additionally, if a quality review of physician coding is being conducted, the vendors should be well versed in the application of E & M Documentation Guidelines that have been approved by CMS in assigning the appropriate level of CPT evaluation and management codes.

- Identify upcoding, undercoding, and coding quality errors that do not affect the DRG assignment when reporting findings to the client. Total compliance involves ensuring complete and accurate coding reflecting the care of the patient. The provider can then be assured that its billing is accurate and that its healthcare statistics provide an accurate view of its case mix for determining future services, managed care contracts, and profiling.

- Charge a fixed fee rather than a contingency fee. Advice provided by the DHHS OIG in its compliance program guidance indicates that compensation for consultants should not provide any financial incentive to improperly upcode claims. By charging the healthcare provider a fixed fee for coding quality reviews rather than a percentage of the money "found," the incentive for upcoding is eliminated.

- Employ only credentialed coding staff and be willing to provide proof of the credential status of each employee who will be providing services. This includes credentials reflecting RHIA, RHIT, CCS, and CCS-P, which indicate that the individuals have met the competencies set for those particular credentials and have maintained continuing education hours on an ongoing basis.

- Justify recommendations for changes to coding or prospective payment system assignment through the use of appropriate references. This would include the use of the Official Coding Guidelines, E & M Documentation Guidelines, *Coding Clinic,* or *CPT Assistant.* If the consultant cannot justify a recommended change, the healthcare provider may want to contact an official source, such as the Central Office for ICD-9-CM for ICD-9-CM questions or the AMA for CPT questions, prior to agreeing with the consultant's recommendation.

- Educate consulting staff on current areas of investigative focus and on consistent application of guidelines. Vendors should be able to document that they provide at least annual or semiannual educational programs for their consulting staff. This may represent an educational meeting developed and presented by the vendors themselves, or it may represent sending their consulting staff to external programs.

- Have their own compliance program and provide a copy of it to potential clients. Vendors' coding compliance programs should adhere to the steps outlined in the OIG's compliance program guidance models. The coding philosophy of vendors should reflect that of the client to ensure complete and accurate coding.

- Educate provider staff as a component of the services. External quality reviews of coding should include education related to upcoding, undercoding, and quality review. It should also provide specific technical or clinical education related to trends identified during the audit process.

- Have never been convicted of fraudulent practices. In keeping with Sections 4301 and 4302 of the Balanced Budget Act (1997), vendors who have been convicted of fraudulent practices should be avoided. This ensures that the healthcare provider receives high-quality, ethical services.

- Provide services under attorney–client privilege. When an attorney who is representing a provider requests auditing services under attorney–client privilege, the vendor works with the attorney designated by the provider. Communication between the vendor and the healthcare provider is limited to protect the results of the coding compliance audit from future "discovery."

- Have credible client references. Healthcare providers should not settle for a prepared list of references—such a list will contain only the names of individuals that vendors want a provider to contact. Instead, the healthcare provider should request a list of the five clients most recently served by the vendors. When contacting them, the healthcare provider should ensure that these clients were satisfied with the vendors' coding philosophy, fees, and quality of service.

Currently, government investigations are focused on healthcare providers. When a trend has been established between the providers under investigation and the use of a particular coding consulting company, however, increased investigations of vendors are likely to occur, as well as investigations of their other clients. Healthcare providers should protect themselves from investigation by ensuring that the company selected for external coding compliance reviews meets the eleven criteria just discussed.

Health Insurance Portability and Accountability Act—Security and Privacy

HIPAA legislation should be evaluated to determine the impact on HIM coding and compliance activities in each facility. The impact should then be translated into effective and efficient processes to protect the security and privacy of coded data.

Code Sets

In addition to ensuring security and privacy of health information, HIPAA legislation includes a provision for the mandatory use of code sets, such as ICD-9-CM, CPT, and HCPCS, for use in reporting healthcare encounters for reimbursement. This provision also includes the current processes in place for updating the code sets, as well as the use of current guidelines.

The rule includes not only federally funded healthcare programs, but also private third-party payers. In other words, all payers will be required to use the same code sets, follow the same processes for updating the code sets, and—most important—use the same guidelines in applying the code sets. Final HIPAA legislation will become effective in 2002 and 2003.

The mandatory use of code sets offers another opportunity for coding managers to shine. Many of the current payers are unaware of the official guidelines in place for code sets, such as ICD-9-CM. Perhaps coding managers could offer educational sessions for local payers about applying guidelines. This would help payers consistently apply code set guidelines to federally funded healthcare programs.

Ensuring the Protection of Coded Data

External vendors who perform backlog coding activities or audit activities are considered business associates under HIPAA. Those vendors will be performing the coding function or auditing function using identifiable health information on behalf of the facility, but they are not internal, permanent employees of the facility. In that type of situation, the healthcare provider must ensure that the vendor (known as a business associate in the HIPAA legislation) has measures in place to ensure the security and privacy of the information to which it has access. This information must be outlined in the form of a contract between the healthcare provider and the business associate.

Terms of the contract must include provisions between the provider and the vendor/business associate that:

- Permit the use of the identifiable health information by the vendor

- Prohibit further disclosure of the identifiable health information by the vendor

- Prevent further disclosure of the identifiable health information by the vendor through the use of internal safeguard mechanisms

- Require a report to the provider of any unauthorized disclosure

- Ensure that subcontractors agree to and follow the same restrictions as the vendor

- Provide for the return or destruction of identifiable health information in cases in which the vendor provides coding services off-site

When vendors do not adhere to the assurances of security and privacy provided to the healthcare provider, they are considered noncompliant with HIPAA regulations. The coding manager must ensure that all contracts with external vendors or agents performing coding audits on behalf of the federal government are in accordance with the HIPAA legislation.

When in doubt, contracts should be reviewed by legal counsel or by the facility's security and privacy officer. The contract should be reviewed to ensure that it safeguards identifiable health information, as well as other aspects of the provider–vendor (business associate) relationship.

Conclusion

Although the federal government's efforts to prevent healthcare fraud and abuse have resulted in some hardships for the provider community, they have also resulted in a renewed effort to ensure quality services that are coded and billed correctly. Support for coders to attend educational programs has never been better. As a major component of complete and accurate coding to ensure appropriate billing, coders are receiving the education needed to enhance their skills and, therefore, their opportunities for advancement.

A whole new field of opportunity has opened up to health information managers. Many compliance officers across the country have come from an HIM background. By taking the initiative, these leaders have proven that their knowledge in coding, billing, and federal regulations made them the obvious choice for ensuring compliance throughout their facilities.

The advent of HIPAA legislation for code sets, as well as legislation related to security and privacy, has resulted in other new opportunities for health information coding managers. Many of them are stepping up to the plate and offering their knowledge of code sets, information systems, confidentiality, and federal regulations. As a result, many health information managers have become their facility's security and privacy officer.

Now and in the future, health information managers need to recognize when a door to opportunity is opened. By stepping through that door and offering their unique expertise, they will advance the profession and increase the credibility of other professionals in the field of health information management.

References and Bibliography

Broussard, K., and C. Hammen. 1999. Twenty pairs the OIG may be targeting for investigation. *Journal of Health Care Compliance* 1(3): 9–14, 36.

Bryant, G., and C. Hammen. 1999. *Healthcare Fraud and Abuse: Compliance from the HIM Perspective (Program in a Box)*. Chicago: American Health Information Management Association.

Hammen, C. 1997. Prevention of health care fraud and abuse is top priority for U.S. government. *Advance for Health Information Professionals* 7(8): 12–13.

_____. 1999. Coding compliance consultants must meet compliance criteria. *Journal of Health Care Compliance* 1(6): 34.

_____. 1999. Performing a manual coding audit. *Journal of the American Health Information Management Association* 70(6): 16–18.

_____. 1999. Specificity in compliance and medical record documentation. *CodeWrite* 8(4).

_____. 2001. Alert: The potential impact of an HCFA position on query forms. *CodeWrite* 10(2): 9, 12.

_____. 2001. Using physician profiling to improve documentation. *Journal of the American Health Information Management Association* 72(3): 19–20.

Hammen, C., and S. Prophet. 1998. Coding compliance: Practical strategies for success. *Journal of the American Health Information Management Association* 69(2): 50–61.

Appendix 8.1

Data Sources

Sources for finding external data for data-monitoring comparisons can be found at the following Web sites:

- CMS Web site, <http://www.cms.gov>. MedPAR data can be found under public use files. It provides information by DRG as to the number of Medicare discharges, as well as other information related to charges, length of stay, and reimbursement.

- American Hospital Directory Web site, <http://www.ahd.com>. Specific hospital data can be obtained through this site. General data are free of charge, while more specific data can be obtained when a subscription is purchased.

- Data Advantage Web site, <http://www.data-advantage.com>. Has comparative data products available for inpatients, outpatients, and physician-office patients.

- Solucient Web site, <http://www.solucient.com> or HCIA Web site, <http://www.hcia.com>. Has comparative data and benchmarking products available.

Appendix 8.2

MedPar Averages for CC Pairs

Medical CC-No CC pairs.xls

DRG	MDC	M/P	Description	% of MedPAR 99 Pair "with CC"
10	1	M	NERVOUS SYSTEM NEOPLASMS W CC	84.7%
11	1	M	NERVOUS SYSTEM NEOPLASMS W/O CC	
16	1	M	NONSPECIFIC CEREBROVASCULAR DISORDERS W CC	76.4%
17	1	M	NONSPECIFIC CEREBROVASCULAR DISORDERS W/O CC	
18	1	M	CRANIAL & PERIPHERAL NERVE DISORDERS W CC	76.5%
19	1	M	CRANIAL & PERIPHERAL NERVE DISORDERS W/O CC	
24	1	M	SEIZURE & HEADACHE AGE >17 W CC	68.2%
25	1	M	SEIZURE & HEADACHE AGE >17 W/O CC	
28	1	M	TRAUMATIC STUPOR & COMA, COMA <1 HR AGE >17 W CC	73.1%
29	1	M	TRAUMATIC STUPOR & COMA, COMA <1 HR AGE >17 W/O CC	
31	1	M	CONCUSSION AGE >17 W CC	67.6%
32	1	M	CONCUSSION AGE >17 W/O CC	
34	1	M	OTHER DISORDERS OF NERVOUS SYSTEM W CC	79.0%
35	1	M	OTHER DISORDERS OF NERVOUS SYSTEM W/O CC	
46	2	M	OTHER DISORDERS OF THE EYE AGE >17 W CC	71.6%
47	2	M	OTHER DISORDERS OF THE EYE AGE >17 W/O CC	
68	3	M	OTITIS MIA & URI AGE >17 W CC	76.0%
69	3	M	OTITIS MIA & URI AGE >17 W/O CC	
79	4	M	RESPIRATORY INFECTIONS & INFLAMMATIONS AGE >17 W CC	95.7%
80	4	M	RESPIRATORY INFECTIONS & INFLAMMATIONS AGE >17 W/O CC	
83	4	M	MAJOR CHEST TRAUMA W CC	81.0%
84	4	M	MAJOR CHEST TRAUMA W/O CC	
85	4	M	PLEURAL EFFUSION W CC	91.2%
86	4	M	PLEURAL EFFUSION W/O CC	
89	4	M	SIMPLE PNEUMONIA & PLEURISY AGE >17 W CC	91.1%
90	4	M	SIMPLE PNEUMONIA & PLEURISY AGE >17 W/O CC	
92	4	M	INTERSTITIAL LUNG DISEASE W CC	89.9%
93	4	M	INTERSTITIAL LUNG DISEASE W/O CC	
94	4	M	PNEUMOTHORAX W CC	88.7%
95	4	M	PNEUMOTHORAX W/O CC	
96	4	M	BRONCHITIS & ASTHMA AGE >17 W CC	67.2%
97	4	M	BRONCHITIS & ASTHMA AGE >17 W/O CC	
99	4	M	RESPIRATORY SIGNS & SYMPTOMS W CC	71.6%
100	4	M	RESPIRATORY SIGNS & SYMPTOMS W/O CC	
101	4	M	OTHER RESPIRATORY SYSTEM DIAGNOSES W CC	79.8%
102	4	M	OTHER RESPIRATORY SYSTEM DIAGNOSES W/O CC	
121	5	M	CIRCULATORY DISORDERS W AMI & MAJOR COMP, DISCHARGED ALIVE (MODIFIED 10/1/97)	66.9%
122	5	M	CIRCULATORY DISORDERS W AMI W/O MAJOR COMP, DISCHARGED ALIVE (MODIFIED 10/1/97)	

Medical CC-No CC pairs.xls

DRG	MDC	M/P	Description	% of MedPAR 99 Pair "with CC"
130	5	M	PERIPHERAL VASCULAR DISORDERS W CC	76.8%
131	5	M	PERIPHERAL VASCULAR DISORDERS W/O CC	
132	5	M	ATHEROSCLEROSIS W CC	95.3%
133	5	M	ATHEROSCLEROSIS W/O CC	
135	5	M	CARDIAC CONGENITAL & VALVULAR DISORDERS AGE > 17 W CC	85.9%
136	5	M	CARDIAC CONGENITAL & VALVULAR DISORDERS AGE > 17 W/O CC	
138	5	M	CARDIAC ARRHYTHMIA & CONDUCTION DISORDERS W CC	71.2%
139	5	M	CARDIAC ARRHYTHMIA & CONDUCTION DISORDERS W/O CC	
141	5	M	SYNCOPE & COLLAPSE W CC	66.8%
142	5	M	SYNCOPE & COLLAPSE W/O CC	
144	5	M	OTHER CIRCULATORY SYSTEM DIAGNOSES W CC	92.0%
145	5	M	OTHER CIRCULATORY SYSTEM DIAGNOSES W/O CC	
172	6	M	DIGESTIVE MALIGNANCY W CC	92.4%
173	6	M	DIGESTIVE MALIGNANCY W/O CC	
174	6	M	G.I. HEMORRHAGE W CC	89.4%
175	6	M	G.I. HEMORRHAGE W/O CC	
177	6	M	UNCOMPLICATED PEPTIC ULCER W CC	72.6%
178	6	M	UNCOMPLICATED PEPTIC ULCER W/O CC	
180	6	M	G.I. OBSTRUCTION W CC	77.8%
181	6	M	G.I. OBSTRUCTION W/O CC	
182	6	M	ESOPHAGITIS, GASTROENT & MISC DIGEST DISORDERS AGE > 17 W CC	74.8%
183	6	M	ESOPHAGITIS, GASTROENT & MISC DIGEST DISORDERS AGE > 17 W/O CC	
188	6	M	OTHER DIGESTIVE SYSTEM DIAGNOSES AGE >17 W CC	87.0%
189	6	M	OTHER DIGESTIVE SYSTEM DIAGNOSES AGE >17 W/O CC	
205	7	M	DISORDERS OF LIVER EXCEPT MALIG,CIRR,ALC HEPA W CC	92.7%
206	7	M	DISORDERS OF LIVER EXCEPT MALIG,CIRR,ALC HEPA W/O CC	
207	7	M	DISORDERS OF THE BILIARY TRACT W CC	76.2%
208	7	M	DISORDERS OF THE BILIARY TRACT W/O CC	
240	8	M	CONNECTIVE TISSUE DISORDERS W CC	80.0%
241	8	M	CONNECTIVE TISSUE DISORDERS W/O CC	
244	8	M	BONE DISEASES & SPECIFIC ARTHROPATHIES W CC	70.7%
245	8	M	BONE DISEASES & SPECIFIC ARTHROPATHIES W/O CC	
250	8	M	FX, SPRN, STRN & DISL OF FOREARM, HAND, FOOT AGE > 17 W CC	59.8%
251	8	M	FX, SPRN, STRN & DISL OF FOREARM, HAND, FOOT AGE > 17 W/O CC	
253	8	M	FX, SPRN, STRN & DISL OF UP ARM, LOW LEG EX FOOT AGE > 17 W CC	64.6%
254	8	M	FX, SPRN, STRN & DISL OF UP ARM, LOW LEG EX FOOT AGE > 17 W/O CC	
272	9	M	MAJOR SKIN DISORDERS W CC	80.3%
273	9	M	MAJOR SKIN DISORDERS W/O CC	

Medical CC-No CC pairs.xls

DRG	MDC	M/P	Description	% of MedPAR 99 Pair "with CC"
274	9	M	MALIGNANT BREAST DISORDERS W CC	91.2%
275	9	M	MALIGNANT BREAST DISORDERS W/O CC	
277	9	M	CELLULITIS AGE >17 W CC	74.6%
278	9	M	CELLULITIS AGE >17 W/O CC	
280	9	M	TRAUMA TO THE SKIN, SUBCUT TISS & BREAST AGE > 17 W CC	69.2%
281	9	M	TRAUMA TO THE SKIN, SUBCUT TISS & BREAST AGE > 17 W/O CC	
283	9	M	MINOR SKIN DISORDERS W CC	74.3%
284	9	M	MINOR SKIN DISORDERS W/O CC	
296	10	M	NUTRITIONAL & MISC METABOLIC DISORDERS AGE >17 W CC	85.0%
297	10	M	NUTRITIONAL & MISC METABOLIC DISORDERS AGE >17 W/O CC	
300	10	M	ENDOCRINE DISORDERS W CC	83.4%
301	10	M	ENDOCRINE DISORDERS W/O CC	
318	11	M	KIDNEY & URINARY TRACT NEOPLASMS W CC	92.2%
319	11	M	KIDNEY & URINARY TRACT NEOPLASMS W/O CC	
320	11	M	KIDNEY & URINARY TRACT INFECTIONS AGE >17 W CC	86.6%
321	11	M	KIDNEY & URINARY TRACT INFECTIONS AGE >17 W/O CC	
323	11	M	URINARY STONES W CC, &/OR ESW LITHOTRIPSY	69.0%
324	11	M	URINARY STONES W/O CC	
325	11	M	KIDNEY & URINARY TRACT SIGNS & SYMPTOMS AGE > 17 W CC	76.3%
326	11	M	KIDNEY & URINARY TRACT SIGNS & SYMPTOMS AGE > 17 W/O CC	
328	11	M	URETHRAL STRICTURE AGE >17 W CC	87.2%
329	11	M	URETHRAL STRICTURE AGE >17 W/O CC	
331	11	M	OTHER KIDNEY & URINARY TRACT DIAGNOSES AGE >17 W CC	90.0%
332	11	M	OTHER KIDNEY & URINARY TRACT DIAGNOSES AGE >17 W/O CC	
346	12	M	MALIGNANCY, MALE REPRODUCTIVE SYSTEM, W CC	92.1%
347	12	M	MALIGNANCY, MALE REPRODUCTIVE SYSTEM, W/O CC	
348	12	M	BENIGN PROSTATIC HYPERTROPHY W CC	84.0%
349	12	M	BENIGN PROSTATIC HYPERTROPHY W/O CC	
366	13	M	MALIGNANCY, FEMALE REPRODUCTIVE SYSTEM W CC	89.9%
367	13	M	MALIGNANCY, FEMALE REPRODUCTIVE SYSTEM W/O CC	
398	16	M	RETICULOENDOTHELIAL & IMMUNITY DISORDERS W CC	91.8%
399	16	M	RETICULOENDOTHELIAL & IMMUNITY DISORDERS W/O CC	
403	17	M	LYMPHOMA & NON-ACUTE LEUKEMIA W CC	88.1%
404	17	M	LYMPHOMA & NON-ACUTE LEUKEMIA W/O CC	
413	17	M	OTHER MYELOPROLIF DIS OR POORLY DIFF NEOPL DIAG W CC	89.6%
414	17	M	OTHER MYELOPROLIF DIS OR POORLY DIFF NEOPL DIAG W/O CC	
419	18	M	FEVER OF UNKNOWN ORIGIN AGE >17 W CC	83.7%
420	18	M	FEVER OF UNKNOWN ORIGIN AGE >17 W/O CC	

Medical CC-No CC pairs.xls

DRG	MDC	M/P	Description	% of MedPAR 99 Pair "with CC"
434	20	M	ALC/DRUG ABUSE OR DEPEND, DETOX OR OTH SYMPT TREAT W CC	60.1%
435	20	M	ALC/DRUG ABUSE OR DEPEND, DETOX OR OTH SYMPT TREAT W/O CC	
444	21	M	TRAUMATIC INJURY AGE >17 W CC	69.6%
445	21	M	TRAUMATIC INJURY AGE >17 W/O CC	
449	21	M	POISONING & TOXIC EFFECTS OF DRUGS AGE >17 W CC	80.6%
450	21	M	POISONING & TOXIC EFFECTS OF DRUGS AGE >17 W/O CC	
452	21	M	COMPLICATIONS OF TREATMENT W CC	82.9%
453	21	M	COMPLICATIONS OF TREATMENT W/O CC	
454	21	M	OTHER INJURY, POISONING & TOXIC EFFECT DIAG W CC	82.2%
455	21	M	OTHER INJURY, POISONING & TOXIC EFFECT DIAG W/O CC	
463	23	M	SIGNS & SYMPTOMS W CC	77.6%
464	23	M	SIGNS & SYMPTOMS W/O CC	
508	22	M	FULL THICKNESS BURN W/O SKIN GRFT OR INHAL INJ W CC OR SIG TRAUMA (EFFECTIVE 10/1/98)	79.5%
509	22	M	FULL THICKNESS BURN W/O SKIN GRFT OR INH INJ W/O CC OR SIG TRAUMA (EFFECTIVE 10/1/98)	
510	22	M	NON-EXTENSIVE BURNS W CC OR SIGNIFICANT TRAUMA (EFFECTIVE 10/1/98)	73.4%
511	22	M	NON-EXTENSIVE BURNS W/O CC OR SIGNIFICANT TRAUMA (EFFECTIVE 10/1/98)	
			TOTAL—% Medical "with CC" Pairs of Total	**81.5%**

Surgical CC-No CC pairs.xls

DRG	MDC	M/P	Description	% of MedPAR 99 Pair "with CC"
7	1	P	PERIPH & CRANIAL NERVE & OTHER NERV SYST PROC W CC	76.6%
8	1	P	PERIPH & CRANIAL NERVE & OTHER NERV SYST PROC W/O CC	
76	4	P	OTHER RESP SYSTEM O.R. PROCEDURES W CC	94.4%
77	4	P	OTHER RESP SYSTEM O.R. PROCEDURES W/O CC	
110	5	P	MAJOR CARDIOVASCULAR PROCEDURES W CC	88.5%
111	5	P	MAJOR CARDIOVASCULAR PROCEDURES W/O CC	
146	6	P	RECTAL RESECTION W CC	82.3%
147	6	P	RECTAL RESECTION W/O CC	
148	6	P	MAJOR SMALL & LARGE BOWEL PROCEDURES W CC	88.4%
149	6	P	MAJOR SMALL & LARGE BOWEL PROCEDURES W/O CC	
150	6	P	PERITONEAL ADHESIOLYSIS W CC	81.9%
151	6	P	PERITONEAL ADHESIOLYSIS W/O CC	
152	6	P	MINOR SMALL & LARGE BOWEL PROCEDURES W CC	69.8%
153	6	P	MINOR SMALL & LARGE BOWEL PROCEDURES W/O CC	
154	6	P	STOMACH, ESOPHAGEAL & DUODENAL PROCEDURES AGE > 17 W CC	82.9%
155	6	P	STOMACH, ESOPHAGEAL & DUODENAL PROCEDURES AGE > 17 W/O CC	
157	6	P	ANAL & STOMAL PROCEDURES W CC	65.0%
158	6	P	ANAL & STOMAL PROCEDURES W/O CC	
159	6	P	HERNIA PROCEDURES EXCEPT INGUINAL & FEMORAL AGE > 17 W CC	59.9%
160	6	P	HERNIA PROCEDURES EXCEPT INGUINAL & FEMORAL AGE > 17 W/O CC	
161	6	P	INGUINAL & FEMORAL HERNIA PROCEDURES AGE >17 W CC	62.0%
162	6	P	INGUINAL & FEMORAL HERNIA PROCEDURES AGE >17 W/O CC	
164	6	P	APPENDECTOMY W COMPLICATED PRINCIPAL DIAG W CC	70.9%
165	6	P	APPENDECTOMY W COMPLICATED PRINCIPAL DIAG W/O CC	
166	6	P	APPENDECTOMY W/O COMPLICATED PRINCIPAL DIAG W CC	53.2%
167	6	P	APPENDECTOMY W/O COMPLICATED PRINCIPAL DIAG W/O CC	
168	6	P	MOUTH PROCEDURES W CC	65.4%
169	6	P	MOUTH PROCEDURES W/O CC	
170	6	P	OTHER DIGESTIVE SYSTEM O.R. PROCEDURES W CC	90.9%
171	6	P	OTHER DIGESTIVE SYSTEM O.R. PROCEDURES W/O CC	
191	7	P	PANCREAS, LIVER & SHUNT PROCEDURES W CC	90.6%
192	7	P	PANCREAS, LIVER & SHUNT PROCEDURES W/O CC	
193	7	P	BILIARY TRACT PROC EXCEPT ONLY CHOLECYST W OR W/O CDE W CC	88.2%
194	7	P	BILIARY TRACT PROC EXCEPT ONLY CHOLECYST W OR W/O CDE W/O CC	
195	7	P	CHOLECYSTECTOMY W C.D.E. W CC	80.4%
196	7	P	CHOLECYSTECTOMY W C.D.E. W/O CC	
197	7	P	CHOLECYSTECTOMY EXCEPT BY LAPAROSCOPE W/O C.D.E. W CC	76.9%
198	7	P	CHOLECYSTECTOMY EXCEPT BY LAPAROSCOPE W/O C.D.E. W/O CC	

Surgical CC-No CC pairs.xls

DRG	MDC	M/P	Description	% of MedPAR 99 Pair "with CC"
210	8	P	HIP & FEMUR PROCEDURES EXCEPT MAJOR JOINT AGE >17 W CC	80.2%
211	8	P	HIP & FEMUR PROCEDURES EXCEPT MAJOR JOINT AGE > 17 W/O CC	
214	8	P	BACK & NECK PROCEDURES W CC (INVALID AS OF 10/1/97)	—
215	8	P	BACK & NECK PROCEDURES W/O CC (INVALID AS OF 10/1/97)	
218	8	P	LOWER EXTREM & HUMER PROC EXCEPT HIP, FOOT, FEMUR AGE > 17 W CC	52.7%
219	8	P	LOWER EXTREM & HUMER PROC EXCEPT HIP, FOOT, FEMUR AGE > 17 W/O CC	
221	8	P	KNEE PROCEDURES W CC (INVALID AS OF 10/1/97)	—
222	8	P	KNEE PROCEDURES W/O CC (INVALID AS OF 10/1/97)	
223	8	P	MAJOR SHOULDER/ELBOW PROC, OR OTHER UPPER EXTREMITY PROC W CC	68.6%
224	8	P	SHOULDER,ELBOW OR FOREARM PROC, EXC MAJOR JOINT PROC, W/O CC	
226	8	P	SOFT TISSUE PROCEDURES W CC	53.0%
227	8	P	SOFT TISSUE PROCEDURES W/O CC	
228	8	P	MAJOR THUMB OR JOINT PROC, OR OTH HAND OR WRIST PROC W CC	69.4%
229	8	P	HAND OR WRIST PROC, EXCEPT MAJOR JOINT PROC, W/O CC	
233	8	P	OTHER MUSCULOSKELET SYS & CONN TISS O.R. PROC W CC	63.0%
234	8	P	OTHER MUSCULOSKELET SYS & CONN TISS O.R. PROC W/O CC	
257	9	P	TOTAL MASTECTOMY FOR MALIGNANCY W CC	51.6%
258	9	P	TOTAL MASTECTOMY FOR MALIGNANCY W/O CC	
259	9	P	SUBTOTAL MASTECTOMY FOR MALIGNANCY W CC	43.7%
260	9	P	SUBTOTAL MASTECTOMY FOR MALIGNANCY W/O CC	
263	9	P	SKIN GRAFT &/OR DEBRID FOR SKN ULCER OR CELLULITIS W CC	86.3%
264	9	P	SKIN GRAFT &/OR DEBRID FOR SKN ULCER OR CELLULITIS W/O CC	
265	9	P	SKIN GRAFT &/OR DEBRID EXCEPT FOR SKIN ULCER OR CELLULITIS W CC	60.4%
266	9	P	SKIN GRAFT &/OR DEBRID EXCEPT FOR SKIN ULCER OR CELLULITIS W/O CC	
269	9	P	OTHER SKIN, SUBCUT TISS & BREAST PROC W CC	76.4%
270	9	P	OTHER SKIN, SUBCUT TISS & BREAST PROC W/O CC	
292	10	P	OTHER ENDOCRINE, NUTRIT & METAB O.R. PROC W CC	93.9%
293	10	P	OTHER ENDOCRINE, NUTRIT & METAB O.R. PROC W/O CC	
304	11	P	KIDNEY, URETER & MAJOR BLADDER PROC FOR NON-NEOPLASM W CC	80.8%
305	11	P	KIDNEY, URETER & MAJOR BLADDER PROC FOR NON-NEOPLASM W/O CC	
306	11	P	PROSTATECTOMY W CC	78.1%
307	11	P	PROSTATECTOMY W/O CC	
308	11	P	MINOR BLADDER PROCEDURES W CC	66.0%
309	11	P	MINOR BLADDER PROCEDURES W/O CC	

Surgical CC-No CC pairs.xls

DRG	MDC	M/P	Description	% of MedPAR 99 Pair "with CC"
310	11	P	TRANSURETHRAL PROCEDURES W CC	74.3%
311	11	P	TRANSURETHRAL PROCEDURES W/O CC	
312	11	P	URETHRAL PROCEDURES, AGE >17 W CC	71.3%
313	11	P	URETHRAL PROCEDURES, AGE >17 W/O CC	
334	12	P	MAJOR MALE PELVIC PROCEDURES W CC	51.1%
335	12	P	MAJOR MALE PELVIC PROCEDURES W/O CC	
336	12	P	TRANSURETHRAL PROSTATECTOMY W CC	57.0%
337	12	P	TRANSURETHRAL PROSTATECTOMY W/O CC	
354	13	P	UTERINE, ADNEXA PROC FOR NON-OVARIAN/ADNEXAL MALIGNANCY W CC	59.0%
355	13	P	UTERINE, ADNEXA PROC FOR NON-OVARIAN/ADNEXAL MALIGNANCY W/O CC	
358	13	P	UTERINE & ADNEXA PROC FOR NON-MALIGNANCY W CC	42.6%
359	13	P	UTERINE & ADNEXA PROC FOR NON-MALIGNANCY W/O CC	
370	14	P	CESAREAN SECTION W CC	48.8%
371	14	P	CESAREAN SECTION W/O CC	
401	17	P	LYMPHOMA & NON-ACUTE LEUKEMIA W OTHER O.R. PROC W CC	79.7%
402	17	P	LYMPHOMA & NON-ACUTE LEUKEMIA W OTHER O.R. PROC W/O CC	
406	17	P	MYELOPROLIF DISORD OR POORLY DIFF NEOPL W MAJ O.R. PROC W CC	78.6%
407	17	P	MYELOPROLIF DISORD OR POORLY DIFF NEOPL W MAJ O.R. PROC W/O CC	
442	21	P	OTHER O.R. PROCEDURES FOR INJURIES W CC	81.7%
443	21	P	OTHER O.R. PROCEDURES FOR INJURIES W/O CC	
478	5	P	OTHER VASCULAR PROCEDURES W CC	83.2%
479	5	P	OTHER VASCULAR PROCEDURES W/O CC	
493	7	P	LAPAROSCOPIC CHOLECYSTECTOMY W/O C.D.E. W CC	66.5%
494	7	P	LAPAROSCOPIC CHOLECYSTECTOMY W/O C.D.E. W/O CC	
497	8	P	SPINAL FUSION W CC (EFFECTIVE 10/1/97)	54.0%
498	8	P	SPINAL FUSION W/O CC (EFFECTIVE 10/1/97)	
499	8	P	BACK & NECK PROCEDURES EXCEPT SPINAL FUSION W CC (EFFECTIVE 10/1/97)	42.2%
500	8	P	BACK & NECK PROCEDURES EXCEPT SPINAL FUSION W/O CC (EFFECTIVE 10/1/97)	
501	8	P	KNEE PROCEDURES W PDX OF INFECTION W CC (EFFECTIVE 10/1/97)	75.9%
502	8	P	KNEE PROCEDURES W PDX OF INFECTION W/O CC (EFFECTIVE 10/1/97)	
506	22	P	FULL THICKNESS BURN W SKIN GRAFT OR INHAL INJ W CC OR SIG TRAUMA (EFFECTIVE 10/1/98)	77.3%
507	22	P	FULL THICKNESS BURN W SKIN GRFT OR INHAL INJ W/O CC OR SIG TRAUMA (EFFECTIVE 10/1/98)	
			TOTAL—% Surgical "with CC" Pairs of Total	**72.3%**

Total CC-No CC pairs.xls

DRG	MDC	Description	% of MedPAR 99 Pair "with CC"
7	1	PERIPH & CRANIAL NERVE & OTHER NERV SYST PROC W CC	76.6%
8	1	PERIPH & CRANIAL NERVE & OTHER NERV SYST PROC W/O CC	
10	1	NERVOUS SYSTEM NEOPLASMS W CC	84.7%
11	1	NERVOUS SYSTEM NEOPLASMS W/O CC	
16	1	NONSPECIFIC CEREBROVASCULAR DISORDERS W CC	76.4%
17	1	NONSPECIFIC CEREBROVASCULAR DISORDERS W/O CC	
18	1	CRANIAL & PERIPHERAL NERVE DISORDERS W CC	76.5%
19	1	CRANIAL & PERIPHERAL NERVE DISORDERS W/O CC	
24	1	SEIZURE & HEADACHE AGE >17 W CC	68.2%
25	1	SEIZURE & HEADACHE AGE >17 W/O CC	
28	1	TRAUMATIC STUPOR & COMA, COMA <1 HR AGE >17 W CC	73.1%
29	1	TRAUMATIC STUPOR & COMA, COMA <1 HR AGE >17 W/O CC	
31	1	CONCUSSION AGE >17 W CC	67.6%
32	1	CONCUSSION AGE >17 W/O CC	
34	1	OTHER DISORDERS OF NERVOUS SYSTEM W CC	79.0%
35	1	OTHER DISORDERS OF NERVOUS SYSTEM W/O CC	
46	2	OTHER DISORDERS OF THE EYE AGE >17 W CC	71.6%
47	2	OTHER DISORDERS OF THE EYE AGE >17 W/O CC	
68	3	OTITIS MIA & URI AGE >17 W CC	76.0%
69	3	OTITIS MIA & URI AGE >17 W/O CC	
76	4	OTHER RESP SYSTEM O.R. PROCEDURES W CC	94.4%
77	4	OTHER RESP SYSTEM O.R. PROCEDURES W/O CC	
79	4	RESPIRATORY INFECTIONS & INFLAMMATIONS AGE >17 W CC	95.7%
80	4	RESPIRATORY INFECTIONS & INFLAMMATIONS AGE >17 W/O CC	
83	4	MAJOR CHEST TRAUMA W CC	81.0%
84	4	MAJOR CHEST TRAUMA W/O CC	
85	4	PLEURAL EFFUSION W CC	91.2%
86	4	PLEURAL EFFUSION W/O CC	
89	4	SIMPLE PNEUMONIA & PLEURISY AGE >17 W CC	91.1%
90	4	SIMPLE PNEUMONIA & PLEURISY AGE >17 W/O CC	
92	4	INTERSTITIAL LUNG DISEASE W CC	89.9%
93	4	INTERSTITIAL LUNG DISEASE W/O CC	
94	4	PNEUMOTHORAX W CC	88.7%
95	4	PNEUMOTHORAX W/O CC	
96	4	BRONCHITIS & ASTHMA AGE >17 W CC	67.2%
97	4	BRONCHITIS & ASTHMA AGE >17 W/O CC	
99	4	RESPIRATORY SIGNS & SYMPTOMS W CC	71.6%
100	4	RESPIRATORY SIGNS & SYMPTOMS W/O CC	
101	4	OTHER RESPIRATORY SYSTEM DIAGNOSES W CC	79.8%
102	4	OTHER RESPIRATORY SYSTEM DIAGNOSES W/O CC	
110	5	MAJOR CARDIOVASCULAR PROCEDURES W CC	88.5%
111	5	MAJOR CARDIOVASCULAR PROCEDURES W/O CC	
121	5	CIRCULATORY DISORDERS W AMI & MAJOR COMP DISCHARGED ALIVE (MODIFIED 10/1/97)	66.9%
122	5	CIRCULATORY DISORDERS W AMI W/O MAJOR COMP, DISCHARGED ALIVE (MODIFIED 10/1/97)	
130	5	PERIPHERAL VASCULAR DISORDERS W CC	76.8%
131	5	PERIPHERAL VASCULAR DISORDERS W/O CC	

Total CC-No CC pairs.xls

DRG	MDC	Description	% of MedPAR 99 Pair "with CC"
132	5	ATHEROSCLEROSIS W CC	95.3%
133	5	ATHEROSCLEROSIS W/O CC	
135	5	CARDIAC CONGENITAL & VALVULAR DISORDERS AGE > 17 W CC	85.9%
136	5	CARDIAC CONGENITAL & VALVULAR DISORDERS AGE > 17 W/O CC	
138	5	CARDIAC ARRHYTHMIA & CONDUCTION DISORDERS W CC	71.2%
139	5	CARDIAC ARRHYTHMIA & CONDUCTION DISORDERS W/O CC	
141	5	SYNCOPE & COLLAPSE W CC	66.8%
142	5	SYNCOPE & COLLAPSE W/O C	
144	5	OTHER CIRCULATORY SYSTEM DIAGNOSES W CC	92.0%
145	5	OTHER CIRCULATORY SYSTEM DIAGNOSES W/O CC	
146	6	RECTAL RESECTION W CC	82.3%
147	6	RECTAL RESECTION W/O CC	
148	6	MAJOR SMALL & LARGE BOWEL PROCEDURES W CC	88.4%
149	6	MAJOR SMALL & LARGE BOWEL PROCEDURES W/O CC	
150	6	PERITONEAL ADHESIOLYSIS W CC	81.9%
151	6	PERITONEAL ADHESIOLYSIS W/O CC	
152	6	MINOR SMALL & LARGE BOWEL PROCEDURES W CC	69.8%
153	6	MINOR SMALL 7 LARGE BOWEL PROCEDURES W/O CC	
154	6	STOMACH, ESOPHAGEAL & DUODENAL PROCEDURES AGE > 17 W CC	82.9%
155	6	STOMACH, ESOPHAGEAL & DUODENAL PROCEDURES AGE > 17 W/O CC	
157	6	ANAL & STOMAL PROCEDURES W CC	65.0%
158	6	ANAL & STOMAL PROCEDURES W/O CC	
159	6	HERNIA PROCEDURES EXCEPT INGUINAL & FEMORAL AGE > 17 W CC	59.9%
160	6	HERNIA PROCEDURES EXCEPT INGUINAL & FEMORAL AGE > 17 W/O CC	
161	6	INGUINAL & FEMORAL HERNIA PROCEDURES AGE > 17 W CC	62.0%
162	6	INGUINAL & FEMORAL HERNIA PROCEDURES AGE > 17 W/O CC	
164	6	APPENDECTOMY W COMPLICATED PRINCIPAL DIAG W CC	70.9%
165	6	APPENDECTOMY W COMPLICATED PRINCIPAL DIAG W/O CC	
166	6	APPENDECTOMY W/O COMPLICATED PRINCIPAL DIAG W CC	53.2%
167	6	APPENDECTOMY W/O COMPLICATED PRINCIPAL DIAG W/O CC	
168	3	MOUTH PROCEDURES W CC	65.4%
169	3	MOUTH PROCEDURES W/O CC	
170	6	OTHER DIGESTIVE SYSTEM O.R. PROCEDURES W CC	90.9%
171	6	OTHER DIGESTIVE SYSTEM O.R. PROCEDURES W/O CC	
172	6	DIGESTIVE MALIGNANCY W CC	92.4%
173	6	DIGESTIVE MALIGNANCY W/O CC	
174	6	G.I. HEMORRHAGE W CC	89.4%
175	6	G.I. HEMORRHAGE W/O CC	
177	6	UNCOMPLICATED PEPTIC ULCER W CC	72.6%
178	6	UNCOMPLICATED PEPTIC ULCER W/O CC	
180	6	G.I. OBSTRUCTION W CC	77.8%
181	6	G.I. OBSTRUCTION W/O CC	
182	6	ESOPHAGITIS, GASTROENT & MISC DIGEST DISORDERS AGE > 17 W CC	74.8%
183	6	ESOPHAGITIS, GASTROENT & MISC DIGEST DISORDERS AGE > 17 W/O CC	

Total CC-No CC pairs.xls

DRG	MDC	Description	% of MedPAR 99 Pair "with CC"
188	6	OTHER DIGESTIVE SYSTEM DIAGNOSES AGE > 17 W CC	87.0%
189	6	OTHER DIGESTIVE SYSTEM DIAGNOSES AGE > 17 W/O CC	
191	7	PANCREAS, LIVER & SHUNT PROCEDURES W CC	90.6%
192	7	PANCREAS, LIVER & SHUNT PROCEDURES W/O CC	
193	7	BILIARY TRACT PROC EXCEPT ONLY CHOLECYST W OR W/O CDE W CC	88.2%
194	7	BILIARY TRACT PROC EXCEPT ONLY CHOLECYST W OR W/O CDE W/O CC	
195	7	CHOLECYSTECTOMY W C.D.E. W CC	80.4%
196	7	CHOLECYSTECTOMY W C.D.E. W/O CC	
197	7	CHOLECYSTECTOMY EXCEPT BY LAPAROSCOPE W/O C.D.E. W CC	76.9%
198	7	CHOLECYSTECTOMY EXCEPT BY LAPAROSCOPE W/O C.D.E. W/O CC	
205	7	DISORDERS OF LIVER EXCEPT MALIG, CIRR, ALC HEPA W CC	92.7%
206	7	DISORDERS OF LIVER EXCEPT MALIG, CIRR, ALC HEPA W/O CC	
207	7	DISORDERS OF THE BILIARY TRACT W CC	76.2%
208	7	DISORDERS OF THE BILIARY TRACT W/O CC	
210	8	HIP & FEMUR PROCEDURES EXCEPT MAJOR JOINT AGE > 17 W CC	80.2%
211	8	HIP & FEMUR PROCEDURES EXCEPT MAJOR JOINT AGE > 17 W/O CC	
214	8	BACK & NECK PROCEDURES W CC (INVALID AS OF 10/1/97)	—
215	8	BACK & NECK PROCEDURES W/O CC (INVALID AS OF 10/1/97)	
218	8	LOWER EXTREM & HUMER PROC EXCEPT HIP, FOOT, FEMUR AGE > 17 W CC	52.7%
219	8	LOWER EXTREM & HUMER PROC EXCEPT HIP, FOOT, FEMUR AGE > 17 W/O CC	
221	8	KNEE PROCEDURES W CC (INVALID AS OF 10/1/97)	—
222	8	KNEE PROCEDURES W/O CC (INVALID AS OF 10/1/97)	
223	8	MAJOR SHOULDER/ELBOW PROC, OR OTHER UPPER EXTREMITY PROC W CC	68.6%
224	8	MAJOR SHOULDER/ELBOW PROC, OR OTHER UPPER EXTREMITY PROC W/O CC	
226	8	SOFT TISSUE PROCEDURES W CC	53.0%
227	8	SOFT TISSUE PROCEDURES W/O CC	
228	8	MAJOR THUMB OR JOINT PROC, OR OTH HAND OR WRIST PROC W CC	69.4%
229	8	HAND OR WRIST PROC, EXCEPT MAJOR JOINT PROC, W/O CC	
233	8	OTHER MUSCULOSKELET SYS & CONN TISS O.R. PROC W CC	63.0%
234	8	OTHER MUSCULOSKELET SYS & CONN TISS O.R. PROC W/O CC	
240	8	CONNECTIVE TISSUE DISORDERS W CC	80.0%
241	8	CONNECTIVE TISSUE DISORDERS W/O CC	
244	8	BONE DISEASES & SPECIFIC ARTHROPATHIES W CC	70.7%
245	8	BONE DISEASES & SPECIFIC ARTHROPATHIES W/O CC	
250	8	FX, SPRN, STRN & DISL OF FOREARM, HAND, FOOT AGE > 17 W CC	59.8%
251	8	FX, SPRN, STRN & DISL OF FOREARM, HAND, FOOT AGE > 17 W/O CC	
253	8	FX, SPRN, STRN & DISL OF UP ARM, LOW LEG EX FOOT AGE > 17 W CC	64.6%
254	8	FX, SPRN, STRN & DISL OF UP ARM, LOW LEG EX FOOT AGE > 17 W/O CC	

Total CC-No CC pairs.xls

DRG	MDC	Description	% of MedPAR 99 Pair "with CC"
257	9	TOTAL MASTECTOMY FOR MALIGNANCY W CC	51.6%
258	9	TOTAL MASTECTOMY FOR MALIGNANCY W/O CC	
259	9	SUBTOTAL MASTECTOMY FOR MALIGNANCY W CC	43.7%
260	9	SUBTOTAL MASTECTOMY FOR MALIGNANCY W/O CC	
263	9	SKIN GRAFT &/OR DEBRID FOR SKN ULCER OR CELLULITIS W CC	86.3%
264	9	SKIN GRAFT &/OR DEBRID FOR SKN ULCER OR CELLULITIS W/O CC	
265	9	SKIN GRAFT &/OR DEBRID EXCEPT FOR SKIN ULCER OR CELLULITIS W CC	60.4%
266	9	SKIN GRAFT &/OR DEBRID EXCEPT FOR SKIN ULCER OR CELLULITIS W/O CC	
269	9	OTHER SKIN, SUBCUT TISS & BREAST PROC W CC	76.4%
270	9	OTHER SKIN, SUBCUT TISS & BREAST PROC W/O CC	
272	9	MAJOR SKIN DISORDERS W CC	80.3%
273	9	MAJOR SKIN DISORDERS W/O CC	
274	9	MALIGNANT BREAST DISORDERS W CC	91.2%
275	9	MALIGNANT BREAST DISORDERS W/O CC	
277	9	CELLULITIS AGE >17 W CC	74.6%
278	9	CELLULITIS AGE >17 W/O CC	
280	9	TRAUMA TO THE SKIN, SUBCUT TISS & BREAST AGE > 17 W CC	69.2%
281	9	TRAUMA TO THE SKIN, SUBCUT TISS & BREAST AGE > 17 W/O CC	
283	9	MINOR SKIN DISORDERS W CC	74.3%
284	9	MINOR SKIN DISORDERS W/O CC	
292	10	OTHER ENDOCRINE, NUTRIT & METAB O.R. PROC W CC	93.9%
293	10	OTHER ENDOCRINE, NUTRIT & METAB O.R. PROC W/O CC	
296	10	NUTRITIONAL & MISC METABOLIC DISORDERS AGE >17 W CC	85.0%
297	10	NUTRITIONAL & MISC METABOLIC DISORDERS AGE >17 W/O CC	
300	10	ENDOCRINE DISORDERS W CC	83.4%
301	10	ENDOCRINE DISORDERS W/O CC	
304	11	KIDNEY, URETER & MAJOR BLADDER PROC FOR NON-NEOPLASM W CC	80.8%
305	11	KIDNEY, URETER & MAJOR BLADDER PROC FOR NON-NEOPLASM W/O CC	
306	11	PROSTATECTOMY W CC	78.1%
307	11	PROSTATECTOMY W/O CC	
308	11	MINOR BLADDER PROCEDURES W CC	66.0%
309	11	MINOR BLADDER PROCEDURES W/O CC	
310	11	TRANSURETHRAL PROCEDURES W CC	74.3%
311	11	TRANSURETHRAL PROCEDURES W/O CC	
312	11	URETHRAL PROCEDURES, AGE >17 W CC	71.3%
313	11	URETHRAL PROCEDURES, AGE >17 W/O CC	
318	11	KIDNEY & URINARY TRACT NEOPLASMS W CC	92.2%
319	11	KIDNEY & URINARY TRACT NEOPLASMS W/O CC	
320	11	KIDNEY & URINARY TRACT INFECTIONS AGE >17 W CC	86.6%
321	11	KIDNEY & URINARY TRACT INFECTIONS AGE >17 W/O CC	
323	11	URINARY STONES W CC, &/OR ESW LITHOTRIPSY	69.0%
324	11	URINARY STONES W/O CC	
325	11	KIDNEY & URINARY TRACT SIGNS & SYMPTOMS AGE > 17 W CC	76.3%
326	11	KIDNEY & URINARY TRACT SIGNS & SYMPTOMS AGE > 17 W/O CC	
328	11	URETHRAL STRICTURE AGE >17 W CC	87.2%
329	11	URETHRAL STRICTURE AGE >17 W/O CC	

Total CC-No CC pairs.xls

DRG	MDC	Description	% of MedPAR 99 Pair "with CC"
331	11	OTHER KIDNEY & URINARY TRACT DIAGNOSES AGE >17 W CC	90.0%
332	11	OTHER KIDNEY & URINARY TRACT DIAGNOSES AGE >17 W/O CC	
334	12	MAJOR MALE PELVIC PROCEDURES W CC	51.5%
335	12	MAJOR MALE PELVIC PROCEDURES W/O CC	
336	12	TRANSURETHRAL PROSTATECTOMY W CC	57.0%
337	12	TRANSURETHRAL PROSTATECTOMY W/O CC	
346	12	MALIGNANCY, MALE REPRODUCTIVE SYSTEM, W CC	92.1%
347	12	MALIGNANCY, MALE REPRODUCTIVE SYSTEM, W/O CC	
348	12	BENIGN PROSTATIC HYPERTROPHY W CC	84.0%
349	12	BENIGN PROSTATIC HYPERTROPHY W/O CC	
354	13	UTERINE, ADNEXA PROC FOR NON-OVARIAN/ADNEXAL MALIGNANCY W CC	59.0%
355	13	UTERINE, ADNEXA PROC FOR NON-OVARIAN/ADNEXAL MALIGNANCY W/O CC	
358	13	UTERINE & ADNEXA PROC FOR NON-MALIGNANCY W CC	42.6%
359	13	UTERINE & ADNEXA PROC FOR NON-MALIGNANCY W/O CC	
366	13	MALIGNANCY, FEMALE REPRODUCTIVE SYSTEM W CC	89.9%
367	13	MALIGNANCY, FEMALE REPRODUCTIVE SYSTEM W/O CC	
370	14	CESAREAN SECTION W CC	48.8%
371	14	CESAREAN SECTION W/O CC	
398	16	RETICULOENDOTHELIAL & IMMUNITY DISORDERS W CC	91.8%
399	16	RETICULOENDOTHELIAL & IMMUNITY DISORDERS W/O CC	
401	17	LYMPHOMA & NON-ACUTE LEUKEMIA W OTHER O.R. PROC W CC	79.7%
402	17	LYMPHOMA & NON-ACUTE LEUKEMIA W OTHER O.R. PROC W/O CC	
403	17	LYMPHOMA & NON-ACUTE LEUKEMIA W CC	88.1%
404	17	LYMPHOMA & NON-ACUTE LEUKEMIA W/O CC	
406	17	MYELOPROLIF DISORD OR POORLY DIFF NEOPL W MAJ O.R. PROC W CC	78.6%
407	17	MYELOPROLIF DISORD OR POORLY DIFF NEOPL W MAJ O.R. PROC W/O CC	
413	17	OTHER MYELOPROLIF DIS OR POORLY DIFF NEOPL DIAG W CC	89.6%
414	17	OTHER MYELOPROLIF DIS OR POORLY DIFF NEOPL DIAG W/O CC	
419	18	FEVER OF UNKNOWN ORIGIN AGE >17 W CC	83.7%
420	18	FEVER OF UNKNOWN ORIGIN AGE >17 W/O CC	
434	20	ALC/DRUG ABUSE OR DEPEND, DETOX OR OTH SYMPT TREAT W CC	60.1%
435	20	ALC/DRUG ABUSE OR DEPEND, DETOX OR OTH SYMPT TREAT W/O CC	
442	21	OTHER O.R. PROCEDURES FOR INJURIES W CC	81.7%
443	21	OTHER O.R. PROCEDURES FOR INJURIES W/O CC	
444	21	TRAUMATIC INJURY AGE >17 W CC	69.6%
445	21	TRAUMATIC INJURY AGE >17 W/O CC	
449	21	POISONING & TOXIC EFFECTS OF DRUGS AGE >17 W CC	80.6%
450	21	POISONING & TOXIC EFFECTS OF DRUGS AGE >17 W/O CC	
452	21	COMPLICATIONS OF TREATMENT W CC	82.9%
453	21	COMPLICATIONS OF TREATMENT W/O CC	
454	21	OTHER INJURY, POISONING & TOXIC EFFECT DIAG W CC	82.2%
455	21	OTHER INJURY, POISONING & TOXIC EFFECT DIAG W/O CC	
463	23	SIGNS & SYMPTOMS W CC	77.6%
464	23	SIGNS & SYMPTOMS W/O CC	

Total CC-No CC pairs.xls

DRG	MDC	Description	% of MedPAR 99 Pair "with CC"
478	5	OTHER VASCULAR PROCEDURES W CC	83.2%
479	5	OTHER VASCULAR PROCEDURES W/O CC	
493	7	LAPAROSCOPIC CHOLECYSTECTOMY W/O C.D.E. W CC	66.5%
494	7	LAPAROSCOPIC CHOLECYSTECTOMY W/O C.D.E. W/O CC	
497	8	SPINAL FUSION W CC (EFFECTIVE 10/1/97)	54.0%
498	8	SPINAL FUSION W/O CC (EFFECTIVE 10/1/97)	
499	8	BACK & NECK PROCEDURES EXCEPT SPINAL FUSION W CC (EFFECTIVE 10/1/97)	42.2%
500	8	BACK & NECK PROCEDURES EXCEPT SPINAL FUSION W/O CC (EFFECTIVE 10/1/97)	
501	8	KNEE PROCEDURES W PDX OF INFECTION W CC (EFFECTIVE 10/1/97)	75.9%
502	8	KNEE PROCEDURES W PDX OF INFECTION W/O CC (EFFECTIVE 10/1/97)	
506	22	FULL THICKNESS BURN W SKIN GRAFT OR INHAL INJ W CC OR SIG TRAUMA (EFFECTIVE 10/1/98)	77.3%
507	22	FULL THICKNESS BURN W SKIN GRFT OR INHAL INJ W/O CC OR SIG TRAUMA (EFFECTIVE 10/1/98)	
508	22	FULL THICKNESS BURN W/O SKIN GRFT OR INHAL INJ W CC OR SIG TRAUMA (EFFECTIVE 10/1/98)	79.5%
509	22	FULL THICKNESS BURN W/O SKIN GRFT OR INH INJ W/O CC OR SIG TRAUMA (EFFECTIVE 10/1/98)	
510	22	NON-EXTENSIVE BURNS W CC OR SIGNIFICANT TRAUMA (EFFECTIVE 10/1/98)	73.4%
511	22	NON-EXTENSIVE BURNS W/O CC OR SIGNIFICANT TRAUMA (EFFECTIVE 10/1/98)	
		TOTAL— % "with CC" Pairs of Total	**79.1%**

Appendix 8.3

High-Risk DRG Pairs

DRG	MDC	M/P	Description	% of MedPAR Pair (FY 99)
14	1	M	SPECIFIC CEREBROVASCULAR DISORDERS EXCEPT TIA	70.4%
15	1	M	TRANSIENT ISCHEMIC ATTACK & PRECEREBRAL OCCLUSIONS	
79	4	M	RESPIRATORY INFECTIONS & INFLAMMATIONS AGE >17 W CC	25.9%
89	4	M	SIMPLE PNEUMONIA & PLEURISY AGE >17 W CC	
79	4	M	RESPIRATORY INFECTIONS & INFLAMMATIONS AGE >17 W CC	74.4%
87	4	M	PULMONARY EDEMA & RESPIRATORY FAILURE	
87	4	M	PULMONARY EDEMA & RESPIRATORY FAILURE	13.5%
88	4	M	CHRONIC OBSTRUCTIVE PULMONARY DISEASE	
88	4	M	CHRONIC OBSTRUCTIVE PULMONARY DISEASE	86.2%
96	4	M	BRONCHITIS & ASTHMA AGE >17 W CC#	
110	5	P	MAJOR CARDIOVASCULAR PROCEDURES W CC	33.0%
478	5	P	OTHER VASCULAR PROCEDURES W CC	
130	5	M	PERIPHERAL VASCULAR DISORDERS W CC	88.5%
128	5	M	DEEP VEIN THROMBOPHLEBITIS	
132	5	M	ATHEROSCLEROSIS W CC	66.6%
140	5	M	ANGINA PECTORIS	
138	5	M	CARDIAC ARRHYTHMIA & CONDUCTION DISORDERS W CC	69.1%
141	5	M	SYNCOPE & COLLAPSE W CC	
140	5	M	ANGINA PECTORIS	29.2%
143	5	M	CHEST PAIN	
174	6	M	G.I. HEMORRHAGE W CC	50.4%
182	6	M	ESOPHAGITIS, GASTROENT & MISC DIGEST DISORDERS AGE > 17 W CC	
182	6	M	ESOPHAGITIS, GASTROENT & MISC DIGEST DISORDERS AGE > 17 W CC	55.6%
143	55	M	CHEST PAIN	
188	6	M	OTHER DIGESTIVE SYSTEM DIAGNOSES AGE >17 W CC	46.7%
180	6	M	GI OBSTRUCTION W CC	
239	8	M	PATHOLOGICAL FRACTURES & MUSCULOSKELETAL & CONN TISS MALIGNANCY	37.8%
243	8	M	MEDICAL BACK PROBLEMS	
271	9	M	SKIN ULCERS	20.1%
277	9	M	CELLULITIS AGE >17 W CC	
296	10	M	NUTRITIONAL & MISC METABOLIC DISORDERS AGE >17 W CC	50.0%
182	6	M	ESOPHAGITIS, GASTROENT & MISC DIGEST DISORDERS AGE > 17 W CC	
316	11	M	RENAL FAILURE	69.0%
331	11	M	OTHER KIDNEY & URINARY TRACT DIAGNOSES AGE >17 W CC	

DRG	MDC	M/P	Description	% of MedPAR Pair (FY 99)
316	11	M	RENAL FAILURE	29.4%
296	10	M	NUTRITIONAL & MISC METABOLIC DISORDERS AGE >17 W CC	
416	18	M	SEPTICEMIA AGE >17	51.9%
320	11	M	KIDNEY & URINARY TRACT INFECTIONS AGE >17 W CC	
475	4	M	RESPIRATORY SYSTEM DIAGNOSIS WITH VENTILATOR SUPPORT	13.8%
127	5	M	HEART FAILURE & SHOCK	

Appendix 8.4

Practice Brief: Developing a Coding Compliance Policy Document

Organizations using diagnosis and procedure codes for reporting healthcare services must have formal policies and corresponding procedures in place that provide instruction on the entire process from the point of service to the billing statement or claim form. Coding compliance policies serve as a guide to performing coding and billing functions and provide documentation of the organization's intent to correctly report services. The policies should include facility-specific documentation requirements, payer regulations and policies, and contractual arrangements for coding consultants and outsourcing services. This information may be covered in payer/provider contracts or found in Medicare and Medicaid manuals and bulletins.

Following are selected tenets that address the process of code selection and reporting. These tenets may be referred to as coding protocols, a coding compliance program, organizational coding guidelines, or a similar name. These tenets are an important part of any organization's compliance plan and the key to preventing coding errors and resulting reimbursement problems. Examples are taken from both outpatient and inpatient coding processes for illustration purposes only. This document cannot serve as a complete coding compliance plan, but will be useful as a guide for creating a more comprehensive resource to meet individual organizational needs.

A coding compliance plan should include the following components:

- A general policy statement about the commitment of the organization to correctly assign and report codes

  Example: Memorial Medical Center is committed to establishing and maintaining clinical coding and insurance claims processing procedures to ensure that reported codes reflect actual services provided, through accurate information system entries.

- The source of the official coding guidelines used to direct code selection

  Example: ICD-9-CM code selection follows the Official Guidelines for Coding and Reporting, developed by the cooperating parties and documented in *Coding Clinic* for ICD-9-CM, published by the American Hospital Association.

  Example: CPT code selection follows the guidelines set forth in the CPT manual and in *CPT Assistant,* published by the American Medical Association.

- The parties responsible for code assignment. The ultimate responsibility for code assignment lies with the physician (provider). However, policies and procedures may document instances where codes may be selected or modified by authorized individuals

  Example: For inpatient records, medical record analyst I staff are responsible for analysis of records and assignment of the correct ICD-9-CM codes based on documentation by the attending physician.

Example: Emergency department evaluation and management levels for physician services will be selected by the physician and validated by outpatient record analysts using the HCFA/AMA documentation guidelines. When a variance occurs, the following steps are taken for resolution (The actual document should follow with procedure details).

- The procedure to follow when the clinical information is not clear enough to assign the correct code

Example: When the documentation used to assign codes is ambiguous or incomplete, the physician must be contacted to clarify the information and complete/amend the record, if necessary. (The actual document should follow with details of how the medical staff would like this to occur, e.g., by phone call, by note on the record, etc.). Standard protocols for adding documentation to a record must be followed, in accordance with the applicable laws and regulations.

- Specify the policies and procedures that apply to specific locations and care settings. Official coding guidelines for inpatient reporting and outpatient/physician reporting are different. This means that if you are developing a facility-specific coding guideline for emergency department services, designate that the coding rules or guidelines only apply in this setting

Example: When reporting an injection of a drug provided in the emergency department to a Medicare beneficiary, the appropriate CPT code for the administration of the injection is reported in addition to the evaluation and management service code and drug code. CPT codes are reported whether a physician provides the injection personally or a nurse is carrying out a physician's order. This instruction does not always apply for reporting of professional services in the clinics, because administration of medication is considered bundled with the corresponding evaluation and management service for Medicare patients.

Example: Diagnoses that are documented as "probable," "suspected," "questionable," "rule-out," or "working diagnosis" are not to have a code assigned as a confirmed diagnosis. Instead, the code for the condition established at the close of the encounter should be assigned, such as a symptom, sign, abnormal test result, or clinical finding. This guideline applies only to outpatient services.

- Applicable reporting requirements required by specific agencies. The document should include where instructions on payer-specific requirements may be accessed

Example: For patients with XYZ care plan, report code S0800 for patients having a LASIK procedure rather than an unlisted CPT code.

Example: For Medicare patients receiving a wound closure by tissue adhesive only, report HCPCS Level II code G0168 rather than a CPT code.

Many of these procedures will be put into software databases and would not be written as a specific policy. This is true with most billing software, whether for physician services or through the charge description master used by many hospitals.

- Procedures for correction of inaccurate code assignments in the clinical database and to the agencies where the codes have been reported

Example: When an error in code assignment is discovered after bill release and the claim has already been submitted, this is the process required to update and correct the information system and facilitate claim amendment or correction (The actual document should follow with appropriate details).

- Areas of risk that have been identified through audits or monitoring. Each organization should have a defined audit plan for code accuracy and consistency review and corrective actions should be outlined for problems that are identified

Example: A hospital might identify that acute respiratory failure is being assigned as the principal diagnosis with congestive heart failure as a secondary diagnosis. The specific reference to *Coding Clinic* could be listed with instructions about correct coding of these conditions and the process to be used to correct the deficiency.

- Identification of essential coding resources available to and used by the coding professionals

Example: Updated ICD-9-CM, CPT, and HCPCS Level II code books are used by all coding professionals. Even if the hospital uses automated encoding software, at least one printed copy of the coding manuals should be available for reference.

Example: Updated encoder software, including the appropriate version of the NCCI edits and DRG and APC grouper software, is available to the appropriate personnel.

Example: Coding Clinic and *CPT Assistant* are available to all coding professionals.

- A process for coding new procedures or unusual diagnoses

Example: When the coding professional encounters an unusual diagnosis, the coding supervisor or the attending physician is consulted. If, after research, a code cannot be identified, the documentation is submitted to the AHA for clarification.

- A procedure to identify any optional codes gathered for statistical purposes by the facility and clarification of the appropriate use of E codes

Example: All ICD-9-CM procedure codes in the surgical range (ICD-9-CM Volume III codes 01.01–86.99) shall be reported for inpatients. In addition, codes reported from the non-surgical section include the following (Completed document should list the actual codes to be reported).

Example: All appropriate E codes for adverse effects of drugs must be reported. In addition, this facility reports all E codes, including the place of injury for poisonings, all cases of abuse, and all accidents on the initial visit for both inpatient and outpatient services.

- Appropriate methods for resolving coding or documentation disputes with physicians

Example: When the physician disagrees with official coding guidelines, the case is referred to the medical records committee following review by the designated physician liaison from that group.

- A procedure for processing claim rejections

  Example: All rejected claims pertaining to diagnosis and procedure codes should be returned to coding staff for review or correction. Any chargemaster issues should be forwarded to appropriate departmental staff for corrections. All clinical codes, including modifiers, must never be changed or added without review by coding staff with access to the appropriate documentation.

  Example: If a claim is rejected due to the codes provided in the medical record abstract, the billing department notifies the supervisor of coding for a review rather than changing the code to a payable code and resubmitting the claim.

- A statement clarifying that codes will not be assigned, modified, or excluded solely for the purpose of maximizing reimbursement. Clinical codes will not be changed or amended merely due to either physicians' or patients' request to have the service in question covered by insurance. If the initial code assignment did not reflect the actual services, codes may be revised based on supporting documentation. Disputes with either physicians or patients are handled only by the coding supervisor and are appropriately logged for review

  Example: A patient calls the business office saying that her insurance carrier did not pay for her mammogram. After investigating, the HIM coding staff discover that the coding was appropriate for a screening mammogram and that this is a non-covered service with the insurance provider. The code is not changed and the matter is referred back to the business office for explanation to the patient that she should contact her insurance provider with any dispute over coverage of service.

  Example: Part of a payment is denied and after review, the supervisor discovers that a modifier should have been appended to the CPT code to denote a separately identifiable service. Modifier -25 is added to the code set and the corrected claim is resubmitted.

  Example: A physician approaches the coding supervisor with a request to change the diagnosis codes for his patient because what she currently has is a pre-existing condition that is not covered by her current health plan. The coding supervisor must explain to the physician that falsification of insurance claims is illegal. If the physician insists, the physician liaison for the medical record committee is contacted and the matter is turned over to that committee for resolution if necessary.

- The use of and reliance on encoders within the organization. Coding staff cannot rely solely on computerized encoders. Current coding manuals must be readily accessible and the staff must be educated appropriately to detect inappropriate logic or errors in encoding software. When errors in logic or code crosswalks are discovered, they are reported to the vendor immediately by the coding supervisor

  Example: During the coding process, an error is identified in the crosswalk between the ICD-9-CM Volume III code and the CPT code. This error is reported to the software vendor, with proper documentation and notification of all staff using the encoder to not rely on the encoder for code selection.

- Medical records are analyzed and codes selected only with complete and appropriate documentation by the physician available. According to coding guidelines, codes are not assigned without physician documentation. If records are coded without the discharge summary or final diagnostic statements available, processes are in place for review after the summary is added to the record

Example: When records are coded without a discharge summary, they are flagged in the computer system. When the summaries are added to the record, the record is returned to the coding professional for review of codes. If there are any inconsistencies, appropriate steps are taken for review of the changes.

Additional Elements

A coding compliance document should include a reference to the AHIMA Standards of Ethical Coding, which can be downloaded from AHIMA's Web site at www.ahima.org. Reference to the data quality assessment procedures must be included in a coding compliance plan to establish the mechanism for determining areas of risk. Reviews will identify the need for further education and increased monitoring for those areas where either coding variances or documentation deficiencies are identified.

Specific and detailed coding guidelines that cover the reporting of typical services provided by a facility or organization create tools for data consistency and reliability by ensuring that all coders interpret clinical documentation and apply coding principles in the same manner. The appropriate medical staff committee should give final approval of any coding guidelines that involve clinical criteria to assure appropriateness and physician consensus on the process.

The format is most useful when organized by patient or service type and easily referenced by using a table of contents. If the facility-specific guidelines are maintained electronically, they should be searchable by key terms. Placing the coding guidelines on a facility Intranet or internal computer network is a very efficient way to ensure their use and it also enables timely and efficient updating and distribution. Inclusion of references to or live links should be provided to supporting documents such as Uniform Hospital Discharge Data Sets or other regulatory requirements outlining reporting procedures or code assignments.

Prepared by

AHIMA's Coding Practice Team and reviewed by the Coding Policy and Strategy Committee and the Society for Clinical Coding Data Quality Committee

Chapter 9

Reporting Issues

Desla R. Mancilla, MPA, RHIA

With the evolution of automated systems, coded data are no longer available only in the form of standard reports from the HIM department. Data can now be customized and used in a variety of ways. HIM department staff or users anywhere in the facility can design and run reports. More important, reports can be used to integrate and summarize data collected and stored in many disparate systems.

The term **information** implies the transformation of raw data into a usable format. Data collected by healthcare facilities are voluminous. The resulting information must be manageable, yet comprehensive enough to accurately depict the overall story of the patient care process.

In the realm of healthcare information, data sources are numerous. Traditionally, paper records were created and analyzed as required data elements were abstracted to a paper document. Subsequently, the paper documents were accumulated and sent to companies to generate reports. Those reports were eventually returned to the originating facility for assessment and interpretation.

Today, with the ever-advancing capabilities provided by automated collection and analysis systems, information is at the fingertips of the user within moments of data collection. However, unformatted data are difficult to understand. Therefore, reports are created, formatted, and distributed to users throughout the healthcare enterprise for a multitude of purposes.

Healthcare facilities everywhere and of every kind—rural, urban, large, small, private, for profit, not for profit, long-term care, ambulatory care, and others—devote significant resources, both financial and human, to the processes associated with collecting, analyzing, maintaining, reporting, and distributing information vital to the organization's success.

Sources of Data

The sources of data must be understood, particularly when those data are converted into diagnostic and procedure codes. Such codes are one step in the process of making data more usable. Coding professionals are charged with the task of analyzing raw data and assigning codes that represent the significant conditions and resources expended on the care of a patient.

Codes, both diagnostic and procedure, are **aggregate data**—a mass or body of data that is treated as a unit. A code represents the sum of the coder's analysis of extensive documentation.

The documentation that coders analyze may be in the form of handwritten notes or reports from healthcare providers but often is computer-generated information from one of many ancillary-, nursing-, or physician-based analysis or treatment systems. For example, an echo-cardiography result may appear as:

- An interpretation handwritten by a physician

- An interpretation dictated by a physician and transcribed into a report by a transcriptionist

- A computer-generated result

The computer-generated result represents the capabilities of knowledge-based systems that require little or no human intervention in the analysis process.

Traditionally, one of the major delays in the coding process has been the time spent waiting for all pertinent test results and transcribed reports. In an effort to speed up the process, and subsequently to reduce billing delays, some facilities have developed great efficiencies in the coding process. They allow coders to access the required information before it is available in its final form. For example, some facilities have developed mechanisms that allow coders to dial into the dictation system to hear a healthcare provider's dictation before it has been transcribed.

In other facilities, interfaces from feeder systems (such as the aforementioned echocardiography system) to the hospital information system allow coders to see the test results on-line and in real time. They do not have to wait for the results to be printed, distributed, and "charted" on the paper record. A **feeder system** is an automated data system that feeds results into a comprehensive database. A **hospital information system (HIS)** is the comprehensive database that contains all the clinical, administrative, financial, and demographic information about each patient served by a hospital.

All of those factors are important in the life cycle of report creation, generation, and distribution. Reports based on coded information are instrumental in promoting managerial efficiency in all aspects of the healthcare facility's operation. Planning, assessment, and development of services, as well as a plethora of financial decisions, are based on reports detailing individual and aggregate coded information.

The remainder of this chapter defines the sources of data as they relate to the coding process, identifies the type of information needed to create reports based on coded data, and describes how various users throughout the healthcare facility need and use coded information.

Abstracting

Abstracting is the process of extracting elements of data from a source document (a paper record, for example) and entering them into an automated system. The purpose of this endeavor is to make those data elements available for later use. After a data element has been captured in electronic form, it generally can be searched for and reported on as a discrete entity. In addition, it can be aggregated into a group of data elements to provide information needed by the user.

Paper versus Electronic Record Systems

Abstracting is not done in the same way if the source document is electronic and the patient record is electronic rather than paper. In this case, the data elements do not have to be abstracted because they already are available in electronic form. However, all electronic data are not searchable. Therefore, if the data elements are going to be searched for inclusion in a required report, they should be stored in indexed data fields that allow for search and retrieval of the required information.

The distinction between the abstracting process in paper and electronic forms must be further detailed to distinguish between a true electronic patient record system and an **optical image–based system.** In a totally electronic record system, all parts of the record are created initially in electronic form. In an optical image–based system, the information is created initially in paper form and then scanned into a system for storage and retrieval. The abstraction process varies depending on the types of electronic systems used within the organization.

Cycle of Capturing Data

To understand how data are captured in an automated system, it is important to understand the flow cycle from the point of registration to the point of discharge. In an acute care facility, it is common for a patient to register for the service being provided. The patient gives admitting department personnel pertinent demographic information that is entered into the registration system. Insurance, emergency contact, and physician data also are generally collected at the point of registration. Throughout the patient's stay, a wide variety of other information is generated, some in paper form and some in electronic form.

In the traditional paper-based facility, the healthcare provider, or some other party authorized to take verbal orders, writes an order for a test in the health record. The order is then generally entered into the HIS. After the order is entered into this system, the responsible ancillary department performs the test. The test is often performed using biomedical or clinical equipment that is itself another type of automated system.

The test result then can be processed in one of the following ways:

- It can be printed and "charted," which is time-consuming and resource intensive.

- It can be sent from the biomedical system to the HIS through an interface or some other direct-access mechanism, which allows nursing, ancillary, and medical staff members to access the result as soon as it is available.

If no automated mechanism is in place to transfer the results to the HIS, the responsible ancillary department typically contacts the physician and the nursing unit with abnormal test results for prompt attention.

Many departments have automated data systems, also called feeder systems, such as those just described. For example, the emergency department may have a system to assist in triage and in tracking patients seen in the department. Respiratory therapy may have a system that not only assists in the interpretation of clinical testing, but also serves as a documentation system for the therapists. In that type of automated data system, therapists no longer write their care notes by hand. Instead, they use the system to create and maintain the history of their treatment services. After the results of all the feeder systems, or automated data systems, are in the HIS, they are integrated with the patient's demographic and financial information, thus creating a comprehensive history of all aspects of care.

Departments that do not have automated data systems create and maintain their information in paper form. The paper records are sent to the HIM department for integration with all other parts of the patient record. In some facilities, these paper documents are scanned into an optical imaging system. The entire record then can be stored in, and retrieved from, an automated system when needed at some point after patient discharge.

The problem for the coder becomes one of timing. He or she must understand where data are stored and how to access them for use in the coding process. Procedurally, coders abide by the guidelines of their organization and of the agencies that direct what information is to be used when determining the appropriate codes to be assigned.

Types of Data Elements

The types of data elements that are abstracted, or defined as indexed fields in an automated system, vary from facility to facility. Generally, however, any data elements that are needed for selecting cases for reports must be abstracted or indexed. Typical data fields that can be searched for the purpose of case finding and reporting include:

- Patient name
- Zip code
- Health record number
- Patient account number
- Guarantor number
- Financial class
- Insurance company and plan number
- Attending physician
- ICD-9-CM diagnosis codes
- ICD-9-CM procedure codes
- DRG number
- APC number
- CPT code

Some of these fields are abstracted; others are present in the system from the point of patient registration onward.

Patient Name Data Field

Patient name fields are searchable for the obvious reason of finding a specific case. A discrete field is generally used to collect both the first name and the last name of the patient. Specific individual records are needed for every imaginable reason—from patient care, to assessment of services, to continuation of medical care.

Zip Code Data Field

Many facilities use the practice of zip code aggregation and analysis to determine populations to which they should market their services. In that way, certain populations can be targeted based on demographics known to be associated with a specific zip code. For example, in communities with young populations, marketing of sports medicine and obstetrical services is commonplace. Conversely, zip codes associated with a largely geriatric population are likely candidates for targeted marketing of long-term and other types of residential care.

Health Record Number Data Field

The health record number is used to identify all occasions of service for a specific patient within a given facility. Moreover, it can be used throughout the entire healthcare enterprise to track a variety of services at different interrelated facilities. Health record numbers are used in reports to identify specific cases meeting selection criteria. In addition, the presence of a health record number on a report assists in the process of finding the record, either in paper or electronic form.

Patient Account Number Data Field

The patient account number is used to separate charges and related services for a specific patient with multiple visits. For example, a patient might have three inpatient visits within a month. In each of those visits, a chest X-ray may have been performed. The account number denotes which X-ray was taken during a specific time frame, essentially allowing for classification of services and charges by date.

An account number is critical for finding specific occasions of service for a particular patient or for identifying groups of related events. For example, a user may need to find all records in which a left heart catheterization was performed. He or she would create a report to search for such cases by procedure code number and would direct the report to print the account number for each case found in the search process. The specific records corresponding to the account numbers listed on the report then would be used in the data analysis project.

Guarantor Number Data Field

The guarantor number identifies all of the patient accounts that a specific party is responsible for paying. In the traditional nuclear family, a married male is the guarantor for his spouse and children, even though his spouse may work and have her own insurance coverage. The guarantor number allows for efficiency in the billing process by grouping active account information together during a billing cycle. In this way, a single statement including all account activity can be sent to the guarantor, or his insurer, instead of multiple statements.

Financial Class Data Field

The financial class is a highly significant data element because it represents the payer, or insurer, of the account. Managed care contracts identify specific criteria that are covered and limitations of coverage. If an organization wants to know which accounts fall out of the specified criteria, a report is often created based on financial class.

In another scenario, a facility that needs to know how many Medicare days of service it has provided over a given time can query its system by financial class code. The query will further be designed to count the days of service for each individual account in order to report a total number of days of service provided within each managed care contract group.

Insurance Company and Plan Number Data Field

The insurance company and plan number also are collected and used in the reporting process because a broad spectrum of insurers may fall into a single financial class. A financial class representing commercial insurance is one possible example. Users needing to run a report for a specific insurance company would be unable to do so based on the financial class data field. Instead, they would have to request further details in the form of the insurance company and plan number.

Attending Physician Number Data Field

Information about the attending physician is extremely important in the reporting process. Many departments within the facility need information based on physician services. The physician is often identified in the system based on a number. Subsequently, reports are run for individual physicians, physicians by service, or even by physicians grouped by medical service department. The concept of physician profiling appears later in this chapter, but it is important to note at this point that the attending physician number is usually held in a separate field from the number fields for the other physicians involved with a case.

The physician numbers of other types of physicians are abstracted for later use in reporting. Numbers for all secondary, consulting, and admitting physicians, as well as surgeons, surgical assistants, and covering physicians, are generally input as part of the data abstraction process. This is necessary to identify all cases in which a physician may have been involved.

The finance department in healthcare facilities also is interested in information trends regarding physicians and patient admissions. For example, an analysis of zip codes can determine that individuals from certain geographic areas in the community are more likely to be admitted through the emergency department than by a general medicine or family practice physician. In such a situation, the healthcare facility may want to develop a facility-sponsored family medicine practice in that geographic area to augment business from that part of the community. Services supported by specialty physicians such as cardiologists, nephrologists, neurologists, and neurosurgeons are generally known to increase reimbursement to the facility. On the other hand, less resource-intensive general practice services create less revenue. Nevertheless, general medical practitioners must be located within the community to ensure initial placement in the facility of patients who then can be referred to specialists as necessary.

ICD-9-CM Diagnosis Codes Data Fields

The ICD-9-CM principal diagnosis code is critical in the process of generating reports. Clinical users select cases based on a specific medical condition, and the principal diagnosis most succinctly describes the clinical assessment and treatment of the patient.

However, the principal diagnosis alone does not fully describe the care provided to a patient. ICD-9-CM secondary diagnosis codes also are important. They provide detailed evidence of the patient's overall condition.

Automated data systems allow for storage of many diagnosis codes. Typically, the principal diagnosis field is listed first and stored as a separate index from the secondary codes. However, there is usually great flexibility in designing reports based on combinations of principal and secondary diagnoses.

ICD-9-CM Procedure Codes Data Fields

The ICD-9-CM primary procedure code and secondary procedure codes are similar to their diagnostic counterparts. When these codes are applied, they are generally associated with detailed information about the physician or caregiver who performed the procedure, along with the date and time of service. Many facilities also choose to associate an anesthesia type with the procedure for future reference.

DRG Number Data Field

The DRG number is of primary significance in reporting because it is the single element that combines clinical care with the resources required to provide it. The DRG is calculated based on a combination of codes and other specific information for inpatient visits. Both clinical and financial users are interested in a multitude of reports based on the DRG number. This combination of clinical and financial resources helps to determine a facility's case mix, which is often used to describe the severity of cases being treated within an institution.

APC Number Data Field

The APC number is the outpatient counterpart of a DRG. Although a relatively new type of payment classification, the APC is poised to be as significant in the early 2000s as the DRG was at its inception in the early 1980s. Outpatient reimbursement will be increasingly tied to APCs. Thus, users throughout a facility will seek to create reports describing outpatient service activities based on the APC number. Many facilities are struggling to ensure that their systems are collecting and storing all information relevant to APC assignment.

CPT Code Data Field

Like ICD-9-CM codes, CPT codes are used throughout a facility to create reports that depict the services provided and the resources expended to provide them. Coders generally assign surgical CPT codes, although some nonsurgical codes are assigned through the item charge process.

Other Data Fields

Other, less-standard data fields are defined by users throughout a facility as fields that must be abstracted for a variety of purposes. For example, nursing administration representatives might ask to have a field collected to indicate whether restraints were used on a patient. This information then could be used to find cases to study for agencies such as the Joint Commission on Accreditation of Healthcare Organizations (JCAHO) that are interested in determining whether the application and maintenance of restraints are appropriate.

Another example demonstrates how abstracting can improve efficiency within a busy HIM department. Mothers of newborn infants frequently call HIM departments to determine whether their children were given an injection to prevent hepatitis. The injection is given on the order of a physician, but not all physicians agree on its necessity. Therefore, there is a fairly even split between physicians on how often these injections are ordered and administered. If mothers do not keep documentation of services provided to their infants by the facility, they will not know what injections their children were given.

In a paper-based system, each time a mother calls for this type of information, the record must be located, pulled, and reviewed to find the answer. In a hospital with an active obstetric and newborn service area, this can mean that staff are involved taking many calls a day and physically accessing many unnecessary paper health records to address a question. In an automated data system, on the other hand, the answer could be abstracted from data in the system.

Role of the Coder in Abstracting

In many facilities, coders are responsible for abstracting required data elements. Some controversy exists in the health information field as to whether this is an efficient use of coders' time. Some argue that staff other than coders can be used to find and extract data elements. Others argue that because coders have to read the record in its entirety to assign appropriate codes, it is more efficient for them to abstract the data elements as they encounter them in the record review process.

Admission Coding versus Discharge Coding

In certain facilities, codes are applied prior to, or at the time of, admission to the facility. This is particularly true in long-term care and other types of facilities that obtain preapproval for the patient to stay in the facility for a prescribed length of time. The approved length of stay (LOS) is often determined based on the admission diagnosis code.

In some facilities, a coding professional determines the admission diagnoses codes; in others, admitting or utilization management personnel or case managers perform that task. In any case, a distinction is made to describe whether codes are admission codes or final codes. This distinction is important in the process of generating reports. Individuals who are building reports must be apprised of the difference between those code fields so that resulting reports are accurate and valid and clearly represent their intended uses.

Chargemaster Description Codes

Yet another distinction is necessary to ensure that all relevant codes are collected and available in the reporting process. A coder traditionally assigns ICD-9-CM procedure and diagnostic codes after the patient has been discharged. However, some CPT codes, particularly those not associated with a surgical procedure, are not assigned by a coder but, rather, are applied to an account through the routine hospital charging mechanism.

When a CPT code is associated with a procedure 100 percent of the time, it is much more efficient to have it applied through the charge description master (CDM) file process rather than have it reviewed by a coder and applied during the coding process. A code applied through the CDM file is referred to as a **hard code.** Using a hard code eliminates the possibility of missing a code assignment through human error. In essence, every time the ancillary department providing the service enters a specific charge, the system applies the corresponding CPT code. The combination of codes—those applied by coders and those entered in the CDM entry process—results in the patient bill.

In this scenario, it is important for the report creator to understand this process. The user may wish to create a report of all CPT codes of a particular type for a specific time frame. In most systems, the user will query a CPT code field to find this information. However, a hard code may not be identified in this manner because it is not usually stored in the same field as a CPT code assigned by a coder. Sometimes a combination of reports or reporting systems must be used to obtain the desired result. As long as the individual creating the report understands the limitations of the system being used and the flow of coding within the facility, a comprehensive report can usually be designed.

System Interrelationships

As described previously, multiple data sources are joined to create a single, complex record used in the process of assigning codes. The validity of data received from disparate systems must be assessed routinely to ensure that all required data reach the final destination in their appropriate form.

If some type of routine verification process is not used to compare data sent from feeder systems with those stored in the primary HIS, the risk of inaccurate reporting is great. When reports are analyzed, the source of the data is generally unknown, which again lends credence to the importance of data integration.

Traditionally, hospital information systems have been strong in their ability to store and process financial information, but weak in their ability to link it to clinical information. Facilities have dealt with this situation by purchasing stand-alone or networked database systems that collect and store clinical data. Integration of the HIS and the database systems results in the ability to create reports based on any collected element. Users are generally trained in extracting required data to create a usable report. Many systems make use of **Standard Query Language (SQL)** or other report-writing programs to pull and integrate data from various sources into a single, comprehensive report.

Uses of Coded Data

Coded data are a valuable resource used extensively throughout the healthcare organization. Users from virtually all areas of healthcare operations have an interest in coded data.

Clinical versus Financial Uses

Some users' needs of coded data are clinical in nature; other users' needs are financial. In either case, individual codes or codes grouped into a DRG, APC, or other grouping category are the basic element used to provide the information needed.

This wide variety of grouping methods adds another level of complexity to the collection and analysis of information. Users comparing reports must understand the grouping system used in each report and base their conclusions on a comparison of like information. From the housekeeping department that analyzes codes on the spread of infectious disease to the hospital administration that plans for expansion of services, diagnostic and procedure codes are the underlying mechanism enabling appropriate case selection and analysis.

Frequency of Use

Daily users of coded data, such as the patient financial services (patient accounts) department, integrate the coded data with other patient-specific financial data such as insurance information to create a single, comprehensive bill of services provided. Other departments, such as the risk management department, need to assess coded data on a less-frequent basis. Nevertheless, in some way or another, all areas within a facility need information arising from coded data.

Use for Given Time Periods

Aggregated coded data succinctly identify the number of cases of each condition within the facility in a given time period. This factor alone is invaluable in planning staff size. For example, a high frequency of cases of congestive heart failure is a cue to nursing administration on how to staff the cardiology unit. Knowledge of the frequency trend of a specific type of case over a significant time period can clarify when to expand certain nursing units or, conversely, when to reduce staff in certain areas. Because coded data are coupled with patient-specific LOS data, even more inferences can be made on how to staff within individual care units.

Use in Decision Making

Both long- and short-term decision making are based on coded data. Reports designed to present coded data are used to support the decision-making process. However, codes alone do not allow for appropriate analysis and management of information. Rather, it is the ability to select codes in conjunction with other significant clinical and financial data that results in reports that support user needs throughout the facility.

Users of Coded Data

Various user areas and departments within a typical acute care facility rely heavily on coded data to perform their functions. Indeed, the success of those departments is closely linked to appropriate analysis of reports depicting ICD-9-CM and CPT codes, as well as DRGs, APCs, and other code groupings.

Cost and Reimbursement Department

The cost and reimbursement department, also called the cost accounting department, has the daunting task of correlating cost to charges and charges to reimbursement. This department is responsible for budgeting, cost reporting, and, in many cases, cost accounting. Under the auspices of the finance division, the cost and reimbursement department is typically separate from the general accounting area, which is responsible for internal accounting practices such as payroll and the preparation of income statements and balance statements.

The integration of clinical and financial information is nowhere more important than in the cost and reimbursement department. Individuals with a strong background in finance are generally found in a hospital's cost and reimbursement department. In some facilities, individuals with an HIM background also are an invaluable component of the cost and reimbursement department. This department is often responsible for the charge description file that is closely related to the coding function within a facility. For this reason, HIM professionals are often involved with chargemaster development and maintenance.

Definitions of Cost, Charges, and Reimbursement

To understand how the cost and reimbursement department uses coded data, it is important to first define the terms *cost, charges,* and *reimbursement.* A detailed analysis of these elements is extremely important to an organization's financial well-being.

Cost
Cost is the dollar amount of a service provided by a facility. The term is closely associated with the accounting method called cost accounting. This accounting method attributes a dollar figure to every input required to provide a service. For example, a patient who receives chemotherapy treatment for a brain tumor will have direct costs, such as medication, and indirect costs, such as the electricity required to heat or cool the patient's room during the hospital stay. These direct and indirect costs are combined to arrive at the total cost per treatment. The total of all the treatments and procedures received by a single patient can then be grouped to arrive at a total cost per case. The CDM file links cost file information and code description.

Charges
Charges are the amount the facility actually bills for the services it provides. The actual charge for a service may be $3,500, but only $2,000 may be paid as a result of contractual allowances agreed on with managed care companies and other insurers. A **contractual allowance** is the difference between what is charged and what is paid. It is commonly known that self-pay patients are usually the only patient type that pays full price for services. Individuals do not

have the same market power to negotiate reductions in bills that managed care companies representing millions of patients have.

Reimbursement

Reimbursement is the amount collected by the facility for the services it bills. Even though $1 million may be billed for a given period, some of this money will never be collected. Rather, it will be written off as charity care or as income that cannot be collected because of a variety of other circumstances.

Another concept to be considered is that of volume to reimbursement. Cognizant financial analysts attempt to build the volume of cases that increase reimbursement, while trying to reduce the volume of reimbursement-losing services. Marketing programs designed to increase awareness of high-income service generators are based on volume-to-reimbursement analyses.

Although high-activity levels are generally sought after, some services are known as "losers." That is, some services are not only unprofitable, but also actually cost the hospital to provide them. Nevertheless, community needs dictate that those services be provided.

DRG Payment System

Prior to implementation of the DRG payment system, comparison of individual cases within a facility based on cost and resources used was difficult. The DRG system created the ability to integrate clinical and financial data. As a result, facilities now can compare costs across the healthcare spectrum.

Although the DRG system has been discredited for causing the financial demise of many a healthcare facility, DRGs actually provide an opportunity for healthcare facilities to more accurately predict their reimbursement for services provided. Even more important, the DRG payment system allows facilities to analyze their own efficiency. Patients now can be classified based on resource consumption. Although it might be obvious that a labor and delivery case is less resource intensive than a cardiac catheterization case, it is not so easy to make comparisons among more similar types of services. For example, facilities now can analyze resource consumption among three or more different types of cardiac catheterizations, as shown in figure 9.1.

The ability to assess data by ICD-9-CM and HCPCS/CPT code numbers and by DRG, APC, and other groups enables facilities to participate in benchmarking. This allows across-the-board comparison among disparate facilities and even among providers and physicians within the same organization. With the recent inception of APC groups, analysis of cost-based data will become even more common.

Case-Mix Reports

Case mix can be referenced to quickly assess the types and severity of cases treated within a facility. **Case mix** is a description of a patient population based on any number of specific characteristics, including age, gender, type of insurance, diagnosis, risk factors, treatment received, and resources used. Ideally, case-mix reports would include both cost- and revenue-based information. However, this is not always the case. Sophisticated cost-accounting systems have been developed and are providing increasingly popular methodologies for ensuring that case-mix reports include both cost and revenue details.

Case mix is the broad category name for a variety of reports. Some of the data elements included in a standard charge-to-reimbursement case-mix report are patient account number, patient name, assigned DRG, actual LOS, charges, predicted reimbursement, and variance (the difference between charges and reimbursement).

Figure 9.1.   Cardiac catheterization comparison report

Anyplace Health Systems
Comparison of All Cardiac Surgeons—Inpatients
Quarter 1, Fiscal Year 01

DRG 104   CARDIAC VALVE PROCEDURES AND OTHER MAJOR CARDIOTHORACIC PROCEDURES WITH CARDIAC CATH

DR. ID #	# of Pts.	ALOS	Case-Mix Index	Estimated Net Revenue	Total Costs	Net Income (Loss)	Net Income % Gross Revenue
						TOTAL	
12554	3	14.0	7.1843	174,945	168,541	6,404	2.0
25874	5	19.8	7.1843	274,468	235,120	39,348	8.7
32682	3	2.7	7.1843	89,265	84,337	4,928	4.7
TOTAL	11	13.6	7.1843	538,678	487,998	50,680	

DRG 105   CARDIAC VALVE PROCEDURES AND OTHER MAJOR CARDIOTHORACIC PROCEDURES WITHOUT CARDIAC CATH

DR. ID #	# of Pts.	ALOS	Case-Mix Index	Estimated Net Revenue	Total Costs	Net Income (Loss)	Net Income % Gross Revenue
						TOTAL	
25874	10	10.6	5.6567	359,286	371,001	(11,715)	(1.7)
36589	1	8.0	5.6567	23,277	31,030	(7,753)	(14.0)
66482	2	12.0	5.6567	50,923	78,915	(27,992)	(19.0)
TOTAL	13	10.6	5.6567	433,486	480,946	(47,460)	

DRG 107   CORONARY BYPASS WITH CARDIAC CATH

DR. ID #	# of Pts.	ALOS	Case-Mix Index	Estimated Net Revenue	Total Costs	Net Income (Loss)	Net Income % Gross Revenue
						TOTAL	
25874	1	5.0	5.3762	22,467	19,124	3,343	7.9
36589	5	9.2	5.3762	122,525	124,070	(1,545)	(0.6)
66482	2	9.5	5.3762	64,599	52,492	12,107	11.5
TOTAL	8	8.8	5.3762	209,591	195,686	13,905	

Case-mix reports can be run and sorted in a variety of ways. Most of them include the assigned DRG, principal diagnoses, principal procedure, charge per case, reimbursement per case, and physician information. For example, one type of case-mix report might show the total number of DRGs sorted by DRG or major diagnostic category (MDC).

The significance of case mix within a healthcare facility is shown by the following example:

For a facility with a case-mix index of 1.47, an increase to an index of 1.62 would result in an average increase in reimbursement of about $600 per DRG-paid case. This increase would depend on the wage index and other factors influencing case-mix calculations. Personnel responsible for analyzing case-mix reports can predict the potential increase in reimbursement by finding the average number of DRG-paid cases within a given time period and multiplying it by $600 per case. Depending on the level of activity, this could result in a multimillion-dollar increase in revenue each year.

Physician Data

In addition to needing DRG information to compare payments received with bills submitted, the cost and reimbursement department also requires associated physician data. The following scenario clearly depicts the importance of assessment by physician:

Dr. Mitchellson (physician I.D. number 4769) is a nephrologist specializing in progressive kidney disease. At sixty-five years of age, he is the hospital's number one revenue-producing physician. An analysis of the physician data report also reveals that no other physicians are waiting in the wings to treat the kind of patients that Dr. Mitchellson does. The cost and reimbursement staff analyzing this type of data should recommend to administration the need to recruit a physician with a skill set similar to Dr. Mitchellson's to ensure the continuation of that revenue source when Dr. Mitchellson retires.

Decision Making and Case-Mix Reports

Major decisions are based on information found in a facility's case-mix reports. With limited funds, most institutions make decisions on whether to purchase major capital equipment or to curtail spending only after a thoughtful review of their case-mix reports. Generally, the cost and reimbursement staff summarizes information in the case-mix reports and forwards it to the administration and to the board of directors. The administration and the board of directors then consider that information in determining how the facility will spend its limited resources.

In addition to the variety of daily and monthly case-mix reports produced for and used by the cost and reimbursement department, innumerable on-demand reports can be created either by the users or at their request to meet a specific, and often transient, need. For example, a facility that wishes to participate in a government-sponsored demonstration project must perform a full assessment of all the relevant information related to the DRGs falling within the project's scope. Although projects of this nature, such as Centers of Excellence programs, lend prestige to the selected organization by identifying it as a high-quality care provider at government-approved pricing, the project's financial cost may not be acceptable.

By evaluating on-demand case-mix reports, the facility can determine whether existing inefficiencies can be reduced to compensate for reduced payment from Medicare program recipients. If the analysis reveals that the facility is already operating as efficiently as it can, the facility can decide to reject or accept demonstration project status based on comparing expected financial losses with the expected benefits of participating in the program.

Knowing the magnitude of the decisions that are based on analysis of DRG and other code-based reports makes the issues related to the quality of coded data readily apparent. In addition to selecting and sequencing appropriate codes, associated quality issues must be addressed. Codes are entered into a system either manually or by automated methods. Manually entered codes are at risk of being miskeyed and subsequently misgrouped. Quality assessment (QA) programs should be in place to routinely compare keyed codes to the source document from which they were entered. Moreover, the routine use of more sophisticated QA mechanisms to validate code assignment and sequencing must be in place to ensure the appropriate collection and reporting of coded data.

Patient Financial Services Departments

The most obvious uses of code-based reports are those that detail the relationship of coded data to the billing process. Entire functional groups within the patient financial services department are devoted to ensuring that bills are produced in a timely fashion. However, because the production of a bill largely depends on the presence of a coded final diagnosis, routine reports are required to track the status of accounts that have not been billed.

Accounts Not Selected for Billing

The **Accounts Not Selected for Billing Report** is a daily report used to track the many reasons that accounts may not be ready for billing, as shown in figure 9.2. Some billing takes place electronically; other bills are created and submitted in paper format. In either case, accounts that have not met all facility-specified criteria for billing are held and reported on this daily tracking list.

Some accounts are held because the consents and authorizations required by the insurer have not been signed by the patient. Others are held because a specific insurer may require a CPT code that has not been assigned. Still others are not billed because the primary and secondary insurance benefits have not been confirmed.

One of the major delays in billing accounts is the lack of final diagnosis and procedure codes. The reasons for that type of delay are varied. In some cases, a physician has not documented the diagnosis. In other cases, test results required to support the written diagnosis may not yet be on the record.

Purposes of the Accounts Not Selected for Billing Report

The purposes of the Accounts Not Selected for Billing Report are to:

- Monitor the total dollars not yet billed

- Monitor the age of accounts not yet billed

- Attribute the delay to one or more circumstances

- Provide a mechanism for users to prioritize their resources for getting accounts billed

Both the HIM and patient financial services departments receive daily copies of this report. However, the report may be modified to show various types of information based on each department's needs.

Figure 9.2.   Accounts not selected for billing report

Issue Date: 5/1/01
Issue Time: 0600

Anyplace Health Systems
Accounts Not Selected for Billing—Inpatients
Patient Financial Services Version

Patient Name	Acct. #	Med Rec #	Status	Unbilled Charges	Days Since Disch.	Pt. Type	Ins. 1	Ins. 2	Ins. 3	Final Dx	DRG	Open Orders	Fin. Class
Axxxxxx, Rxxx	1452585	124785	Discharged	18,139.45	13	E-Inpt	Yes	Yes	Yes	No	000	No	J
Bxxxx, Vxxxx	4568972	258564	Discharged	1,173.75	26	Inpt	No	No	No	Yes	466	No	T
Cxxxx, Axxxx	7456594	256632	Discharged	10,286.70	5	E-Inpt	Yes	Yes	Yes	Yes	277	Yes	Q
Fxxxx, Txxxxx	7458961	148965	Discharged	3,425.45	15	Inpt	No	Yes	Yes	Yes	000	Yes	F
Plxxxxx, Gxxxxx	8585964	745321	Discharged	15,452.25	8	Inpt	Yes	Yes	Yes	Yes	321	Yes	J
Sxxxxxxx, Cxxxx	8569741	154428	Inpt-In-house	52,846.25	0	E-Inpt	No	No	No	No	000	Yes	T
Zxxx, Mxxxxxxx	7458946	147589	Discharged	25,584.55	20	E-Inpt	Yes	Yes	Yes	No	000	No	B

Totals

		Unbilled Charges	Reason for Rejection		Final Dx		Open Orders
I/P Discharged	6	74,062.15	Insurance Not Verified	4	4	No Final Dx	4
I/P In-House	1	52,846.25	Open Orders	4	4	Invalid DRG	0	0

Issue Date: 5/1/01
Issue Time: 0600

Anyplace Health Systems
Accounts Not Selected for Billing—Outpatients
Patient Financial Services Version

Patient Name	Acct. #	Med Rec #	Status	Unbilled Charges	Days Since Disch.	Pt. Type	Ins. 1	Ins. 2	Ins. 3	Final Dx	DRG	Open Orders	Fin. Class
Cxxxx, Jxxx	5869751	586462	O/P - Recur.	1,377.50	34	Recur.	No	Yes	Yes	Yes	131	No	T
Dxxx, Axxx	7469832	154783	O/P – Surg	10,850.40	16	Surgical	Yes	Yes	Yes	Yes	479	Yes	L
Gxxx, Dxxxxx	7459831	852697	O/P	12,587.75	4	Out	Yes	Yes	Yes	No	000	No	Q

Totals

		Unbilled Charges	Reason for Rejection		Final Dx		Open Orders
Recurrent Outpatients	1	1,377.50	Insurance Not Verified	1	1	No Final Dx	2
Outpatient Surgical	1	10,850.40	Open Orders	1	1	Invalid DRG	0	0
Outpatient General	1	12,587.75					

271

For example, the HIM department may be interested in accounts not billed based on the responsible physician number. In that way, the department can strategize how to elicit cooperation from a physician who is not providing sufficient documentation for coding. In another example, the HIM department may wish to sort the list by health record location so that a needed record can be found quickly and supplied for completion. The patient financial services department, on the other hand, may be more interested in knowing which accounts are being held because the appropriate payment authorization forms are not yet available. Both departments, however, keep close track of the highest-dollar cases and the oldest cases because billing those accounts is their highest priority.

Matching Payments to Billed Amounts

In addition to simply billing the account, ICD-9-CM coding–based reports are required to match payments to billed amounts. An account is often billed at a specific amount, but the payment received and accepted by the facility is less than the billed amount. This situation arises because agreements have been made with managed care companies and other insurers to pay certain DRGs at a lower rate.

For example, a facility may have a contract with a managed care company to carve out DRG 104 for payment at a rate of 60 percent to charges. A **carve out** occurs when a payer cuts the applicable service from the contract and pays it at a different rate. Instead of receiving the full, expected payment, the facility receives only 60 percent of the amount it charged. The carve-out process is commonplace and is used as a mechanism to control costs for the managed care company. The facility agrees to the carve outs to increase the volume of patients it treats. Thus, even though the facility receives less money per case, it receives more money in total.

Reports designed to show payments by case and payer include fields for charges compared with payments. An analysis of those reports over time can reveal whether carve outs are effective in meeting the facility's financial goals.

The fact that so many insurers exist, each with its own rules for billing, makes for numerous complications in the prebill process. Some insurers require CPT codes for certain nonsurgical procedures and others do not. To complicate matters further, insurers do not always communicate their billing requirements before receiving the bill, which results in a duplication of work and in delays in receipt of payment for services provided. Tracking such occurrences and entering them in a database can generate reports that identify trends in information requested by payers after the fact. Once reported, process or system interventions can be put in place on the front end of the process to ensure that the required elements are coded before a bill is generated.

Nonstandard Reasons for Bill Holds

Reports also can facilitate communication between departments. Not every issue that causes a bill to be held is included on the daily Accounts Not Selected for Billing Report. Those issues that occur less frequently are generally more difficult to manage. Their infrequency means that no procedure is in place for reaching an efficient resolution to a problem. Some facilities have created automated programs to deal with those types of issues.

Examples of situations that could require extensive communication on a less-than-routine basis might include:

- The need to assign specific accounts to an APC group instead of a DRG
- The need to code an ICD-9-CM procedure code for a Class IV procedure group

- The need for a nonstandard E & M code to be applied to a specific account based on individual agreements with insurers

In such instances, the patient financial services and HIM staffs enter system-generated standard notes, or customized notes, into a specific account file with directions for what must occur to process the bill. The note stays with the account until it is billed, thus providing an efficient account management process. Each department then can generate reports grouping all accounts-pending billing based on a specific note type. This permits processing en masse, which is more efficient than resolving situations on a case-by-case basis.

Rebilling Process

The hospital information system usually generates the bill, and the data from the HIS are often passed on to other systems for future reporting of integrated clinical and financial information. At times, certain accounts are manipulated or revised after the bill has been produced. The process of rebilling is an important concept that relies heavily on reports of coding revisions. The timing of data transfer from one system to another is essential for accuracy in reporting.

Report Validation

Medicare program requirements include provisions for self-auditing of billed accounts. In some cases, Medicare outlines the specific CPT codes to be audited. At times, the CPT code might be applied through the CDM charge process. In many facilities, the CDM codes are not stored in the abstract file of the HIS but, rather, are printed directly on the UB-92 claim form. In such cases, pulling together a full listing of accounts to be audited becomes difficult.

Moreover, reporting in these situations becomes difficult, and the need to validate the report contents becomes critically important. Whenever data are drawn from multiple, disparate sources, the results must be reviewed to ensure that the report creator selected the appropriate data elements to appear on the report. Moreover, even if the correct elements were selected, the results must be further validated to ensure that technical issues did not result in report discrepancies.

Rigorous testing of system interfaces and data exchange protocols are essential to ensure that valid data are being reported. First-time reports must be reviewed thoroughly to confirm data validity. After a critical assessment of the report has been performed, the report can be considered reliable. However, subsequent random reviews of reports for the purpose of assuring data validity must be performed, particularly after any system change that might affect the report's results.

Quality Management Departments

The quality management (QM) department interprets a variety of code-based reports. Issues of current significance being reviewed by JCAHO include rates of cesarean sections and of vaginal deliveries after cesarean sections within a facility. Both of these statistics are inferred from ICD-9-CM procedure codes. Reports designed to clarify the frequency of those procedures help the QM department prepare summarized data for JCAHO review purposes.

Another area of concern is patient length of stay (LOS) by diagnosis. QM data analysts review LOS reports to determine whether physicians are deviating from the mean LOS. After a deviation is noted, the department implements performance improvement initiatives to bring outliers within an acceptable standard deviation for the specific LOS indicator. This type of information is also used in the physician reappointment process as a reflection of how physicians compare with their peers or with a national standard.

Code Validation

In many facilities, the QM department staff acts as a secondary level to ensure coding accuracy within the facility. Although it may be an inefficient use of resources to have the QM department staff validate every code assigned by the HIM department staff, random validation can be considered a judicious use of staff time.

By identifying trends in code assignment errors, the QM department can focus on areas of concern. Code validation becomes particularly important when physician discipline is based on deviation from acceptable care standards, as identified by diagnosis and procedure codes combined with other clinical details.

Work Lists

Facilities with electronic patient record systems can use codes to create work lists for secondary users in departments such as QM. Rather than retrieving paper records to review the assigned codes, the records to be reviewed can be retrieved based on the assigned codes. This is a subtle difference, but one that makes for an efficient use of staff resources.

Source Documents

Reports alone, however, do not always provide enough detail to support QM practices. Sometimes the QM staff must review the actual source documents to fully evaluate the indicator being assessed. For example, a facility wishing to determine its risk-adjusted mortality rate would have to review each mortality case to ascertain comorbid conditions because these types of conditions are not generally detailed in standard mortality reports.

Ancillary Departments

Various ancillary departments use coded data for different reasons. Generally, ancillary users of coded data are interested in CPT codes to assess the volume of procedures provided in their area. For example, the clinical laboratory management staff might be interested in assessing the frequency with which glycohemoglobin tests are performed. Patients with diabetes should have at least one glycohemoglobin test each quarter. By determining the volume of this type of test and by performing a correlated assessment of ordering practices of physicians for this type of test, a laboratory can prepare a marketing plan to ensure that diabetic patients and their physicians are aware of the standard recommended protocol for the assessment and treatment of diabetes.

CPT code assessment also lends itself particularly well to comparisons across the healthcare spectrum. Laboratory test profiles can vary from facility to facility, but because a CPT code is applied to each test, a national standard of comparison becomes available. This enables users to compare provisions of like services, regardless of the ordered laboratory test profile. Using an external database such as that of the College of American Pathologists allows laboratories to compare their staffing efficiency against other laboratories, as well as across shifts within their own facility.

With continued movement toward case management, further extrapolation of code-based data can be expected. For example, laboratories might want to evaluate coded data from all hospital-affiliated sources. This might include home healthcare and facility-managed physician offices. In that way, clinical laboratories could ensure that appropriate disease management and clinical pathway methodologies are being followed. (Radiology, diagnostic, and other ancillary departments use reports that detail CPT codes for reasons similar to those for clinical laboratories.)

Managed Care Departments

Summarized reports of ICD-9-CM codes are valuable in determining the scope of managed care contracts. Analyzing codes as an isolated data element is rarely useful. However, when assessed with other data elements using demographic assessment software, trends can be identified and programs developed to meet a specific population's needs. For example, certain areas of the country are at a higher risk for cardiovascular diseases. Cancer rates are higher in highly industrialized areas where air pollution is more common than in less-industrialized areas. Analysis of ICD-9-CM codes can help to identify these types of trends.

Strategically, facilities should provide the product lines most needed by the community they serve. For example, a facility located in a community with an aging population should provide an appropriate level of geriatric services. In that type of situation, the managed care program manager would assess coded data to identify conditions associated with the aging process. Then the manager would recommend development of product lines such as adult exercise and rehabilitative services. Employers that represent the community's patient population contract with facilities that are strategically committed to providing needed services.

A variety of code-based reports, such as Net Income by Product Line (figure 9.3), Physician Profile, and Managed Care Summary, are used to assess business efficiencies and contract success. Managed care departments generally receive coding data through system collection processes. They further manipulate those data by using spreadsheet programs to develop scenarios that compare best practices in managed care with the practices within their specific facility.

Medical Staff Departments

The medical staff department requires access to information for a variety of reasons. Assessing the legitimacy of accessing information has become a concern of medical staff departments. This issue is of increasing importance, particularly in light of the Privacy Regulations in the Health Insurance Portability and Accountability Act of 1996 (HIPAA). Reports required by physicians often include demographic information about patients that falls into the realm of protected health information as outlined in the regulations. After reviewing appropriate authorization to use the information, the HIM practitioner will create reports that help physicians meet both their office practice- and hospital-based information needs.

Certification Reports

Physicians seeking to become board certified in their area of medical expertise must provide evidence of the number of cases and the outcome of each case of the specified type in which they participated. Cases identified on reports of this type are found by using case-finding programs. Such programs search abstracted or indexed fields to find cases that match the entered selection criteria.

Many physicians request reports that identify all their cases for a specific time period. Other physicians request only specific cases based on a particular ICD-9-CM diagnosis or procedure code, CPT code, or DRG. Those reports then are compared to the codes submitted by their office billing staff to ensure that appropriate coding practices are taking place in their office.

Figure 9.3. Net income by product line of four selected product lines

Anyplace Health Systems
Net Income by Product Line—Inpatients and Outpatients
Quarter 1, Fiscal Year 2001

Product Code (MDC)	Description	# Of Patients	ALOS	Case-Mix Index	Total Charges	Deductions	Est. Net Rev.	Variable Costs	Contribution Margin	Cont. Margin %	Fixed Costs	Net Income	Net Income %
001	Cardiac Cath	302	1.1	1.2043	2,070,907	880,809	1,190,098	653,758	536,341	25.9	348,569	187,771	9.1
005	Cardiology	938	3.4	1.1516	8,309,282	3,778,766	4,530,515	3,426,684	1,103,831	13.3	1,545,018	−441,186	−5.3
055	Neonatology	158	8.4	1.9519	2,320,429	568,621	1,751,808	835,249	916,559	39.5	276,314	640,245	27.6
160	OP and ER	26,286	.0	.0000	16,679,820	6,087,147	10,592,673	3,834,331	6,758,342	40.5	2,791,237	3,967,105	23.8

Physician Reappointment Summaries

The medical staff department also is particularly interested in the ICD-9-CM codes associated with each physician. Because diagnostic codes can identify untoward events that occur during hospitalization, the quality of a physician's services can be identified through reports called physician reappointment summaries. These summaries outline the number of cases by diagnosis and procedure type, LOS, and infection and mortality statistics.

At initial credential confirmation (generally referred to as credentialing), initial appointment, and reappointment to a facility's medical staff, code-based reports are required. These reappointment reports identify all cases and procedures in which a specific physician was involved as an attending physician, a consultant, a surgeon, or a surgical assistant.

Reappointment reports are available by specific code number or by narrative description of a code. When such reports are combined with information regarding the physician's previous utilization of hospital facilities, quality improvement actions, and insurance claims, the full picture of a physician's history becomes clearer. The medical staff department accumulates these reports and works with the elected or appointed medical staff leadership to ensure that a thorough analysis of each physician's activities takes place before he or she is reappointed to the staff.

Preceptor Programs

Preceptor programs also make use of code-based reports. In many organizations, when new physicians join the staff, they are appointed a preceptor. A preceptor is an experienced physician responsible for ensuring that the new physician has appropriate on-the-job experience to perform certain types of medical procedures. As part of the preceptor program, the experienced physician must work alongside the new staff member in surgery. When surgical procedures are abstracted, the new physician is credited with performing the procedure, but the experienced physician's number also is abstracted. When a preceptor relationship terminates, reports are generated by a specific ICD-9-CM procedure code to summarize the new physician's activity level.

Reports for Method of Approach

When a surgical innovation is first used in an organization, a procedure code may not always be available. For example, when laparoscopic tools first became widely used, the surgery could be coded, but there was no way to specify that it was a laparoscopic method of entry or approach. This detail was important because many studies were necessary both to ensure that postsurgical complications did not increase because of the new method of approach and to give credit to physicians experienced in performing these "new" procedure types. To report on these details, some facilities chose to create a special modifier code. This special code was used with the procedure code number to identify the method of approach.

Corporate Compliance Departments

The corporate compliance department ensures that fraudulent coding and billing practices are not being performed within an organization.

Auditing Programs

The corporate compliance department uses record-auditing programs to review both source documents and summarized code-based reports. The record-auditing programs also identify trends in the frequency of high-profit tests and procedures that are coded and billed.

Coding audits can be performed by hospital-based staff or by agencies with which organizations contract for review. In either case, an objective review of the assigned codes is necessary to minimize the risk of civil and criminal penalties for inappropriate code assignment.

The MedPar Database

Each bill submitted to Medicare is tracked in the MedPar database system. All of the fiscal intermediaries in the country submit their information, including charges, DRG, and payment information, to this same database. The Office of Inspector General (OIG) analyzes this database to identify suspicious billing and charge practices. Medicare fraud and abuse investigations continue to increase in numbers, as the efficiency of analyzing Medicare's MedPar file increases.

Hospitals do not typically have the resources to assess the information found in the MedPar file. For-profit reporting agencies, however, have found them to be an area in which they can provide a useful service to healthcare facilities. These agencies have developed tools to create reports based on the MedPar file information. They then sell the reports to healthcare facilities that use them to compare their billing and charge practices with those of neighboring facilities.

Nursing and Infection Control Departments

Nursing services and infection control department staff members review code-based reports to identify specific patient records that must be evaluated for a variety of reasons. Quality improvement programs are developed and implemented based on cases that are identified through the process of electronically searching the record-abstracting software program.

Automated Case-Finding Programs

An automated case-finding program is an efficient way to locate specific records that meet selection criteria. The case-finding program should perform a search of the database based on the following elements:

- A specific time period
- A single patient visit type or a group of patient visit types
- A single or combined group of physician identification numbers
- ICD-9-CM diagnosis and procedure codes separated by principal and secondary code assignment levels and CPT codes

Additionally, user-defined fields should be eligible for use in case selection. For example, a nursing staff might be interested in finding specific cases in which restraints were used. Infection control staff might want to identify cases with an elevated postoperative temperature. The output of those abstract searches can be either a screen display or a printed report.

Paper-Based Records

If a paper-based record system is being used, the health record's location should also appear on the report or the screen so that the HIM staff can more efficiently locate records to be pulled for study. Such reports are typically user-generated and created on an ad hoc basis. Predesigned routine reports, on the other hand, can be prepared and run daily, monthly, or quarterly to track frequently requested health record review criteria.

The Reporting Process

In the early days of health information management, users requiring information on health records had nowhere to go but the HIM department. With the advances made in automated systems, this is no longer the case. Individual user departments now use departmental information systems to report on data elements stored within their own systems. However, it is still generally the function of the HIM department to assist users in creating reports based on an analysis of all types of information.

Security Issues

Security access to report development programs should be limited. Such limited access ensures that only authorized users can create or receive reports based on protected health information. Therefore, departmental users generally have access to data only from their own departments' system. If users need integrated information detailing not only their department's input, but also other parts of the record, they must request such reports through the HIM department. In its role as guardian of patient information, the HIM department tracks requests for information and ensures that a legitimate need for access to it is present.

Frequency of Reports

Some ICD-9-CM code-based reports such as the Accounts Not Selected for Billing List are generated daily and often appear in the form of large, paper-based reports. Other reports such as case-mix and physician-profile reports are run on demand, or as needed, by the user or the HIM department representative. Still other reports are created through the use of ad hoc reporting programs that allow users to customize reports based on any collected data element.

Report information can be requested through many automated systems that produce the output and store it in a "queue." The output queue then can be downloaded onto stand-alone or networked personal computer (PC) programs. The PC user can format the data in the desired fashion.

Verification of Report Data

Verification of report data is essential. Random checks of the selected data must be performed. Ensurance of data validity requires that selected data be compared with the source documents and that all system integration elements be functional.

Conclusion

The massive amounts of data stored in automated systems create a plethora of information. However, unless reports are thoughtfully designed and distributed, the information may not be comprehensible. For that reason, users must develop the skills necessary to succinctly define the information they really need. The creators of reports must become equally skilled in developing reports to meet users' needs.

Formatting reports for readability and ease of use is an important step in presenting code-based data in an organized and useful manner. A report's length should guide its creator in determining the spacing, font size, and other advanced formatting options. The flexibility afforded by automated report-writing programs allows users to sort, group, and summarize information as needed. Some reports require great detail; others provide summaries. Sometimes reports are printed in code-number or DRG-number order. At other times, they are sorted by code within a specific medical staff specialty and then grouped by physician number. Some data lend themselves well to summarizing features such as totaling, subtotaling, or counting.

As the information age continues to advance, new and more efficient reporting mechanisms will become available. However, the essential process of ensuring appropriate access to and use of code-based health information will become even more challenging. With each new system, another integration element will be required. With each new integration element, the need for data validation will become even more important. Finally, HIM practitioners will be evaluated on their ability to create a flexible and secure system that generates reports to meet the needs of every user.

Part III

Financial Implications

Chapter 10

Accounts Receivable

Loretta S. Miller, RHIA, CCS-P

Accounts receivable (A/R) has become a topic frequently discussed within the healthcare setting. As third-party payers impose more regulations on the payment process, healthcare facilities must work to reduce costs and receive more timely payments.

Because A/R experts are scarce and demand a high salary, many healthcare facilities are educating staff members about their roles in the A/R process. By involving staff, facilities hope to optimize reimbursements, collect payments more rapidly, and reduce the number of days accounts are held in A/R.

What Is Accounts Receivable?

The **accounts receivable** function in any organization is the enumeration and management of the amounts owed to it by customers or clients who have purchased goods or services from the organization and who plan to pay for them at a future time. Accounts receivable in a healthcare facility consists of the charges for patient services that have been billed and for which the facility is awaiting payment. In other words, claims have been submitted or statements sent, but payment has not yet been received. In the healthcare setting, A/R is also the record of the cash the facility will receive for the services they have provided. **Cash** is the actual money that has been received and is readily available to pay debts.

When a service is performed, the amount of money owed the facility for the service is placed in the A/R account while the facility waits for payment from the payer. When a payment is made, that amount is deleted from the A/R account and is placed in a cash account. The remaining balance is then billed to a secondary payer or to the patient, or it is treated as a write-off, or adjustment. **Write-offs** occur when partial payment has been made and all avenues of collecting full payment have been exhausted. An **adjustment** is the process of writing off an unpaid balance on a patient's account to make the account balance.

Thus, a situation is created in which the amount the facility charged for services is different from the amount of payment it received or expects to receive. According to principles of finance, revenue and receivables should be valued the same. In other words, the account should **balance.** To achieve a balance, the debt, or money not received, is eliminated from the patient's account, or is written off as a **bad debt.** Because the money written off must be accounted for, it is placed in the healthcare facility's **write-off account.**

Accounts receivable represents cash that will be collected in the future. Because most healthcare facilities have no other means of generating revenue, cash is needed for the facility's day-to-day operations. If the facility is waiting to receive hundreds of thousands of dollars and payers are taking longer than expected to send payments, the facility must make other arrangements—such as borrowing money or withdrawing funds from an interest-bearing account—to pay for the facility's operations. Having large amounts of dollars in A/R for long periods of time can jeopardize a facility's financial position and cause it to lose money.

Days in Accounts Receivable

Simply stated, days in accounts receivable is the A/R balance at the end of a specific period divided by an average day's revenues from that period, as shown in the following formula:

$$Days\ in\ accounts\ receivable = \frac{Ending\ accounts\ receivable\ balance\ for\ the\ period}{Average\ revenue\ per\ day}$$

Many accounting systems can generate a Days in Accounts Receivable Report. This report shows the days in A/R for each financial class, or type of payer. An example of a report for days in A/R is shown in figure 10.1. The numbers represent the average number of days it takes each payer to pay claims.

By examining the report in figure 10.1, a facility can easily determine which payers have a problem with timely payment. For example, the days in accounts receivable for Blue Cross is only as high as 65.7 days; but Medicare Part B is as high as 108.1 days; Workmen's Compensation rises to 140.0 days; and self-pay is at the peak with 166.6 days. Weekly review of such a report will keep a facility's staff focused on reducing the days in A/R.

The Collection Process

The **collection** process, or the process of obtaining payment for services rendered, is timely and complicated. Healthcare facilities should think of the collection process as part of the complete billing process and should educate staff to the fact that not all money billed is collected. In fact, as accounts age, the chances of collecting the money are reduced, as shown in the Aging Accounts Receivable Report in figure 10.2.

Aging of Accounts

Aging of accounts is the practice of counting the days, generally in thirty-day increments, from the time a bill has been sent to the payer to the current day. If an account has not been paid by thirty days after billing, that account is considered "aged thirty days."

The Aging Accounts Receivable Report (figure 10.2) shows that when an account is more than ninety days old, or aged ninety days, the chance that it will not be collected is 60 percent. Such a high percentage of noncollection is another reason to have the lowest possible number of days in A/R.

Dollars in Accounts Receivable

Dollars in accounts receivable is the amount of money owed a healthcare facility when claims are pending. **Pending** simply means waiting for the payment. Monitoring the dollars in A/R is just as important as keeping track of the days in A/R. Payment of claims with high dollar amounts results in the facility receiving a large amount of cash—quickly decreasing the total dollars pending in A/R.

Figure 10.1. Days in accounts receivable by financial class

| | 2000–2001 | | | | | | | | | |
| Month | A | B | C | D | E | F | G | H | I | J |
	AR Days Blue Cross	AR Days Private Insurance	AR Days PPO/HMO	AR Days Medicare A	AR Days Medicare B	AR Days Medicaid	AR Days Self-Pay	AR Days Workmen's Comp	AR Days Other	AR Days Total
January	64.8	74.8	69.2	55.6	59.7	74.1	137.1	93.9	48.1	76.4
February	65.7	74.6	69.2	51.7	62.5	76.1	122.1	140.0	56.1	76.7
March	52.7	74.8	61.4	55.6	68.2	91.7	150.8	70.5	62.4	75.8
April	56.7	72.5	68.0	57.9	72.0	74.9	166.6	79.9	31.6	79.0
May	49.8	67.4	70.2	55.9	63.7	60.8	132.0	107.7	68.4	72.4
June	53.4	66.2	72.0	57.8	68.3	84.5	141.0	95.4	52.1	75.3
July	52.1	78.4	95.5	81.3	86.1	95.1	116.0	111.1	71.2	89.3
August	56.1	67.7	79.4	95.2	94.1	93.6	108.7	116.0	74.4	91.6
September	60.2	71.4	74.1	99.8	96.7	91.8	103.3	124.3	68.7	94.3
October	58.9	73.5	84.8	79.7	106.3	61.2	75.2	127.7	58.8	86.5
November	54.7	64.3	62.4	54.9	108.1	62.0	92.1	101.3	100.5	78.1
December	57.1	71.9	76.7	64.3	106.1	82.2	86.3	108.2	131.0	83.7
January	58.5	66.4	70.8	67.9	83.5	64.7	100.6	98.3	63.0	77.0
February	57.3	70.1	74.4	52.5	76.3	58.0	114.5	93.5	43.7	72.1
March	56.4	76.0	62.6	52.0	70.6	77.2	140.8	84.5	53.3	72.7
Ave 2000	56.9	71.5	73.6	67.5	82.7	79.0	119.3	106.3	68.6	81.6
Ave 2001	57.4	70.8	69.3	57.5	76.8	66.6	118.6	92.1	53.3	73.9
Change	0.5	-0.6	-4.3	-10.0	-5.9	-12.4	-0.6	-14.2	-15.3	-7.7
Change %	1.0%	-0.9%	-5.8%	-14.8%	-7.4%	-15.7%	-0.5%	-13.4%	-22.2%	-9.3%

Figure 10.2.   Aging accounts receivable report

Anywhere Hospital Aging Accounts Receivable Bad Debt Estimation May 2001			
Number of Days Past Due			
Category	**Amount**	**Estimated Percentage Uncollectable**	**Estimated Amount Uncollectable**
Current	$657,874.00	1%	$6,578.74
Past Due			
1–30 days	$3,676,526.00	4%	$147,061.04
31–60 days	$4,678,763.00	10%	$467,876.30
61–90 days	$7,865,467.00	40%	$3,146,186.80
Over 90 days	$18,909,872.00	60%	$11,345,923.20

Another report that a facility's accounting system can generate is the Dollars in Accounts Receivable Report, as shown in figure 10.3.

The information in the report in figure 10.3 shows the amount of money each payer owes the facility for each month of the year. By using information from the reports in figure 10.1 and figure 10.3, a facility can compare the days in A/R with the dollars in A/R. For example, figure 10.3 shows that Medicare Part B owes more than $1,000,000, and figure 10.1 shows that the facility might have to wait more than three months to collect the payment.

When Does Days in Accounts Receivable Start?

Healthcare facilities use one of the following dates to start counting the days in A/R:

- The date the patient registers

- The date the patient is discharged

- The date the bill drops

Although any of these dates can be considered the starting time for days in A/R, a bill cannot be collected until it has been sent to a payer. Most healthcare facilities start counting the days in A/R at the time the bill drops. The bill drop occurs when a bill is completed and the claim is actually sent, either electronically or through the mail, to a payer. In the healthcare setting, the UB-92, or HCFA-1450, is used for Medicare Part A billing, and the HCFA-1500 is used for Medicare Part B billing.

Medicare Part A Billing: UB-92/HCFA-1450

The UB-92 is the uniform billing form used to bill the third-party payers for the healthcare facility's services under Medicare Part A. Hospital services covered for Part A for a Medicare patient include medically necessary and reasonable services such as:

- Bed and board
- Private room when medically necessary
- Intensive care unit services
- Regular nursing services
- Operating room services
- Drugs furnished by the hospital
- Laboratory tests
- Radiology services
- Medical supplies, appliances, and equipment furnished by the hospital
- Physical, speech, and occupational therapy
- Respiratory therapy
- Inpatient stays for rehabilitation and psychiatric hospital services (St. Anthony 2001)

Figure 10.3.   Dollars in accounts receivable report

2000–2001									
Month	Blue Cross	Private Insurance	PPO/HMO	Medicare A	Medicare B	Medicaid	Self-Pay	Workmen's Comp	Other	Total
January	573,768	720,451	292,867	758,318	1,019,403	193,195	614,424	147,756	5,590	4,325,772
February	656,468	741,835	358,686	698,779	1,042,331	176,917	572,631	232,276	4,501	4,484,424
March	594,604	746,692	306,763	742,571	1,125,824	102,406	648,054	150,691	7,532	4,425,137
April	495,364	676,418	281,832	950,681	1,009,354	189,437	653,390	220,799	3,880	4,481,155
May	621,359	676,428	240,285	764,532	1,187,654	245,643	675,434	224,543	3,880	4,639,758
June	578,987	676,567	345,432	789,876	1,123,432	156,676	678,765	234,543	3,005	4,587,283
July	567,654	678,567	365,787	909,678	1,167,876	174,567	567,483	394,776	3,456	4,829,844
August	523,455	667,098	267,885	1,189,098	1,342,345	245,342	587,467	367,875	3,644	5,194,209
September	621,898	547,898	345,898	879,098	989,076	156,432	678,654	213,456	3,237	4,435,647
October	567,654	676,546	245,654	987,378	1,189,097	217,876	578,987	239,878	3,876	4,706,946
November	490,987	789,098	324,098	987,238	1,298,732	321,123	678,543	267,653	3,667	5,161,139
December	556,879	890,987	389,097	966,787	1,076,554	267,567	689,882	267,987	3,876	5,109,616
January	689,097	628,987	389,098	876,787	1,198,907	245,678	789,876	378,987	4,356	5,201,773
February	589,878	793,678	298,767	978,909	990,766	317,899	722,345	347,862	3,667	5,043,771
March	478,965	765,948	278,678	1,156,733	1,178,963	178,987	733,456	233,678	3,887	5,009,295
Ave 2000	717,251	889,767	394,236	1,136,372	1,411,693	265,812	822,449	326,897	5,171	4,698,411
Ave 2001	585,980	729,538	322,181	1,004,143	1,122,879	247,521	748,559	320,176	3,970	5,084,946
Change	−131,271	−160,229	−72,055	−132,229	−288,814	−1,8291	−73,890	−6,721	−1,201	386,536

Medicare Part B Billing: HCFA-1500

The HCFA-1500 is the billing form for Medicare Part B services that cannot be paid under Part A. The patient may have exhausted all Part A benefits, but coverage can continue under Part B. The HCFA-1500 is also used to bill physician services performed in the hospital or office setting.

What Affects Days in Accounts Receivable?

Healthcare workers should not think that A/R can be affected only after the patient has been discharged. Nothing could be further from the truth. Although days in A/R do not actually begin until the bill drops, any part of the process from registration to billing can delay payment.

Healthcare facilities can minimize days in A/R by monitoring the following stages or intervals of the billing process:

- Admission to discharge

- Discharge to bill completion

- Bill completion to receipt by payer

- Receipt by payer to mailing of payment

- Mailing of payment to receipt by hospital

- Receipt by hospital to deposit in bank (Cleverly 1992, 4)

For example, by examining the number of days from admission to discharge, a facility might improve the length of stay by implementing care plans or other standards.

Coding at Registration

Medicare now requires facilities to issue an advanced beneficiary notice (ABN) to patients receiving services that may not be covered. If this notice is signed before the patient is seen, the facility can bill the patient for the noncovered services. This requirement has forced many institutions to use registration personnel to place ICD-9-CM codes on the patient's registration form or face sheet. Because registration personnel are often not trained in coding principles and conventions, a delay in A/R can start at this point.

A facility's HIM department should inform registration coding staff about payment policy resources such as the Local Medical Review Policies (LMRP) for Medicare. The HIM department should always share information with registration coding personnel, and coding accuracy should be included in the review process.

If registration personnel place an incorrect code on the UB-92 that is submitted, the claim may be rejected and returned to the facility. Then the claim must be corrected and resubmitted. When a claim is rejected, the business office is notified and staff must investigate the reason for the rejection, thus causing a significant delay in payment. If the code entered at registration is not consistent with documentation in the health record or with the actual condition of the patient, not only could revenue from third-party payers be missed, but compliance issues also could arise.

Verifying correct insurance information at registration can also reduce the days in A/R. A claim submitted to the wrong payer or with incorrect patient information will be subject to delayed payment, thus considerably lengthening the days in A/R.

Delay in Charge Entry

A delay in entering charges can also affect the days in A/R. For example, a bill is to be dropped within five days from the discharge of the patient, but some areas or departments of the facility have not entered their charges. The bill drop, therefore, cannot take place so complete payment for services is thus delayed. However, if the bill is dropped without all the charges, missed revenue results. Although facilities are paid on the basis of DRGs for inpatient services, all charges must be captured to allow an accurate tracking of charges. Capturing all services is also important in determining the cost of treatment to a patient. If charges are placed on hardcopy forms, such as charge tickets or encounter sheets, and entered by hand, facilities should have a written policy for daily entry.

Coding Accuracy: Entering Correct Codes

Entering ICD-9-CM, CPT, and HCPCS codes is often the responsibility of the HIM department. In some facilities, coding is left to a department that does not have personnel with the training or expertise to provide accurate codes for claims. To ensure correct coding for billing, the HIM department should have access to and provide input to the chargemaster and work closely with the A/R department. Certified coding staff should review health records and provide the diagnosis and procedure codes for healthcare services.

The entire facility is affected when coding and billing errors lengthen the days in A/R. For example, the facility may have to change the time of buying budgeted items, or it may not be able to meet payroll demands.

Coding and billing errors and omissions can also result in lost revenue. Even if payers do not reject claims, they might instead pay a lower amount because of coding errors or missing codes. If no one on staff is checking for coding errors and making sure that charges are complete, the missing part of payments will be written off, resulting in lost revenue.

Coding to the Highest Level of Specificity

Coding must also be done to the highest level of specificity. Payers may deny or reduce payment for diagnoses with unspecified codes (codes ending with .x8 or .x9). Coding staff must be informed concerning payer requirements, and physicians must also be educated to document specific diagnoses and to avoid using unspecified terms whenever possible. Coding must always be done from documentation that reflects clinical facts, and there may be times when more specific codes are not available.

Facilities can perform an analysis to determine the amount of revenue lost because of payment denials for nonspecific codes. To conduct this analysis, personnel who work with denials must track the claims denied because of nonspecific principal diagnosis codes. The form in figure 10.4 can be used to conduct a nonspecific code analysis. The analysis should be conducted monthly. The report of total revenue lost should then be presented to the medical staff. The results of such an analysis should be used to educate physicians about coding concerns and the need for using more precise and specific terminology in documentation. Physicians can be given their information in confidence. Instead of the physicians' names, physician numbers may be used on the form for confidentiality purposes. If the same physicians are commonly using nonspecific codes, the medical staff may need to support education of these physicians.

Coding Errors That Cause Claim Rejections or Denials

Figure 10.5 shows a portion of a UB-92 claim with several coding errors that would cause the claim to be rejected or denied. A rejection occurs when a facility submits a claim that is not accepted for processing by the payer. The facility then corrects the errors and resubmits the claim, or rebills the payer. In a denial, the claim has been accepted, but payment has been denied.

Coding Errors That Cause Claim Rejection

The following common coding errors would cause the claim in figure 10.5 to be rejected and returned for correction:

- The statement covers the period for the day of 5/8/00, but the procedure date is listed as 6/8/00.

- The principal diagnosis code 789 (abdominal pain) is not an acceptable code for the CPT code 95860 (EMG, one extremity).

Figure 10.4.   **Nonspecific principal diagnosis code analysis**

Month of January						
Patient Account Number	Date of Service	Payer	ICD-9-CM on UB-92	Recommended ICD-9-CM Code	Amount of Claim Not Paid	Attending Physician
12345	1/25/01	Medicare	236.90	236.0	$1,265.41	Dr. W. Smith
23456	1/28/01	Medicare	461.9	461.1	$629.14	Dr. J. Miller
Total for Month **$1,894.55**						

Figure 10.5.   **UB-92 claim with coding errors**

PATIENT NAME	STATEMENT COVERS PERIOD FROM	TO
	5/8/00	5/8/00
42 REV.CD.	43 DESCRIPTION	44 HCPCS RATES
922	Other diagnostic services	95860
PRIN DIAG CODE	OTHER DIAG CODES	
789		
PRIN PROCEDURE CODE	DATE	
93.0	6/8/00	

- The diagnosis code 789 is not coded to the highest level of specificity, because the category requires both a fourth and a fifth digit to specify the location of the pain.

- The principal procedure code is missing the fourth digit and is also inconsistent with the listed diagnosis. Physical therapy is not a usual therapy or diagnostic aid for abdominal pain.

Many payers place "reason codes" and a key for interpreting the codes on the rejection notice or on the explanation of benefits (EOB) form. In this way, the facility can determine the errors that caused the claim to be rejected, correct them, and resubmit the claim.

Coding Errors That Cause Claim Denial

Coding errors could also cause denial of the claim in figure 10.5 for the following reasons:

- Lack of medical necessity

- Inconsistent procedure codes

- Incorrect ICD-9-CM diagnosis and procedure codes

- Incompatible dates of service

Denial of a claim may result in a lengthy appeal process, requiring a letter of appeal along with a resubmission of the claim before payment can be received. Once again, the delay in payment increases the days in A/R.

The requirements of the appeal process can vary by fiscal intermediary (FI). The FI is the contractor appointed by the federal government to process Medicare Part A and some Part B claims. All facilities should have a written appeal process issued by their local FI to ensure that appeals are handled correctly.

Coding Audits

In large facilities, a coding supervisor is responsible for regularly scheduling and conducting coding audits. The coding supervisor may assign coding staff to assist in this task or may hire a consulting firm to perform the audit. In smaller facilities, the health information manager generally conducts the audit and may ask coding staff to assist in the process.

The coding audit process should include reviewing claim rejections and denials against the health record. Such a comprehensive audit helps identify:

- Departments and/or personnel from which coding errors are originating

- Information that coding staff members can put into effect as they review and correct code assignment errors

- Additional education needed by staff as part of an action plan for correcting coding errors

Responsibility for Coding Accuracy

The first step toward decreasing the number of days in A/R is to assign responsibility for coding accuracy to a staff member. This person not only should have access to A/R reports, denial statements, and coding audit reports, but also should work in partnership with the patient accounting department and the clinical staff.

Coding errors cannot be eliminated unless personnel are informed about errors, and adequate explanations and references are provided to support the corrections. Many payers now furnish an LMRP that contains acceptable diagnoses for many procedures, including laboratory tests and radiology procedures. Facilities should request this information and make it available to coding staff, as well as to ordering physicians. Using up-to-date resources with correct codes can considerably decrease the denial rate, as well as the number of days in A/R.

Correcting Coding Errors

When a payment is denied or rejected because of a coding error, a facility corrects the error according to its written policy on changing codes. If possible, all coding changes should be done in the HIM department. The health record must be pulled, and coding must be done from the documentation. If the documentation in the record shows evidence of an acceptable code that the physician did not specify clearly, the physician should be contacted for clarification and asked to amend the health record.

When coding changes are made in the business office rather than in the HIM department, personnel making the changes should never do so without access to the clinical documentation and the consent of the attending physician. Because claims waiting for corrections of coding errors cause the days in A/R to increase, good rapport among the HIM department, business office, and medical staff offices optimizes reimbursement and decreases the number of days in A/R.

Managed Care Contracts

Many payers negotiate contracts with healthcare facilities to predetermine payment for specific services. Because these payments are similar to DRG payments, many payers follow Medicare guidelines. Managed care contracts can be vague, allowing the payer much discretion in determining payment. To effectively contract with managed care companies, a facility should know each company's allowable diagnosis and procedure codes, as well as the payment for each service.

Managed Care Contracts and the Coding Staff

The coding staff should take an active role in reviewing contracts to learn how the payer wants selected services reported by specific codes and how codes are used in the payment process. Because managed care contracts often require a specific method of code reporting or billing, coding personnel must be informed about all coding requirements for all contractors. However, some payers do not update their codes in a timely manner, thus requiring deleted or expired codes to be handwritten onto the bill. When possible, any variances in coding guidelines should be outlined and explained by the payer before the contract is signed. For example, some payers may use obsolete codes, pay supplies separately, or not reimburse for certain procedures.

When the coding staff is not aware of the specific payer guidelines, they cannot generate clean claims. A clean claim has all billing and coding information entered correctly on it so that it can be paid by the payer the first time it is submitted. This can only happen if the chargemaster, revenue codes, diagnosis and procedure codes, and patient information are accurate. One goal of the A/R team should be to produce clean claims. Coding professionals, however, should never report services contrary to official coding guideline policies, however, without attempting to resolve a mutually satisfactory reporting solution. Chapter 7 provides a more detailed discussion of the coder's responsibilities in this regard.

Carve Outs

The facility's contract negotiator should discuss carve outs for procedures that require special and expensive services and/or supplies. A **carve out** means that the payer will cut out the applicable service from the contract and pay it at a different rate. Reviewing the EOB can determine what procedures are not being paid, or are being paid at less than the charge or at less than the cost of doing the procedure. By writing precise and concise terms for payment into the contract, days in A/R are kept at a minimum and reimbursement is optimized.

Other Billing Policies

Another factor the contracting party should examine in a managed care contract is the policy for late billing. Many payers have time limits for sending a claim. Members of the A/R team and especially the coding staff should be informed of the time line for dropping the bill. Some payers also allow only one claim to be sent for a single service. If all charges are not on that claim, no additional claim may be submitted. Other payers allow only one procedure to be billed per service. Regardless of the payer's requirements, code assignment may be important for other facility needs. Therefore, codes should not be omitted from a case on the basis of a payer's mandates.

Accuracy of Revenue Codes

Revenue codes are four-digit codes that must be used in field 42 on the UB-92 claim form. These codes are used to indicate to the payer the type of service performed, a specific accommodation, or the place of service. For example, revenue code 301 tells the payer that a laboratory chemistry test was performed; revenue code 510 tells the payer the patient was seen in a clinic; and revenue code 112 denotes obstetrics accommodations. The first digit of a revenue code is a zero and is placed automatically on the UB-92 for electronic claims. The zero allows for future additions to revenue codes. Medicare allows for this digit, but many payers accept a three-digit code, omitting the zero. When UB-92s are printed for review or when the code is placed in the chargemaster, only the three-digit number is used.

Payers who use their own revenue code criteria are responsible for furnishing these criteria to the healthcare facility. The facility then has a responsibility to educate all involved personnel about the criteria.

Inaccurate revenue codes cause denials of claims. For example, in figure 10.6, revenue code 360 (operating room services) tells the payer that a surgery was performed. However, the

Figure 10.6.   Incorrect revenue code billing

42 REV.CD.	43 DESCRIPTION	44 HCPCS RATES
360	OPERATING ROOM	97001

procedure is incorrectly coded with CPT code 97001 (physical therapy evaluation). Because physical therapy does not take place in an operating room, the claim will be rejected.

HIM personnel have become more knowledgeable about revenue codes because they are involved with chargemaster management, denial reviews, and accounts receivable processes. The business office staff also has experts in revenue code reporting. The HIM department and business office, therefore, should work together to correct revenue code errors and to resubmit claims quickly.

The *UB-92 Editor* contains a list of revenue codes, the definition for each code, and a list of CPT/HCPCS codes with their acceptable revenue codes. This publication is a solid reference for revenue codes because it follows Medicare guidelines on these codes.

The Accounts Receivable Team

Many healthcare facilities have established an accounts receivable team that informs all personnel involved with billing and coding processes about the importance of submitting clean claims and keeping days in A/R to a minimum. Personnel for this team should include appointment schedulers, registration clerks, charge entry personnel including nursing and ancillary staff, coding staff, accounts receivables clerks, claims reviewers, and a finance department representative. A compliance officer could also be included on this team.

Documenting the Charging Process

One of the first actions of the accounts receivable team should be development of a flowchart that documents, step-by-step, the charging process for a patient from registration to discharge. Because some areas, such as radiology, enter codes on their own unit via the chargemaster while others allow the HIM department to do the coding, all patient areas should document their charging process. A sample flowchart illustrating the charging process for an outpatient laboratory service is shown in figure 10.7.

The team should then examine each component of the charging process to see how it affects the days in A/R. From this examination, the team can establish standards and perform quality studies that identify parts of the charging process that require corrective action.

Functions of Personnel on the Accounts Receivable Team

Staff members in each position on the accounts receivable team play an important part in submitting clean claims, thus reducing the days in A/R.

Appointment Schedulers

Appointment schedulers assign patients a time for an office visit or other services. Before scheduling an appointment, the scheduler should determine whether a referral is required. If so, an appointment should not be scheduled until the referral is completed. When patients receive services without a requisite referral, a collection issue is created and days in A/R are lengthened.

When scheduling appointments over the telephone, appointment schedulers should have a script to read to patients. The script should tell patients what is required of them at the time of their visit, such as the need for and the amount of a copay.

Figure 10.7.   Flowchart for charging process

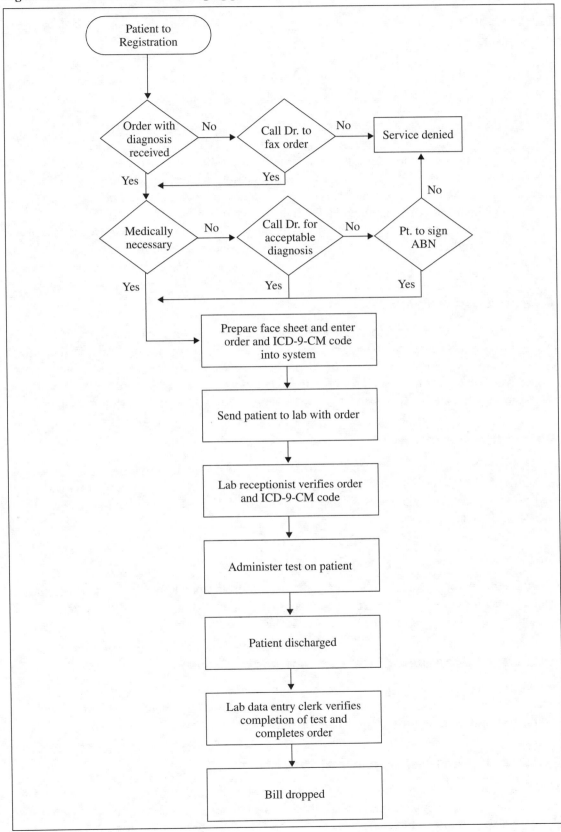

Registration Clerks

When patients arrive at the facility and register for their office visit or other services, registration clerks perform the following tasks:

- Obtain the correct insurance information
- Verify that an order has been received for any test to be performed
- Make sure that patients' names and addresses are correct

Registration clerks should know enough medical terminology to correctly transcribe diagnoses onto the face sheet. Some facilities expect registration clerks to assign ICD-9-CM codes at registration. In such cases, registration clerks should have completed a coding course, and the facility should provide adequate code books.

When patients are not registered correctly, days in A/R are increased just by the time it takes to find and correct the errors. A claim may be sent several times before all errors are caught.

Charge Entry Personnel

After patients have received services, charge entry personnel enter patient charges on paper charge forms or on a computer charge screen. Personnel using charge forms must update the form as needed with additions or deletions of services and codes. Personnel using a computer charge screen will want the charge screen to be up-to-date with current procedures performed. More information about charge forms and computer charge screens appears later in this chapter.

Data Entry Personnel

Data entry personnel may enter charges from charge forms on a daily basis if this process is not automated at their facility. Charges should be entered every day from the previous day. If charges are more than two days old, papers might get lost or set aside, eventually resulting in missed or delayed revenue.

Coding Staff

Coding staff members place codes on claims through an abstracting process or by manual assignment for data entry in patient accounts. Some codes are automatically placed on claims through the chargemaster and the automated order entry process.

Accounts Receivable Clerk and Claims Reviewers

Accounts receivable clerks post, or record, the payment received from the payer. Claims reviewers examine the EOBs to determine where the delay of payment lies. Claims reviewers should communicate claim rejections and denials to all members of the A/R team.

Finance Department Representative

The finance department representative is responsible for obtaining reimbursement and for maintaining the facility's financial viability. This member of the accounts receivable team should help create procedures and systems for billing, collections, cash flow, and forecasting.

Compliance Officer

The compliance officer's responsibility is to assign conditions and boundaries for audits and for other monitoring performed in the facility. The compliance officer's primary role should be overseeing the compliance plan. A compliance plan is a written document that guides a facility in preventing, detecting, or resolving any issues that do not follow government requirements and regulations for healthcare facilities.

Forms and Tools Used in the Coding Process

Throughout the accounts receivable process, codes are entered from various charge forms, computer screens, superbills, and the chargemaster. Such forms and tools must be regularly updated to ensure coding accuracy.

The Chargemaster

If the chargemaster has incorrect codes and/or descriptions of procedures, the claim will not be accurate when submitted to the payer. When chargemaster updates are made, all billing forms, including computer billing screens, must also be updated. When these updates are made, all personnel using any charge form or charge screen should be informed about the changes. Coding personnel often memorize certain codes or charge items. If coders are not informed about changes, they will continue to charge items that have since been deleted or updated. The chargemaster must be kept current to ensure billing and payment compliance and coding accuracy.

Knowing which payers require special coding, such as a HCPCS Level II code instead of a CPT code, can help keep the days in A/R low because a clean bill will be sent the first time the bill drops. If the chargemaster does not have the capability of editing the line items for specific payers, then a manual coding process is required to ensure that correct codes are placed on the UB-92.

An example of chargemaster editing is shown in figure 10.8. Medicare requires the use of HCPCS code G0001 for routine venipuncture, while other payers accept CPT code 36415. The procedure can be on the same line in the chargemaster if proper edits are in place.

Not all similar HCPCS II and CPT procedures can be placed on the same line item in the chargemaster, as shown in figure 10.9. For example, CPT code 90780 (IV infusion, other than chemo, up to one hour) must be placed on a separate line item from HCPCS code Q0081 (IV infusion, other than chemo, per visit). Because the payment structure is different, there must be two line items in the chargemaster.

If the chargemaster cannot edit the correct code to the payer and separate line items are not used for different payment stuctures, an incorrect code will be placed on a claim. Such action will cause a delay or denial of payment and an increase in days in A/R. (See chapter 5 for a thorough discussion on the chargemaster.)

Figure 10.8.   Example of chargemaster editing

CDM #	RevCd	Mcare	Mcaid	Commercial	BWC	Description
12345	361	G0001	36415	36415	36415	Venipuncture

Charge Forms and the Computer Charge Screen

Paper charge forms are used to document a service for payment. The computer charge screen is used for the same purpose. Often the charge item on the form or on the computer screen does not match the line item in the chargemaster. Whenever a new service is added in a department, the charge form should be updated. Every department that provides patient services should review the chargemaster at frequent intervals and validate that information with the charge form and/or charge screen. A sample chargemaster and a sample charge form for the echo department are shown in figures 10.10 and 10.11. When comparing the charge form to the chargemaster, all charge numbers, CPT and HCPCS II codes, and descriptions should match. The charge for the service can also be reviewed at this time.

Superbills

Superbills are a type of encounter form used in some physicians' offices and specialty clinics to document services rendered. These documents usually have CPT, HCPCS Level II, and ICD-9-CM codes already printed on them. The physician or clinician checks off the correct service lines and ICD-9-CM codes, and the data entry clerk enters the charges into the information system for billing.

Superbills should be reviewed each time that new codes are made available—in October for ICD-9-CM codes and in January for CPT codes. Because of a shortage of certified coders, physicians sometimes use consulting companies to conduct superbill reviews. These companies are better able to keep up with current coding and billing issues. The sample superbill in figure 10.12 demonstrates the importance of maintaining correct codes on this form.

Figure 10.9.   Example of a correct chargemaster

CDM #	RevCd	Mcare	Mcaid	Commercial	BWC	Description
23456	636		90780	90780	90780	IV infusion, other than chemo, up to 1 hour
34567	260	Q0081				IV therapy, other than chemo, per visit

Figure 10.10.   Chargemaster for the echo department

CDM NO.	DEPT. NO.	DEPARTMENT NAME	REV CODE	CPT CODE	DESCRIPTION	HOSPITAL CHARGE
4001111	4001	ECHO	483	93312	ECHO-TRANSESOPHAGEAL	$700.00
4001112	4001	ECHO	483	93307	ECHO-2D & M-MODE	$350.00
4001113	4001	ECHO	483	93350	ECHO-STRESS TREADMILL	$300.00
4001114	4001	ECHO	483	93320	ECHO-DOPPLER, ADD-ON CODE	$170.00
4001115	4001	ECHO	483	93325	ECHO-COLOR FLO, ADD-ON CODE	$150.00
4001116	4001	ECHO	483	93350	ECHO-STRESS DOBUTAMINE	$300.00
4001117	4001	ECHO	254		ECHO OPITSON CONTRAST 3CC	$150.00

Figure 10.11.   Sample charge form for the echo department

CHARGE NUMBER	DESCRIPTION	CHECK SERVICE COMPLETED
4001111	ECHO-TRANSESOPHAGEAL	
4001112	ECHO-2D & M-MODE	
4001113	ECHO-STRESS TREADMILL	
4001114	ECHO-DOPPLER, ADD-ON CODE	
4001115	ECHO-COLOR FLO, ADD-ON CODE	
4001116	ECHO-STRESS DOBUTAMINE	
4001117	ECHO OPITSON CONTRAST 3CC	

Figure 10.12.   Sample superbill

OFFICE VISIT	NEW	EST	ICD-9	INCISION AND DRAINAGE		MISCELLANEOUS	
Minimal		99211		Abscess, simple	10060	Induce sputum, initial	94664
Focused	99201	99212		Abscess, compl	10080	Induce sputum, subsequent	94665
Expanded	99202	99213		Hematoma	10140	Burn tx. 1st degree, local	16000
Detailed	99203	99214		Nail evacuation	11740		
High complex	99204	99215				SUPPLIES	
Postop F/U no charge		99024		LACERATION REPAIR		Ace wrap, any width	A4460
THERAPEUTIC INJECTIONS				Simple, scalp, trunk < = 2.5	12001	Ankle brace, aircast	L4350
IV infusion 1st hour		90780		2.6–7.5	12002	Splint, finger	A4570
IV infusion ea. addl hour		90781		Simple, face, ears < = 2.5	12011	Splint, wrist/ forearm	L3908
Benadryl 50mg		J1200		2.6–5.0	12013		
Bicillin 1.2 units		J0540					

Coding Tools: Books and Software

It is critical that facilities have current coding information because not all payers keep their coding materials current. A payer may deny a claim for a coding error when in fact the health-care facility entered the correct code. If such a denial occurs, the facility must alert the payer to update its code book. (See chapters 2 and 3 for information on coding and coding resources.)

If a facility is coding from an encoder, it should receive updates whenever coding additions or changes are approved by the Cooperating Parties or by the AMA. All departments of the facility that use CPT and/or HCPCS Level II codes need access to an updated version of the code book every year. Some of those departments are respiratory therapy, laboratory, radiology, physical therapy, occupational therapy, mental health, and cardiology. Coding staff from the HIM department can review all additions, deletions, and description changes with those departments. Whether coding is done by hand or generated by the chargemaster, codes must be current.

Timeliness of Coding and Dropping Bills

Because many factors can delay sending a claim, all departments must work together to drop the bill in a timely fashion. Healthcare facilities should set a standard number of days from the discharge of the patient to the bill drop, keeping the 72-hour window in mind for Medicare. The goal should be to have all charges entered, all documentation on the chart, and the coding completed to achieve bill drop within four to five days after discharge. This may or may not be consistent with medical staff requirements for health record completion, however.

Unbilled Accounts

As previously mentioned, the days from discharge of the patient to the bill drop are not included in days in A/R. Those days are included, however, in days of **unbilled** accounts—accounts that have not yet had a bill drop. Unbilled accounts are not included in accounts receivable, but they are tracked to inform the finance department about the amount of money waiting to be billed. By evaluating the time it takes to drop a bill, personnel become aware that delays in bill drop in turn cause delays in payment.

If certain departments constantly contribute to delayed bill drops, the facility's A/R team should take corrective action to improve those departments. Some actions the team can take include:

- Educating all staff about the importance of timely billing
- Sharing financial reports with department managers at their meetings
- Encouraging department managers to share financial information with staff

When bills cannot be dropped because physicians have not completed components of the health record, physicians must be informed of their delinquency. Although a facility's administration should support educating physicians about timeliness of bill drops, they can also hold the threat of possible suspension of privileges if there is no improvement.

Bill Holds

In some circumstances, a facility must hold a bill for further information, such as coding changes, loose reports that are not attached, or laboratory tests. This action is called a bill hold.

Holding bills for a week or more to collect loose reports is unacceptable. This not only delays billing, but also delays the completion of the health record. Coding performed without the completed health record, on the other hand, can place the hospital at risk for compliance issues of inaccurate coding.

All loose reports should be collected within three days of discharge. A bill should be held only if the facility is waiting for a report, such as a pathology report, to optimize coding.

Submitting the Claim

When a claim is submitted electronically, the claim reaches the payer within a few hours. Many healthcare facilities utilize a billing company because edits are in place before dropping the bill to the payer. If the billing company has not kept current on payer requirements, the facility may experience delays in the payer receiving the bill. The healthcare facility, therefore, must keep apprised of all payer requirements and not rely solely on the electronic biller.

Claims that are sent through the mail usually take from two to four days to arrive. If payment has not been received within forty days, the facility should contact the payer about the status of the claim.

In general, payers respond within thirty days to a claim with either a rejection, a denial, partial payment, or full payment. When reviewing days in A/R, facilities should pay close attention to the number of days each payer takes for payment. For example, a payer might have a claim for sixty days, find a coding error, and return the claim unpaid. After the facility recodes and resubmits the claim, it then might wait another sixty days for payment.

Receiving the Payment—The End of Days in Accounts Receivable

Many payers now make electronic transfer of payment directly to a facility's bank. This considerably reduces days in A/R. Other payers continue to send payments through the mail. When the facility receives those payments, the facility should deposit them immediately—within one to three days. In other words, "The quicker receivables are converted to cash, the quicker cash is available to support current liabilities" (Costales and Szurovy 1994, 59).

The days in A/R end when all payments, adjustments, and/or write-offs are completed and there is a zero balance. **Zero balance** occurs after an established length of time has passed, and the finance department decides to write off the balance of certain accounts. Accounts that have received some payment may also have a zero balance. When zero balance is achieved, the account is closed. A closed account can be reopened, however, if the possibility exists that further payment can be made.

Setting the Budget to Days in Accounts Receivable

A departmental budget is a detailed plan outlining the future use of financial resources in the department. Budgeting involves how resources will be acquired and used during a budget period. By being aware of the cash flow in accounts receivable, a department manager can prepare a more effective and accurate budget.

When preparing the budget, the coding manager must consider days in A/R. If a department plans on receiving a set amount of revenue each month and suddenly the days in A/R increase by twenty or thirty days, a cash flow deficit is created and the budget cannot be maintained.

Before a department's budget can be set, the manager must understand the difference between dollars billed and dollars received. **Dollars billed** is the amount of money a facility bills for services rendered. **Dollars received,** on the other hand, is the actual amount of money reimbursed to a facility. The amount billed for healthcare services usually differs from the actual amount of the payment because of DRG selection, contractual arrangements, or participation agreements with third-party payers.

Sometimes healthcare facilities want to set their budget by the amount of dollars billed. They look at the chargemaster fee and multiply it by service volume instead of looking at actual dollars reimbursed. This creates a false sense of the actual revenue that the department generates. For example, if the chargemaster shows a volume of 100 units of service for a physical therapy evaluation at a charge of $100.00 per unit, it would be a mistake to assume that the physical therapy department will receive $10,000.00 for those services.

When preparing a budget, the department manager must have a basic understanding of the cost of services. Also needed is an understanding of the expected reimbursement of a service compared with the charge. It is the responsibility of department managers to be familiar with the reimbursement policies of their patients' healthcare plans to set their budget parameters accordingly.

Constructing a budget is often the first encounter a department manager has with accounting information. Reviewing A/R reports and knowing how to interpret the chargemaster will assist department managers in planning their department's budget, in controlling costs, and in planning future services. For example, if days in A/R are not within the expected number, a department may not be able to acquire a budgeted item. Thus, controlling the days in A/R also allows department managers to control the budget.

Summary

ICD-9-CM, CPT, and HCPCS coding identifies services that have been provided to the patient and communicates that information to the party being asked to pay for those services. These codes appear on the claim form submitted to the payer and may also appear on the patient's statement. The descriptions on the charge forms and in the chargemaster, however, are not displayed on the claim form.

A clean, accurate claim can be submitted only if there are no breakdowns in the coding, charging, and billing processes. Submitting clean claims can greatly reduce the days in A/R, thus helping the healthcare facility meet its budget and maintain a positive cash flow.

By taking the following actions, a facility can move closer to its goal of submitting clean claims:

- Form an A/R team to establish policies and procedures for billing.

- Train registration personnel to start each claim with correct information.

- Ensure an accurate chargemaster by checking a random sample of charts to verify that the code selected validates the UB-92 with the chargemaster.

- Purchase current coding books.

- Code to the highest specificity possible provided in the documentation.

- Observe Medicare and Medicaid code requirements for HCPCS Level II or Level III reporting.

- Monitor coding requirements in managed care contracts.

- Train appropriate staff to read A/R reports and to review them no less than monthly.

- Share A/R reports with the coding staff.

- Emphasize the importance that correct coding has in decreasing days in A/R.

- Keep communication open among departments and with the medical staff.

- Have policies in place for timely coding and billing processes.

- Negotiate with managed care contractors for timely payment and for compliance with official coding guidelines.

Accomplishing these tasks may require a new way of thinking in some healthcare facilities. Staff members must be educated about the demands of billing and collecting. They must then be held responsible for reducing days in A/R. Additional benefits may accrue in facilities that adopt such thinking: improved accountability of staff and increased job satisfaction for staff (Sherwin 1998, 4).

References and Bibliography

Cleverley, W. O. 1997. *Essentials of Healthcare Finance.* Gaithersburg, Md.: Aspen Publications.

Costales, S. B., and G. Szurovy. 1994. *The Guide to Understanding Financial Statements.* New York: McGraw-Hill, Inc.

Sherwin, D. M. 1998. *Toward an Ideal Accounts Receivable Process.* <http://www.physiciansnews.com/business/1298.html> (Accessed September 28, 2001).

St. Anthony. 2001. *UB-92 Editor.* Reston: Va.: St. Anthony Publishing.

Chapter 11

Case-Mix Management

Margaret M. Foley, MBA, RHIA, CCS

The **case mix** of a patient population is a description of that population based on any number of the following characteristics:

- Age
- Gender
- Type of insurance
- Diagnosis
- Risk factors
- Treatment received
- Resources used

Case mix has also been defined in the following ways:

- "The method by which patients are grouped together based on a set of characteristics, e.g., resource consumption, diagnosis or procedure" (Abdelhak 2001)

- "The categories of patients (types and volumes) treated by a hospital representing the complexity of a hospital's caseload" (Amatayakul 1985)

- "An interrelated but distinct set of patient attributes which include severity of illness, prognosis, treatment difficulty, need for intervention and resource intensity" (3M 2000)

Case-Mix Methodologies

Coding professionals employ various methodologies to perform case-mix analysis. The specific methodology used to develop a case mix depends on the nature and intended purpose of the grouping of the patients and any further analyses that might be performed. Case-mix analyses may be performed for the following reasons:

- Determining reimbursement
- Describing a population to be served
- Identifying differences in practice patterns or coding complexity

In some instances, a classification of patients may be based simply on one variable, such as the type of insurance. That kind of case-mix analysis may reveal a great deal of information about a patient population. In a more complex approach, an analysis may be performed using several variables. That type of case-mix analysis develops distinct patient groups (Carpenter et al. 1999; National Health Information 1997).

The key factor that distinguishes each case-mix methodology is based on the type of data used, including the following data sets:

- Claims data

- Demographic characteristics

- Disease- and procedure-based classifications

- Severity-of-illness systems

Using Claims Data

In some methodologies, only claims data are provided for the case-mix analysis. This information is limited to all charge-related data for both inpatient and outpatient visits to the provider. Claims data also include all diagnostic and procedural codes.

In more complex methodologies, additional clinical information supplements claims data. This additional information might include findings from the patient's health history, physical examination, and laboratory, radiology, and pathology results. Because the additional data elements provide a more complete view of each patient, the ultimate analysis of each group of patients may be more accurate.

Using Demographic Characteristics

A number of case-mix methodologies include demographic characteristics such as age, gender, race, type of insurance, level of education, level of income, employment status, and place of residence—urban, suburban, or rural area (Zaslavsky et al. 2000; National Health Information 1997; Hofer et al. 1999). Those characteristics are routinely included in case-mix analyses because they are readily available, they lend themselves to analysis, and they are objective in nature. Moreover, a wealth of information may be gained from a minimal set of those data elements.

Age and Gender Data

A case-mix analysis of a patient population limited simply to age and gender data may prove quite revealing. For example, the case-mix analysis might show a concentration of elderly patients. From this information, the healthcare facility could plan for a greater incidence of chronic diseases, such as emphysema and hypertension.

In another example, the case-mix analysis might show that children less than fifteen years of age are a significant part of the population. Accordingly, the healthcare facility might conclude that this group will require more well-child visits and routine immunizations. Such services follow a rather prescribed schedule. From this analysis, the facility could plan the use of resources, such as examination rooms and personnel, for well-child visits.

As a third example, the case-mix analysis might also reveal a large group of women of childbearing age. From that information, the facility might conclude that more gynecological, obstetrical, and family planning services will be needed. Because obstetrical services also follow a regular schedule, the facility could appropriate its resources to the best advantage (Muldoon, Neff, and Gay 1997).

Racial and Socioeconomic Data

A case-mix analysis limited to racial and socioeconomic data may prove illuminating, as well. For example, it might reveal that cultural or linguistic factors are creating barriers that result in some patients not receiving the healthcare they need (Zaslavsky et al. 2000).

Studies have noted that the use of certain healthcare services varies across racial groups, educational levels, and areas of residence. This is true of services such as mammograms and immunizations (Zaslavsky et al. 2000).

Type of Insurance Coverage Data

A number of studies have correlated types of insurance coverages to resource use. Because managed care organizations routinely offer preventative services, their members generate more well-child and routine vaccination visits. A healthcare facility could anticipate decreased use of emergency department (ED) services from a patient population covered by managed care organizations. This population uses preventative services for health problems before they reach the point that warrants a visit to the ED.

Decreased use of ED services for nonemergent care has also been noted among populations covered by specific types of insurers. These insurers include financial disincentives to minimize nonemergency visits to the ED. Thus, members of those insurance plans may be more inclined to arrange care through a visit to their primary care provider (Peabody and Luck 1998).

Case-mix analyses have revealed that populations covered by specific insurers demonstrate different kinds of health issues. For example, Medicaid populations differ from patient groups that are not covered by Medicaid. Medicaid is administered at the state level to a state's indigent population. This section of the population is routinely associated with a number of health risk factors including increased prevalence of chronic conditions such as diabetes and asthma (Muldoon, Neff, and Gay 1997). Moreover, some studies have shown that the length of stay for the Medicaid population is longer after inpatient admission to an acute care hospital (Arndt et al. 1998).

In contrast, a private insurance plan may have fewer members with neuromuscular conditions, such as muscular dystrophy and paralytic syndromes, because patients suffering from these illnesses are typically covered by Supplemental Security Insurance (SSI) for the disabled (Muldoon, Neff, and Gay 1997).

Using Disease- and Procedure-Based Classification Systems

Many of the more familiar case-mix classification systems, such as DRGs and APCs, group patients according to diagnoses and/or procedures reported in claims data. (See chapter 1 for a complete explanation of DRGs and APCs.) Diagnosis- and procedure-based classification case-mix systems are often criticized. Critics believe those methodologies do not distinguish between different levels of a specific illness (Carpenter et al. 1999). For instance, although two patients may carry a diagnosis of diabetes mellitus, a patient who presents with well-controlled diabetes will have very different issues than one with fluctuating glucose levels.

Because the DRG system was designed to classify patients into groups based on clinical and hospital resource-consumption patterns, the level of an illness may not be directly related to the use of services. Clearly, a patient with end-stage breast cancer has a much more severe form of the disease than a patient presenting with stage I breast cancer. However, the patient with stage I cancer may actually require more resources for workup of the disease. The patient with end-stage breast cancer may only need supportive services (3M 2000). Because the DRG system does include complications and comorbidities in calculating the DRG, this methodology tends to minimize the effect of the severity of the illness.

Using Severity-of-Illness Methodologies

Some case-mix methodologies address the weakness inherent in the DRG system. Those methods group and analyze patient data according to the following variations (Estaugh 1998; 3M 2000):

- Extent of the disease
- Risk of death
- Need for intervention
- Urgency of care
- Intensity of resources
- Difficulty of treatment

One case-mix index (CMI) approach, developed by Jefferson Medical College and Syste-Metrics, Inc., uses disease staging as the basis for classifying patients with similar conditions. The CMI determines patterns of resource use (Plomann 1984). The CMI is covered more fully later in this chapter.

Adjusted Clinical Groups

After the implementation of the DRG system, physicians repeatedly criticized the DRG methodology for not adequately addressing severity-of-illness differences among provider caseloads. In response to that criticism, Johns Hopkins University Hospital developed the adjusted clinical groups (ACGs). This software application classifies individuals into groups that are likely to have similar resource requirements. Then it maps diagnostic codes into 1 of 106 diagnostic groups based on age, gender, and the number and type of diagnostic-group morbidity clusters.

NACHRI Classification

The National Association of Children's Hospitals and Related Institutions (NACHRI) has developed a classification of congenital and chronic health conditions. This **NACHRI classification** employs disease progression factors for case-mix analysis that are based on the anticipated course of the disease, as well as on the treatment goal, disease progression, and severity of the disease (Muldoon, Neff, and Gay 1997).

The Medical Outcomes Study Short-Form Health Survey

The **Medical Outcomes Study Short-Form Health Survey** also uses such factors as the severity of the disease and health status measures. In this survey, patients are asked to report on their disease and symptom intensity to characterize the total burden of the disease (Hofer et al. 1999).

The Atlas System

The *Atlas System,* formerly referred to as the medical illness severity grouping system (MedisGroups), is perhaps the most commonly used severity-of-illness system employed by hospitals in the United States and Canada. In fact, as a result of the Health Care Cost Containment Act, all acute care providers in the Commonwealth of Pennsylvania must provide an

Atlas score for all discharges. The score is based on claims data supplemented by key clinical findings abstracted from the health record and includes data from the following sources:

- Health history

- Physical examination

- Laboratory, radiology, and pathology results

The *Atlas System* specifically excludes the patient's diagnosis in the scoring process (Abdelhak 2001).

Using Other Clinical Characteristics

In addition to diagnosis and procedure information or severity-of-illness factors, some methodologies include other clinical characteristics in the case-mix analysis.

The Resource Utilization Group Version III

The **resource utilization group version III (RUG-III)** is such a case-mix classification system. It is used for reimbursement of skilled nursing services for Medicare patients (Mueller 2000). Because of the unique nature of patients in a nursing home setting, this case-mix methodology includes clinical factors such as:

- Cognition

- Sensory deficits

- Psychological well-being

- Nutrition patterns

- Medications taken

This case-mix methodology also considers clinical conditions such as complications or comorbidities that may affect the level and extent of care provided to the patient.

The Functional-Related Group System

The functional-related group (FRG) system is a case-mix methodology used in rehabilitation settings. Clinical factors considered for case-mix analysis in the rehabilitation setting include the patient's ability to perform activities of daily living and the patient's level of spinal cord injury (Tesio, Bellafa, and Franchignoni 2000).

The Home Health Resource Grouping System

The home health resource grouping system (HHRG) includes the following clinical attributes in the case-mix analysis:

- Extent of pain

- Respiratory status

- Integrity of the integumentary system (as indicated by the presence of stasis ulcers and so forth)

309

Moreover, in determining the HHRG assigned to a patient, the following social factors are considered as key factors (U.S. Health Care Financing Administration 1999; 2001):

- The caregiver who has primary responsibility for the patient
- The current residence of the patient
- The principal residence of the primary caregiver

Case-Mix Index

After the patient population has been classified into groups based on one of the case-mix methodologies previously described, the professional coder can analyze the groupings and compare the results to those of other facilities. From this comparison, the coding professional arrives at the facility's or physician's case-mix index (CMI).

The **case-mix index** is the average of the relative weights of all cases treated at a given facility or by a given physician. The CMI is calculated by adding the relative weights of all cases and then dividing that total by the number of cases in the population. A case-mix index (CMI) score, or relative weight (RW), reflects the resource intensity or clinical severity of a specific group in relation to the other groups in the classification system. The theoretical "average" case-mix index is 1.00. (See chapter 1 for additional information on CMI.)

Morbidity Index in the ACG System

In the ACG system, a key factor in the physician profile is the specific physician's morbidity index. This figure indicates the severity of the physician's case mix compared with his or her peers (National Health Information 1998). The overall peer-group morbidity index, or the overall average weight, is valued as 1.00. Each physician is then compared with this average to determine his or her morbidity index relative to that of the overall peer group. If his or her morbidity index is greater than 1.00, he or she has a more severely ill group of patients than his or her peers. Conversely, a morbidity index of less than 1.00 indicates that a physician has a healthier pool of patients than the average physician has.

The relative weight also indicates variance from the norm. If a physician has a morbidity index of 1.10, his or her pool of patients has a morbidity rate 10 percent higher than the peer group.

Case-Mix Index in the DRG System

In a hospital setting, the CMI is usually based on the relative weights assigned to DRGs. (See chapter 1 for an explanation of assigning relative weights to DRGs.)

Case-Mix Index as a Measure of Resource Use and Severity of Illness

The coding professional can calculate an overall score that reflects the resource intensity of the service provided, or the population's severity of illness. For example, DRG 34, Other disorders of the nervous system with complication or comorbidity, has a relative weight of 1.0099. DRG 209, Major joint and limb reattachment procedures of lower extremity, has a relative weight of 2.0912. In this example, the resource intensity and subsequent Medicare reimbursement for DRG 209 is approximately twice that of DRG 34.

A typical Medicare DRG CMI for a university hospital that provides heart surgery, organ transplants, and neurosurgery might be 2.11. On the other hand, a community hospital that does not offer such complex services and provides more routine care, such as general surgery and medicine, might have a CMI of 1.14. The difference between those indices reflects that the average case at the university hospital is more resource intensive than the average case at the community hospital.

CMI as a Basis for Reimbursement

Some case-mix systems use the CMI as a basis for reimbursement. In that way, the CMI is also a measure of the average revenue received per case. Many hospitals closely monitor the movement of their CMI for inpatient populations for which payment is based on DRGs and for outpatient populations for which payment is based on APCs.

Influences on a Facility's CMI

A host of factors influences a facility's CMI (Holland 1998). Coding managers must be aware of the following influences on their facility's case-mix index:

- Changes made by CMS to DRG relative weights

- Changes in services offered by the facility

- Accuracy of documentation and coding when assessing changes in the CMI

Changes Made by CMS to DRG Relative Weights

Annually, CMS reviews and then increases or decreases, as appropriate, the relative weights for DRGs. Those changes are based on predictions of variations of resource consumption caused by technological advances in medicine.

For example, during the 1980s, surgical methods for a number of procedures shifted from an incisional to a laparoscopic approach. A laparoscopic approach is significantly less invasive and usually requires a shorter recovery period, or length of stay. Therefore, an admission for such a procedure is considered less resource intensive. Accordingly, CMS reevaluated the relative weight for the DRG associated with the procedure to reflect the change in resource consumption.

Sometimes a substantial proportion of a facility's inpatient admissions is associated with a DRG that was revised. In that case, the overall CMI for the facility would be altered as well.

Changes Caused by Shifts in Services

In addition to modifications in the CMI that may be imposed by CMS, changes in services rendered by a facility may also impact its case-mix index. For instance, surgical DRGs tend to have higher relative weights than medical DRGs. If a facility shifts from a medical to a predominantly surgical caseload, its CMI will be higher.

Table 11.1 presents a list of the eleven most frequently used DRGs for Medicare patients in a hypothetical hospital. The CMI for that hospital is depicted as 1.2094. If a large orthopedic practice responsible for caring for a majority of patients assigned to DRG 209 were recruited by a competing facility, the CMI would be lower.

Table 11.2 displays the effect of reducing the patient volume for DRG 209 by 229 patients, from 359 (as shown on table 11.1) patients to 130. Such a change in the DRG distribution for the facility results in a drop in the hospital's CMI from 1.2094 to 1.0892.

Table 11.3 displays the effect on the hospital's CMI if those 229 orthopedic patients (from table 11.1) became internal medicine patients and were divided among the medical DRGs 127, 089, and 088. Although the CMI increases to 1.1468 on table 11.3 from 1.0892 in table 11.2, the shift in patient volume to the medical DRGs is still insufficient to compensate for the loss of the surgical patients. In other words, even though the patient volume is unaffected, the shift

Table 11.1.   Typical community hospital's Medicare DRG case mix

DRG	DRG Title	R.W.*	Discharges	ALOS**
127	Heart failure and shock	1.0130	818	5.4
089	Simple pneumonia and pleurisy age > 17 with CC	1.0647	512	6.0
088	Chronic obstructive pulmonary disease	0.9317	399	5.2
209	Major joint and limb reattachment procedures of lower extremity	2.0912	359	5.2
014	Specific cerebrovascular disorders except TIA	1.2070	356	6.1
116	Other perm cardiac pacemaker implant or PTCA with coronary artery stent implant	2.4190	309	3.7
430	Psychoses	0.7644	273	8.2
462	Rehabilitation	1.2401	251	11.7
174	G.I. hemorrhage with CC	0.9985	237	4.8
296	Nutritional and miscellaneous metabolic disorders age >17 with CC	0.8594	235	5.2
182	Esophagitis, gastritis and miscellaneous digestive disorders age >17 with CC	0.7922	235	4.4
	Case-Mix Index	**1.2094**	**3,984**	

*R.W.: Relative Weight
**ALOS: Average Length of Stay

in the caseload to a more medical orientation resulted in a reduction in the CMI—from 1.2094 in table 11.1 to 1.1468 in table 11.3.

As mentioned previously, surgical DRGs typically have higher relative weights than medical DRGs and thus can increase a hospital's CMI. Orthopedic, vascular, and general surgical cases typically have DRG relative weights greater than 1.25. However, higher relative weights are not apparent for urological and gynecologic procedures (Holland 1998).

Effect of Coding Accuracy on CMI

Accurate documentation and subsequent coding can also affect a hospital's DRG case-mix index. Incomplete documentation or **undercoding**—missing diagnoses or procedures that should be coded—could result in a CMI lower than that warranted by the actual service intensity of the facility.

Risk Adjustment

Often the purpose of a case-mix analysis is to identify differences among patient populations. To compare diverse populations, coding professionals must adjust the data to make a fair comparison. Such an adjustment may be referred to as a risk adjustment, a case-mix adjustment, or a severity-of-illness adjustment (Hagland 2000).

Risk adjustment is defined as ". . . any method of comparing how sick one group of patients is, compared with another group of patients. The compared group might be defined as all patients of individual doctors, physician groups or hospital systems. Or they might be membership of different health plans" (Hagland 2000).

Table 11.2.   Medicare case mix with decline in orthopedic patient populations

DRG	DRG Title	R.W.*	Discharges	ALOS**
127	Heart failure and shock	1.0130	818	5.4
089	Simple pneumonia and pleurisy age > 17 with CC	1.0647	512	6.0
088	Chronic obstructive pulmonary disease	0.9317	399	5.2
209	Major joint and limb reattachment procedures of lower extremity	2.0912	130	5.2
014	Specific cerebrovascular disorders except TIA	1.2070	356	6.1
116	Other perm cardiac pacemaker implant or PTCA with coronary artery stent implant	2.4190	309	3.7
430	Psychoses	0.7644	273	8.2
462	Rehabilitation	1.2401	251	11.7
174	G.I. hemorrhage with CC	0.9985	237	4.8
296	Nutritional and miscellaneous metabolic disorders age >17 with CC	0.8594	235	5.2
182	Esophagitis, gastritis and miscellaneous digestive disorders age >17 with CC	0.7922	235	4.4
	Case-Mix Index	**1.0892**	**3,755**	

*R.W.: Relative Weight
**ALOS: Average Length of Stay

Table 11.3.   Medicare case mix with increase in internal medicine patients

DRG	DRG Title	R.W.*	Discharges	ALOS**
127	Heart failure and shock	1.0130	895	5.4
089	Simple pneumonia and pleurisy age > 17 with CC	1.0647	588	6.0
088	Chronic obstructive pulmonary disease	0.9317	475	5.2
209	Major joint and limb reattachment procedures of lower extremity	2.0912	130	5.2
014	Specific cerebrovascular disorders except TIA	1.2070	356	6.1
116	Other perm cardiac pacemaker implant or PTCA with coronary artery stent implant	2.4190	309	3.7
430	Psychoses	0.7644	273	8.2
462	Rehabilitation	1.2401	251	11.7
174	G.I. hemorrhage with CC	0.9985	237	4.8
296	Nutritional and miscellaneous metabolic disorders age >17 with CC	0.8594	235	5.2
182	Esophagitis, gastritis and miscellaneous digestive disorders age >17 with CC	0.7922	235	4.4
	Case-Mix Index	**1.1468**	**3,984**	

*R.W.: Relative Weight
**ALOS: Average Length of Stay

Risk adjustment is applied to prevent providers with more severely ill populations of patients from being unfairly penalized (Berlowitz et al. 1998). For example, Physician A sees a predominantly aged population that presents with a host of chronic conditions and comorbidities. Physician B's practice is primarily composed of patients between the ages of twenty and sixty that present for routine visits or for acute illnesses of limited duration. Accordingly, a comparison between Physician A's and Physician B's patient population would be unfair: Physician A's patient population consumes more resources because of the severity of their illnesses (Hagland 2000).

Age and Gender Adjustments

Typically, a managed care program provides a fixed rate per month to a primary care provider for each **capitated** patient in the practice. A capitated patient is one who, upon enrollment in a managed care program, selects his or her primary care provider. Based upon this selection, the managed care program directs the fixed monthly payment to the identified primary care provider. This patient is considered a capitated patient for that primary care provider.

The managed care program may adjust the fixed rate slightly based on a patient's age and gender. This risk adjustment method has been criticized because age and gender attributes account for only 5 percent of the variability in anticipated resource use for a patient (National Health Information 1997).

Clinical Risk Adjustments

Sophisticated approaches using clinical data for risk adjustment have also been developed. For example, a method based on patient treatment episodes relies on the following clinical data:

- Physician charges
- Number of outpatient visits
- Number of inpatient days
- Prescription drug charges
- Laboratory and radiology charges

From those data, adjustments are made to the capitated payments of the primary care physician. The adjustments are based on the patient's severity-of-illness level (National Health Information 1997).

Situation-Specific Risk Adjustments

Risk adjustment may also be applied to specific clinical conditions and to specialty providers.

Risk Adjustment for Specific Clinical Conditions

A study reviewed the medical outcomes for patients with the following specific clinical conditions:

- Blood pressure ≥160/90 mmHg for hypertension
- Glucose level of ≥240 mg/dl for diabetes mellitus (DM)
- Hospitalization for chronic obstructive pulmonary disease (COPD)

The study revealed that exacerbation of those conditions in the prior year indicated patients with a poorly controlled disease. Such patients had more complex conditions and would be expected to have poorer clinical outcomes than patients with well-controlled diseases (Berlowitz et al. 1998).

Some criticism has been directed at disease-specific risk adjustment methods applied at the provider level. For those methods to be appropriately administered, the provider must have a sufficiently large group of patients with a particular disease. This ensures that a risk adjustment is statistically sound. Because primary care providers see a diverse population, the issue of insufficient patient volume for disease-specific risk adjustment may be more prevalent in that setting (Hofer et al. 1999).

Risk Adjustment for Specialty Providers

Situation-specific risk adjustment may also be applied to specialty providers. For example, a hospital's rate of cesarean sections is an outcome that is often analyzed from both quality and cost perspectives (Whitsel et al. 2000). **Outcomes measures** assess what happens or does not happen to a patient as a result of healthcare processes provided.

The following situations are high-risk factors for cesarean sections:

- Multiple gestation

- Malpresentation of the fetus

- Preterm labor

- No trial of labor permitted for medical reasons

In one study, the crude rate of cesarean sections for a hospital-based practice versus a community-based practice was estimated at 24.4 percent and 21.5 percent, respectively. However, after adjusting for the high-risk factors, the adjusted cesarean rates were 20.1 percent and 21.5 percent, respectively. Those percentages showed no statistically significant difference between the two practices in cesarean section rates (Lieberman et al. 1998).

Use of Comparative Data in Case-Mix Analysis

Comparative data are provided by a host of sources, including the following:

- CMS

- State-mandated databases, such as the Health Care Cost Containment Council of the Commonwealth of Pennsylvania

- Professional associations, such as the Medical Groups Management Association (MGMA)

The data sets from those sources allow individual healthcare providers or organizations to identify other organizations with similar case mixes with which they may conduct comparisons. Alternatively, those comparative data may reveal the characteristics upon which one facility varies from seemingly similar ones. In turn, those differences may promote a more focused case-mix analysis. Such an analysis can assess variances among facilities in outcomes or in patterns of resource use.

For example, figure 11.1 lists comparative data provided by CMS for home healthcare agencies. A specific facility may generate a report in which the facility's case-mix profile is

Figure 11.1. Comparative data provided for CMS for home healthcare organizations

Agency Name: Faircare Home Health Services	Requested Current Period: 09/1999–08/2000
Agency ID: HHA01	Actual Current Period: 09/1999–08/2000
Location: Anytown, USA	Number of Cases in Current Period: 601
Medicare Number: 007001	Number of Cases in Reference Sample: 29983
Medicaid Number: 999888001	Date Report Printed: 11/30/2000

All Patients' Case-Mix Profile at Start/Resumption of Care

	Current Mean	Reference Mean	Sig.		Current Mean	Reference Mean	Sig.
Demographics				**ADL Disabilities at SOC/ROC**			
Age (average in years)	70.75	72.78	**	Grooming (0–3, scale average)	1.02	0.86	**
Gender: Female (%)	69.4%	62.9%	**	Dress upper body (0–2,			
Race: Black (%)	1.7%	10.7%	**	scale average)	0.56	0.59	
Race: White (%)	97.5%	85.5%	**	Dress lower body (0–3,			
Race: Other (%)	0.8%	3.8%	**	scale average)	1.22	1.10	*
				Bathing (0–5, scale average)	2.15	2.03	
Payment Source				Toileting (0–4, scale average)	0.63	0.57	
Any Medicare (%)	80.4%	82.6%		Transferring (0–5, scale average)	0.64	0.70	**
Any Medicaid (%)	12.9%	14.3%		Ambulation (0–5, scale average)	1.05	1.07	
Any HMO (%)	3.0%	5.8%	*	Eating (0–5, scale average)	0.33	0.32	
Medicare HMO (%)	1.3%	2.2%		**ADL Status Prior to SOC/ROC**			
Any third party (%)	19.9%	21.9%		Grooming (0–3, scale average)	0.66	0.52	**
				Dress upper body (0–2,			
Current Residence				scale average)	0.35	0.35	
Own home (%)	74.7%	78.7%		Dress lower body (0–3,			
Family member home (%)	20.5%	14.1%	**	scale average)	0.70	0.63	
				Bathing (0–5, scale average)	1.33	1.20	
Current Living Situation				Toileting (0–4, scale average)	0.39	0.38	
Lives alone (%)	28.6%	29.4%		Transferring (0–5, scale average)	0.38	0.44	**
With family member (%)	66.7%	64.2%		Ambulation (0–5, scale average)	0.70	0.71	
With friend (%)	1.3%	1.6%		Eating (0–5, scale average)	0.22	0.21	
With paid help (%)	2.3%	3.3%		**IADL Disabilities at SOC/ROC**			
				Light meal prep (0–2, scale average)	1.02	0.90	**
Assisting Persons				Transportation (0–2, scale average)	1.05	0.99	**
Person residing in home (%)	57.0%	55.9%		Laundry (0–2, scale average)	1.62	1.51	**
Person residing outside				Housekeeping (0–4, scale average)	2.89	2.68	**
home (%)	44.3%	53.0%	**	Shopping (0–3, scale average)	2.10	2.06	
Paid help (%)	9.3%	14.1%	**	Phone use (0–5, scale average)	0.63	0.72	
				Mgmt. oral meds (0–2,			
Primary Caregiver				scale average)	0.69	0.70	
Spouse/significant other (%)	31.0%	33.6%		**IADL Status Prior to SOC/ROC**			
Daughter/son (%)	33.0%	26.4%	**	Light meal prep (0–2, scale average)	0.65	0.56	*
Other paid help (%)	3.7%	6.1%	*	Transportation (0–2, scale average)	0.78	0.69	**
No one person (%)	21.7%	20.2%		Laundry (0–2, scale average)	1.10	0.96	**
				Housekeeping (0–4, scale average)	1.93	1.73	*
Primary Caregiver Assistance				Shopping (0–3, scale average)	1.45	1.32	
Freq. of assistance (0–6,				Phone use (0–5, scale average)	0.49	0.59	
scale average)	4.11	4.10		Mgmt. oral meds (0–2, scale average)	0.53	0.54	
Inpatient DC within 14 Days of SOC/ROC				**Respiratory Status**			
From hospital (%)	69.1%	68.4%		Dyspnea (0–4, scale average)	1.33	1.19	
From rehab facility (%)	7.2%	6.4%					
From nursing home (%)	1.8%	3.3%		**Therapies Received at Home**			
				IV/infusion therapy (%)	4.3%	3.7%	
Med. Reg. Chg. w/in 14 Days of SOC/ROC				Parenteral nutrition (%)	0.5%	0.3%	
Medical regimen change (%)	67.7%	81.2%	**	Enteral nutrition (%)	2.2%	1.8%	
Prognoses				**Sensory Status**			
Moderate recovery				Vision impairment (0–2,			
prognosis (%)	85.3%	85.9%		scale average)	0.32	0.30	
Good rehab prognosis (%)	62.6%	68.2%	*	Hearing impair (0–4, scale average)	0.38	0.45	**
				Speech/language (0–5,			
				scale average)	0.45	0.47	

Figure 11.1. (Continued)

	Current Mean	Reference Mean	Sig.		Current Mean	Reference Mean	Sig.
Pain				**Home Care Diagnoses**			
Pain interf. w/activity (0–3, scale average)	0.95	0.98		Infectious/parasitic diseases (%)	13.0%	4.5%	**
Intractable pain (%)	14.0%	137%		Neoplasms (%)	11.8%	12.3%	
				Endocrine/nutrit./metabolic (%)	29.0%	27.1%	
Neuro/Emotional/Behavioral Status				Blood diseases (%)	8.2%	6.7%	
Moderate cognitive disability (%)	10.8%	11.9%		Mental diseases (%)	20.1%	9.9%	**
Severe confusion disability (%)	5.7%	6.9%		Nervous system diseases (%)	13.8%	9.4%	**
Severe anxiety level (%)	16.7%	11.7%	**	Circulatory system diseases (%)	61.6%	55.3%	*
Behav probs > twice a week (%)	14.0%	5.7%	**	Respiratory system diseases (%)	24.3%	19.5%	*
				Digestive system diseases (%)	13.8%	12.0%	
Integumentary Status				Genitourinary system diseases (%)	10.7%	10.4%	
Presence of wound/leson (%)	31.6%	31.2%		Pregnancy problems (%)	0.5%	0.2%	
Stasis ulcer(s) present (%)	3.7%	2.9%		Skin/subcutaneous diseases (%)	6.2%	7.4%	
Surgical wound(s) present (%)	21.1%	22.3%		Musculoskeletal system diseases (%)	26.1%	23.5%	
Pressure ulcer(s) present (%)	8.2%	5.4%		Congenital anomalies (%)	1.8%	0.8%	
Stage 2–4 ulcer(s) present (%)	6.5%	4.5%		Ill-defined conditions (%)	24.1%	19.6%	*
Stage 3–4 ulcer(s) present (%)	4.0%	1.4%		Fractures (%)	12.0%	9.1%	
				Intracranial injury (%)	0.2%	0.3%	
Elimination Status				Other injury (%)	9.5%	5.9%	**
UTI within past 14 days (%)	22.5%	9.7%	**	Iatrogenic conditions (%)	2.2%	3.1%	
Urinary incont./catheter present (%)	12.6%	16.7%	**				
Incontinent day and night (%)	10.0%	9.3%		**Length of Stay**			
Urinary catheter (%)	6.0%	5.9%		LOS until discharge (average in days)	49.52	40.35	**
Bowel incont. (0–5, scale average)	0.29	0.23		LOS from 1 to 31 days (%)	46.6%	54.0%	**
				LOS from 32 to 62 days (%)	28.0%	30.0%	
Acute Conditions				LOS from 63 to 124 days (%)	17.8%	11.8%	**
Orthopedic (%)	18.5%	21.5%		LOS more than 124 days (%)	7.7%	4.3%	**
Neurologic (%)	13.1%	9.3%	*				
Open wounds/lesions (%)	33.0%	31.8%					
Terminal condition (%)	5.7%	5.6%					
Cardiac/peripheral vascular (%)	27.0%	30.9%					
Pulmonary (%)	17.3%	16.9%					
Diabetes mellitus (%)	7.7%	8.4%					
Gastrointestinal disorder (%)	12.5%	11.5%					
Contagious/communicable (%)	9.8%	3.0%	**				
Urinary incont./catheter (%)	6.0%	8.1%					
Mental/emotional (%)	9.3%	3.1%	**				
Oxygen therapy (%)	11.2%	11.2%					
IV/infusion therapy (%)	4.3%	3.7%					
Enteral/parenteral nutrition (%)	2.7%	2.0%					
Ventilator (%)	0.0%	0.1%					
Chronic Conditions							
Dependence in living skills (%)	42.1%	35.9%	*				
Dependence in person care (%)	37.9%	22.9%	**				
Impaired ambulation/mobility (%)	14.0%	13.4%					
Eating disability (%)	4.2%	3.2%					
Urinary incontinence/catheter (%)	13.1%	13.7%					
Dependence in med. admin. (%)	44.1%	39.9%					
Chronic pain (%)	7.7%	5.7%					
Cognitive/mental/behavioral (%)	28.6%	23.5%	*				
Chronic pt. with caregiver (%)	40.4%	34.0%	**				

*The probability is 1% or less that the difference is due to chance, and 99% or more that the difference is real.

**The probability is 0.1% or less that the difference is due to chance, and 99.9% or more that the difference is real.

compared with a national reference sample. The report provides detailed information on patient characteristics, such as the following:

- Living situation
- Activities of daily living scores
- Presence of pressure ulcers
- Presence of acute and chronic conditions
- Length of time receiving home healthcare services

The report also identifies statistically significant differences between the specific facility and the reference sample.

Summary

There are many approaches to and uses for case-mix data. Case-mix analyses have been employed for outcomes analysis, strategic planning, budget forecasting, and staffing analysis. Moreover, results of case-mix analyses can be applied to assign patients more appropriately to disease-management programs, to provide more equitable compensation to providers, and to track quality indicators. The key factor in case-mix analysis is to select a case-mix methodology that is most appropriate to the analysis under consideration.

References and Bibliography

Abdelhak, M., ed. 2001. *Health Information: Management of a Strategic Resource.* Philadelphia: W. B. Saunders Company.

Amatayakul, Margret. 1985. *Finance Concepts for the Health Care Manager.* Chicago: American Health Information Management Association.

Arndt, M., et al. 1998. A comparison of hospital utilization by Medicaid and privately insured patients. *Medical Care Research and Review* 55(1): 32–53.

Baker, Judith. 2000. *Health Care Finance: Basic Tools for Nonfinancial Managers.* Gaithersburg, Md.: Aspen Publishers.

Berlowitz, D. R., et al. 1998. Profiling outcomes of ambulatory care: Case mix affects perceived performance. *Medical Care* 36(6): 928–33.

Carpenter, C. E., et al. 1999. Severity of illness and profitability: A patient-level analysis. *Health Services Management Research* 12(4): 217–26.

Dunn, R. 1999. *Finance Principles for the Health Information Manager.* Chicago: American Health Information Management Association.

Estaugh, S. R. 1998. *Health Care Finance: Cost, Productivity, & Strategic Design.* Gaithersburg, Md.: Aspen Publishers.

Goldberg, H. B., and D. Delargy. 2000. Developing a case-mix model for PPS. *Caring* 19(1): 16–19.

Hagland, M. 2000. Risk adjustment: Medicare's latest move to tinker with your income. *Medical Economics* 77(16): 126–28.

Hofer, T. P., et al. 1999. The unreliability of individual physician "report cards" for assessing the costs and quality of care of a chronic disease. *Journal of the American Medical Association* 281(22): 2098–2105.

Holland, R. P. 1998. Case-mix index. *For the Record* (July 27): 40–41, 43.

Lieberman, E., et al. 1998. Assessing the role of case mix in cesarean delivery rates. *Obstetrics and Gynecology* 92(1): 1–7.

Mueller, C. 2000. The RUG-III case-mix classification system for long-term care nursing facilities: Is it adequate for nursing staffing? *Journal of Nursing Administration* 30(11): 535–43.

Muldoon, J. H., J. M. Neff, and J. C. Gay. 1997. Profiling the health service needs of populations using diagnosis-based classification systems. *Journal of Ambulatory Care Management* 20(3): 1–18.

National Health Information. 1997. Use this statistical tool to analyze practice patterns and develop capitation rates. *Capitation Management Report* (May): 77–81.

_____. 1998. Adjust utilization for case mix and make physician responsible for remaining variation. *Data Strategies & Benchmarks* (Feb.): 25–28.

Peabody, J. W., and J. Luck. 1998. How far down the managed care road? A comparison of primary care outpatient services in a veterans affairs medical center and a capitated multispecialty group practice. *Archives of Internal Medicine* 158(21): 2291–2299.

Plomann, M. P. 1984. Understanding case-mix classification systems. *Topics in Health Record Management* 4(3): 77–87.

Tesio, L., A. Bellafa, and F. P. Franchignoni. 2000. Case-mix in rehabilitation: A useful way to achieve a specific goal. *Clinical Rehabilitation* 14(4): 112–14.

3M Health Information Systems. 2000. *Diagnosis Related Groups Version 18.0: Definitions Manual* (prepared under Health Care Financing Administration Contract 500-99-0003).

U.S. Health Care Financing Administration. 1999. *Medicare Fact Sheet: The Home Health Prospective Payment System.* November 29. <http://www.hhs.hcfa.gov/medicare/hhfact.htm> (Accessed October 1, 2001).

_____. 2001. *Sample Case Mix and Adverse Event Report.* Satellite Broadcast (January 19).

Whitsel, A. I., et al. 2000. Adjustment for case mix in comparisons of cesarean delivery rates: University versus community hospitals in Vermont. *American Journal of Obstetrics and Gynecology* 183(5): 170–75.

Zaslavsky, A. M., et al. 2000. Impact of sociodemographic case mix on the HEDIS measures of health plan quality. *Medical Care* 38(10): 981–92.

Part IV

Future Considerations

Chapter 12

The Changing Landscape of the Professional Coding Community

Rita A. Scichilone, MHSA, RHIA, CHC, CCS, CCS-P

As conditions in the healthcare industry have become more challenging, many positions within the HIM profession have evolved, making management of the coding process a dynamic undertaking. In a variety of ways, coding professionals are making their mark in the industry.

Forces inside and outside the profession have profoundly affected the role of the coding professional in the last few years. To be effective, coding managers must recognize and make use of new tools and technology as they become available to meet the needs of healthcare delivery systems fueled by information. Today, changes in coding system requirements are part of a major revolution in healthcare delivery systems and claims processing.

In Search of the "Good Record"

"The only fee for which the doctor pays for the use of a thoroughly equipped and serviced workshop, the hospital, is the good medical record," wrote Betty Wood McNabb (1958, p. 8). Coding professionals have always had to contend with records that are not "good" for optimal data capture, and this is still true at the close of the year 2001. Healthcare organizations still strive to paint an accurate clinical picture from code assignments for external agencies and for internal use. Coding professionals work with good records of bad patient care, bad records of good care, bad records of bad care, and most often—excellent records of excellent care. The form and formats of the records are different than they were in 1958, and keeping up with changes still ahead will keep coding managers busy for quite awhile.

Clinical coding continues to be a process of piecing together data elements to create a consistent and uniform data set that accurately represents what was done for the patient and why. At one time, the uniform data set was the HCFA-1500 or the UB-92 (HCFA-1450) form used for health insurance processing. The Health Insurance Portability and Accountability Act (HIPPA) of 1996 has proposed standards for electronic transmission of health data that transcend former requirements and further refine data elements and data requirements. In many ways, these new mandates create a better process for a more consistent application of coding guidelines.

McNabb (1958, p. 20) warned prospective coding professionals that the ". . . career you have chosen is a career; it is complex, responsible, and professional in caliber—you are not a clerk. Decide to learn as much as you can about medical record science, and you will find every medical record librarian, everywhere, ready to help you." Although the coding profession changed dramatically in the last few years of the twentieth century, coders and HIM professionals are still distinguished by their dedication and willingness to innovate and supply the industry with quality data. As a group, they have developed unique skills because of the specific requirements of their jobs.

The Transition of Coding Education

In the past, many coders were trained on the job. Even though coding education moved from the workplace to the academic setting more than thirty years ago, the on-the-job training process continues even now because of a continuous influx of new technology and tools and a shortage of qualified coding professionals.

Health Information Technology Programs

The traditional two-year program awarding an associate's degree in health information technology (HIT) has produced many clinical coders. In the past, most graduates of HIT programs accepted hospital coding positions. Today, diverse career opportunities exist for HIT graduates and fewer of them are interested in jobs that are strictly limited to hospital coding. Complicating the situation, many HIT programs are struggling to fill their traditional day program enrollment. To be more attractive to working individuals, many HIT programs have transitioned to evening and weekend programs. Yet, the demand for coders still exceeds the supply of HIT graduates.

Many HIT programs have added one-year certificate programs in clinical coding and/or reimbursement. A one-year program usually consists of twenty-four to thirty semester hours and focuses on the knowledge and skills required for entry-level coding in both hospital and physician-office settings. Although programs of this type are new, they have increased the supply of clinical coders ready to enter the marketplace. However, employers may not perceive these individuals to be potential coding employees because most employers want coders to be "certified." The current AHIMA coding credentials, certified coding specialist (CCS) and certified coding specialist—physician based (CCS-P), recommend that candidates have several years of experience before attempting either examination. The certificate program graduate with no coding experience may have difficulty passing either examination. Some employers understand that the new certificate graduate will require time to prepare for these exams. These employers have created "junior coder" or "coding assistant" positions to take advantage of the person's knowledge and skills while giving the person time to gain the coding experience necessary to pass a credentialing examination.

Internet-Based and On-Site Training

The academic setting has not met the needs of all employers, and many have been forced to look for alternatives. Some organizations now provide Internet-based training to help employees develop skills in coding systems. In this way, persons with clinical backgrounds in radiology, laboratory, nursing, and other areas are learning how to assign codes. This may seem like a return to the early days of on-the-job training for coders. However, the advantage of a structured training program has been recognized by many organizations, and they have worked with local colleges and remote companies to bring that training on-site to their facility.

Boom Times for Coders

The expansion of prospective payment systems (PPSs) from acute care hospitals into skilled nursing facility care, rehabilitation services, home health agencies, hospital outpatient services, and physician professional services has created a universal theme of "what you code is what you get"—in reimbursement, that is. All government-sponsored healthcare reimbursement is now linked to the reported clinical codes that describe the services and conditions of the encounter or stay.

In the hospital setting, coders have traditionally been employed in the HIM department. Today, clinical coding is beginning to be decentralized within hospitals, putting coders closer to patients so health information can be translated into ICD-9-CM and CPT/HCPCS codes for immediate use. Coders now work in emergency rooms, primary care clinics, admitting and scheduling departments, patient accounting or business offices, and off-site patient care centers. From these settings, coders can have coded data ready for billing as well as for use by their healthcare facility for future patient encounters.

Healthcare facilities other than hospitals are hiring clinical coders for their internal data needs. Home health agencies and physician group practices have been the most active in recruiting and hiring clinical coders. These facilities have come to understand the importance of coded data to their financial bottom line.

Other organizations that use clinical data also are recognizing the knowledge and skill sets of clinical coders and are starting to recruit them. Such organizations include coding software developers and marketers, health insurance companies, and pharmaceutical companies. With the new demand for coders outside the traditional hospital setting, the boom time for coders continues.

New Roles, New Opportunities

HIM professionals are the best candidates for data management and reimbursement coordinator roles. They possess the knowledge of disease processes and reimbursement principles and have been trained in documentation requirements. The role of coding professionals is no longer that of literal translators of diagnostic statements into codes. Their new and widening role is that of clinical coding advisors for correct code selection based on clinical evidence in the health record. This new role is expected to expand even more with the implementation of natural language processing (NLP) systems that automatically assign clinical codes to text documents. Even though these NLP systems are showing great promise, HIM professionals will be needed in oversight and editing roles. They will have to make sure that the software is appropriately interpreting the materials and that the code assignments are accurate and complete.

Technology has changed coding practice significantly. At one time, a few reference sources kept coders current with coding principles. Today, they must use a variety of resources just to keep abreast of constant changes in reimbursement methods, advanced therapies, and new health conditions. Coders can look forward to a time when they will no longer use any type of "coding manual." Instead, they will be downloading code sets from an Internet site. Because coding systems of the future are expected to be much larger than can be contained in book form, computer skills and Internet data retrieval skills will be essential for coding professionals.

Analysis and use of coded data have revolutionized the industry by providing consistent and reliable clinical data that are accessible in electronic formats. Coding professionals have learned how to be real "detectives," finding data within health records that legitimately improve reimbursement by DRG, APC, ASC, or RBRVS. Coders analyze abnormal findings, medications, and surgical therapies so that complications, comorbidities, or valid operating room procedures overlooked by a physician in a final diagnostic statement may be used to optimize hospital reimbursement. They also apply confusing CMS/AMA guidelines to physician documentation for professional services so they can assign the appropriate level of service or validate levels assigned by physicians, thus helping physicians avoid audits and overpayment.

In the twenty-first century, ICD-9-CM and CPT/HCPCS code numbers became the universal product code of the healthcare service marketplace. Coding professionals can expect these systems to become increasingly sophisticated as they evolve to take advantage of new technology. Use of a universal procedural coding system will likely replace the dual reporting now common for hospital outpatients. It is inevitable that the current systems, which were developed in a preelectronic age, will not endure much longer in their current form.

The use of ICD-10-CM will be implemented at some point to create a more universal language that can be used throughout the international community for mortality and morbidity reporting on a global scale. As political unrest unfolds and threats of bioterrorism emerge, a more sophisticated public health system may require greater uniformity and granularity in clinical data reporting than the current systems allow.

A Crystal Ball for Coding

Recently, the AHIMA Coding Futures Task Force was convened to study how several dominant forces in the area of medical vocabularies and enabling technologies could affect the domain of coding practice. **Enabling technologies** produce innovative devices that facilitate data gathering or information processing in ways not previously possible. For example, a handheld computer that works with a wireless network enables clinicians to collect health data at the point of care in a new manner that is more efficient than dictation, transcription, and filing pages in a paper health record. Composed of nationally recognized authorities in the development of medical vocabularies, standards development, and use of coded data, the task force looked beyond current frames of reference to illuminate what the future will likely hold. A complete report of their findings was published in the January 2000 issue of the *Journal of the American Health Information Management Association* (Johns 2000). All current and future coding professionals and managers should read this important information.

The task force evaluated the effect of the following three forces on coding:

- The evolution and growth of medical vocabularies

- The development and application of information and enabling technologies for coded data

- The emergence of the information economy

To assess the combined effects of these forces, the task force used a process called "scenario planning" to create stories about the future based on environmental variables. The results are a provocative collection of scenarios about the future of the coding industry. These scenarios forecast changes in the way HIM professionals will work with data, technology, standards, and patients. The task force also developed recommendations for the best actions for HIM professionals and for AHIMA to take in the future so that the profession benefits no matter which scenario proves to be true.

Looking into the Crystal Ball

The task force's "crystal ball" yielded four scenarios that developed around the key factors of technology, standards development, the cost-driven environment, and consumer demands.

Rapid Changes in Technology

The first scenario is dominated by rapid changes in technology that include a better technology infrastructure and the development of a true computer-based patient record. In this scenario, forward-thinking organizations anticipate technological breakthroughs and accordingly reengineer to capitalize on them. Conversely, professional organizations that do not anticipate, shape, and stake their positions feel the aftershocks of technological change.

Standards Development

The second scenario is dominated by development and implementation of standards—a "virtual" approach to data management. Organizations that cling to inefficient practices and have not developed methods for data and knowledge management are left behind. Similarly, professions that have not transformed themselves and are overly invested in old conceptual frames of reference suffer.

Cost-Driven Environment

In the third scenario, cost drives the healthcare industry. Financial, consumer, and professional interests clash over new, cost-efficient delivery models that have little or no room for negotiation with payers and regulators. Algorithmic technologies for interpreting coded data support best practices and compliance with fraud and abuse regulations. Failure to deploy such technology sounds alarms. For all parties, hindsight reveals that misplaced and misordered priorities resulted in costly mistakes.

Consumer Demand for Information and Quality

In the final scenario, a consumer demand for better information and for a better quality of life dominates. Healthcare yields to the preferences and purchasing decisions of millions of people. In this scenario, what originally was a private fiduciary relationship between doctors and patients now looks and feels more like a relationship between suppliers and customers at multiple levels. Only organizations that listen, hear, and respond to their customers' collective voice will survive.

Be Prepared

What do these scenarios tell about the future of coding practice? In a sense, they offer a mixed bag. On the one hand, the convergence of forces and major trends in technology, medical vocabularies, and the information economy offers many new opportunities for HIM professionals who specialize in coding. On the other hand, these opportunities will only be available to those who are prepared to develop and assess technology at deeper levels than they currently do. Those who wish to take advantage of these opportunities must develop new skills, especially in areas such as the development of:

- **Algorithmic translation.** This process involves the use of algorithms to translate or map clinical nomenclatures among each other or to map natural language to a clinical nomenclature or vice versa (Johns 2000, 33).

- **Concept representation.** A concept is a unit of knowledge created by a unique combination of characteristics. The SNOMED-CT is a clinical terminology that is based on clinical concepts represented by unique numbers. Concept representation is a methodology that has been used in the construction of the Unified Medical Language System (UMLS) developed by the National Library of Medicine (Johns 2000, 33).

- **Vocabulary mapping processes,** especially among clinical nomenclatures and reimbursement methods. A clinical vocabulary is a dictionary containing the terminology of a particular subject field. A vocabulary mapping process would connect or crosswalk one clinical vocabulary to another.

In the future, according to the task force, thanks to the development of enabling technologies, automatic coding systems, and the maturity of natural language processing, the critical shortage of individuals to assign diagnostic and procedural codes will all but disappear. Instead, an acute urgency will arise for leadership in the creation, maintenance, and oversight of the vocabulary mapping process. Many individuals will be needed to monitor the output of these processes and to ensure overall data quality. Individuals with the knowledge and skills to position themselves as authorities on the cutting edge of healthcare nosology (the classification of diseases) will also be needed.

Ultimately, the task force's findings show that the HIM profession must define itself in an open-ended way to take full advantage of opportunities in the electronic world. First and foremost, according to the task force, HIM professionals who specialize in coding must define themselves as information managers with a focus on data as opposed to records. They should position themselves as visible agents of change in coded data activities and in furthering new methods of concept representation, extraction, and use of clinical data.

In the near future, the education of coders must prepare them to go beyond the assignment of diagnostic and procedural codes. With implementation of advanced technologies, code assignment will be largely automatic. Coders also must be trained and retrained in **coding formalization principles** broader than ICD and CPT codes. Coding formalization refers to the transition from analysis of health records to a process that involves data analysis using more sophisticated tools such as algorithmic translation, concept representation, and vocabulary or reimbursement mapping. Skills and knowledge in the creation, development, and research validation of new coding systems will be premium competencies that the marketplace seeks.

Unveiling a New Trajectory of Practice

Having analyzed the possible scenarios, the task force offered some insights about factors that will have direct and lasting impact on HIM professionals who specialize in coding. The most fundamental insight is that merging external forces are producing a new trajectory for HIM practice. This "trajectory" is a way of describing a fundamental change from a records management to a data management focus. The trajectory depends on a number of corresponding critical initiatives.

The task force believes that the new trajectory of practice would affect numerous parts of the coding picture in the following ways:

- Innovative methods of professional development training and retraining. The evolution of HIM practice is producing a critical need for new training (and retraining) of HIM professionals who carry out coding functions. At each level of practice, new tasks along the growth trajectory must be identified, and opportunities for "special skills" training must be developed for newly and rapidly evolving roles. Coders must be prepared to develop and assess technology at deeper levels than they currently can, especially in areas of data security, data structures, system implementation, data integrity, process flow, information modeling, and concept representation. **Information modeling** involves the use of clinical code sets with application software to create information meaningful to the end user. **Concept representation** is a methodology that is being used in the construction of medical language systems.

- Certification title changes. As the trajectory continues to move away from records management, current certification titles must change to reflect the movement toward data and information management. AHIMA's 1999 House of Delegates approved new credential titles of registered health information administrator (RHIA) and registered health information technician (RHIT), which replace the RRA and ART, respectively. With this step, the profession has already recognized the new trajectory of practice.

- A need for leadership in standards development. To be a valued and competitive player in the new coding roles, HIM professionals who specialize in coding must expand their participation in standards and vocabulary groups. The merging of external forces will create new roles, but these roles will require a broader and deeper knowledge in areas of information modeling and concept representation. HIM professionals must be actively involved in this process and also must contribute to the development of nomenclatures.

- An opportunity for leadership in compliance activities and in ethics. Coding professionals should take advantage of opportunities created by the HIPAA and compliance programs. Ethical practices and the integrity of patient and coded data are major areas of future practice that coding professionals should aggressively pursue.

- An opportunity for leadership in the creation, maintenance, and oversight of the vocabulary mapping process. Coders should be educationally prepared to go well beyond assigning diagnostic and procedural codes. In the future, leadership in the creation, maintenance, and oversight of the vocabulary mapping process will be critical. For example, HIM professionals who specialize in coding should be leading enterprisewide efforts to design and implement systems that provide a set of nonoverlapping controlled vocabularies that together cover the concepts needed to document patient problems and the process of care.

Taking the Lead: Capitalizing on Opportunities

Because data management has traditionally been an information systems function, HIM professionals who specialize in coding now must emphasize their unique contributions to this area. In that way, they can maintain and create new value for their role in the marketplace. How can HIM professionals do this? Capitalizing on current and future opportunities requires:

- Special skills training and retraining in newly and rapidly evolving roles

- A long-term strategy for credential management that reflects a general core of competency complemented with subspecializations

- Expanded leadership and volunteer activity in standards and classification systems development and in oversight of vocabulary mapping processes

- Transformational organizational change that makes AHIMA's organizational structure and its component parts sufficiently nimble to provide new services and products ahead of the curve

Coding specialists can prepare to capitalize on these opportunities by applying lifelong learning strategies and by updating their knowledge and skills in technology application and healthcare vocabularies. Some specific informal learning tactics include:

- Keeping current on technology and vocabulary issues such as those covered in the *Journal of the American Health Information Management Association*

- Expanding their knowledge of medical vocabularies beyond ICD and CPT by becoming knowledgeable about the content, construction, use, and development of healthcare vocabularies. More than thirty vocabularies are currently contained in the National Library of Medicine's *UMLS Metathesaurus*.

- Widening their reading horizons through key sources of information, such as the *Journal of the American Health Informatics Association, Proceedings of the American Medical Informatics Association, Nursing Informatics,* and *Methods of Information in Medicine*

- Attending conferences and symposia that focus on medical vocabulary issues

- Visiting the National Library of Medicine's Web site at <http://www.nlm.nih.gov> and investigating issues relating to development of the Unified Medical Language System

- Updating their knowledge and skills by reading books devoted to topics related to nosology, technology, and healthcare vocabularies

- Participating in national and international vocabulary standards groups

No one knows what scenario will "come true" in the following years. One thing is clear, however: For HIM professionals who specialize in coding, the future will be very different from the present. Those who succeed will be those who are prepared—and the time for preparation is now.

What the Future Holds

The use of handheld computers and "palm" devices has already shown coding managers a glimpse of the health record of the future. Some insurance companies now market personal health records for consumers in the form of smart cards. These cards provide healthcare professionals with the information needed to provide appropriate healthcare services and to receive the appropriate reimbursement according to patient's/card carrier's health insurance plan. Can it be long before Medicare adopts this type of system to simplify coverage and better serve its beneficiaries?

The health record of the future increasingly will be an audio or video image rather than a text-based account of care. These dynamic media will provide more useful healthcare observations. The clinical data specialist will continue, however, to be an essential member of the healthcare team—managing and displaying clinical data sets, evaluating clinical trends, and assuring data quality. The clinical skills that serve coding professionals today will continue to serve them in this new role. By determining to learn all that they can, coding professionals will remain gainfully employed for years to come.

Technology now makes it possible to perform coding from remote locations—the "coding-from-home" phenomenon has just begun. Imaging and Internet-based platforms are now commonplace for moving health records to coders for analysis, whether it is across the street or across the ocean. Just as transcription is increasingly outsourced to companies providing specialized service under contract, so also coding is being performed more often in this manner rather than only within HIM departments.

Looking Ahead

The sheer complexity of the systems required to manage these new processes will keep coding system managers in demand well into the middle of the twenty-first century. Although the coding systems will change and the technology will support better ways of collecting, storing, and reporting clinical data, the future is very bright for coding management.

"Due to the complexities involving coding and reimbursement, physicians, allied health professionals, reimbursement specialists, and third-party payers become focused on that 'piece' of the healthcare environment in which they directly work," Denise Stace-Naughton, RHIA, CPC, writes (1999, p. xiii). There are many pieces in the puzzle called healthcare delivery. Management of the coding process is an essential part of the puzzle. For that reason, teams of dedicated HIM professionals will still be needed to deliver consistent, accurate results that satisfy the requirements for clinical information in a form easily digested by information systems and data warehouses.

Conclusion

Effective Management of Coding Services was intended to explore what is currently known about coding models, the coding function, and the professional practice aspect of clinical code reporting. The authors have included material about related issues such as process improvement, quality control, documentation, and compliance monitoring. They hope this textbook will be a useful tool for managing coding systems and personnel well into the future.

References

Johns, M. 2000. A crystal ball for coding. *Journal of the American Health Information Management Association* 71(1): 26–33.

McNabb, B. W. 1958. *Medical Record Procedures in Small Hospitals.* Chicago: Physicians' Record Co.

Stace-Naughton, D. 1999. *Coding and Reimbursement: The Complete Picture within Health Care.* Chicago: American Hospital Association Press.

Glossary

Abstracting: The process of extracting elements of data from a source document (a paper record, for example) and entering them into an automated system.

Accounts Not Selected for Billing Report: A daily report used to track the many reasons why accounts may not be ready for billing.

Accounts receivable (A/R):   Billed charges for patient services for which the facility is awaiting payment.

Activity date or status: The element in the CDM that indicates the most recent activity of an item.

Adjusted clinical groups (ACGs):   A classification that groups individuals according to resource requirements and reflects the clinical severity differences between the specific groups.

Adjustment: The process of writing off an unpaid balance on a patient account to make the account balance.

Aggregate data: A mass or body of data that is treated as a unit. A code is an aggregate form of data that represents the sum of the coder's analysis of documentation.

Aging of accounts: The practice of counting the days, generally in thirty-day increments, from the time a bill has been sent to the payer to the current day.

Algorithmic translation: A process that involves the use of algorithms to translate or map clinical nomenclatures among each other or to map natural language to a clinical nomenclature or vice versa.

Assumption coding: The practice of assigning codes based on clinical signs, symptoms, test findings, or treatment without supporting physician documentation.

Atlas System: A severity-of-illness system that is commonly used in the United States and Canada.

Benchmarking survey: A survey in which a healthcare facility compares elements of its operation with other, similar healthcare facilities.

Bill drop: The point at which a bill is completed and electronically or manually sent to the payer; most facilities start counting days in A/R at bill drop.

Bill hold period: The time that a bill is suspended in the billing system awaiting late charges, diagnosis and/or procedure codes, insurance verification, and so on.

Bill holds: Circumstances when a facility must hold a bill for further information (coding changes, loose reports not attached, waiting for lab tests, etc.).

Brainstorming: A technique used to promote creative thinking and generate ideas for process improvement.

Capitated patient: A patient enrolled in a managed care program that pays a fixed monthly payment to the patient's identified primary care provider.

Carve outs: When a payer cuts the applicable service out of the contract and pays it at a different rate.

Case mix: A description of a patient population based on any number of specific characteristics including age, gender, type of insurance, diagnosis, risk factors, treatment received, and resources used.

Case-mix index (CMI): The average of the relative weights of all cases treated at a given facility or by a given physician, which reflects the resource intensity or clinical severity of a specific group in relation to the other groups in the classification system.

Case-mix system: A grouping of cases that are clinically similar and that ordinarily use similar resources, used to provide information about the types of patients treated by a facility.

Cash: The actual money that has been received and is readily available to pay debts.

Charge code: The numerical identification of a service or supply that links the item to a particular department within the CDM.

Charge description master (CDM): A document that contains the entire list of eligible charges that corresponds with a list of supplies and services by department within a healthcare facility and that is used for UB-92 billing. The CDM is stored in the main computer of the healthcare facility and is used for coding procedures and services.

Chargemaster: Another name for the CDM.

Charges: The dollar amounts actually billed by healthcare facilities for specific services or supplies and owed by patients.

Classification: A system that groups related entities to produce necessary statistical information.

Clean claim: A claim that has all the billing and coding information correct and can be paid by the payer the first time it is submitted.

Clinic cases: Patient encounters that take place on an outpatient basis in a clinic within a teaching environment.

Clinical abstract: A computerized file that summarizes patient demographics and other information, including reason for admission, diagnoses, procedures, physician information, and any additional information deemed pertinent by the facility.

Clinical terminology: A set of standardized terms and their synonyms that can be mapped to broader classifications.

Code look-up: A computer file with all of the indexes and codes recorded on magnetic disk or CD-ROM.

Coder: A title that denotes that the person holding that position is assigned solely to the function of coding.

Coder/biller: A title that denotes a person who works in ambulatory care or a physician-office setting and who is generally responsible for processing the superbill.

Coding formalization principles: A term that refers to the transition of coding from analysis of records to a process that involves data analysis using more sophisticated tools such as algorithmic translation, concept representation, and vocabulary or reimbursement mapping.

Collection: The part of the billing process in which payment for services performed is obtained.

Comorbidity: A secondary condition that exists at the time of admission.

Complication: A secondary condition that arises during hospitalization.

Computerized patient record (CPR): An electronic repository of patient information that includes all clinical, administrative, and financial data relating to the delivery of healthcare services to the patient.

Concept representation: A concept is a unit of knowledge created by a unique combination of characteristics. The SMOMED-CT is a clinical terminology that is based on clinical concepts represented by unique numbers. Concept representation is a methodology that has been used in the construction of the Unified Medical Language System (UMLS).

Concurrent coding: Coding that takes place while the patient is still in the hospital and receiving care.

Contract coder: A coder who is hired on a temporary basis to work on-site.

Contractual allowance: The difference between what is charged by the healthcare provider and what is paid by the managed care company or other payer.

Cooperating Parties: The American Health Information Management Association (AHIMA), American Hospital Association (AHA), Centers for Medicare and Medicaid Services (CMS), and National Center for Health Statistics (NCHS). The Cooperating Parties develop coding rules and guidelines for correct use of ICD-9-CM.

Cost: The dollar amount of a service provided by a facility.

Data quality review: An examination of health records to determine the level of coding accuracy and to identify areas of coding problems.

Days in accounts receivable: The ending accounts receivable balance divided by an average day's revenues.

$$Days\ in\ accounts\ receivable = \frac{Ending\ accounts\ receivable\ balance\ for\ the\ period}{Average\ revenue\ per\ day}$$

Demand bill: A bill that is generated and issued to the patient at the time of service.

Denial: The circumstance when a bill has been accepted, but payment has been denied for any of several reasons (e.g., sending the bill to the wrong insurance company, patient not having current coverage, inaccurate coding, lack of medical necessity, etc.).

Discharged, not final billed (DNFB) list: A detailed list of all discharges for which no bill has yet been dropped.

Dollars billed: The amount of money billed for services rendered.

Dollars in accounts receivable: The amount of money owed a healthcare facility when claims are pending.

Dollars received: Payments agreed upon through DRG selection, contractual agreements, or other payer payment methods.

DRG creep: A rise in a case-mix index that occurs through the coding of higher-paying principal diagnoses and of more complications and comorbidities even though the actual severity level of the patient population did not change.

Drivers and passengers: A name for exploding charges wherein the driver is the item that explodes into other items and appears on the bill.

Enabling technologies: Any newly developed equipment that facilitates data gathering or information processing not possible previously. For example, a handheld computer that works with a wireless network enables clinicians to collect health data at the point of care in a new manner that is more efficient than dictation, transcription, and filing pages in a paper health record.

Encoder: A computerized software program used to assign codes.

Exploding charges: Charges for items that must be reported separately but are used together, such as interventional radiology imaging and injection procedures. When grouped together, such items will be included automatically on the bill.

Feeder system: An automated data system that feeds results into a comprehensive database.

General ledger (G/L) key: The two- or three-digit number in the CDM that assigns each item to a particular section of the general ledger in the healthcare facility's accounting section.

Granularity: The level of detail that a system is able to capture.

Grouping: A system of assigning patients to a classification scheme (DRG or APC) via a computer software program.

Hard code: A code applied through the CDM file.

Hard coding: The process of attaching an HCPCS code to a procedure so that the code will automatically be included on the patient's bill.

Hierarchical system: A system structured with broad groupings that can be further subdivided into more narrowly defined groupings or detailed entities.

Home health resource grouping (HHRG) system: A case-mix methodology used in rehabilitation settings.

Hospital information system (HIS):   The comprehensive database that contains all the clinical, administrative, financial, and demographic information about each patient served by a hospital.

Independent consultant: An individual who works as an independent contractor to provide coding services to healthcare facilities.

Information: The result of transforming raw data into a usable format that accurately depicts the overall story of the patient care process.

Information modeling: The use of clinical code sets with application software to create information that is meaningful to the end user.

Insurance code mapping: The methodology that allows a hospital to hold more than one CPT/HCPCS code per CDM item.

Item description: The actual name of the service or supply listed in the CDM.

Job sharing: A situation in which two or more individuals share the tasks of one or one full-time equivalent position.

Local medical review policies (LMRPs): Documents that define Medicare coverage of outpatient services via lists of diagnoses defined as medically reasonable and necessary for the services provided.

Master patient index (MPI): The link tracking patient, person, or member activity within an organization (or enterprise) and across patient care settings. The MPI identifies all patients who have been treated in a facility or enterprise and lists the medical record or identification number associated with the name. An index can be maintained manually or as part of a computerized system.

Medical Outcomes Study Short-Form Health Survey: A patient survey that reflects the patients' disease and symptom intensity to characterize the total burden of the disease.

MedPar database system: A database that contains information submitted by fiscal intermediaries about all Medicare billing. The MedPar (Medicare Provider Analysis and Review) database is used by the Office of Inspector General to identify suspicious billing and charge practices.

Multiaxial system: A system that can classify an entity in several different ways.

Multiservice contractor: A small company that provides coding services or services that are related to coding.

NACHRI classification: A classification of congenital and chronic health conditions that employs disease progression factors for case-mix analysis.

Needs assessment: An analysis of departmental or organizational requirements.

Nomenclature: A system of names used in any science or art.

Optical image–based system: A patient record system in which information is created initially in paper form and then scanned into an electronic system for storage and retrieval.

Outcomes measures: A way to assess what happens or does not happen to a patient as a result of healthcare processes provided.

Outpatient coder: A title for a person who is responsible for assigning ICD-9-CM and CPT codes to ambulatory surgery or emergency department cases each day.

Outsourcing: Hiring outside personnel to do work in-house that would otherwise be done by full-time staff.

Parents and children: A name for exploding charges wherein the parent is the item that explodes into other items and appears on the bill.

Pending: The condition during which a facility waits for payment after a bill is dropped.

Physician champion: The title for a person who assists in educating medical staff on documentation procedures for accurate billing.

Pointer: An item that has no dollar value and no code attached to it that is mapped to two or more items with separate charges.

Principal diagnosis: The disease or condition that was present on admission, was a principal reason for admission, and received treatment or evaluation during the hospital stay or visit.

Probationary period: A period of time in which the skills of a potential employee's work are assessed before he or she assumes full-time employment.

Process Improvement Team: An interdepartmental task group formed to redesign and change processes in the coding department.

Productivity bonus: A monetary incentive used to encourage employees to improve their output.

Pull list: A list of requested records to be pulled for review during the audit process.

Rebill: Resubmitting a corrected bill to the payer after it has been rejected.

Reimbursement: The amount collected by the facility for the services it bills.

Rejection: The process of having a submitted bill not accepted by the payer. Rejection differs from denial in that corrections can be made and the claim resubmitted.

Relative weight (RW): A multiplier that determines reimbursement; a measure of the resource intensity or clinical severity of a specific group of patients based on a specific case-mix methodology.

Request for proposal (RFP): Means used by a facility to solicit information from vendors about their services and costs.

Resource utilization group version III (RUG-III): A case-mix classification system used for reimbursement of skilled nursing services for Medicare patients.

Retrospective coding: Coding that takes place after the patient has been discharged and the entire health record has been routed to the HIM department.

Revenue code: Three- or four-digit number in the CDM that is used for Medicare billing. It totals all items and their charges for printing on the UB-92.

Risk adjustment: Any method of comparing the severity of illness of one group of patients with that of another group of patients. Also referred to as case-mix adjustment or severity-of-illness adjustment.

Service bonus: Monetary reward given to long-term staff in recognition of their skills and commitment to the facility.

Service-line coder: A title that denotes a person who excels in coding one particular service line, such as oncology or cardiology.

Sign-on bonus: A monetary incentive used by a facility to encourage a candidate to accept employment.

Standard Query Language (SQL): A report-writing program that pulls and integrates data from various sources into a single, comprehensive report.

Superbill: The office form used for physician-office billing that is initiated by the physician and that states the diagnoses and other information for each patient encounter.

Telecommuting: Arrangement in which an employee works at home and communicates with the office via electronic means.

Unbilled account: An account that has not been billed and that is not included in accounts receivable.

Unbundling: The practice of using multiple codes that describe individual steps of a procedure rather than the appropriate single code that describes all steps of the comprehensive procedure.

Undercoding: Incomplete documentation that results when diagnoses or procedures are missing that should be coded.

Upcoding: The practice of using a code that results in a higher payment to the provider than the code that actually reflects the service or item provided.

Vocabulary mapping process: A clinical vocabulary is a dictionary containing the terminology of a particular subject field. A vocabulary mapping process would connect or crosswalk one clinical vocabulary to another.

Weight: The numerical assignment that is part of the formula by which a specific dollar amount, or reimbursement, is calculated for each DRG or each APC.

Work imaging study: A technique for analyzing the coding time required of full-time equivalent employees (FTEs) to established productivity standards.

Write-off: The action taken to eliminate the balance of a bill after the bill has been submitted and partial payment has been made or payment has been denied and all avenues of collecting the payment have been exhausted.

Zero balance: The result of writing off the balance of an account, which closes off the account and ends the days in accounts receivable.

Index